Returning the Gaze

Anna Everett

RETURNING THE GAZE

A Genealogy of

Black Film Criticism,

1909–1949

DUKE UNIVERSITY PRESS   Durham and London   2001

©2001 Duke University Press

All rights reserved

Printed in the United States of America on acid-free paper ∞

Designed by C. H. Westmoreland

Typeset in Adobe Caslon by Keystone Typesetting, Inc.

Library of Congress Cataloging-in-Publication Data appear on the last printed page of this book.

FOR LENA M. EVERETT AND A. L. NIELSEN

Contents

Acknowledgments

This work has been made possible because of the efforts of many people. First and foremost, I want to express my eternal gratitude to my mentor and friend Lynn Spigel for her unwavering support, encouragement, and brilliant critical suggestions in the development and completion of this manuscript. I thank David James, Endesha I. Holland, Todd Boyd, and Darnell Hunt for reading and offering invaluable insights on an earlier version of this work. I particularly want to acknowledge the intellectual generosity and support of my colleagues both in the film studies program at the University of Colorado at Boulder and in the film studies department at the University of California at Santa Barbara. Also, the research time and faculty development grants from the University of Colorado at Boulder and the University of California at Santa Barbara were essential to the timely production of this manuscript. The Ford Foundation has provided financial assistance and inestimable intellectual stimulation from the inception of this project to its conclusion. I owe so much to my fearless editor Ken Wissoker, whose faith in, and support of, this work were so constant that I remained inspired even during those inevitable moments of doubt, fatigue, and frustration that accompany any major writing project. Katie Courtland and the rest of the editorial staff at Duke were wonderfully reassuring and a delight to work with. I must add a special note of gratitude to Rebecca Johns-Danes and William Henry whose exceptional care and meticulous attention contributed so much to this manuscript. I also want to thank my Duke University Press readers for their attentiveness and valuable contributions. To Lisa Johnson, I thank you for being the best research assistant in the world. It is truly the case that without the generous support and assistance of Colonel Eugene F. Scott, and the *Chicago Daily Defender,* this project would be greatly diminished—thank you so very much, Colonel Scott. The able and cordial staff members at the Library of Congress Manuscript and

TV and Motion Picture Divisions, the A. C. Bilbrew Research Center in Black Culture, UCLA Special Collections, and the Moorland-Spingarn Research Center at Howard University made my archival digs productive, efficient, and pleasant. I want to express special thanks to Messrs. Jim Huffman, Wayne Furman, and Marc Andreas at the Manuscripts, Archives, and Rare Books Division–Schomburg Center for African American Research, the New York Public Library, Astor, Lenox, and Tilden Foundations, for their incredible generosity and assistance. I am grateful to the *Spectator* and *Cinema Journal* for publishing different versions of portions of this work. I also want to acknowledge Teshome Gabriel's guidance and influence early in my academic career, and his continuing influence on my work today. To George Lipsitz, who read this work in its entirety and offered valuable suggestions and support, I thank you very much. All photos from the *Pittsburgh Courier* are reprinted by permission of GRM Associates, Inc., agents for the *Pittsburgh Courier*.

To my family, especially my mother, Lena Everett, thank you for constantly expressing faith and confidence in my ability to persevere against many formidable obstacles. Finally, I want to thank my stalwart husband, Aldon L. Nielsen, for keeping me sane during the creation and re-creations of this work, and for his support, patience, humor, understanding, and very beneficial input and advice. Even with the phenomenal help and support that I received in the preparation of this work, I am ultimately responsible for its final form.

Introduction RETURNING THE GAZE

It is remarkable that even after numerous fin de siècle celebrations of the cinema's first centenary, the history of African American film criticism and commentary continues to be marginalized in both popular and scholarly histories and critical reevaluations. These high-profile recuperations of America's cinematic past argue convincingly for its costly preservation despite what many believe is the cinema's inevitable eclipse in the face of new digital media technologies' global impact. It is equally important that the history of black film criticism be preserved and positioned alongside the canonical histories of white critical writing on the cinema. This is one of the primary goals of the present volume. Although there has been a revival of interest in the pioneering works of James Baldwin, Donald Bogle, Thomas Cripps, Henry Sampson, and others who focused necessary attention on the history of the African American image in cinematic representations, the fact remains that little has been written about the proliferation of early film literature produced by African Americans. Because this rich literary and journalistic history has languished at the periphery of mainstream film history and criticism, it is a little known fact that at least from 1909 onward, African Americans regularly returned the motion picture camera's often distorting gaze by scrutinizing the medium closely, vigilantly, and forcefully, and by publishing their criticisms and observations in the extensive network of publications that made up the black press.

Compounding the relative obscurity of much of the earliest black film literature is the misperception that significant black writing on film began and ended with the black press's well-documented campaign opposing D. W. Griffith's 1915 film *The Birth of a Nation*. Unwittingly, the nearly exclusive focus of most film histories on the black press response to this film has contributed significantly to this now-untenable historical myopia. And although this controversial film's catalyzing impact must not be minimized, neither should it continue to obscure from view the enormous amount of African American literature dealing with a host of other films that came before and afterward. In fact, there exists a sustained discourse on the cinema by African Americans from the turn of the century through the Black Arts movement of the 1960s. Yet another major impediment to recovering the totality of black film criticism is that too much of the early literature is unknown, underappreciated, and, worst yet, inaccessible.

It is still the case that too much of the history of African American film criticism from 1909 to 1949 remains buried away in special collections or scattered across the country in library microfilm vaults without benefit of comprehensive indexes. This is especially the case for the earliest writing. My own page-by-page searches of black publications in several university and public institutional research centers and special collections divisions, particularly for the literature produced during the first half of the twentieth century, have yielded an impressive array of early film literature in black newspapers, magazines, monographs, and scholarly journals. Even though the preponderance of film-related literature I uncovered appears in publications located in the Northeast, the Northwest, and the West, a sampling from southern publications rounds out this national survey. Because so much of this material is nearly inaccessible, I have found lengthy excerpts from some articles to be necessary so as to provide the reader a better sense of the specifics and nuances of the literature, namely, the modes of address, the magnitude of the issues at stake, the dynamic rhetorical and stylistic approaches and conceits, and the historical facts and contexts.

Although this work collects what was once considered ephemera, its historical and sociopolitical impact should not be ignored. Although turn-of-the-century commentary and criticism appearing in the nation's black newspapers may still appear inconsequential to many scholars and students, during the first half of the twentieth century, the rigidly segregated nature of American society imbued the black press with a potent force for social change that redounds even today. It is well to remember that the imperatives of America's rigid racial separation, which persisted even through the last half of the century, meant that the black press was the only dedicated forum for the mass cultivation, appreciation, and dissemination of African American ideas, culture, values, talent, literature, thought, and analysis.

Indeed, as early as 1827, members of the black press recognized the necessity "to offset any misrepresentations . . . originating from others who 'too long have spoken for us'" (Pride and Wilson 1997, 13). These words from the editors of America's first black newspaper, *Freedom's Journal*, enable us to understand why Samuel E. Cornish and John B. Russwurm founded *Freedom's Journal* on the premise that as an oppressed group, "We wish [and need] to plead our own cause" (13). Clearly, it was the black-owned and -operated presses that made it possible historically for black writers and other culture fighters to plead their own causes through the years. Following the War of Independence, the numbers of black pamphlets, periodicals, and other modes of communication increased. The importance of print publications for black causes such as the Abolition and the Negro Convention movements in the northern states before the outbreak of the Civil War, and for African Americans in the post-Reconstruction era and beyond, has been extensively documented. The seminal work on the history and significance of the black press is I. Garland Penn's 1891 book *The Afro-American Press and Its Editors*. Beginning with *Freedom's Journal*, Penn covers all the black newspapers and magazines, their editors and missions, and their relationship to the white press through 1891.[1]

In later years, more specialized critical histories of the black press have ensued. Notable among them is *Propaganda and Aesthetics: The Literary Politics of African-American Magazines in the Twentieth Century*, written in 1979 by Abby Arthur Johnson and Ronald Maberry Johnson. Their work centers on nationally renowned black-owned and -operated journals such as *The Crisis*, *Opportunity*, and *Phylon* and on some of the more experimental small magazines including *Fire*, *Harlem*, and *Negro Story*. Given the breadth of black publications' histories, the Johnsons narrowed their focus to magazines "most significant to the course of black literature" (xviii). Other black press histories include Henry Lewis Suggs's *The Black Press in the South, 1865–1979*, Walter C. Daniel's *Black Journals of the United States*, Penelope L. Bullock's *The Afro-American Periodical Press: 1838–1909*, Roland E. Wolseley's *The Black Press, U.S.A.*, and Clint C. Wilson II's *Black Journalists in Paradox: Historical Perspectives and Current Dilemmas*. More recently, *A History of the Black Press*, by Armistead S. Pride and Clint C. Wilson II, and Charles S. Simmons's *The African American Press: With Special Reference to Four Newspapers, 1827–1965* contribute to this voluminous body of research on the role of black journalism in the overall development of American literary culture and history. The present work centering on black film criticism that draws on the wide spectrum of black press outlets and their rich histories aims not to duplicate but to deepen and widen this historical enterprise.

At stake in this project of historical rediscovery are important precedents and implications for contemporary black film criticism. Any careful and thoughtful archaeology of this impressive and underused literary legacy will go far to ensure that important contemporary African American film texts such as bell hooks's *Reel to Real* and *Black Looks,* Jesse Rhines's *Black Film: White Money,* Mark Reid's *Redefining Black Film,* Ed Guerrero's *Framing Blackness: The African American Image in Film,* and James Snead's *White Screens, Black Images: Hollywood from the Dark Side* will not be viewed exclusively as recent phenomena devoid of historical anchorage and aesthetic foundations. Just as the slave narratives established a venerable history for past and present African American literature in a tradition of belles lettres, so does the early black press engagement with the history of the cinema situate contemporary black film literature in an enduring legacy of film discourse.

The relevance here is that despite such formidable fin de siècle obstacles circumscribing black life—namely, the 1896 *Plessey v. Ferguson* Supreme Court decision and the retrenchment from Reconstruction-era progressive politics and their related goals of black education and enfranchisement—African Americans craved and indeed attained literacy. Moreover, their tenacious quest in the aftermath of slavery led them to found approximately three hundred black newspapers and magazines by 1910 (Du Bois 1910, 3). Contained within this significant literary output are palimpsestic tracings of a vital and vibrant African American literary film history too often erased by official histories of the American cinema, especially histories of the cinema in embryo. This historical back story is necessary to mention for what it contributes to our understanding of both the black community's refusal to remain subjugated by widespread illiteracy and its surge to literariness and modernity, evinced dramatically in the Great Migration itself.[2] It also situates our present knowledge in a corpus of texts that document unequivocally the significant participation of such early African American writers as Walton, Russell, Bragg, and others in the totality of American film history and not merely in the well-worn paper trail detailing the black press's opposition to *The Birth of a Nation* beginning in 1915. Clearly, this infamous film represents a watershed event in both black and white film histories. However, let us be clear that nearly from the cinema's inception to the present day, African Americans not only were inscribed in the early cinema but also were prolific in their literary inscriptions of the primitive cinema.

Brian Stock's term "textual community" (quoted in Marvin 1988, 12) provides a useful concept for describing the dialogic relationship existing between black publishers and black readers in terms of a shared language code, but the term needs to be augmented for our study because we need a heuristic framework that can incorporate the caste and class divisions existing within the heterogeneous black community. After all, whereas many rural African Americans who migrated from the South during this era were illiterate, many from the Northeast and Midwest were highly literate. Still others were in between these poles. If we add Renate Holub's paradigm of language communities sharing in "a dialect or some elements of a common 'structure of feeling'" (24), we can get a more nuanced conceptual framework within which to consider the incredible sway of the black press during this schizophrenic era of racial segregation and general societal progressivity.[3] Recall here that some readers spoke the highly circumscribed language and specific dialects of the postemancipation South (the unwashed masses), while others spoke the more mainstream and traditional language of the northern free states (the black elite). But what unified this "textual community" most was a common "structure of feeling" organized around racial and sociopolitical uplift. Again, we must not lose sight of the fact that the myth of the black monolith has served to obscure many fundamental antinomies that existed between the black bourgeoisie and its often tolerated other, the great mass of rural and urban "wretched of the earth," in Fanon's terms. From the skin-color caste hierarchy to the competing high-art and folk traditions of cultural expressions, the black community of that epoch often was more distinguished by its sociocultural differences than by its forced racial affinities.[4]

Discussing African American journalistic praxis in his autobiography, Walter White (1948) observed that the absence of a strong advertising base in the black press resulted in "the perpetuation in the Negro press of personal journalism, with its advantages and disadvantages" (209). Accordingly, he enables us to see the distinctive character of the black press as evolving out of its reader-driven, versus advertiser-directed, interests

(210). For African Americans at this historical moment, the white newspapers offered precious little; the black press forged its niche market in
direct response to this near invisibility. It is therefore not unexpected that
newspapers such as the *New York Age,* the *New York Amsterdam News,* the
Baltimore Afro-American, the *Pittsburgh Courier,* the *Chicago Defender,*
and the *California Eagle,* among many, became African America's voice
with which to "talk back" to mainstream American society, but more
importantly, to communicate with itself at this crucial moment of self-
reinvention. Vilma R. Potter points out in her study of reader expectation
in the black press that "the newspaper editorial thus becomes the articulate voice of an inarticulate interest" (1993, 17). I do not believe it to be an
overstatement to assert that, to the displaced masses of African Americans, the black press was in effect the social, political, and cultural lifeline
in a hostile white world.

For African American migrants from the South, often aware that illiteracy was a lingering marker of slavery's degradation, black press publications symbolized an entrée for the requisite orientation and accultura-
tion to their newly modernized existences. As well, it is clear that within
the pages of the black press they sought strategies for individual improvement, political empowerment, and overall racial uplift. For the aspiring
working- and middle-class blacks who impelled this journalistic miracle
(as Walter White has so described it), these weekly newspapers filled in
the glaring absence of useful news and information about African American progress and setbacks that typified the major white dailies. Consequently the dialogism that developed between the black press and its
constituency of heterogeneous readers complicates traditional notions
of narrative form, authorial voice, mode of address, and narrative intent generally thought to constitute the communication act. The black
journalist-reader dynamic was constituted generally by two-way messages that provided black readers more direct participation in public
matters than was available via the major white presses at this time.

In the black press's ever increasing role as the cultural arbiter of an
emerging film culture in black metropolises across America, the entertainment pages placed a new emphasis on the films and movie houses,
with each theater generally commanding its own share of a newspaper's
amusements column. Through all this, black theater critics and writers
regularly filled their embryonic film discourses with exhortations that

their readers should "join the crowd" and "*get the habit*" (italics mine) of filmgoing ("Jottings"). I might add that the tremendous social and cultural influence exerted by black newspapers and the new film medium did not go unchallenged by the historical leaders of the African American community, namely, the church. In fact, it did not take long for the church to recognize and react to the threat posed by the cinema to the church's long-standing hegemony. Consequently, as occurred in mainstream society, the African American church's response to the cinema's growing influence spurred a major debate within this fragmented community about the cinema's role in the race's social-uplift agenda. Following this, it should come as no surprise that the African American press began to scrutinize the cinema more closely.

The present work is divided into five chronological parts, with each demonstrating some significant elements of intertextuality between African American and more mainstream cinema histories. For example, chapter 1, "*The Souls of Black Folk* in the Age of Mechanical Reproduction," is explicitly concerned with the earliest writing on the cinema by African American journalists that has not, at this writing, been reprinted elsewhere. A significant aspect of this chapter is its foregrounding of the relationship between the contents of the black press and a number of the major sociocultural vicissitudes that typified race relations at the turn of the century. Thus the reader is invited to recognize within northern newspapers such as the *New York Age*, the *New York Amsterdam News*, and the *Chicago Defender* a cultural discourse so influential that it helped engender the first wave of the great migration of African Americans from the economically depressed and racially polarized South to the imagined promised land of the industrial North. Once established as an important labor force in cities such as Chicago, New York, Baltimore, and Pittsburgh, this migrant community's eventual possession of leisure time and money easily transformed them into a substantial audience for the new cinema. As chapter 1 will demonstrate, it was not only as avid spectators that black migrants interacted with the early cinema. Since many were also possessed of a sense of Du Boisian racial consciousness, these avid filmgoers interacted with the cinema as critics as well. As black film fandom increased during these early years, so too did the black press's critical and celebratory commentary on film. On behalf of a burgeoning black readership caught up in the modernizing process of social, political, cultural, and economic transformation, African American journalists and other race leaders understood from the outset that blacks needed to be as passionately engaged with the cinema as the cinema was with them.

Protest literature against *The Birth of a Nation* is the one aspect of black film criticism with which most film historians and scholars are familiar. Chapter 2 not only revisits well-known aspects of this legendary journalistic history but also introduces articles that have not previously been collected or referenced in discussions of this highly controversial film. For example, in 1919, the *New York Age*'s resident theater and film critic, Lester A. Walton, wrote an important article discussing the international repercussions of *The Birth of a Nation* in terms that prefigure contemporary debates about American cultural imperialism. Also, analyses of pre–*Birth of a Nation* articles are incorporated because they constitute necessary components of this volatile issue to the extent that they document the vigilant campaign waged by the black press against Thomas Dixon's race-baiting narrative from the start. In this chapter, *Chicago Defender* columnist Sylvester Russell's 1911 pre–*Birth of a Nation* article "Tom Dixon's Latest Play," along with Walton's series of remonstrations against his fellow black journalists and black spectators who failed to join in the protests against the film, are included because they counter the myth of a monolithic response by African Americans to *The Birth of a Nation*. These essays are important commentaries on this issue, especially in view of cultural studies theorizing about resistant or transgressive readings of literary and cinematic significations. Another meaningful shift that becomes apparent in this section is the fact that film essays begin to expand in length. This is an interesting corollary to the expanded narrativization of the American feature film inaugurated by the unprecedented success of *Birth of a Nation*.

In chapter 3 we will see that African American film criticism exhibits an optimism that is absolutely consistent with, and determined by, the particular historical milieu created at the juncture of the Roaring Twenties and the Harlem Renaissance. As the southern plantation "darky" effected a timely self-reinvention as the northern "New Negro," the critical posture of these black writers toward the cinema was transformed accordingly. Generally, the critical trend in black writing on film during the twenties was ebullient, optimistic, and ultimately naive. This was the silent-film era, and resourceful African American entrepreneurs such as William Foster (also known as Juli Jones), Oscar Micheaux, Emmet J.

Scott, and George and Noble Johnson entered the fray of independent filmmaking. It is important to note that this early entrepreneurial activity flourished before the economic cartel of the powerful studio system and the advent of vertical integration, factors that virtually foreclosed the competitive ability of black independent filmmakers to function within the newly configured entertainment industry as the decade drew to a close. Until that time, African Americans seized the opportunity to master the relatively primitive and inexpensive film technology for crafting new self-representations and generating economic self-sufficiency. Unlike the legitimate stage, which was nearly completely closed to African Americans (with the exception of minstrelsy and burlesque), pre-Hollywood independent filmmaking presented a means by which black artists could break the manacles of minstrelsy and reflect their changing social and cultural status. Consequently black filmmakers and critics of the era were among the cinema's strongest proponents during those heady days. Some black filmmakers, particularly Micheaux and Jones, produced for the black press some of the most insightful and cogent film commentary and analysis available at the time to black or white print media outlets.

Chapter 4 will focus attention on the growing sophistication of black film criticism that developed during the period between the two world wars. Black film commentary produced in the thirties and forties is symptomatic of the political schism that bisected the African American community along radical and conservative lines, a schism dating back to the notorious debates between W. E. B. Du Bois and Booker T. Washington over their competing philosophies of racial uplift. Coming of age as it did in the wake of the Harlem Renaissance, black film criticism during this epoch grew increasingly more complex, for here the African American literati as well as journalists and academics were disillusioned by the demise of the black renaissance, the financial devastation of the Great Depression, and the technological barriers erected by the sound revolution in film. All together, these devastating events ushered in a period of critical reevaluation for African Americans writing about the cinema during the ascendancy of the now-classical studio system. Some of the film essays in this chapter convey a radical response to these events adopted by one segment of African American society during those days. Most notable in this regard are the radical critiques of the cinema that appeared in the far-left black newspaper the *Harlem Liberator*, which later changed its name to the *Negro Liberator.* The *Liberator,* in both incarnations, adhered to a Marxist political perspective, and each weekly edition carried two film columns, one entitled "Camera Eye" and the other "Movie Snapshots." In these columns, the critics promoted the efforts of the Workers Film and Photo League and invariably stressed the need for black spectators to resist the ideology of capitalism codified and reified in mainstream Hollywood films, and they routinely denounced what they considered capitalism's exploitative industry practices. At the other critical pole were the accommodationist writers, who often rationalized their uncritical celebratory film discourse in the guise of supporting struggling black film actors. Having set forth this critical polarity, in the interest of fairness, it is important to acknowledge the moments of intersection between these camps that yield striking ambiguities and contradictions. In the main, these contradictions surface when these African American writers attempt to reconcile the conflicting imperatives to at once condemn and celebrate talented black actors who perform demeaning stereotypical roles with aplomb. The profuse criticism centered around the film *Imitation of Life,* and its black stars Louise Beavers and Fredye Washington, is telling.

The brand of criticism suggesting a sort of jaded acquiescence by black writers to the intractability of Hollywood's racial bias is the focus in chapter 5. The film literature from this era reveals the limits of black critics' dialogic encounter with Hollywood's short-lived but self-serving reformist moment calculated to enlist maximum African American support for the war effort. At the behest of the U.S. military, Hollywood did produce select films featuring blacks that broke temporarily with its usual stereotypes. Nothing illustrates this tenuous united front better than the nation's split "Victory at War" campaign. Whereas Hollywood and the majority population crafted rhetoric around the "V" for victory campaign in terms of success abroad, the black press upped the ante literally to make the slogan serve double duty. The black press rechristened it the "Double V" campaign to symbolize not just victory over Fascism and Nazism in Europe but "victory at home and abroad." After the war, however, frustrated black film critics were forced to turn their attention to the hypocrisy of Hollywood and its betrayal of patriotic African Americans who were sacrificed yet again, on the altar of the southern box office. At the same time, black film criticism of this era reveals Hollywood's feeble attempt to use the "social problem" films to reimpose the nation's prewar Jim Crow racial images on America's shell-shocked post-war generation. Recognizing the anachronism of its antebellum mammy and coon stock types, Hollywood cleverly devised transitional black stereotypes such as the Hottentot Saphire and the hep cat or urbane entertainer, for instance. These were the character staples of the genres of musical short subject films (or precursors to television's music videos) and feature-length musicals of the 1940s. The polite but segregated world that Hollywood musicals accommodated provided black critics less overtly vitriolic but equally insidious racial stereotypes with which to concern themselves. Consequently cynicism becomes a more discernible undercurrent in many of these articles as black cultural workers attempt "the management of ruptures."[5] In the years following World War II, the management of ruptures in Hollywood's progressive treatment of black themes and characters led black writers to extend their criticisms to include Hollywood's increasingly worrisome competitors, primarily television, but black music and radio as well. While they maintained a recalcitrant gaze on Hollywood, black critics both encouraged and covered black film performers' migration to these seemingly promising newer modes of cultural expression.

In a landmark 1944 essay, Lawrence Reddick demonstrated that American cinema, from its inception, posited African Americans in radical alterity to white norms. Listening to today's debates about the NAACP initiative to protest blacks' exclusion from leading roles in network television programming, one cannot help being reminded of the organization's earlier efforts with the film industry. But although popular attention to black engagement with the moving image seems always to begin with no knowledge of what has gone before, the fact remains that contemporary black criticisms of the media rest on, and evolve from, a long and complicated history of critical thinking and viewing.

1

The Souls of Black Folk

in the Age of Mechanical Reproduction

BLACK NEWSPAPER CRITICISM AND

THE EARLY CINEMA, 1909–1916

By means of its technical structure, the film has taken the physical shock
effect out of the wrappers.—Walter Benjamin, *Work of Art*

While passing a moving picture theater . . . The writer was surprised to
see . . . JOHN SMITH of PARIS, TEXAS, BURNED at the STAKE. HEAR
HIS MOANS and GROANS. PRICE ONE CENT!
—Lester Walton (*Degeneracy*)

We seldom study the condition of the Negro today honestly and carefully.
It is so much easier to assume that we know it all.
—W. E. B. Du Bois (*Souls*)

The American cinema was born during the era Rayford Logan described as "the nadir" of the African American experience in post-
Reconstruction America, from 1897 to 1917. African American film criticism was born likewise amid this political maelstrom, characterized by
the nation's retrenchment from the goal of racial justice once advanced
during Reconstruction. Emerging as it did within the late-nineteenth-
century historical milieu marked by the 1897 *Plessey v. Ferguson* Supreme
Court decision that inaugurated the sweeping system of "separate but
equal" Jim Crow legislation, early American cinema at once reflected and

influenced this fateful aspect of the nation's racial politics. From the outset, many of the era's one-reel films, such as American Mutascope and Biograph Company's (AMBCO) *Who Said Chicken* (1902), *The Gator and the Pickaninny* (1903), *While Strolling in the Park* (1904), *Kiss in the Dark* (1904), *The Misdirected Kiss* (1904), *A Bucket of Cream Ale* (1904), and *A Nigger in the Woodpile* (1904), yoked the cinema's earliest signifiers to the potent theatrical idiom of blackface minstrelsy. More important, since the cinematic apparatus was considered at one with other modern scientific instruments—namely, the microscope, thermometer, and telegraph (Winston 1993, 37), with their strong claims on "truth," "reality," and empirical verifiability—early cinematic narratives, often minstrel derivatives, were even more formidable in popularizing and reifying America's politics of white racial supremacy. Now the power of scientific inscription was put in the service of ultrareactionary race politics, as these early film shorts convey. At the same time, efforts to countermand this political blacklash against African Americans' sociocultural strivings must be recognized as a motivating factor in the rise of the critical discourse—inchoate as it may be—about the early cinema by African American literary figures, scholars, journalists, and cultural leaders.

Indeed, as effective as Jim Crow laws were in undermining any lingering ideals of racial equity between European and African American citizens in post-Reconstruction America (Janken 1993, 7), they became even more efficacious when aligned with America's ascendant institutions of mass culture. This separatist trend had clearly gained momentum in the mid– to late nineteenth century with the rise of antebellum minstrel theater, regarded by some observers as "'the only true American drama' or an 'American National Opera'" (Toll 1974, v). In his book *Blacking Up: The Minstrel Show in Nineteenth Century America*, Robert Toll identifies blackface minstrelsy as the first national entertainment "shaped by and for the masses of average [white] Americans" (26). With the arrival of the motion picture industry, the kinds of distortions popularized by minstrelsy were taken up and promulgated by the new cinematic regime of representation.

Meanwhile, certain mainstream writers and theorists of the age entered into heated debate over the relative merits of these new mass arts in terms of "high" and "low" cultural norms and specificities, the dichotomy of art versus science, and the role of mimetic and nonrepresentational art in America's cultural institutions. In contrast, many turn-of-the-century African American cultural critics regarded the issues in less esoteric terms. For them, the advent of mass culture, especially the cinema, represented a fundamental transformation of the very nature of art itself. No longer was the matter a simple question of whether scientific innovations such as photography and film could be deemed worthy of the appellation "Art." More pressing for them was the potential of these new media to craft and legitimate even more destructive renderings of black life and culture. It is precisely this point that troubled the African American intellectuals writing about art and culture in America during this era, men such as the *New York Age*'s drama columnist Lester A. Walton, scholar and activist W. E. B. Du Bois, clergyman Adam Clayton Powell Sr., and minstrel performer George Walker, among many others. Moreover, in keeping with what Dolan Hubbard (1994) terms the "sermonic hermeneutics" of the African American "preacherly voice,"[1] these writers foregrounded the sociopolitical pragmatics of these new cultural forms and their impact on the newly self-reinvented black masses. Accordingly, these respected black leaders began to advance their own interpretive theories to explain the difficulties and potentialities of art's modernist transformation. From their often "messianic" writings, it becomes apparent that many of these black intellectuals understood clearly W. E. B. Du Bois's (1926) statement that "all art is propaganda and ever must be, despite the wailing of the purists" (514).

Taking the lead in articulating some important consequences of traditional cultural productions was the incomparable George Walker (1906). In an early instance of cultural critique, Walker's sage deliberations on blackface minstrelsy and its powerful naturalization of African Americans' racial subordination illustrate Du Bois's point well:

> Black faced white comedians used to make themselves look as ridiculous as they could when portraying a "darky" character. In their "make-up" they always had tremendously big red lips, and their costumes were frightfully exaggerated. The one fatal result of this to the colored performers was that they imitated the white performers in their [own] make-up as "darkies." *Nothing seemed more absurd than to see a colored man making himself ridiculous in order to portray himself.* (243; italics mine)

At once a celebrated cultural performer and astute critic, Walker, one-half of the world-renowned Williams and Walker black minstrel duo, experienced firsthand the difficulties of "double-consciousness'" incongruities. Walker well understood the absurdities inherent in the black minstrel's valiant attempt to reconcile the conflicting natures of his Eurocentric and Afrocentric cultural legacies. Even though Walker's essay "The Negro on the American Stage," published in 1906 by *Colored American Magazine,* is a specific analysis of the stage and thus is precinematic, its applicability to early film criticism is evident. Here, Walker's sophisticated critique of the African American minstrel's complicity in his own victimization, a complicity that aids and abets minstrelsy's antiblack rhetorics, is quite simply a brilliant instance of self-reflexivity. It is important to understand that Walker and partner Bert Williams established their minstrel act by rejecting the burnt-cork makeup convention instituted by white minstrels. Unfortunately, their reform efforts could go only so far. By articulating African Americans', indeed his own, conflicted participation in minstrelsy, a participation purchased at the exorbitant cost of negating more authentic black cultural expressions, Walker suggests clues whereby we might begin to appreciate the nascent cinema's powerful allure for early-twentieth-century African Americans.

Initially, the new entertainment medium seemed to promise an alternative to the limitations of black theatrical minstrelsy, so eloquently delineated by Walker. It is important to bear in mind, however, that this attenuated black theatricality flourished only as the national preoccupation with white minstrel shows waned (Toll 1974, 135). Notwithstanding the early cinema's predilection for crafting vituperous and dehumanizing caricatures of black life, the "nickelettes," as black minister Adam Clayton Powell Sr. referred to film exhibition houses in 1910, were immensely popular among the reconstituting African American communities on both sides of the Mason-Dixon line.[2] Against this backdrop, it is telling that the optimism and enthusiasm of the cinema's first black audiences rarely, if ever, corresponded to the brutal reality of the cinema's early racist narratives, of which Edison's *The Watermelon Patch* (1905), and AMBCO's *The Chicken Thief* (1904) are exemplars.[3] Put another way, turn-of-the-century African American spectators were seduced into a painfully unrequited and yet enduring love affair with the primitive cinema.

Although some contemporary film historians have taken a second look at the earliest film literature in an effort to chronicle unofficial histories of European immigrants and other now-mainstream groups (Carbine

Preeminent black entertainer George W. Walker performing in sophisticated antiminstrelsy garb, ca. 1900s. Courtesy of the Manuscripts, Archives, and Rare Books Division–Schomburg Center for Research in Black Culture, the New York Public Library, Astor, Lenox, and Tilden Foundations–Lester A. Walton Photograph Collection.

Advertisement for a black minstrel show displays the blackface caricatures that the Williams and Walker duo rejected. *Chicago Defender,* 1910.

Bert Williams and George Walker, the first black minstrels
who refused the burnt-cork, blackface makeup tradition. Courtesy
of the Manuscripts, Archives, and Rare Books Division—Schomburg
Center for Research in Black Culture, the New York Public
Library, Astor, Lenox, and Tilden Foundations—Lester A. Walton
Photograph Collection.

1990, 9), there still remains a conspicuous lack of concern for, and interest in, African Americans' literary contributions to American film history. To fill this void and to explore the love-hate dialectic suffusing the first African American cultural leaders' and spectators' interaction with the early cinema, it is necessary to recover the numerous black press articles and columns that were devoted to news of this technological innovation. In refocusing attention on the first decade of literary production by African Americans on the cinema, specifically from 1909 to 1916, we must first begin with the prolific doyen of early African American film criticism, the *New York Age*'s resident drama critic Lester A. Walton, and his contemporaries at the *Chicago Defender,* Sylvester Russell, Minnie Adams, Columbus Bragg, and Tony Langston.

Lester A. Walton and the Birth of Cinema's *Ecriture Noire*

For more than a decade, Lester A. Walton edited the *New York Age*'s popular entertainment page, which included music, stage, and film reviews. Until his 1920s promotion to managing editor of the newspaper and his subsequent return to stage theatrical management, Walton was the *New York Age*'s, and by extension most of black America's, cultural arbiter. In this capacity, he can be regarded as African America's first major mass-culture griot. Many features of Walton's penetrating analyses are recognizable today in such yet-to-be developed aspects of film study as genre criticism, narratology, spectatorship and reception, apparatus and textual analysis, and industry practices. It should also be pointed out that Walton's mixing of several of these critical approaches in a single essay does not represent a weakness in thematic unity as much as it underscores the cinema's interdisciplinarity. Additionally, his ever-vigilant gaze on the stages and screens of New York's theatrical establishments and his prolific literary output on the subject construct a historical and cultural blueprint for tracing African America's early tradition of responding to those early filmic narratives that Kay Sloan (1988) has dubbed "the loud silents." In effect, Walton used his public voice to "talk back," as bell hooks (1989) would term it, on behalf of the silenced mass of African Americans, a necessary act of opposition to the emerging hegemony of the country's nascent culture industries. "'Talking back,'" hooks writes, "meant speaking as an equal to an authority figure. It meant daring to disagree and sometimes it just meant having an opinion" (hooks 1984, 5). Indeed, Walton had a number of audacious opinions that he dared to express in his weekly column, entitled "Music and the Stage." As a matter of course, Walton's critiques became increasingly fixated on cinematic objectifications of the black body.

Beginning with his 1909 essay "The Degeneracy of the Moving Picture Theatre," which followed a more customary theatrical review, and extending through the more complete discussions of the cinema that frequently commanded the entire column, Walton's talking back instigates the early cinema's first black writing. On 15 December 1910, for example, Walton addressed the ongoing battle for the souls of black folk being waged by the cinema and the church. On 23 February 1911, he covered the "Change Wrought by Motion Picture Craze"; on 5 June 1913, the column was devoted to "The Motion Picture Industry and the Negro"; in October of that year, it was "Motion Picture Concern Makes Film Ridiculing Race"; and in 1914 he wrote a column on African Americans and the push for representation on film censor boards in the Northeast, as well as "New Yorkers Have Gone 'Dippy' over the Movies." From his cultural pulpit at one of the most influential black newspapers of its day, Walton forged his column as a potent cultural force with which to talk back against what he saw as a tendency of "degeneracy" in America's emergent commercial cinema.

Walton's writings signify an early intervention in the new medium's ability to diminish and somehow displace the horror and national shame of black lynchings. His recourse to acts of literary defiance begins with his 5 August 1909 article for the *New York Age*, entitled "The Degeneracy of the Moving Picture Theatre." In this first critical essay on the cinema, Walton chafes at the P. T. Barnum promotional stratagem deployed by early movie theater establishments to lure unsuspecting film enthusiasts into venues aiming to profit from the spectacularization of this horrific aspect of African American pain and suffering:

> While passing a moving picture theatre on Sixth avenue several days ago, the writer was surprised to see a sign prominently displayed in front of the place bearing the following large print: JOHN SMITH of PARIS, TEXAS, BURNED at the STAKE. HEAR HIS MOANS and GROANS. PRICE ONE CENT! A crudely-painted picture of a colored man being burned at the stake completed the makeup of the offensive as well as repulsive-appearing

sign. Judge the great surprise of the writer when two days later while walking down the Bowery a similar sign met his gaze, the same earnest appeal being made by the proprietor of the moving picture theatre to the public to walk in and *enjoy* [italics mine] the sight of a human being meeting death by burning, with the moans and groans thrown in for a penny. . . . The promoters of moving picture theatres make the assertion that their pictures are of an educational nature. . . . We would like to know where do the elements of education come in so far as the picture in question is concerned? (Walton 1909a)

Walton's righteous indignation at the ease with which early filmmakers hijacked the cinema's formal properties to aestheticize such "barbarism" (Walton's term) is certainly warranted. In recognizing the obvious racialized appeal of these shockingly desensitizing images to the film's implied white audience, Walton is correct to challenge the narrative intent of these loathsome and highly suggestive representations of black victimization in a society beset by routine racial conflagrations and deep-seated antagonisms.[4] Walton lucidly protests the cinematic effect in overpowering and ultimately supplanting an individual's moral thought processes during those heightened moments of spectatorial suturing and identification. His essay, in effect, demystifies the lynch film's incredibly seductive and affective powers to inhibit moral outrage even as it flaunts the film's ability to engender sociopolitical acquiescence. By suggesting further that the abhorrent lynching film will likely be exhibited in theaters across the nation, Walton warns against the very real and present dangers that mass communication of these incendiary images poses for the nation's divided body politic.

Decrying the moral bankruptcy informing the text of the theater's promotional placard, Walton makes clear his position that the scandal was not confined to the mere production and exhibition of these loathsome pictures. Consumption of them was equally ignoble in Walton's estimation because it meant "the planting of the seed of savagery in the breast of those whites who even in this enlightened day and time are not any too far from barbarism" if, indeed, their spectatorial pleasure could so easily be purchased by such wanton displays of barbarous violence.

Not content to leave his "sermonic hermeneutics" to revelation or exposé alone, in his preacherly mode, Walton then shifts to a prescriptive. In the article's conclusion, Walton issues a call to action (a call, incidentally, he repeats in subsequent articles). Having thus laid out the urgency of the situation, he implores ministers and lay readers alike to protest and, implicitly, to boycott such cinematic mendacity. Presciently, he ends with a caveat: "If, we do not start now to put an end to this insult to the race, expect to see more shocking pictures with the Negro as subject in the near future" (this quote has added saliency because the warning preceded the national protests of *The Birth of a Nation*). As his impassioned plea attests, Lester Walton refused to avert his gaze from the cinema's deliberate or unwitting vitiations of the shame and horrors of black lynchings, both literal and figurative. By refusing to mute his outrage over the commodification of black pain and suffering, Walton notified the commercial interests of the day that certainly he refused to participate in the conspiracy of silence and indifference that authorized the reduction of the lynched black body to the latest aesthetic feature in America's early cinema of attractions.

Apparently Walton's call for a moral rejection of such images did not go unheeded. So compelling was this article that certain white newspapers were moved or shamed into endorsing his position. Two weeks after the publication of his "Degeneracy" essay, Walton reported that his antilynching film commentary had struck a responsive chord in the larger community, evidenced by the essay's reprint in the white motion picture trade journal *Moving Picture News*. Walton and his readers must have felt a vindication of sorts when this white industry journal, during the height of the Jim Crow era, not only reprinted this African American criticism but included such sympathetic comments as "We would like to ask the writers and film makers to read [Walton's criticism] and let it burn into their consciences and cease giving offense to vast numbers of our population" (quoted in Walton 1909b). In addition to his critical interventionist approach to the new cinema, Walton's early film criticism was also characterized by a reformist propensity that enabled him to envision the cinema's dormant emancipatory potential.[5]

In the year following the "Degeneracy" article, Walton used his column to explore the growing tensions between the black church and the increasingly popular cinema. Exacerbating the controversy over what religious leaders saw as the secular erosion of the moral center of black life was the inability of the African American clerics to mount a united front in opposition to the major culprit in all this, the moving pictures. Positioned on one side of the hotly contested issue of whether moving picture theaters should be banned, with Godspeed, in the African American community were conservative ministers galvanizing support for a nationwide crusade against all moving picture establishments. On the other side stood clerics of a more moderate inclination. This group perceived the cinema as a relatively innocuous social outlet for the working masses, and even perhaps as a modern tool that might somehow be used for revitalizing the church itself. Endorsing this latter position, Walton nevertheless decided to submit the matter to his readers. In a mode that typifies the communal orientation of the black press at that time, Walton turned his column over to the Reverend Adam Clayton Powell Sr., "for the benefit of the readers of the *Age,* and for the Rev. Powell to tell, in his own words, 'why he is opposed to the church starting a crusade on the five and ten cent theaters'" (Walton 1910). In principle, it might appear that Walton should be predisposed in the opposite direction, especially with this article coming so soon after his own spirited campaign against cinematic sensationalism. According to this logic, Walton's support of the dissenting ministers might seem inconsistent. Although such a charge is understandable on the surface, a more probing review suggests that the two calls for censure operating here are sufficiently differentiated so as to make such a reduction or conflation of the two shortsighted. Whereas ministers Dr. Clair of Washington, D.C., and the Reverend E.W. Daniels of New York were agitating for a complete disavowal of all films and all movie theaters, Walton, even with his stage bias, judiciously confined his opposition only to those theaters exhibiting the repulsive lynch films.

Whereas Walton's articles from 1909 to 1910 outline his concerns with the micropolitics of the cinema's racial themes, his 1911 article entitled "Change Wrought by Motion Picture Craze" indicates his growing interest in the cinema's more far-reaching macropolitics of the racial discourse. At this time, he also begins to concentrate more on the institutional nature of cinema's encroachments on the entire entertainment establishment. In this column, Walton talks about the seemingly benign trend in Brooklyn and Manhattan theaters of abandoning their mainstays of musical comedy and dramatic plays in favor of the more popular vaudeville and the wildly successful motion pictures that, in many cases, accompanied them. But Walton's point is the imminent devastation these new entertainment policies could wreak on the newfound viability of the struggling African American theatrical establishments. Walton knew only too well how tenuous the present inroads African Americans had made on the so-called Great White Way were, and he put the case thus:

> The information [this entertainment shift] advanced did not occasion much of a flurry in theatrical circles over Brooklyn, being regarded merely as an incident in the meteoric career of the motion-picture business, which has had a marvelous growth in recent years—so much so that the entire theatrical map has undergone a decided change by its invasion. It is doubtful if there are many playgoers in Manhattan who are aware of the change of policy inaugurated by the management of the Court Street Theatre, and even so, they, too, do not attach much significance to the announcement. And yet, the desertion by the Court of musical comedy and drama for vaudeville and motion pictures means a great deal to one branch of the show business—the colored musical shows. (Walton 1911)

As one of the first generation of African American writers to earn a livelihood as a journalist specializing in the dramatic arts, Walton was not only in a unique position to read the proverbial handwriting on the wall; he also seems to have fully embraced his calling as the uniquely qualified and equipped messenger capable of deciphering these troubling new cultural codes. To be sure, Walton wanted his readers to understand the significance of the fact that the Court Theatre had "become inoculated with the motion-picture germ," as he described it. And here, as in most of Walton's rhetorical style, his linguistic choices demand a serious reckoning. His witty and accessible rhetorical style often veiled an assiduous and trenchant investigation: "For the past two seasons the Court Theatre has been the one bright and particular spot for colored shows. It has been the oasis of the local theatrical desert and the only popular-priced house in Greater New York that furnished financial encouragement to colored productions." In one of the few contemporaneous rationalizations of Bert Williams's Faustian decision to ally himself with the white minstrelsy establishment when he joined the Ziegfeld Company, Walton asserts: "That is the reason Bert Williams judiciously joined a white Broadway show, and early last season Cole and Johnson, seeing the hand writing on the wall, concluded not to take out a production. The situation is truly a trying one for colored shows." Left unstated here is Walton's understanding of the trying time this transition betokened for his own newly established profession.

As was his usual practice, Walton appended to this analysis a related follow-up article reprinting relevant responses to a prior column. Many of the responses reprinted by Walton emanated from white writers and white establishments compelled to refute or reaffirm his searing critiques, as the earlier "Degeneracy" responses illustrate. In this case, however, the response was a letter from a white music publisher taking umbrage at Walton's charge of pervasive racist practices in the music publishing industry. The company involved was the Harry Von Tilzer Music Publishing Company. Although this particular reply concerned the music business, Walton's conjoining of the distinct scenarios establishes the necessary correlation between the racist practices underlying the transformation of the theater houses and this related music industry episode. Walton seems motivated to disclose the formidable pattern of racial exclusion endemic to all sectors of the white-controlled entertainment industry. He also had no compunction about taking on the white journalists whom Paul Laurence Dunbar would have considered "captious critics" (Dunbar 1913, 189) because of their ability to turn the racial problematic on its head by representing whites as the true victims of the nation's oppressive race-based policies.

In 1909 James Metcalfe, a white drama critic for *Life* magazine, wrote about racial matters and the cinema in a vein that resonates with current appeals to reverse discrimination and anti–affirmative action rhetoric. "It is a curious fact," Metcalf asserts, "that practically the Negro has more rights with respect of the theaters under the laws of New York than the white man has." In addition to reprinting Metcalfe's disingenuous argument in the 18 November 1909 column, Walton responds to the bogus claims and articulates well the deep-seated frustrations experienced by African Americans as true victims of American racism, whose oppression under Jim Crow laws was in little jeopardy of being inverted. Walton's effectiveness in literary contests of this sort hinges on a reprint strategy that permits the internal contradictions of opposing arguments to be self-disclosed, thereby bolstering his own contestations of specific points at issue. In this case, Walton had the easy task of countering Metcalfe's spurious claims that blacks somehow were privileged by a new law of equal access to New York theater seats. Walton reminds Metcalfe and *Age* readers, by quoting Metcalfe's own words, that there is always an available panacea for theater owners desiring to subvert the legal process: "[Where] Negroes have insured seats and insisted on their rights to be seated an ingenious solution has been found. . . . Under some pretext these representatives of the managers pick a row with the Negroes, create a disturbance, a policeman is called in and all hands are taken to the station house. The rest, of course, is easy." That Metcalfe willfully ignores society's de facto antiblack social contract that encourages such "easy" racist maneuvers is not the most important element of Walton's 18 November article. More to the point for Walton is society's refusal to recognize the Americanness of African Americans when the nation was experiencing a tidal wave of foreign immigration to its northern shores. Clearly, there was not the same difficulty of securing public accommodations for the nation's newly arriving European immigrants. Walton frames the national identity question in this way: "What is particularly galling to us is the thought that we who are native-born American citizens are discriminated against solely on account of color, and that an organized effort is being made to deprive us of rights and privileges to which we are justly entitled by law." Regarding the consensus by white theater managers that blacks should not insist on first-floor seats even during a performance of an African American show, Walton goes on to state: "The Negro race was [not] put on the earth to conform with every wish and desire of the Caucasian, and the fact that it was presumed that we were not wanted did not necessarily mean that we should not aspire to make an effort to realize our ambition" (1909c).

In 1912 Walton tuned his critical antennae toward the international response to the cinema's influence. In his 12 March column, Walton relays to his readership this bit of European news: "Moving picture shows are not only bringing about a new condition of affairs in the United States but in Europe, according to a [dispatch] to the *New York Sun* from Germany." In the reprinted *Sun* communiqué was a line that must surely have worried Walton's theater-loving heart: "At a meeting of actors and dramatists in Berlin, Ludwig Fulda said that in consequence of the competition of moving picture shows the 120 theatres in Germany would soon be hopelessly bankrupt." Though it may be true that Walton has excerpted this specific international communiqué because it echoes his own anxieties about the cinema's displacement of his beloved stage entertainments, the fact that he monitored, transmitted, and contextualized news of the global impact of the cinema is remarkable for that time period. Walton's recourse to this globalist strategy is not such an anomaly when viewed diachronically and in terms of the historic tradition of black letters. It is true, after all, that as Frederick Douglass and other former and fugitive slaves found an international audience for their antislavery messages, the American abolitionist movement gained momentum and increased support in progressive white communities in antebellum America. In this context, Walton's internationalist view falls within a historical continuum of audacious African American intellectual freedom fighting. Walton's reprinted *Sun* article goes on to add:

> There is a law in force now which restricts the cinematographs, and the managers and dramatists are looking for further legislation on this subject. The announcement that the new Royal Opera has granted the rights for the summer season to a Parisian film company has aroused angry protests. (Walton 1912a)

Given his past desire to curtail the cinema's destructive reach, Walton's ulterior motives seem justified, especially when counterposed to the cinema's threat to the future of African American theatricality in general, and its corresponding jeopardy to African American safety in particular, especially at this political moment in Jim Crow America. In his closing commentary, Walton underscores the seriousness of the cinematic threat by issuing a prophetic observation: "The majority of theatrical men confess that they do not see any prospects of the moving picture craze waning in popularity in the near future."

In 1949 Nicholas Vardac wrote *Stage to Screen, The Theatrical Origins of Early Film: David Garrick to D. W. Griffith*. In this book, Vardac traces what is now regarded as the early cinema's effort to borrow prestige from the legitimate stage by crafting early film dramas as filmed theater. With the evidence of Walton's discussion of the intense rivalry between the cinema and the stage during American cinema's formative years, there emerges a more complete picture of the origins of the "proscenium bias" that gave impetus to the early one-reelers, also known as filmed theater. Walton's detailing of the economic determinants responsible for the cinema's encroachments on the theater's audience base becomes an indispensable corollary to Vardac's subsequent work on the evolution of this cinematic aesthetic. Vardac begins his study by referencing the mutuality of influence occurring early on between the stage and screen: "Naturally, in these early years, the film and the stage were hardly differentiated from one another; the cinema frequently borrowed from the theatre, while the theatre, in an attempt to counter the new attraction, in its turn borrowed from the film" (xxvi). But in Walton's writings we are made privy to the more problematic dimensions of this "natural" evolutionary process outlined by Vardac. Contained in Walton's 5 March 1914 column, "New Yorkers Have Gone 'Dippy' over the Movies," is his lament over the cinema's "Broadway Invasion." This piece is remarkable for the glimpse it provides into the fierce internecine battles between theatrical luminaries such as David Belasco and Oscar Hammerstein over the cinema's rise to preeminence and the ultimate capitulation by Broadway to its powerful sway. Divulging the telling statistics of the phenomenal growth in the number of nickelodeons and picture palaces mushrooming throughout Greater New York (which the New York Bureau of Licenses tallied at about 950 to 1,000, with new additions daily), Walton clues us in to some of the fascinating facts behind these 1914 numbers:

> The greatly changed attitude of theatrical promoters toward the movies within the last twelve months has been interesting. Three or four years ago . . . representative theatrical managers, those who produced first-class attractions, turned up their noses at the motion picture industry and motion picture theatres, and this turning up of noses was more in a literal sense than figurative. But recently their olfactory organs quickly assumed a different angle. . . . David Belasco, the lessee, decided to sublet [The Republic] to a firm for the presentation of pictures. To this plan Oscar Hammerstein, the owner, vigorously demurred and sought to enjoin Mr. Belasco in the courts from carrying it out. The courts decided against Mr. Hammerstein. . . . And so the conquest of the movies goes merrily on. Additional surrenders are likely to be chronicled at any moment. (Walton 1914b)

On one level, Walton seems to relish the financial chaos inflicted by the cinema on the Great White Way; his message of comeuppance suggests a poetic justice in this state of affairs that ultimately compensates for the years of discrimination practiced against African American thespians, impresarios, and audiences. On another, he wants to pillory the powerful theater barons for their complicity in endangering the future of the legitimate theater. Overall, this article, with its nostalgic reminiscences of the great bygone days of Broadway and its stellar casts and productions, at once eulogizes those theaters that "succumbed to the hypnotizing influences of the movies" and attempts to blunt "the force of the shock sustained by the advent of the movies." Adding further complexity is Walton's own ambivalent response. Even as he despairs over the cinema's

meteoric ascent, he demonstrates apparent pleasure at being able to report on the sensational "electrical display" of a new movie theater debut-
ing with a film version of Alexander Dumas's *Three Musketeers* that "be-
dimmed the luster of the Vitagraph Theatre's electrical exhibition" just
across the street. Significantly, this lengthy article is accompanied by a
large lithograph image of the novelist Alexander Dumas, a writer of
African descent with roots in the Caribbean. Walton's delight in seeing
Dumas's name emblazoned in neon lights along Broadway must have
diminished, temporarily, his apocalyptic view of the cinema's "invasion."
For what other African diasporic writer's name had Walton seen so il-
luminated on the Great White Way?

The broadening of Walton's film criticism becomes more evident as he
encompasses analyses of cinema news apart from "the familiar cry of
drawing the Color Line" (1911) that so hobbled American entertainments. An example of this is Walton's commentary on the proliferation
of "fake pictures" purporting to be of the *Titanic* disaster, which he titles
"Ban on Titanic Moving Pictures." In this 2 May 1912 column, Walton
excoriates the early film industry propensity to pander to "morbid curiosity" in the rush to supply "fake pictures . . . in connection with such an
appalling disaster as the sinking of the *Titanic.*"

> The sinking of the Titanic, accompanied by such a great loss of life, is too
> serious in character to be treated along cheap, melodramatic lines. Then
> even those who were not principals in this great sea tragedy, who secured
> their information through the newspapers, indulged in sufficient realism
> by reading the accounts of the sinking of the ship and drawing on their
> imagination. To see fake pictures was not necessary. (Walton 1912b)

Walton is incredulous when he acknowledges that "morbid curiosity, of
course prompted some to spend their change to see a 'reproduction' of
the great sea tragedy, *knowing, however, before entering that they would
look at fake pictures*" (italics mine).

Here Walton communicates to his readers, in subtle fashion, that seeing a world represented in films is not always believing. He further informs them that "only a few days after it had been made known that the
Titanic had gone down with hundreds on board several film concerns advertised that they could furnish pictures of the 'Sinking of the *Titanic.*'"
This admonition to his constituency warns against being taken in by a
cinematic ruse that trades on "morbid curiosity." More to the point,

however, is Walton's understanding that the "willing suspension of disbelief" credo indeed authorizes such fantastic and often disingenuous cinematic claims to veracity. Walton's questioning of the limits of verisimilitude governing the enormously popular actuality films problematizes the veracity of filmic representation on the whole. Moreover, he indirectly challenges the presumed sanctity and irrefutability of the very principles of scientific inscription on which early film spectators uncritically based their mediated knowledge of the complex and often unknowable world that existed outside the narrow confines of their everyday lives. Besides noting how the fake *Titanic* pictures compromise the newsreels' privileged claims to verisimilitude, Walton also calls attention to other questionable examples of the actuality films' reliance on instances of "staged authenticity" (to borrow a phrase from Dean MacCannell).

Writing once again on the cinema in his 5 June 1913 column, Walton interrogates the role of the motion pictures "in properly presenting to the world at large the American Negro." Here Walton contrasts the Pathe Weekly newsreel depiction of black migrants from Memphis, Tennessee, moving to the nation's capital, with the newsreel's coverage of German peasants going to Sunday services. Pointing out the racial economy served by the filmmakers' conscious decision to inscribe this scene of black misery in the comedic vein, Walton observes:

> All the refugees in line were colored. Then the operator who took the pictures must have made up his mind to inject a bit of comedy. The spectacle of this long line of hungry, homeless men, women and children did not touch his sympathetic chord, nor did it awaken a feeling of sadness. . . . So he arranged three little black, half-starved pickannies in a row, sat a bowl of mush and a piece of bread before each and then waited to see the fun. Even a cultured grown-up person, when nearly famished, thinks but little of etiquette, and these youngsters did not disappoint the operator for the Pathe concern. . . . A negro woman was also put on exhibition. (Walton 1913b)

Walton then juxtaposes the documentary effect or naturalizing tendencies of the newsreel's comedic scenario of blackness to the more flattering travelogue footage signifying normative whiteness in the world of the German peasants:

> From the "comic" pictures the audience was taken abroad and the Kaiser of Germany figured in one scene. The peasants going to church on Sunday in

one of the German towns was next shown, and as I gazed at the reproduction showing the German boys and girls making their way to church in large numbers, I wondered why it was that the Pathe people had seen fit to depict to the world the lowest type of the Negro—the ignorant, half-starved, homeless and deformed—while the peasantry of Germany was presented in Sunday clothes and at their best. (1913b)

Walton's Socratic irony in describing the racial binary oppositions this scene constructs is clarified in his cogent analysis of the ideological function of the abject images of blackness. To thwart this naturalizing of the first wave of the great black migration in terms of an undesirable social burden, Walton recalls the harm to African American sociopolitical advancement incurred by demeaning and pernicious stereotypes already circulating in America's polarized society. Although Walton does not address the fact that Pathe is predominantly a French film company, he is concerned with the global construction of racial difference that such juxtapositions of images advance. Consider this biting interrogative:

Certain Negro stage types have been instrumental in making thousands of whites in this and in other countries believe us to be as a whole what we are not, and if the motion picture concerns continue to do as the Pathe people in showing the refugees at Memphis, or rather the colored refugees, the impression of the Negro in America will grow worse instead of better. (1913b)

When we situate this analysis in the context of the massive influx of new arrivals to the nation's northeastern industrial centers and the subsequent social and cultural vicissitudes it impelled, Walton's assessment takes on added significance. James Weldon Johnson's important study of the African American presence in New York from slavery through the Harlem Renaissance sheds further light on the sociopolitical stakes involved here. Originally published in 1930, Johnson's *Black Manhattan* (1968) census figures on the staggering number of Europe's first wave of Anglo-Saxon immigrants to New York, nearly four million by the turn of the century (45), provide the necessary background for a nuanced reading of Walton's discourse on the cinema's role in fomenting antiblack sentiments while at once fostering attitudes of tolerance for, and acceptance of, the first- and second-generation European immigrants. Even though Walton's critique of Pathe's newsreels predates the swell of the great migration of African Americans that ensued during and after World War I, it is clear that Walton's remarks do address the precipitous decline in the quality of life for black New Yorkers who "lost ground" as a result of their reduced competitiveness "in the wider fields of domestic service, common labor, and the so-called menial jobs" amid this cultural upheaval (Johnson 1968, 45). Through Walton's vigilant gaze we apprehend the contribution of these early cinematic images in authorizing society's tacit rules of interracial coexistence in turn-of-the-century New York. In "talking back" against this balkanization of racial prejudice directed at African Americans, he continues: "Even in the United States the white and colored citizens are living practically side by side, with the white citizens, in general, knowing very little about us." Additionally, Walton contends, "If the motion picture concerns are sincere in their desire to educate the masses, they ought to make pictures showing the better elements of the race, not the lowest" (1913b). As if to counteract Pathé's skewed cinematic portraiture of modern blackness, Walton printed a photo next to his article of an obviously refined, fair-skinned, middle-class black vaudeville performer named Ada Guiguesse. The photo suggests that if filmmakers would not present "pictures showing the better elements of the race," Walton certainly would.

Rather than leave this important matter up to white theatrical establishments profiting, in more ways than one, from such racially divisive film portrayals, Walton implores those "motion picture houses conducted by colored managers [to] make it their business to prevail upon the manufactures of motion picture films to present the Negro under more favorable conditions."

> The motion picture industry can wield an influence for good and serve as an educational medium in helping to solve the so-called Negro question if it will; but setting up to the world from time to time the very lowest types of the race, whether intentionally or unconsciously done is harmful. (1913b)

Here Walton demonstrates his profound understanding of the mediating function of films that prefigures later arguments against reflection theories of film and other media representations. As a member of a group most denied, as a matter of course, true cinematic reflections or mirrorings of its lived realities—even in actualities or newsreels—Walton knew firsthand how limited, though politically efficacious, claims to cinematic verisimilitude could be, especially in race matters. Moreover, it is evident

Refined black woman vaudevillian who displays "the better elements
of the race" that Walton believed white motion picture firms put
under erasure. *New York Age*, 1913.

that Walton understood films' incomparable ability to influence social attitudes on important issues of the day. In 1914 Walton begins his preemp-
tive strikes against the unrelentingly demeaning portrayals of the race.

Walton's advocacy of African American representation on New York's
Film Censor Board arises out of the study he made of black Chicago's
parallel struggle. This 19 March 1914 article, entitled "Want Representation on Film Censor Board," not only advances this interventionist
strategy but also denounces the culpability of negligent black entrepreneurs. "Severest criticism," he asserts, "should be directed at the colored
people . . . who are not progressive enough to take advantage of the wonderful opportunities offered to make money in the amusement world"
(1914a). Not one to turn a blind eye to the responsibility of intragroup
critique, Walton is willing to lay partial blame for the dismal state of

affairs at the feet of his own upwardly striving community. Instead of condoning a censuring of enterprising whites who endeavor to erect theaters for the black market, Walton instead seeks to prod African Americans along the same lines: "That white men are able to see the commercial possibilities existing among colored people [as avid film-goers] and colored men are not is a reflection on the business acumen of the latter." With that, Walton quotes the following statement provided by certain white theater promoters preparing to launch their black movie house in Norfolk. The remarks are telling:

> As you know, there is not a theater in the city that will seat a colored person, no matter how refined, anywhere except in the peanut gallery, where they are not only segregated to a disadvantage but are exposed to great danger in the case of fire. This theatre will obviate the necessity of colored people . . . subjecting themselves to "Jim Crow" conditions in order to see a decent theatrical production. (1914a)

To further provoke those "colored people fast asleep" and to awaken them as the cinematic revolution was gaining momentum, Walton adds yet another reprint, this time from an article appearing in the 14 March 1914 edition of the *Philadelphia Bulletin*. The article details an ordeal suffered by a twenty-one-year-old African American woman arrested for her noncompliance with the segregation practices of a Philadelphia movie theater. When the young woman screamed as an usher tried to force her to a seat located in the rear of the theater, her screams caused a near stampede as other women in the theater bolted for the doors. The theater proprietors implored the judge to sentence the young woman to prison. Instead, he refused, and on discharging her, the judge suggested that she bring suit against the theater (Walton 1914a). Presumably Walton hoped to cause enough of a stir to galvanize the emergent black bourgeoisie to a proactive stance and thereby circumvent such common-place injustices. For Walton, this meant ushering in a new era of wide-spread black participation in the production, distribution, and exhibition of motion pictures. No doubt Walton's familiarity with the 1913 arrival of the Foster Photoplay Company of Chicago motivated his desire to see a viable black film industry emerge in New York and counter such systemic outrages. Walton wants to make it clear that until blacks themselves create the conditions for bringing about a more hospitable environment

Lester Walton, ca. 1920s.
Courtesy of the Manuscripts,
Archives, and Rare Books
Division–Schomburg
Center for Research in
Black Culture, the New York
Public Library, Astor, Lenox,
and Tilden Foundations–
Lester A. Walton
Photograph Collection.

for black theatergoers (Carbine 1990, 9), such abuse, heaped daily on decent African American citizens whose only offense was attempting to indulge their movie fandom, would surely prevail.

By the end of the decade, Walton's concern with the interrelationship of the cinema and the nation's collective political unconscious had deepened. His last series of regular articles on the cinema for the *Age* appeared in 1919 and are representative. In his 15 March column, entitled "Stop German Opera; Un-American Film Allowed on Screen," Walton inculpates white America in its hypocrisy on matters concerning the public good. Written during America's involvement in the final stages of World War I, this article takes issue with white America's selective view of what constitutes political art. Occasioned by the violent protests of white servicemen against the performances of German operas in New York, Walton uses the situation to unveil the racist logic that permits whites to politicize the German operas as unacceptable "German propaganda" unfit for the wartime economy, and yet to depoliticize the blatant and unrelenting "un-American propaganda," as he puts it, in such films as Griffith's wildly popular opus *The Birth of a Nation*, among others.

> To colored Americans the campaign against German opera is a trivial matter compared to the un-American propaganda which upholds such vicious screen presentations as "The Birth of a Nation" and teaches the false doctrine of "All white men on top and all black men down." After all, aversion against German opera is a mere matter of sentiment; the anti-Negro propaganda strikes at the very roots of the fundamental principles of democracy. (Walton 1919a)

By couching his criticism in terms suggestive of the limits of American liberal humanism, an ethos that fails to include black humanity in its purview, Walton's strategy is twofold. First, he seems to be demanding an acknowledgment that African American lives are on the line in the fight for democracy against German imperialism. And Walton demonstrates that black soldiers, for all their patriotism, can expect no parallel rush to censor antiblack films. Second, he suggests the likelihood that this anti-German sentiment is a temporary, knee-jerk reaction merely projected on, and delimited to, the realm of art, as against the long-standing history of persecution of African Americans that pervades all spheres of American life, without benefit of future rescission. Although his relativizing of the dangers of intolerance in this piece creates another set of problematics, his larger aim to unmask the political unconscious of the nation regarding its racial myopia cannot be minimized.

In "World to Be Americanized by Such Films as 'Birth of a Nation,'" published on 7 June 1919, Walton continues his attack. In this instance, however, he forgoes the local for the global implications that stereotypical films pose. Again, he takes for his object the scrutiny of the highly celebrated text *The Birth of a Nation*. If nothing else, Walton's early example of a popular literature engagé must be seen as contesting and correcting errant notions about African Americans' passive engagement with the cinema's earliest discourses before *The Birth of a Nation*. As these early articles by Walton aptly demonstrate, African American cultural workers were not complacent with nor had they acquiesced to their historically prescribed places at the margins of early film criticism and literary development.

Leaving Walton's specialized discourse on the cinema, for the moment, we now turn to his contemporaries at the *Chicago Defender* and to the phenomenon of the cinema as front-page general news in the black press.

Sylvester Russell and the *Chicago Defender*'s Coterie of Critics

The *Chicago Defender*'s "Musical and Dramatic" column from 1910 to 1914 bore a structural and functional resemblance to its counterpart at the *New York Age*, though there were significant thematic and ideological differences. Unlike the *Age*, with its decade-long history of relatively consistent and evolving film criticism characterized by the tenacious probings of Lester Walton, the *Defender*'s early cinematic discourse is marked by a more sporadic and truncated engagement with the new medium. This was necessarily the situation during those early years at the *Defender*, due in large measure to its revolving door of theatrical critics. The *Defender*'s cadre of critics consisted of Sylvester Russell (the *Defender*'s self-styled "foremost dramatic critic"), Minnie Adams, Tony Langston, and Columbus Bragg. Another distinction separating the early film literature of these two major African American newspapers was each paper's ideological agenda regarding the merits of the cinema. The *Age*'s "Music and the Stage" column, under the philosophical guidance of Walton, took a generally dim view of the cinema as an apparatus for African American uplift or an agent for broader social change, even though Walton did agitate for the establishment of an autonomous African American cinema institution. In contrast, critics at the *Defender* tended toward the more optimistic view. This is perhaps because as early as 1905 Chicago could lay claim to operating the nation's first black-owned movie theater (Carbine 1990, 9). Given the magnitude of this achievement, it is easy to appreciate these critics' embrace of the new medium and the promise it represented.

The *Defender*'s earliest writings on the cinema were contributed by Sylvester Russell, whose 12 March 1910 column reveals that African American stage criticism was poised to enter its second decade, and that "it takes a very capable man in these days to handle it" (Russell 1910a). Of course, Minnie Adams's arrival as critic for the *Defender* complicates Russell's masculinist claim. By April of that year, Russell was making his own tepid overture to discoursing on the new celluloid art. For example, in his 9 April 1910 "Musical and Dramatic" column, Russell's enthusiastic, albeit scant, mention of the cinema amounts to little more than an acknowledgment that "the moving picture theater craze" had developed what he considered "a wonderful stampede among Negro and Yiddish theater goers" (1910b). That Russell's early musings on the cinema pale in

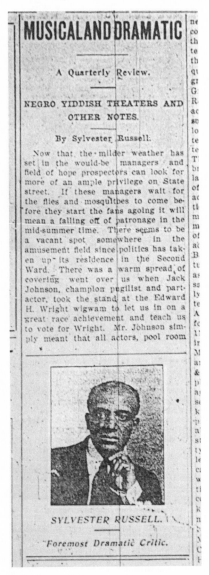

MUSICAL AND DRAMATIC

A Quarterly Review.

NEGRO YIDDISH THEATERS AND
OTHER NOTES.

By Sylvester Russell.

Now that the milder weather has
set in the would-be managers and
field of hope prospectors can look for
more of an ample privilege on State
street. If these managers wait for
the flies and mosquitoes to come before they start the fans agoing it will
mean a falling off of patronage in the
mid-summer time. There seems to be
a vacant spot somewhere in the
amusement field since politics has tak-
en up its residence in the Second
Ward. There was a warm spread of
covering went over us when Jack
Johnson, champion pugilist and part-
actor, took the stand at the Edward
H. Wright wigwam to let us in on a
great race achievement and teach us
to vote for Wright. Mr. Johnson simply meant that all actors, pool room

SYLVESTER RUSSELL.

"Foremost Dramatic Critic."

Sylvester Russell, the *Chicago
Defender*'s self-styled "foremost
dramatic critic." 1910.

comparison to Walton's is clear. Nevertheless, what Russell contributes is
a revealing look at the theatrical critic's role and function at the black
presses of that moment, at least from his self-interested position. First of
all, there is some significance in the fact that Walton, Russell, and Adams
were not mere cultural informants or detached discussants. Each was a
participant-observer of the local theatrical scene. Walton also possessed
impressive theatrical credentials as a member of New York's influential

theatrical association of the 1900s called the Frogs (Hughes and Meltzer 1967, 60). In addition to their journalistic activities, Russell was a vocalist; Adams, a musician; and Bragg, a playwright. In one of his more candid moments, Russell makes this revelation:

> Negro stage criticism is now over ten years old and it takes a very capable man in these days to handle it. And it must be handled carefully and cautiously. And much depends upon who the man is who ventures to tell tales out of school. . . . But actors can't afford to trust the best of us; we are mean to the meager and [magnanimous] to the meritorious. We can't help it. That's our business. (1910a)

It is the case that Russell ignores the obvious fact that meritocracy too often attaches to a highly subjective set of perceptions and pronouncements, and he seems perfectly at ease with its economic determinants. The 30 December 1911 column discussing theatrical competition on State Street, Chicago's black theater district, continues Russell's informative disclosures on the symbiosis of theatrical production and the promotional agenda of critics:

> The most delicate point with managers is the box office, and no intelligent critic of honorable reputation, of long, reliable service has ever been known to criticize the box office system of any theater unless the public had complained and the critic himself had experienced the same unfair treatment and insult from the management. The days of ignorant managers who think they have the divine right to dictate to an intelligent newspaper representative of honest capability is past. . . . Unlawfully prohibiting a newspaper man from a theater . . . is generally the most disastrous thing a manager can do, even in a city where a manager has corrupt assurance of winning law suits by influence and money. . . . I have often been told that Colored newspapers are a joke. . . . The newspapers I represent are far from being a joke. . . . The power of public sentiment is great. (Russell 1911d)

Apart from drawing attention to the imbrication of the critical establishment in the system of mass entertainments, Russell's comments veer into even more intriguing cultural thickets, especially as they concern the racial problematic. First, in tandem with the previous quote, Russell's assertions serve to acquaint both theatrical consumers and producers with his importance as a cultural aesthete or middleman capable of arbitrating their respective desires. For the newly urbanized mass of untutored African American migrants from the South, Russell positions himself as the voice of experience to whom decisions regarding their hard-earned leisure time and money should be entrusted. With the increased competition for black patronage along the Stroll, as State Street was also known, it is not unreasonable to presume that Russell's position of influence grew accordingly. If Russell is attempting here to inspire confidence and loyalty in the hearts of his readers, on the one hand, on the other, he aims to instill a sense of fiduciary anxiety in the minds of bigoted theater operators regarding race matters and box office receipts. At bottom, Russell is reminding "ignorant managers" that, indeed, the new day has brought with it the New Negro, whose newfound socioeconomic status dictated a new approach in the area of public accommodations. One is also left with the distinct impression that Russell betrays his personal frustrations and anger at having suffered the indignities of second-class citizenship in these race theaters during the execution of his duties as theater and film critic. Furthermore, Russell makes it clear that his constituency is not unaware of the judiciary's complicity in perpetuating the theatrical managers' discriminatory cabals. The subtext of Russell's message, however, seems to be that though such treatment of the average Negro patron may go unpunished in a court of law, no such immunity would be granted in the court of Negro public opinion, especially when a respected newspaper man such as himself was victimized (Russell 1911d).

Russell's comment that "no intelligent critic of honorable reputation, of long, reliable service has ever been known to criticize the box office system" underscores E. Franklin Frazier's (1957) concern about black businesses' wholesale adoption of the capitalist ethos. Instead of challenging or opposing the "box office system," Frazier reminds us of the intoxicating nature of the profit motive. He observes that the "Negro professional men engage in the same 'rackets' as the successful Negroes in the underworld" (110) and their white counterparts. Thus Russell's own willful compliance with the "box office system," save the indignities of racism, suggests a sort of uncritical adherence to middle-class consumerist ideology.[6] Although class lines were drawn and blurred to a lesser extent among the second-class African American community in its racial uplift quest, Russell's expectation of enjoying the privileges and prerogatives of an elite class of newspaper men as against those of the average Negro attest to his susceptibility to Lizabeth Cohen's embourgeoisement idea.

Over the course of the following year, the changes in Russell's column to accommodate "the motion picture craze" were minimal. Lacking the critical depth that we see in Walton, Russell's early, inauspicious film commentary appears as little more than footnotes wherein he simply catalogs the weekly film offerings at the neighborhood nickelodeons. These brief mentions of the cinema began with a subtle addition to his column as offset subheadings denoting the latest film schedules at the different theater houses on the Stroll. And thus began the budding commentary on the cinema as an autonomous topic in the high-profile entertainment page of the *Defender*. Accordingly, the first film commentary found in Russell's column stated, "The Phoenix Theatre Shows Good Pictures." Appearing on 1 July 1911, this subheading typified the manner in which the "Musical and Dramatic" column demarcated the boundaries of its theater and film commentary. Although the tone of the short paragraph, which primarily announced the Phoenix Theater's moving picture fare for the week, is uninspiring, it nevertheless carves out a narrative niche for the paper's later, more expanded versions. Generally, in Russell's discussions of films, the narrative tone is subjective, passionate, and suasive; for example, he writes that "the Phoenix theatre is the place for the children, and we are glad to see them go. The picture plays are moral and humorous" (1911b). Here, as before, Russell not only touts the merits of the cinema where children are concerned but also extols its benefits as a suitable and wholesome amusement for young adults.

In his 22 July 1911 column, Russell proclaimed that the Phoenix theater's films were of "high moral character." In his view, "the good class of young people who attended" these moral films should serve to reassure any skeptical parents concerned about the leisure activities of their impressionable youths. In stressing the high moral character of the films at the Phoenix, Russell sought to disabuse dubious parents of the notion that film theaters were equivalent to those other notoriously amoral dens of iniquity littering the crowded tenement districts of southside Chicago, the burlesque houses, saloons, and juke joints, for example. It is through such passages that the *Defender* and Russell's articles often divulge their strong assimilationist ideology (as Franklin and Cohen might argue), or their adherence to bourgeois norms of social progress that critics such as Russell then pass on to their readers. It is important to bear in mind that the *Defender*'s readers are both the dislocated black masses from the South and their slightly less downtrodden brethren hailing from the

North, and that both classes were seeking useful clues to effect their respective sociopolitical transformations. Viewed from this vantage point, Russell's endorsement in the article of the songs accompanying the film, "Battle Hymn of the Republic" and "Wages and Wage Earners," which he says "were especially good" (1911c), is revealing. It reveals that conservative and patriotic values as conveyed through these songs were appealing to, and expressive of, African Americans' Americanness.

One noticeable change early on in the *Defender*'s entertainment column occurred with Russell's exit from the paper. During Russell's tenure as the "Musical and Dramatic" column's resident critic, his distinguished and pensive-looking photo gazed out at readers. At that time, Russell was the *Defender*'s only columnist identified by a photo in addition to a byline. On some level, it seemed that his photo and his theatrical credentials functioned to authorize and legitimize Russell's more grandiloquent journalistic prose, and to distinguish it from the sensational and everyday prose of the paper's "hard" news sections. With Russell's eventual departure, the removal of his photo, and the abandonment of his unique writing style, the more quotidian style of his immediate successor, Minnie Adams, became the column's narrative standard.

Adams's arrival on the entertainment column signaled the column's transitional shift in tone and mood. J. Hockley Smiley, of the *Defender*, notes that "as a critic, she [Adams] is plain but just, and concerns her own self more about whether her efforts are more clearly understood" (Smiley 1911). Whether Smiley's remarks amount to a direct imputation of Russell's more idiosyncratic style is unclear, but the inference seems fair. Ultimately, Russell's photo gave way to Adams's aphorism "All Passes, Art Alone Endures." This decidedly less personalized mode of address also marks the column's linguistic shift from Russell's author-centered, high-art aesthetic of theatrical reviews and critiques to Adams's more circumspect and reportorial prose style. Perhaps the decline of theatrical productions brought about by films, coupled with Russell's own apparent discomfiture with discoursing on the new medium, more an attraction than art, precipitated the increased prominence of film news, for a time, in the entertainment pages of the *Defender*. During her critical reign, the column moved away from discussions of theater syndicates, quarterly assessments, and the role of the critic to more parochial matters. The broader-based discussions of topics such as "The Advisability of a Colored and White Managers' Alliance," "Important Issues of the Negro

Stage Profession," "The Duty of Colored Actor Organizations," and comparative analyses of Negro and Yiddish theaters clearly were Russell's domain. Adams's work, instead, is defined by a more localized sensibility. Her commentary most often was restricted to local reviews of African American vaudeville shows, dramatic plays, and musical concerts and rare discussions of film. However, the most notable contribution Adams made to the early corpus of African American film literature is her essay "In Union Is Strength." Published on 24 February 1912, this article, with its chastisement of Chicago's black community's lack of economic solidarity, was to become Adams's most substantive critique on the cinema. Here Adams holds up the tarnished mirror reflecting the community's failure to adequately patronize the black-owned Pekin Theater, the only such "race" establishment on the Stroll. In so doing, her aim to instill shame and foment a sense of business loyalty in her readers is paramount:

> It is a shame so great that we should blush when we realize how little we care for the welfare of our own. The efforts of individuals for the betterment and the pleasure of the race should be met by the hearty cooperation of every man and woman. . . . One might argue that the offerings at the above named house were not creditable, perhaps not at all times, but on whom can the blame be laid? By all means on the community. Give the [Pekin] theater your support and watch its policies improve. What other house has given our local talent as much consideration as the Pekin? And for that reason if no other, it should have our approval and patronage. . . . We wish to . . . entreat the people to wake up to the fact that they are not letting charity begin at home. (Adams 1912)

In voicing her scorn for this dereliction of group responsibility, Adams fails to recognize the incredible lure of the better-equipped venues for a downtrodden people anxious to experience the best their meager and hard-earned monies could procure. It would be unreasonable, after all, to expect black audiences not to be attracted by the luxury or elegance of theaters featuring decorated foyers, stairways, and ceilings. As Robert Sklar (1976) observes in another context, these amenities greatly enhanced the film experience for early spectators and the profit margins for theater owners who could afford the costly renovations (45). A *Defender* announcement for one of the Star Theater's weekly offerings illustrates the point. " 'The Mad Hermit,' in three reels, will be presented. . . . 'The

Flash of Fate,' a two reel Bison picture, will be thrown on the screen. Both are first runs and well worth seeing. . . . Mr. William Riley, the genial manager, spares no pains or expense in making this the coziest and most attractive movie house on The Stroll. Get the Habit" ("Jottings Theatrical" 1914). These important factors in the totality of the filmgoing experience seem lost on Adams, but apparently not on the film enthusiasts among her readership. Her self-help argument, nonetheless, is well-advised. It is striking that Adams makes it clear that she is not advocating wholesale abandonment of the other, white-owned theaters, but she insists that her readers be mindful of this disquieting reality:

> Many [white] theaters in the city we go to and are admitted on sufferance and more than apt to be relegated to the rear of the house, but we grin and bear it. . . . For those who only laugh in your face for your money and then are willing to lynch you if given half a chance, or, if they become prosperous after having bled you sufficiently they will turn you down. With all due respect for the theaters on State Street, and their managers . . . I feel they are of the opinion that a race is crazy who would not assist to upbuild its own. . . . There are sufficient of the race in Chicago to give to each of the theaters excellent box-office receipts, so that all might live and flourish. (Adams 1912)

Functioning here as a repository of cultural memory for readers expecting perhaps too much from their new urbanized existences, Adams refuses to let them lose sight of the ever present danger of black lynchings as a coercive force in assuring white power and dominance, even in the North. To militate against this formidable obstacle, it is her position, as well as that of most of the black elites, that successful black businesses and subsequent economic strength were the only real leverage against the repressions of white supremacy. In spite of it all, Adams states, "I approve of all the playhouses, the Grand and the Monogram are delightful places of amusement." Her point is not to foreclose the option blacks exercised in attending theaters better appointed than the Pekin along the Stroll. She simply believes that the community should occasionally sacrifice their temporary specular pleasures for a bit of permanent community "upbuilding."

Aside from this rare instance of protracted discourse on the black community's involvement with the cinema, Adams's critical reign displaced Russell's interpretive mode of engagement with the theatrical arts and featured instead description and précis. Occurring as they did before the advent of the feature-length film, Adams's modifications appear a somewhat fitting discursive move for what was largely regarded as the early cinema's passage through its mere recording function. In this light, it is easy to understand how the manifest content of the primitive cinema seemed to eschew critical depth and thorough interpretation (although Walton's lengthy exegeses trouble this proposition somewhat—Walton's case must be contextualized in terms of his consistent and autonomous reign as the *Age*'s solitary critic, and not as one among many). Unlike Russell, Adams would often not be the sole author of the column. Whereas Russell's authorship was never in question, during Adams's one-year or so tenure there were times when the "Musical and Dramatic" column displayed no byline whatsoever.

Eventually, Columbus Bragg and Tony Langston replaced her, each in his turn, as the durable column's critics-at-large. Both Langston and Bragg contribute something to our understanding of the cultural dynamics existing between the black press and its heteroglot readership, a readership speaking multiple regional dialects. This dialogism of the mass and the elite is a crucial intragroup dynamic suffusing the spoken and written languages in the diverse black community at this time. (Because African Americans tend to be regarded as a monolithic group, the complexity of their linguistic practices is too often essentialized and described unproblematically as "black English.") However, it is well worth noting the historical existence of marked language variations within the African diasporic community in America from the turn of the century onward, which are attributable to significant educational, regional, and even national differences in the case of West Indian immigrants. Before shifting our focus to the black press's treatment of the cinema as general rather than entertainment news, one particular column by *Defender* writer Columbus Bragg deserves mention.

By mid-1914, with the "Musical and Dramatic" column under the editorial control of Columbus Bragg, news and promotion of the cinema as an autonomous category becomes even less pronounced. When limited coverage of the cinema does occur, there is, however, an echo of Sylvester Russell's critical style. For example, Bragg begins his column, which he calls "On and off the Stroll," by announcing his arrival and by inserting himself into the narrative:

> Starting on my journey into the Holy Mount of Muses and reflections and
> close observations on the mental calisthenics of the gay white way or the
> stroll. . . . The saying that goodness draws children but beauty draws men,
> heroism draws women, accounts for the big crowds at [the Elite café]
> nightly. (Bragg 1914)

Here Bragg not only restructures the column to suit his own more figurative linguistic approach but also resuscitates the theater, music, and society news that for a time had become overshadowed by the passively
descriptive and uncritically celebratory billboarding of the cinema house
offerings. As with Russell before him, Bragg took advantage of the pedagogical possibilities of this entertainment column. In this 1 August 1914
article, Bragg educates readers about the subtleties of cinematic, as opposed to theatrical, performance techniques. In response to readers' inquiries about employment in films, Bragg articulated the distinctions
between the two performative modes. In his "On and off the Stroll" section of the column, Bragg delves into the specificities of the cinematic art
not broached by the other critics, including Walton. In response to "so
many letters asking of [cinematic] work," Bragg sets out to explain a few
distinguishing properties and specific requirements of the cinema. To
assist aspiring thespians seeking to break into film work, Bragg writes:

> It is not necessarily actors or actresses that have worked on the stage, as
> they are seldom successful in motion picture work or photo-play produc-
> tions. To act before a camera requires special qualities. The pantomime
> actor of 100 years ago who depended for effects solely upon actions and not
> words would have made an ideal motion picture actor today, who must
> necessarily rely upon facial expression and gesture for the interpretation of
> any scene or incident which he may desire to portray. Now an experienced
> motion picture actor or actress very rarely looks direct at the camera, but
> does his part as though it were non-existent. (Bragg 1914)

Such commentary written in 1914 is remarkable indeed, and it marks a
foray into aspects of the cinema clearly separate from the usual concerns
with the racial problematic. Bragg demonstrates a familiarity with the
dictates of silent-film performance techniques that even predates the
theories of cinema as art contained in Vachel Lindsay's 1915 book *The Art
of the Motion Picture*, Hugo Munsterburg's 1916 seminal study *The Film:*

A Psychological Study, and Rudolph Arnheim's anthology of writings from the 1930s, *Film as Art.* Although Bragg's reflections on these issues are not sustained and sophisticated treatises on the subject, his early albeit limited articulations of them do portend the eventual development along these aesthetic lines in both black and mainstream film criticism. It is impressive that Bragg addresses in this one essay such broad themes as techniques of performance, dialogue and rhetoric, lighting effects, and what he calls "the art of condensation." He makes the point that

> the beginner always has to be cautious that every action is not definitely recorded by the machine. I have noticed that in all big studios that I have visited you cannot depend on your makeup for facial expressions. Very little is used as the immense enlargement the film undergoes when thrown on the screen would intensify the paint and powder to such an extent you would look ridiculous. The light which is so strong from the arc lights that are used in the studio forms a striking contrast of lights and shade: Now the time of a play only takes a very short time, the rehearsal might be a day or a month. . . . A minute or two is sufficient to film a play, as all dialogues are cut out, as action is the important thing wanted. The successful film producer is a past master in the art of condensation, being capable of boiling down a four-act play into say 500 or 600 feet of concentrated actions. (Bragg 1914)

Here Bragg's apt explication of the cinematic codes that characterize what Nicholas Vardac (1949) calls the film "storyette," the one- to three-reelers that preceded feature films, demonstrates Bragg's prescience in concentrating on the cinema's visual aesthetics as well as its narrative themes. In this passage, he engages such issues as cinematic naturalism and photographic realism as conveyed through character direction, camera techniques, spatiotemporal manipulation, and both theater and film acting styles. It is obvious that Bragg's assessments of the specificities of the silent film form unquestionably are on target. His response to "questions that have been mailed me this week by readers of the *Defender*" exceeds our expectations. Later in the article, he highly recommends *The Fall of the Mighty,* a film by the Bartlett Film company: "the best Afro American picture for real clean comedy with a moral to it, well posed, well acted and the plot was clever." Now, these perfunctory comments on the film *The Fall of the Mighty* create a dissonance in comparison to his foregoing analysis, especially because both appeared in the same column.

Bragg's meager film reviews compared to his brilliant revelations about the unique demands of the silent cinema leave us quite disappointed, perplexed, and yearning for more. How does this film production, for instance, fulfill or abnegate Bragg's prior statements? We are left to ponder this obscure film's merits relative to Bragg's own fitting criteria for successful silent cinema techniques. This critical absence becomes all the more intriguing and elusive when we learn finally of Bragg's departure from journalistic criticism to pursue his successful theatrical production of *The Ahjah,* a "classic Ethiopic drama" featuring "the sacred songs of Solomon." Bragg's obvious training in the art and craft of the classical theater informs his brilliant assessment of the requisites of silent cinema and promises so much more than his anemic film review delivers. Bragg concludes his article by jokingly threatening to "tell on some people" in next week's issue, and after a Machiavellian confession that he is "talking out of school," he ends with "Nuff said." We, however, respectably disagree and wish this able critic had said more about *The Fall of the Mighty.* As concerns Bragg's production of *The Ahjah,* it is important to note that owing to the lack of theatrical venues available to African American theatrical impresarios, the production was staged at a church, and according to Tony Langston, it was a major hit. Alas, there is no further information in the *Defender* about Bragg's subsequent activities along these lines.

Bragg's legacy was the column's return to privileging African American music and stage productions, too long overshadowed by the rush to embrace the new mainstream cinematic offerings. His reapportionment of the column's ratio of film commentary to reviews of other amusements is symbolized by the appearance of a new subheading, "Jottings Theatrical and Otherwise." Gone for a time is the billboarding of State Street's various nickelodeon offerings that had dominated the column previously. Bragg tended to incorporate his film commentary into the larger theater and society news, as Russell had done three years earlier. It is important to stress, however, that with the formal shift, the silent cinema news remained an important feature of the 1914 "Musical and Dramatic" column.

As Bragg's foregoing address to his readers indicates, the *Defender*'s readers did not suffer their media expectations and disappointments in silence. "Southern black men and women" especially, Vilma Raskin Potter (1993) points out, "wrote to editors as though they knew them personally," and they wrote about everything, including their opinions of, and desires for, balanced entertainment and amusement coverage. Under the subheading "Resents Criticism," a letter from a self-identified "constant reader" was printed on 18 July 1914 in the "Musical and Dramatic" column and placed directly adjacent to the weekly entry. The letter's content serves as a forceful example of the author-reader interaction that informed much of the black press's journalistic philosophy at the turn of the century. As early as the late 1840s, the black press understood well its mission "partly to relieve 'the inability of the colored people to bring their inflicted wrongs and injustices before the public.' . . . Any person of color asking for correction of an error in a white paper or for the chance to reply in kind to a story offensive to the Negro would be likely to get the runaround or an outright refusal" (Pride and Wilson 1997, 56). Addressing the editor, the author of the letter complains that "the dramatic critic overworked himself, and went way beyond the boundary line of the unwritten rules of criticizing talent and art," because "the great writer had a little too much time on his hands or lacked the material to fill the allowed space" ("Resents Criticism" 1914). This breach was wholly unacceptable to this particular reader for several reasons. Most unforgivable was the fact that the critic was disparaging in his comments about the one musician in all of Chicago responsible for black orchestras procuring work in State Street's film theaters. "Had the writer [critic] made any inquiries," the letter continues, he would have discovered that the piano player he panned was responsible for compelling "every house along State Street to put in orchestras." Although the "constant reader" concedes that "everybody in public life is open to criticism," he or she feels compelled to "read" the critic in this way: "No critic is beyond the opinion of his readers, but when a writer [especially this unidentified critic] dabs his pen to comment on a moving picture orchestra, the limit has been reached." As the unnamed, pilloried film critic who drew the ire of that "constant reader" soon learned, early-twentieth-century African American film spectators did love the early cinema, but once introduced, they loved equally well, if not more, the role their traditional music played alongside this technological marvel. Because early films were considered mere novelties, the letter writer seems reconciled to critics' need for dabbing their "pen to comment on a moving picture," but to have a critic's pen trifle with the reputations of black orchestras, which often were more of a draw for black spectators than the films they accompanied—that was "the limit."[7]

By the end of 1915, the *Defender*'s "Musical and Dramatic" column found a way to accommodate a regular film review section featuring synopses of the latest offerings at the movie theaters all along Chicago's State Street Stroll. Each theater, including the New Grand, the Lux, the Merit, and the States, had its name prominently featured and its weekly program separately discussed in the column. And as might be expected, the column's film space expanded to reflect the increasing popularity of this phenomenal urban pastime with routine news of black spectators' attendance patterns. The cinema's onslaught was now evident as its coverage had begun, once again, to eclipse that of music and the stage.

Extra! The Black Press Discovers the Newsworthiness of the Cinema

When we recall the trenchant legal and de facto prohibitions against black literacy in America from slavery and beyond, the fact that Lester Walton, Sylvester Russell, and their peers and a vibrant African American literary tradition even existed at all, to say nothing of its amazing flourishes, during this era is remarkable in and of itself. News of the cinema that tended to grab front-page headlines and other general news columns focused largely on racially explosive topics (like biased seating and pricing policies in local theaters, and defamatory themes), on the cinema's technological advances, on black filmmaking enterprises, and on African American responses to the new medium. "Discusses Fight Pictures" was the headline referring to the Johnson-Jeffries championship fight that grabbed black Harlemites' attention when it appeared on the front page of the *New York Age* in 1910. The language of its reportage on the efforts of the Washington, D.C., chief of police to get the pugilist film suppressed, owing to its potential to impassion racial animosities, hints at the *Age*'s cautious endorsement of the contested measure. But the *Age* betrays the conditional nature of its endorsement of this suppression measure by joining the controversy over this fight picture to that over Thomas Dixon's race-baiting play *The Clansman:* "If the fight pictures could be barred in theatres on the grounds that they incited race against race and inflamed the passions of those who attended . . . Then certainly on the same grounds such plays as Thomas Dixon's 'The Clansman' would be barred from the established theatres as being more harmful than beneficial" ("Discusses Fight" 1910).

While the tenor of cool reason and the expectation of civic fair play regarding this racial powder keg governs the *Age*'s coverage in the turbulent aftermath of the Johnson-Jeffries match (for this was the one social arena where a black and a white man were permitted to compete on relatively equal terms), prior coverage of the much anticipated event in the white trade journal *Moving Picture World* points up the futility of the *Age*'s reasoned approach to such an unreasonably motivated and promoted public spectacle. On 21 May 1910, *Moving Picture World* ran a near-full-page advertisement for the film footage of Jack Johnson training for his competition with James Jeffries. The ad featured in this white journal ran the following promotional copy:

> Moving pictures of Jack Johnson, *Champion of the World* in training for the Big Fight of July 4, 1910 with James J. Jeffries, consisting of 6 rounds with his sparring partners. . . . And the features incidental to training quarters— The Best Ever Seen—Approximate length 1,000 feet. Ready for delivery May 16, 1910. States Sold: Massachusetts, Connecticut, Rhode Island, Vermont, New Hampshire, Maine, Ohio, Indiana . . . Illinois, Nebraska, Colorado, Utah . . . Tennessee, Kentucky, Virginia, West Virginia . . . Balance of States Rights For Sale: Write or Wire at Once. ("Fight Film" 1910)

One month later, the same *Moving Picture World* printed a fascinating full-page story on the Johnson-Jeffries fight wherein speculations about the untold millions of dollars to be made on this fight film pending "the unmistakable victory of Jefferies" ran rampant. In contrast, the article states unequivocally that if Jeffries, the "Great White Hope," were to be defeated by Johnson, "*It is commonly believed that the pictures would then be of comparatively little value* [italics mine] especially amongst the white section of the community" ("Pictures" 1910).

Hanging in the balance, of course, were the already strained race relations of polarized communities across the nation. While the *World*'s article voiced its concern about the "racial pride" Johnson's victory would signify for African Americans and the subsequent elevation of Johnson's status to "demigod," it is revealing that no such corollary regarding white racial pride pending Jeffries's success was even entertained. Jack Johnson was the victor, and melees of violence did ensue ("Discusses Fight" 1910). Clearly, then, it is in the context of the fight's violent aftermath that the *Age*'s conciliatory position on suppressing the fight pictures must be adjudicated. More substantial, however, is the strategic use to which the *Age* puts the words of Major Sylvester, the D.C. chief of police and chief censor. Before printing Sylvester's personal appeal to the paper's readership, the *Age* frames his remarks in a legitimating discourse of sincerity: "Major Sylvester, some are willing to believe, is sincere in this matter. He has previously waged successful fights against billboards, which display criminal actions, on account of the influence these have upon children." Though the major's comments do specifically address the "fights" among children of both races that occurred in the wake of Johnson's victory, as with the *World*, no issue is made of the white adults' participation in the racially motivated discord. It is unlikely that white children were responsible for the injuries sustained by "the vice president of the Negro Business League, A. H. Underdown" ("Discusses Fight" 1910) during the riots that broke out after news of Johnson's victory was publicized. Instead of confronting the systemic racism responsible for such wanton displays of violence, both Sylvester and the *Age* were content to blame the "lower class of both races." Be that as it may, by taking the opportunity to conflate the racism surrounding the Jeffries-Johnson fight with the racism of *The Clansman* in this article, the *Age* must be seen as striking a strategic oppositional blow to the nation's racial status quo and its propagandistic perpetuation in the popular media.

A 1910 *Chicago Defender* front-page story apprised its readers of early efforts to develop talking pictures. Below the heading "Talking Pictures," which was typeset in big, bold print, a short article reported on a demonstration at the Edison laboratories in New Jersey. This news item briefly explains some basic principles of the new kinetophone while simultaneously tempering reader expectation of its imminence by cautioning that Edison "thinks he needs one year more to so improve the mechanism." The earliest news of, and commentary on, the cinema in the black press that I have located dates back to 1909 editions of both the *Baltimore Afro-American Ledger* and the *New York Age*. Judging from the profusion of theater, music, and sports news in these papers, it appears that racial segregation governing the public sphere, from which the moving picture theaters were by no means exempt, militated against the widespread access of African American audiences to the new medium at its founding. The national commitment to racial separation, and the consequent inability of African American writers to screen the bulk of the early film releases, no doubt greatly impeded the formation of a systematic and far-reaching black press foundation for early black film reviews and criticism. Still, it is possible to assess a typology of general trends in the nature and tone of the critical responses to the cinema forged by those black critics (as discussed earlier) fastidious enough to meet the challenge. Starting with the *Afro-American Ledger*, we can see one example of an early film story in which the sizable headline "Moving Pictures Doing Good Business" hardly merits the scant copy corresponding to it. The *Age*'s earliest film news, by comparison, manages a full column of information that continues beyond page 1 of its 21 July 1910 film story. As both these papers enjoyed national circulations (and in the case of the *Age*, limited international circulation), they were able to extend their interpretations of the early cinema outside their regional borders. Thus these earliest reports on the cinema in the black newspapers convincingly illustrate black publishers', editors', and writers' recognition of, and interest in, the growing fascination the African American masses were developing with the movies. The purpose of foregrounding these articles is not to overstate the merits of these early writings in terms of a cohesive or consistent body of work on the early cinema by African American journalists at the dawn of the century. The point is to cull this early material from 1909 onward so as to point the way to an emergent critical discourse in the black press on the cinema's inauguration that would expand significantly in the decades that followed. Our introduction of Walton's emergence as a film critic during the first decade of the 20th century clearly signals black newspapers' and periodicals' increasing interest in serving and influencing the black community's growing fascination with the then-promising new technology.

Obviously, fiscal concerns were another motive force driving the black press's interest in the early cinema. For editors of the black press, moving pictures were doubly newsworthy both as regularly scheduled entertainments with built-in advertising revenue and as a source of genuine headline news, as the front-page news of the Johnson-Jeffries "fight picture" discussed earlier amply conveys. Also, cinema news blended well with the established social and entertainment pages so important in the black press of this era. In fact, the *Age* and the *Defender* vigorously promoted their entertainment columns.

Typically, when the black press covered cinema news in the early years, they frequently engaged in a myopic celebration of what they saw as the medium's emancipatory potential, that is, the liberation of the black image from the damning iconography of what Donald Bogle (1989) has described as "Toms, coons, mulattos, mammies, and bucks." There are, however, many reasons for this seeming naïveté. For the organic intellectuals who founded and wrote for the black press, the cinema represented a break with the old representational arts (namely, literature and the stage) because of its mechanical ability to record or hold up a less biased mirror to the progressive reality of black life. Clearly, New Negro self-representations were anathema to the retrograde mythologies underlying the national belief system that reified black backwardness and pathology. The black press's optimism about the cinema might also be contextualized within its collective faith in the establishment of nationwide boards of censors coupled with an inverted sense of technological determinism.

Whereas much has been written about the antimachinery Luddite tendency among many white Americans,[8] who were anxious or hostile in the face of employment competition from machine technologies that impelled the modern industrial age, many black Americans, it seems, did not share that same anxiety about the machine technologies' usurpation of their employment opportunities. Perhaps this attitude can be explained by blacks' incredulity that technology could plunge them any lower than their present positions at the bottom of America's racially stratified civil society. Thus, after more than three hundred years in bondage, it is easy to imagine that news of technological progress would not necessarily represent the same threat for blacks as it might for working-class whites. A passage from the *Ledger*'s 1909 front-page article proclaiming "Moving Pictures Doing Good Business" convincingly demonstrates the black press's embrace of motion picture technology and the promise it suggests for African Americans: "The Hiawatha Theater is doing all the business it can handle. . . . An important member of the Hiawatha staff is Mr. Raymond Murray, who operates the moving picture apparatus in the machine room. . . . The Hiawatha is helping the proscribed Negro to solve their amusement problem" ("Moving Pictures" 1909). Immediately striking in this passage, besides the pro-machine apparatus statement, is the hopeful tone of the article, which is symptomatic of black America's desperation for any mechanism to alleviate the nation's repressive racial order at this historical juncture. One senses, in all probability, that the Mr. Murray identified here is a member of the race. On balance, then, it is likely that Murray is cited not so much for his singular ability to participate in this modern industry as a skilled projector in the age of Jim Crow but as material proof of African American socio-economic uplift theory put into practice despite Jim Crow.

In proffering the cinema as the black entertainment remedy for the decades of discrimination holding sway on the Great White Way, for its part, the *Ledger*'s "Moving Pictures Doing Good Business" performs two acts of cultural intervention on behalf of its readers. First, the paper serves notice to white theater owners that black entertainment dollars can no longer be ignored or taken for granted, especially with such a rival and democratizing medium as the cinema looming large on the horizon. Second, the paper reveals to its "textual community" of New Negroes that the modern cinema industry manifests America's latent capacity to do the right thing, particularly since Mr. Raymond Murray's achievement provided confirmation that even prestigious employment opportunities were available to the race in this modern and exciting medium. An essay by Bill Foster appearing under his professional pseudonym, Juli Jones, in the 9 October 1915 edition of the *Defender*, entitled "Moving Pictures Offer the Greatest Opportunity to the American Negro," reinforces the point:

> Thus hundreds and hundreds of talented colored ladies and gentlemen who would really join the ranks of the moving picture business, that would not entertain the idea of going on the stage, because the stage, with a few exceptions, never offers the Negro an opportunity to display any real talent as a playwriter. . . . In a moving picture the Negro would offset so many insults to the race. . . . The world is very anxious to know more of the set-aside race, that has kept America in a political and social argument for the last two hundred and fifty years. . . . Any one can buy cameras and machines of all kinds in open market. A picture show can be turned into a church very profitably with a very little outlay of money to start with. (J. Jones 1915)

Jones's statements focus attention on several important matters. From him we begin to see that the purchase on the black press's faith in the cinema is attributable in part to expectations of its radical potential to manumit the black image from the shackles of blackface minstrelsy. Also, the popularity of the early cinema among the black masses represented a viable means for black entertainers, impresarios, and writers to avoid altogether the intractability of racist practices on the legitimate stage. As Jones attests, speaking from his enlightened position as founder of one of the first African American film production companies ("Foster Photoplay"), "any one can buy cameras and machines of all kinds in open market." The hour of black self-articulation in the mechanical arts clearly had arrived. Having himself produced such film shorts as *The Fall Guy, The Butler, The Grafter and the Girl,* "and that sensational comedy, *The Railroad Porter,*" when Jones writes on 9 October 1915, "The time is now,"[9] his challenge that blacks should seize the moment is no mere hyperbole. Rather, his brash observations and bold recommendations issued from his insider knowledge and years of film production experience.

To better appreciate the transition early-twentieth-century black writers and editors made from covering cinema news as a novel but promising curiosity and as entertainment staple to treating it as a more legitimate and consistent source of real news, it is useful to consider, in a bit more detail, news of the cinema as it matured in the pages of both the *New York Age* and in the *Chicago Defender* from 1909 to 1916. On an empirical level, in the case of the *Defender,* we notice the shift occurring as the news of the cinema encroaches spatially on theatrical and music news, the traditional mainstays of the paper's social and entertainment page. Noticeably, the moving picture news's spatial gain often was inversely proportional to the music and theatrical news's loss. This logistical shift seems also to have contributed to, if not precipitated altogether, the marked decline in the cultural prominence of the black theater of this era, with its compromising links to both the racism of white minstrelsy and the ribaldry of burlesque. Both papers, but especially the *Age,* do engage in a bit of self-criticism when they lay blame for much of black theatrical loss squarely on the shoulders of black businessmen and black theater patrons because of their respective lack of vision and racial unity.[10] In analyzing these entertainment columns over time, it is possible to map the cultural ascendancy of the white-dominated cinema in segregated black communities, an ascendancy, I might add, secured uneasily at the expense of black cultural workers, including writers, theatrical impresarios, drama critics, and thespians.

From 1914 on, we begin to see a modification in the rhetoric of the black press regarding news of the cinema. After having sold its readers on the virtues of the cinema, with such hyperbole as "solving the Negro's entertainment problem," and with such boosterism as "get the habit" and "join the crowd," the black press—especially the *Defender*—was now emboldened to rail against it. Repositioning itself as a media watchdog of sorts, the paper printed a blistering front-page denunciation of one particular film. In a big, bold headline stating " 'Hit the Nigger,' New Film Insult," the *Defender* uses the film *Levinsky's Holiday* to reproach the board of censors, the film's exhibitor, and the film's black spectators, although not in equal measure. Leading into the article is a subtitle: "Major Funkhouser and his board of censors fail to suppress moving pictures that breed race hatred and Afro-Americans keep silent." In a move that anticipates, by one year, the furor that was to follow *The Birth of a Nation*, this article takes aim at the institutional racism responsible for the circulation of such biased cultural productions as *Levinsky's Holiday* and others of its ilk.

> In its last issue, *The Chicago Defender* called attention to the fact that on the moving picture censor board every race was represented but the Afro-American. The ink was hardly dry before the New Grand Theater . . . put on a film "Levinsky's Holiday" which shows a Jew on a frolic. "Hit the Nigger" is Levinsky's delight and runs through the entire film. . . . And as usual the house was crowded with Afro-Americans evidently insult-proof for they laughed and applauded. . . . [Funkhauser's board allows] the race to be insulted and ridiculed for they know no complaint will be made. It used to be "Hit the Jew" or "Down with the Irish," but alert members of those races watch with hawk-like eyes any attempt to belittle their people. . . . However, all concerned must remember that *The Chicago Defender* never sleeps. ("Hit the Nigger" 1914)

Interestingly, the paper's front-page editorial bite does not exact the pound of flesh from the exhibitor as might be expected in this article. By resting the blame for this film's screening solely at the feet of an employee of the New Grand Theater, it is clear that the paper saves face even as it promotes regularly the same theater's weekly schedule, and it blunts its own criticism of the theater for "being unfair to the people to whom they cater." Whether the leniency shown to the proprietor, whom the article claims was too busy to have prior knowledge of the incident, was based on fiscal concerns remains uncertain. What is certain, however, is that the black press' stormy honeymoon with the white-dominated cinema was rapidly disintegrating. Just three months later, yet another front-page condemnation of the cinema appeared in the *Defender*. This time banner headlines alerted readers to a new cinematic offense.

On 30 May 1914, the *Defender*'s readers saw "States Theater Shows Colored Men Stealing Chickens" emblazoned across the paper's front page. Contrasting this article to the prior one, it becomes obvious that the paper's editors are no longer willing to soft-pedal their criticism of a theater proprietor a second time around. Perhaps it was the States Theater's audacity to screen two racially offensive films that the paper and black spectators found particularly egregious. Another factor may have to do with the fact that the States Theater did not employ blacks as did the Grand. The two films in question are *The Tale of the Chicken* and *Mother of Men*. Whereas the *Defender*'s article chose to lay stress on the antiblack theme of the former title, I want to call attention to the eerie resonance of the latter film's theme with the antiblack sentiments that propelled a late-1990s national news story of a carjacking hoax in Union, South Carolina, to national prominence. Consider the 1914 *Defender*'s brief synopsis of the film *Mother of Men*:

> Another picture equally as bad was entitled "Mother of Men," by Warren. This was supposed to show a slave stealing a white child, the hunt for her, and other exciting things. In the first place, this picture is foolish. Slaves do not steal white children, and if they did they could not find a place to hide them. The Chicago *Defender* disapproves of such depraved pictures and brands the last one as a lie from start to finish. ("States Theater" 1914)

This passage suggests that it is the existence of America's irrational antiblack collective consciousness that licenses the manufacture of such "vile race pictures" (as the *Defender* terms them). To that I would add, very little seems to have changed in the eighty years since this article was published. At any rate, the article goes on to reiterate the culpability of the black audiences and the Board of Censors in the latest conflagration over race and representation in the new cinema. Unlike the previous article, here the paper indicts the theater owner explicitly for booking the "objectionable and insulting" pictures. Another sign of the paper's tried patience on this issue is the acknowledgment of the newspaper's conflict of interest. The *Defender* asserts that "this newspaper has no thought of advertisements when it makes this complaint, as it has done the same thing with its best advertisers."

It is interesting to speculate about how the paper's ideal readers are inscribed in the black newspapers' bipartite coverage of the cinema both on the front pages, as general important news, and inside the paper, as fodder for the community entertainment calendars. Can we assume, as perhaps did the editors, a schizophrenic reading subject who, on the one hand, can refuse the disparaged cinema of the front pages and, on the other, become wholly seduced by it a few pages later in the entertainment and promotions pages? Whatever the answer, it is apparent that theories of the mimetic versus creative nature of art and aesthetics confront a more thorny set of problems when the art form in question is the cinema, and when its thematic content is race and representation.

The Birth of a Nation

and Interventionist Criticism

RESISTING RACE AS SPECTACLE

Five years ago, when "The Clansman" was originally produced in New York, I was present at the first performance. . . . I discerned at a glance that in spite of all its ghastly features . . . there was one prominent figure in it that would dethrone the white race and benefit the Negro and that was the mulatto politician. . . . I hold to this day that plays against the Negro are not damaging to him but helpful to his cause.
—Sylvester Russell, "Sins"

The most striking thing about the merciless plot on which *The Birth of a Nation* depends is that, although the legend of the nigger controls it . . . there are really no niggers in it. The plot is entirely controlled by the image of the mulatto.—James Baldwin, *The Devil Finds Work*

Once many plantations grew cotton; today, some grow movies.
—Ed Guerrero, *Framing Blackness*

D. W. Griffith's 1915 magnum opus, *The Birth of a Nation,* has a secure place in the annals of American and international film histories. Conjoined as it is with an endless cache of past and recent critical, aesthetic, and historical texts dedicated to its perpetuity, this classic, problematic film narrative of racial intolerance will be shown and celebrated for generations to come. There has not been a similarly sustained effort to preserve and study the reams of protest literature produced contemporaneously against the film by African American and other critics. It has been almost a century since their demand for a complete reckoning with the film's racist agenda, and yet the call continues to go unheard by many mainstream scholars, historians, film archivists, and cinephiles. Content, for the most part, to subsume the film's racist vitriol under the imprecise and ameliorating rubric of "controversial," or to treat the subject in asides mentioning the black press's opposition to the film, many contemporary cultural workers and audiences alike persist in leveraging America's cultural supremacy (narrative film and jazz music representing America's ironic but unique cultural gifts to the globe) on the currency of racial demagoguery and divisiveness.[1]

Unveiling the Clansman Within

PRE–*BIRTH OF A NATION* CRITICISM IN THE BLACK PRESS

When Thomas Dixon dramatized his novel *The Clansman* for the stage, it met with a strident resistance in the black press that presaged the volcanic eruption of protests directed at Griffith's subsequent cinematic adaptation. Starting in 1906 and 1907, the *Iowa State Bystander* was among the first black publications to alert its readership to this latest attempt by a son of the South to foment racial strife beyond its traditional stronghold in the southland.[2] On 15 June 1906, the *Bystander* ran a substantial front-page article on *The Clansman*.[3] One year later, the paper carried a shorter follow-up article on Dixon's play. With the provocative headline "Is the Negro a Man?" the first article takes "Dixon, Senator Tillman and other race agitators" to task for embracing the play and its agenda of igniting the embers of racial antagonisms. The *Bystander* countered Dixon's revisionist lore of Reconstruction both directly and indirectly. The direct attack called attention to the play's deliberate misrepresentations of certain historical facts to legitimate and influence prevailing racial antagonisms. Indirectly, the paper used its design layout strategically to position a routine report of brutal black repression under Jim Crow racism adjacent to critical commentary on the play. Juxtaposed to the article on *The Clansman* and its baleful effects was a news story detailing an incident of racial violence perpetrated against an African American minister en route from Boston to deliver a commencement address at a black industrial school in the South. Upon reaching Tennessee, the minister was brutally mobbed and driven from a Pullman train compartment by white passengers. In pairing the articles in this way, the paper opposes Dixon's romantic fictionalization of the Klan's murderous exploits by exposing an actual instance of white supremacist terror, as meted out on 2 June 1906, to one defenseless black man, the Reverend R. C. Ransom. The contiguity of the two articles serves to create an even stronger affective response in the reader than each could command singly and apart. For instance, under the subhead "Effect of Play," the writer reports overheard audience remarks during a performance of *The Clansman:* "At the play, I heard a lady say, 'I'd like to kill that nigger.'" Another is quoted as saying, "When I came out, I wanted to kill every nigger I saw" ("Is the Negro a Man?" 1906). While such visceral responses might normally be dismissed as inert figurative speech momentarily induced by the play's inflammatory rhetoric, the actual case of the racialized assault on the black minister renders these remarks chilling indeed.[4] The rationale given for the minister's unprovoked, violent ejection from the train was attempted fraud. Because his luggage bore a tag denoting travels to France, the minister was accused of fraudulent impersonation of a Frenchman. In an era noted for making whites masquerading in blackface national entertainment superstars, that a black man's possession of a stamp from France could spur such a reaction underscores the absurdities of early-twentieth-century race relations. The *Bystander*'s coverage of the incident conveys the ever-present danger to African American safety in the nation's racialized public sphere at that juncture. Moreover, the twinned articles bring into view the specter of far more lethal consequences inspired by Dixon's glorification of lynchings, ostensibly to protect the virtue of white womanhood from the imagined threat of rapacious black male desire.

In telescoping the argument against the play with such offset subheadings as "Race War Imminent," "Effect of Play," "Comparative Civilization," and "Who Made the Negro Immoral?" the writer not only lends a heightened sense of urgency to his rebuke but demands as well a closer scrutiny of lynchings and other racial atrocities in the nation's hellish encounter between blacks and whites:

> It [the "Negro problem"] is not to be solved by the lurid and despicable sentiments of . . . "The Clansman," for, unless race hatred is allayed and not aroused, there will be a race war and it is not as yet sure that it will be the Ne-

gro who goes to hell any more than the white man. . . . Nothing could be more unfortunate just now when the best men of the South are putting their brains and hearts to solve the Negro question. . . . Nothing could be more unfortunate . . . than that Tom Dixon should have launched his novels upon the public and should go about with his play fanning all that is worst in us to new life and create murder in our hearts. ("Is the Negro a Man?" 1906)

By noting the fragile attempt at cooperation between the races at that point, the article makes clear its imperative to circumvent any threat to destabilize the hard-fought interracial harmony obtaining in that jurisdiction. The passage communicates well the dual nature of the article. First, it seeks to reinforce the tenuous efforts at resolving "the Negro question" by the "best men of the South." Second, it calls for an unqualified rejection of Dixon's dissimulation of Reconstruction lest it be mistaken for the thing itself. Here the writer casts doubt on the white audiences' ability to satisfy their "fatal curiosity" about such an art of dissimulation while holding at bay its imperative to fan the flames of murderous intent that societal indifference and historical ignorance ignite. To emphasize his point, the writer considers the fact versus the fiction of lynchings and rape:

> The impression that seems to prevail and to which Tom Dixon so effectively appeals to the galleries, that the antipathy to the Negro rises from his crimes against womanhood, is simply not true. . . . But what are the facts? Between the years of 1866 and 1900 there were 504 lynchings and of these only 96 were for rape. ("Is the Negro a Man?" 1906)

In an effort to delegitimate the play's premise that rape somehow authorizes or justifies the draconian measure of lynching black males accused of this crime, the writer takes an empiricist stance on the evidence of rape to refute Dixon's calamitous vision of rampant black criminality. Equipped with statistical proof of the disproportionate number of lynchings to rapes, the author aims to alert readers to some otherwise hidden truths. If there are lynchings not precipitated by rape or murder, the writer asks, then what could be the rationale for this excess? Obviously, the writer concludes, the lynch statistics hanging in the balance and not affiliated with rape "must be put down to mere race prejudice" ("Is the Negro a Man?" 1906). This article and others like it in the black press that contest Dixon's retelling of Reconstruction history advance what

Robert Allen and Douglas Gomery (1985) describe as "the realist response" (13) to conventional film history.[5]

Because this black press literature represents the vanguard of opposition to Dixon's and Griffith's adaptation of the play to the cinema, for our purposes, they can be seen as adhering to Allen and Gomery's (1985) concept of the realist response scenario, which holds that "it is because most film history books treat questions of historical evidence and explanation as if they were unproblematic that it is necessary to devote admittedly tortuous discussion to them: Film histories are the works of historical explanation, and as such cannot escape basic questions of historiography" (13). Because mainstream reviews and commentary produced contemporaneously with *The Clansman* and *The Birth of a Nation* tended to evade or obscure the texts' pro-lynching discourses, their black press counterparts that did address this issue must be incorporated into the film's metahistory because they describe "not only the observable layer of reality but also the workings of *the generative mechanisms that produced the observable event*" (15). This *Bystander* article and others are unequivocal in naming racial hatred and national acceptance of it as among the generative mechanisms responsible for producing the spectacle of black lynchings and society's tolerance of them during the early part of the century. In addition, the increasing militancy of black press editorial philosophies often emboldened it to speak out forcefully against the abysmal conditions in all phases of black life in America.[6] This included consistent indictments of *The Clansman* and *The Birth of a Nation* particularly as "generative mechanisms" in the era's revitalization of the Ku Klux Klan.

To further undermine the play's seduction and the affective fallacy on which it is based, the *Bystander* article adopts an unexpected tack. The writer poses the enigmatic question "Who Made the Negro Immoral?," which necessitates an interesting sort of ratiocination:

> He is immoral, fearfully and degradingly immoral, and it is the lament both of the leaders of the South and of his own race. He was stolen nearly three hundred years ago from the wilds of Africa and after three hundred years contract [*sic*] with the white man he is still Immoral? You denied him the possession of a soul and you called him a beast and in all the years he was with you, you treated him as one. The charge that he is immoral is the worst indictment that can be brought against slavery and the slave's master. . . . If slavery was such a beneficent institution it ought to have more to

show for the three hundred years in which the slave was in daily contact with the Christian white man. ("Is the Negro a Man?" 1906)

It is striking that the writer deploys this reified notion of black immorality to subvert its ontological assumptions. To the extent that black immorality is granted in this writer's formulation, its cause is attributed to the institution of slavery that enriched and benefited "the Christian white man" for centuries. In effect, black immorality has been transposed into white corruption. This transposition absolves black immorality by folding historical white culpability in the slavery experience back onto itself, whereby charges of black immorality become indictments not against black victims but against white systems of domination. After displacing received notions of black criminality and amorality onto white repressive regimes responsible for the miseducation of the Negro,[7] as Carter G. Woodson (1933) would put it, the writer ratchets up the rhetoric in a section called "Comparative Civilization." The point in this subsection is to expose the nation's double standard of morality. How, the writer seems to ask, can a people degraded for three hundred years be expected to live up to a moral code evidently not binding on the bearers of the nation's moral standard? This double standard places a particularly unjust burden on African Americans in the writer's estimation, when even after "1500 years of civilization and Christianity" Tillman and Dixon, who have not sufficiently evolved out of barbarity, and still "have the molars, the claws and the blood-thirst of the beast of prey," are nonetheless counted among the civilized. By contrast, the writer posits the example of "Booker Washington who could say," after only a four-decade remove from slavery, " 'I will never allow any man to drag me down by making me hate him' " ("Is the Negro a Man?" 1906, 1). For the writer, Senator Tillman and playwright Dixon, as legatees of centuries of Western civilization, still were not so enlightened. In his view, these prominent white citizens were symptomatic of a widespread white immorality rendered invisible because of the nation's preoccupation with charges of African American immorality. In his comparison of the relative moral degradation of both groups, the writer asks, what about "white thieves, white murderers, white rapists, white bribers of legislatures, and it has been whispered that there have been white looters of life insurance funds—'first pluck out the beam [from] thy white eye then thou shalt see clearly to pluck out the mote [from] thy brother's eye" ("Is the Negro a Man?" 1906, 1).

In an 8 March 1907 front-page article, the *Bystander* printed follow-up information on African American protest activity against performances of *The Clansman* at a local opera house. Under the heading "The Clansman," the paper congratulates certain of the community's "race men" for their efforts in "getting a resolution through the city council whereby it will be unlawful for it or similar plays to be given here." The story applauds the community's success in garnering a temporary injunction against the play, but it also is careful to caution readers that the sweet victory, nevertheless, was subject to repeal because "the Mayor, Geo. W. Mattern, who attended [the play], gave an interview in the evening paper [stating] that there was nothing bad about it." The writer's incredulity is evident when he opines that either "our Mayor is dull of comprehension or densely prejudiced (some of his past actions have proven the latter), or else he is framing his way to veto the resolution which prohibits the play in our city" ("The Clansman" 1907). This sanguine parenthetical aside serves to remind the *Bystander*'s African American readers that they certainly could not count on the kindness or morality of their mayor.

On 17 March 1906, the *Baltimore Afro-American Ledger* took up the fight in an editorial denouncing *The Clansman*. In addition to excoriating Dixon for his "perversity" in producing the play with its "tendency to disturb the pleasant relations existing between the races" ("*The Clansman* and Its Effect" 1906), this article broaches a new consideration, the inextricability of class concerns in racial antagonisms. After reporting on the play's failure in some southern cities, the writer attempts to account for its success in Baltimore. To explain the seeming discrepancy, the article suggests that a shift has occurred in the city's cultural sensibilities as a result of the influx of southern whites who migrated to that area over the course of three decades. The article goes on to situate the large number of southern students in the region's universities at the forefront of this cultural shift. It is primarily to this group, with its sectional politics of counter-Reconstruction ideology, that the article attributes the play's triumph. According to the article's writer, any attempt at reinstating the racial and class ethos of the southern aristocracy would be applauded by these self-exiled southerners resentful of their diminished social status, which placed them in the loathsome position of common laborers forced to compete with black men for the same jobs (Du Bois 1935, 670).[8] Given this economic reality, the article sums up the situation as follows:

A decent, self-respecting, well-dressed colored man, is to them as flaunting a red rag before an infuriated bull. Anything which seems to have a tendency to degrade a colored man or woman appeals to them in the highest sense, and makes them laugh with glee. ("The Clansman and Its Effect" 1906)

Since southerners have historically referred to the "self-respecting, well-dressed colored man" contemptuously as "uppity," the writer goes on to propose this class-inflected rationale for the play's appeal to many southern white students in Baltimore. The argument is that for these students, "many of whom are too poor to make their way through school without doing some kind of work" to finance their education, a new class jealousy is responsible for exacerbating the historical race prejudices. By bringing in class considerations, the article expands the debate beyond the usual parameters of racial bigotry and confrontation. The white audiences of Baltimore might be seduced by Dixon's message of white supremacy, but the writer of the article aims to frustrate their nostalgia and wish fulfillment desires with contrary pronouncements of this sort:

If anyone thinks that anything can be done in this late day to stop the progress of the Negro, he is much mistaken. The Negro is bound for a higher sphere and he will attain it no matter how many obstacles may be placed in his way. And the more obstacles that may be thrown across his pathway only make him the more ambitious to surmount them. ("The Clansman and Its Effect" 1906)

That the unfinished business of Reconstruction enlivens this message of inevitable black social and economic progress seems clear. Coupled with it, however, is the racial reconciliation message that "noble white men and women of the North, who have done so much and are still doing much" should not be deterred in their just cause "for the betterment" of both races, lest they inadvertently contribute to an "imminent race war."

Whereas the *Iowa State Bystander* and the *Baltimore Afro-American Ledger* sought to expose Dixon's hate mongering overtly, Sylvester Russell, columnist for the *Chicago Defender*, refuted Dixon's racist agenda through a covert strategy of indirection. Surely one of the era's unique interpretations of Dixon's theatrical legacy is Russell's 8 April 1911 "Musical and Dramatic" column entitled "The Sins of the Father, at the Princess Theater: Tom Dixon's Latest Play Visits the Two Races to

Which It Belongs." Taking the interpretative road less traveled, Russell explains what he believes are unintended but beneficial ideas for African Americans lurking beneath the surface of Dixon's tales of Dixie. Russell was convinced that black leaders and citizens were wrongheaded in their responses to Dixon's play. For him the play's preoccupation with the miscegenation taboo would be its own undoing. Dixon's plays, in Russell's view, contained the seeds of their own narrative subversion because "it is [the miscegenation theme], it must be, all a story of consanguinity, smuggled up in the ice chest of a Southerner's hatred of the sins of his own father" (1911a). Although these comments are directed at Dixon's later play, *The Sins of the Father*, further into the article Russell connects these narrative problematics to Dixon's earlier work, *The Clansman*.

> Five years ago, when the *Clansman* was originally produced in New York, I was present at the first performance. The Negro race had raved over the coming production and wanted it stopped, but when I saw the play, I discerned at a glance that in spite of all its ghastly features, there was one prominent figure in it that would dethrone the white race and benefit the Negro and that was the mulatto politician. . . . My manuscript was not accepted for publication and that settled it, and I hold to this day that plays against the Negro are not damaging to him but helpful to his cause. . . . But the people in Chicago had no faith in my contention. (Russell 1911a)

Russell's unique interpretation of Dixon's writing clearly exemplifies what cultural studies theorists consider as a resistant or transgressive reading of a presumably transparent or closed system of meaning.[9] Although Dixon may have conceived of his work as an unambiguous recuperation of the vainglorious and genteel days of a bygone era, save for the specter of a savage blackness (Cripps 1993b, 42), Russell's reading ruptures this narrative intent. In so doing, Russell's essay also enacts a rhetorical reversal of the terms of mastery. Like the *Iowa State Bystander*'s "Is the Negro a Man?" Russell's "The Sins of the Father" displays what Houston Baker Jr. (1987) has termed "virtuoso mastery of form" (15). Russell's rhetorical virtuosity undercuts Dixon's racist imaginary at the same time that his reading deforms the mastery assumed by Dixon and his white readers.

By rereading Dixon's messages to make them beneficial for blacks, Russell redeploys Dixon's texts so as to undermine their ideal narrative meanings and exploit the indeterminacy of their linguistic formations (Hall 1980, 129). Following this logic, Russell is able to imagine a transcendent truth in Dixon's narrative of miscegenation whereby the plays' overdetermined meanings, especially on the mulatto issue, can be made to "benefit the Negro race because of the true love and pity [the play will generate] for the colored people, and against the white race" (Russell 1911a). Russell clearly expects the sympathetic response toward African Americans to inhere in society's remembrance that nearly all mulattoes, especially during that epoch, were produced by the coercive and rapacious white slave masters. Though Russell apparently is alone in his decoding practices,[10] his, nonetheless, is a truly transgressive reading, one that affirms cultural studies' emphasis on use value approaches to mass-cultural texts that often go unobserved when the focus is limited to the exploitative exchange value of the tragic-mulatto discourse. Even James Baldwin's 1976 contemplation of the iconography of the mulatto in *The Birth of a Nation* fails to invest this overdetermined racial icon with such subversive thematic potential as Russell imagines.[11] Although Russell may have constituted a subcultural audience of one, capable of discerning such transcendent and subversive aspects within Dixon's narratives, by the time *The Clansman* was adapted in cinematic form, the black press was already alert to the widespread damage the film's more conventional reception might engender. What must not be overlooked, however, in Russell's idiosyncratic decoding strategy is the notion that a specific text or discourse can be imbued with an unexpected use value separate and apart from an otherwise expected coercive exchange value. And while Russell's aberrant reading of Dixon attests to the ultimate indeterminacy of linguistic signification, it is clear that the erstwhile critic expected a large number of people (e.g., his readers) to be swayed ultimately by his alternative decoding logic. How else are we to account for his position that "plays against the Negro are not hurtful but beneficial to his cause"?

This essay by Russell conflates several of Dixon's works to make the relationship among the texts override the damaging ideology each might advance individually, at least in Russell's view. Russell expropriates "the intentional possibilities" (Bakhtin 1981, 289) of Dixon's language to his own ends. Put another way, Russell attempts to go beyond the seeming transparency of Dixon's individual prose pieces and instead puts the individual texts in dialogue with each other so that an overall narrative preoccupation might be adduced. In the process, Russell helps dispel the convenient assumption that African Americans were monolithic in their reception of, and response to, *The Clansman*.

A more characteristic response, however, to Dixon's literary legacy can be found in an article written by James Weldon Johnson for the *New York Age* on the occasion of the release of the film adaptation of *The Clansman,* Griffith's *The Birth of a Nation.* In "Uncle Tom's Cabin and the Clansman," published on 4 March 1915, Johnson, an important African American literary figure of the era, represents the more familiar oppositional stance. Johnson uses the discourse of Dixon to critique the duplicitous motives of white authorities who, on the one hand, could deem it necessary to prohibit public performances of works considered disparaging to whites and, on the other hand, could feign an inability to reciprocate in kind when the beneficiaries of such "benevolent" censorship practices were African Americans. Johnson then contrasts the response of white authorities in Atlanta, Georgia, to the play version of "Uncle Tom's Cabin" with the response of white New York officials regarding the film *The Birth of a Nation.*

> [A] theatrical company was forbidden to play the usual version of "Uncle Tom's Cabin." . . . The [censorship] action was taken on account of a protest by some local organization. . . . The play was changed and given the Arcadian title of "Old Plantation Days," the offensive parts were expurgated. . . . And so a performance was given that was no doubt a great success and offended nobody's sensibilities. All of which is very amusing. . . . "The Clansman" did us much injury as a book. . . . It did us more injury as a play. . . . Made into a moving play it can do us incalculable harm. Every minute detail of the story is vividly portrayed before the eyes of the spectators. A big, degraded looking Negro is shown chasing a little golden-haired white girl for the purpose of outraging her, she, to escape him, goes to her death by hurling herself over a cliff. Can you imagine the effect of such a scene upon the millions who seldom read a book, who seldom witness a drama, but who constantly go to the "movies"? This play was passed by the Board of Censors, and is scheduled to open in one of the New York theaters this week. (J. W. Johnson 1995b, 12)

Although Johnson convincingly challenges this duplicitous standard of censorship, more important is his point concerning the relative measure of injustice in the two scenarios because of the unparalleled power of the cinema to "do incalculable harm" as compared with its literary and theatrical precursors. Although Johnson's observations predate structuralist theories of cinematic signification and referentiality, it is clear that his lamentations resonate with contemporary structuralism's project of cultural demystification. Johnson seems attuned to the potency of the representational power of the cinema because of its "analogous or iconic relationship" to its referent (Nichols 1981, 21), as compared with the more indexical or arguably ambiguous significations that literary codes often engender. When Johnson makes the points that Dixon's book appealed to "those already prejudiced against us," and that "a great deal of what it attempted to tell could not be represented on the stage" (whereas the film could do incalculable harm "because of its vivid portrayals"), his observations cohere well with Bill Nichols's comment that "it is easy to confuse the realms of the image and the physical world by treating the image as a transparent window . . . by assuming that something like its essence has been transferred or reproduced in the image" (21). For Johnson, it is the cinematic image's received acceptance of transparency that makes its racist ideology more dangerous than that of the novel and the play. It might be assumed that Johnson was anticipating the incalculable harm that would follow in the wake of the film's presumed veracity of transparency when he asked, "Can you imagine the effect of such a scene upon the millions," who have no alternative point of reference? For a largely illiterate audience devoid of the mediating influences of literature and dramas that might controvert the opinions of those "already poisoned by racism," Johnson is rightly concerned about the incalculable harm the cinema could effect on impressionable minds nationwide not already predisposed to its racist telos. This essay not only marks Johnson's literary acumen insofar as the power of language and its ideological and aesthetic functions are concerned but also points to his intuitive understanding of the cinema's ability to augment such functions exponentially. Although Johnson's article is one of the first such critiques of *Birth*'s racial and political narrative economies, it functions as an avatar of black press reactions to come.

Breaking Out of *The Birth of a Nation*'s Prison House of Racial Language

Recalling his conclusion of *The Prison-House of Language*, Fredric Jameson (1990) makes the point that formalist analyses often project "form onto content" (quoted in *Signatures of the Visible*, 127) in cinematic discourses. Formalist assessments of *The Birth of a Nation* have been successful in extricating the film's structural and aesthetic advancements from its troubling ideology of white supremacy and racial hate. Because most official histories of Griffith and Dixon's film text privilege this approach, the task of interpolating its racist agenda and contravening this formalist project has not advanced a great deal from contemporaneous critiques of the film that appear in the black press from 1915 and beyond. It is not simply the case that "Blacks, though, saw no art; they saw the retelling of Reconstruction history as a Gothic horror tale haunted by the black brutes," as Thomas Cripps (1993b) would leave us to believe (42). Although it is true that African Americans rejected the film's revisionist view of Reconstruction—with good cause—it is not true that they "saw no art."

From the moment that black press representatives got wind of the news that Griffith and Dixon were adapting *The Clansman* for the screen, they embarked on a public awareness campaign to prevent the film's exhibition. This opposition should not be equated with an unwillingness or inability of the black press to recognize or appreciate the artistic merits of the film. On the contrary, African American critics of that era understood only too well that the film's artistic merits could function to sublate and obfuscate its more wrenching sociopolitical agenda of fomenting racial discord. It is important to recall that black press opposition to the film was not simply a knee-jerk reaction to a racist book cum play cum film. Theirs was a resistance forged in the trenches of battle against decades of damaging fallout from pernicious blackface theatrical minstrelsy and pervasive antiblack discourses in popular American literature. Those African American writers were intent on contextualizing the film within that hazardous narrative trajectory. Even in their scathing denunciations of *The Birth of a Nation*, several black critics acknowledged the film's artistry in some way.

The *New York Age* and the *Chicago Defender* were among the first African American publications to assail the film. They were joined later by *The Crisis, California Eagle,* and countless others. In each instance, the overarching theme concerned strategies for the suppression, censuring, and censorship of *The Birth of a Nation,* and failing this, they initiated widespread disclosure of the film's destabilizing tendencies in disrupting the nation's race relations détente. Because a full accounting of the black press's strident opposition to this important film text is beyond the scope of this work, we will consider, as exemplary, selected articles from the above mentioned publications.

On 4 March 1915, the *Age* printed news of the suppression campaign being waged by the National Association for the Advancement of Colored People (NAACP) against *The Birth of a Nation* during its scheduled New York run. As with other film stories it considered significant enough to warrant front-page coverage, the *Age*'s editorial strategy of denouncing the film on page 1 signals the editors' desires to apprise readers of the cinema's strong influence beyond the escapist realm of mere entertainment. Given the compartmentalization and stratification of information in newspaper layout design, the editors clearly want to send the message that this film represents important news bearing on the interests of the entire readership, not just on those interested in entertainment and leisure time activities. By highlighting the active involvement of the NAACP and the National Board of Censors in the controversy, the *Age* further conveys the message that the film poses a new racist threat to the community that must not go unchallenged. It is noteworthy that the article's subheadings stress that "'Birth of a Nation' [Is] Based on Dixon's *Clansman.*" As a way to ensure that readers understand the larger ramifications of the film, in the body of the text, the article recalls the hard-fought efforts to get Dixon's play prohibited "from nearly every theatre in the country" ("Vicious Picture" 1915). The subtext here, of course, is that nothing short of a similar act of unified protest against the film is acceptable. The article goes on to specify that the NAACP and the Board of Censors rejected the entire second half of the film and that suggestions were made for overall modifications. However, in a tone expressing both cautious optimism and pragmatic resignation as to the inevitability of the film's New York exhibition, the story reports that "the board has no legal power, but its findings are accepted by eighty per cent of the moving picture producers" ("Vicious Picture" 1915). The article concludes with the unsettling information that a private screening of the film was held for President Woodrow Wilson and Supreme Court Justice White, and that the two foremost moral enforcers in the land "expressed approval" ("Vicious Picture" 1915). It is also telling that the NAACP initially was only agitating for the film's revision rather than outright revocation, for this response does not accord necessarily with the view that African Americans "saw no art" in this highly compromised film.

One week later, the *Age* ran "Still Showing Vicious Picture: Local

Officials Refuse to Suppress 'The Birth of a Nation'" as the lead story on 11 March 1915. In addition to reiterating the black community's demand for the film's suppression, this follow-up article prints a chronology of sorts that highlighted the *Age*'s role in efforts to thwart the film's exhibition. Attached were the less-than-satisfactory responses of the city officials involved. The article featured texts from telegrams sent by Lester A. Walton, the drama editor and columnist for the *Age,* and by Fred R. Moore, the paper's general editor. Walton wrote to the mayor of New York City cautioning against the outbreak of "serious racial conflicts" should the film be permitted on the city's screens. Not surprisingly, the evasive response from the mayor's office was to have the matter "referred to the Commissioner of Licenses, with the request that he make a careful investigation of the conditions . . . and take proper action," and in the interim the film's exhibition was unimpeded. Perhaps in an effort to offset such a tactic, the *Age*'s managing editor, Fred R. Moore, sent communiqués opposing the film both to the mayor and to the license commissioner stressing the deleterious effects of the "vicious film." In an astute move to appeal to the mayor's political acumen, Moore presented this well-reasoned argument:

> This play is very obnoxious and places the Negro in a false light before the public. It represents him as beastly and seeks in every way to degrade the members of my race. I am quite sure that you as the Mayor of *all* the people will not permit any part of the citizenship of this community to be so misrepresented [italics mine]. . . . We feel that we have a right to appeal to you as you appealed to us for our votes when you were candidate for the high position to which you were elected. At that time you said that you believed in a square deal. We are now asking you to give us that square deal by insisting that the people responsible for this play eliminate from it every phase that will tend to degrade a part of the citizenship of this community. ("Still Showing" 1915)

The covert admonishment contained in this message is clear; if the mayor is not concerned about the present-day quality of life of his African American constituency, then he should not expect this community to be concerned about his political life in the future. Moore's desire to have the mayor appreciate the seriousness of the black community's resistance to this film beyond mere partisan politics seems explicit enough. As Ed Guerrero (1993) points out in *Framing Blackness,* "considering the racism, discrimination, and brutality at large in that historical moment, African Americans had every reason to fear that what was depicted on the screen could easily be acted out against them in reality" (14). And to the extent that this plea might fall on deaf ears, the paper's editors adopted another textual strategy in its arsenal of words.

Besides its frontal attack on the white establishment's willing complicity in agitating racial antagonism through high-profile endorsements of the racially polarizing film, the paper used this particular front page to insinuate several retaliatory options available to a unified African American populace forced to react in its own interest. While column 1 ran "Still Showing Vicious Picture," the story opposing the film, in which a bold subheading reads "Both Races Protest," an adjacent story in column 3, the only other column on the page with a prominent headline, carried the following: "Want Negro's Support on Female Suffrage: White Women Ask Colored Voters to Rally to Their Aid in the Fall." At the heart of this bit of metacommentary is the paper's effort to advance the idea of coalition politics between the races. That the *Age*'s editors recognized the exploitable nature of the white gender divide on the matter of suffrage speaks volumes about their political savvy. If white women wanted black men to support them in their fight for suffrage, the message is that white women should be willing and were expected to support the black-led protest against the film. One prominent white woman political activist, Jane Addams, did just that in later weeks.[12]

Column 4 of that same edition reports, "Race Taking Advantage of Evening Schools." And scattered throughout page 1 are incidental but related news items: "Colored Voters Want Another Councilman," "Negro Hater Defeated in 'White City Primary,'" and "Modern Abolitionists Denounce Race Hatred." Even though these articles are not directly concerned with the anti–*Birth of a Nation* discourse of column 1, it is apparent that they are imbricated in a larger signifying chain of counternarratives on the refusal of blacks to be mistaken for Dixon's, Griffith's, and other southern sympathizers' nostalgic dissimulation of blackness. If white suffragists and white politicians want the support of black male voters, then an ethics of reciprocity seems to be the point authorizing the strategic agglomeration of these articles. No longer, they seem to suggest, can black loyalty and support be taken for granted. No longer can whites expect the unconditional support of a mythic subservient and faithful Negro popularized by southern lore. Speaking as much to its black readership as to the white elite, who routinely monitored the black press for indications of the Negro's "progress,"[13] it is obvious that the editorial contents of this *Age* front page were carefully calculated as contestations of *The Birth of a Nation*'s deliberate misrepresentations. Though its efforts at having the film suppressed or censored were to no avail, the *Age* nevertheless used its voice to "talk back" against Dixon and Griffith's malevolent blackface ventriloquism.[14]

By 25 March 1915, the *Age*'s campaign against the film had shifted in location and in tone. After having deployed sensational headlines to draw widespread attention to the general threat posed by the film, in much the same way that theater marquees, white newspaper endorsements, and larger-than-life advertisements were used to promote the film, now the *Age* used its front page and its entertainment columns to broadcast its opposition. In this third week of protest, after the film had been allowed ample time to promote its antiblack vitriol, it was left to Lester Walton and his entertainment column to debunk the film in more specific and pointed terms. Beginning with his 23 March essay entitled "Colored Citizens' Weakness Shown in Photo Play Incident," Walton initiates the discussion with information about the status of the stalled legal proceedings against the film, after which he chastises African Americans for their "refusal to properly organize for their own good." In addition to upbraiding blacks for their lack of racial solidarity, Walton also stresses the fact that the film's agenda buttressed "the strength of the radical Southerners" who had been embraced by the northern elite in their ongoing efforts to reunify the nation in the wake of the Civil War at the expense of African Americans. In a comment on the "extremely cautious manner in which local authorities find it necessary to move in response to the demand that 'the Birth of a Nation' be suppressed for the good of the public," Walton's tongue-in-cheek comment on the city officials' befuddlement on the finer points of its legislative authority in suppressing the film recalls James Weldon Johnson's essay on the double standard of censorship rules discussed earlier. Walton questions the "ulterior motive" of the New York officials in view of their stalling tactics in the matter of blacks' requests that the film be suppressed:

> The "celerity" shown by the city officials in exerting their authority in this instance is in marked contrast to their usual methods. For instance, all theatre managers using motion pictures are constantly receiving communi-

cations from the Commissioner of Licenses instructing them not to show certain pictures that have been officially banned as vicious and a menace to public morals. Managers are informed that if they disobey instructions, their theatre license will be revoked. Why the manager of the Liberty theatre [the venue showing *Birth*] enjoys special privileges and is immune from such regulations is tinged with an air of mystery. (Walton 1915a)

While it is clear that Walton aims to demystify the racial imperative that informs this double standard, his rhetorical strategy succeeds because it avoids the intentional fallacy predicated on evidentiary proof. By pointing out previous instances of theaters' compliance with official instructions "not to show pictures that have been officially banned as vicious and a menace to public morals," Walton makes plain his accusation that race is the determining factor in the Liberty Theater's immunity from license revocation even as it profits from a film widely reputed to be "vicious and a menace to public morals." As incensed as Walton was with this bitter pill of second-class citizenship, he meted out special scorn to the black religious leaders of the city because, in his view, "few colored ministers regard the theatre as a fit subject for discourse, as it does not deal with the spiritual." It pained Walton to have to admit that "the strongest sermons against the presentation of 'The Birth of a Nation,' have been delivered by white ministers." It was Walton's impatience, justified or not, with the lack of foresight in matters of secular reality on the part of black religious leaders that prompted him to conclude that "sooner or later members of the race in New York City and elsewhere will learn that the Negro, not the white man, is our worst enemy, and that until we possess race consciousness, race respect, race confidence, and [learn to] organize, we must expect to be ridiculed and humiliated" (1915a).

Meanwhile the *Chicago Defender* ran a special front-page story on the *Birth* controversy with a New York dateline. The story, entitled "*Birth of a Nation* Arouses Ire of Miss Jane Addams," outlined "an exclusive interview she gave the *New York Evening Post* [on] March 13."[15] Although Addams's sentiments against the film might be expected owing to her progressive politics and affiliation with the NAACP, her critique of the film's deliberate misuse of history is important. For Addams's analysis interjects the matter of ethical responsibility incumbent on historians to be fair in their representations or else be held accountable for the damag-

ing social and political consequences that historical inaccuracies precipi-
tate. Addams's rejection of the film on the grounds that it "does not tell
the whole truth" underscores a persistent refrain found in many black
press articles that were circulated against the Dixon and Griffith film.
Addressing the film's calculated distortions of blacks during the Reconstruction era, Addams writes:

> It would be easy enough to go about the slums of a city and bring together
> some of the criminals and degenerates and take pictures of them purport-
> ing to show the character of the white race. It would no more be the truth
> about the race than this [film] is about the black. . . . It is claimed that the
> play is historical, but history is easy to misuse. . . . You can use history to
> demonstrate anything when you take certain of the facts and emphasize
> them to the exclusion of the rest. ("*Birth of a Nation* Arouses" 1915)

What is troubling to Addams is the film's claims to historicity and that
such claims function to endow the film's fictions with an unwarranted
status of narrative veracity. And as Hayden White (1978) has pointed out,
"there are always more facts in the record than the historian can possibly
include" (51) in any historical retelling. Addams's remarks that history
can be used to demonstrate anything when certain facts are emphasized
and others elided make this very point about the selective use of historical
facts in *The Birth of a Nation*'s construction of a "pernicious caricature of
the Negro race" ("*Birth of a Nation* Arouses" 1915). Given the contents of
her principled stand against the film, it is little wonder that the *Defender*
carried a reprinted excerpt from Addams's interview prominently on
page 1. Addams was a white suffragist and social reformer who founded
Chicago's famous Hull House, a settlement hospice for Chicago's poor
and immigrant communities. Her reputation as a progressive social
worker was widespread, and undoubtably her experience with the white
criminal and degenerate elements dwelling in the slums gave her comments about the fundamental unfairness of "gathering the most vicious
and grotesque individuals . . . and showing them as representative of the
truth about the entire race" a special salience for readers of the *Defender*.
Here was a prominent white citizen taking a public stance against the
historical inaccuracies of the film that throngs of admiring white spectators were rushing to behold. This tactic of reprinting anti–*Birth of a
Nation* commentary from sympathetic whites became a frequent occur-

rence during the black press's unrelenting campaign against the film and
its supporters. Addams's attack, furthermore, illustrates Walton's barb
that some influential whites were more willing than hesitant black religious leaders to take the lead in opposing the baleful effects of this
"vicious film." James Weldon Johnson also commented on the willingness of several white New York papers to speak out against the film.[16]

In returning to the *Age*'s opposition to *Birth* under the auspices of
Walton's entertainment column, we notice that on 13 June 1915, Walton
has focused his critical attention on the reception of the film in the white
press, specifically that of the *Chicago Tribune*. In so doing, Walton finds
new terrain on which to mount his latest challenges. This approach
enables him to consider several aspects of the film's remarkable resiliency
in the face of an unprecedented mass public repudiation. The willingness
of city officials and theater proprietors to ignore adverse public opinion
marks a significant turnaround for the principals involved. The previous
tendency of both groups was to eschew any negative public reaction that
might jeopardize the film industry's aim to legitimize itself in the eyes of
a skeptical public.[17] In view of this reversal, Walton's fear that the nation's
unresolved racial politics were somehow a crucial determinant in the
matter is understandable. In "*Chicago Tribune* Laments over Barring of
Photo Play: A Patron of the Arts," Walton (1915b) seizes on the profit
principle motivating some of the film's staunch proponents, the film's
historical misrepresentations, and the veiling of the film's racist enuncia-
tions behind the claims of art.

In terms of the film's enormous profit potential, attributable to its
exorbitant admission price of two dollars minimum (Sklar 1976, 58),
Walton zeroes in on the minor advertising fortune to be made by the
Tribune in promotional fees. Walton sees this financial incentive as a
taint on the *Tribune*'s claim to being "a patron of the arts." Thus Walton
is not convinced that the *Tribune* is "highly incensed" over the Chicago
authorities' decision to ban the film from that city because "Chicago
citizens will be denied the rare privilege of seeing 'the greatest piece of
work done for the films by American producers.'" On the contrary, Walton believes that the paper's real concern is with the denial of its privilege
to see its percentage of the huge profits this film promises. Displaying his
usual sardonic wit, Walton interrogates the *Tribune*'s "patron of the arts"
posturing:

If poverty was knocking at the door of the *Tribune* business office and the high financial rating it so proudly enjoys was not generally known, one would be led to suspect that this wailing and gnashing of teeth evidenced the bitter disappointment felt by the editors over failure to secure a share of the huge fund raised by the producers of the picture for advertising purposes. (Walton 1915b)

There can be little doubt that Walton here seeks to foreground the pecuniary impetus of the *Tribune*'s cultural gatekeeping function where this film was concerned, a gatekeeping that conveniently reaffirms and ossifies the nation's discourse on the race problem whereby the very existence of African Americans, rather than the prejudices against them, is proffered as the cause of social disunion in the nation's body politic. In addition to pointing out what he considers the *Tribune*'s masking of its profiteering in the guise of altruistic public service, Walton also repudiates the *Tribune*'s characterization of the movement to suppress this particular film as a referendum on censorship in general. The call to reject the film had been misrepresented by the *Tribune* as a call for indiscriminate censorship or tyranny by the minority. What Walton is struggling with is the paper's representation that "minute minorities" are opposing the film out of "a disposition to use power when it is created," whereas proponents of the film are viewed as protectors of free speech whose only interest is in granting Chicagoans "the rare privilege of seeing 'the greatest piece of work done for the film by American producers'" (Walton 1915b). Appended to a lengthy excerpt from the *Tribune*'s statement in support of the film is Walton's rebuttal. Here he contests the *Tribune*'s laudatory comments about the film, taking claims for "its artistic appeal," and its claims to represent history, as important points of departure.

To the claims that *Birth* symbolizes the quintessence of "the greatest piece of work done for the film by American producers," Walton responds, "this may be true." Nonetheless, he complicates this aesthetic myopia concerning the film's artistic merits with a sobering analogy:

In Germany the sinking of the Lusitania by a submarine is regarded as "the greatest piece of work done since the advent of the submarine." But do we Americans share the views of the Germans? Some stilettos are artistically carved and very pretty, as are some revolvers, but notwithstanding their artistic value they are dangerous and objectionable, and so is "The Birth of a Nation." (Walton 1915b)

This passage outlines Walton's desire to fuse the aesthetics of representation with the ethics of social responsibility, conveniently disconnected in the *Tribune*'s consideration of the matter. To separate the two, according to Walton's formulation, is to invite charges of social malfeasance and irresponsibility. That a well-respected paper such as the *Tribune* would participate in this mean-spirited project of cultural hate strikes Walton as being especially odious. By equating the film's racial polemics with such highly charged images of military weapons of destruction, Walton hopes to demonstrate the limits as well as the dangers of a perspective that champions aesthetics divorced from ethics. Proffering a corrective to the film's skewed depiction of Reconstruction history, Walton writes:

> If at any time during the Reconstruction Period colored members of the legislature walked about in their bare feet, drank liquor and committed other acts of indiscretion during the session of the legislature as described by the film (shown to instill in the minds of white citizens that the colored man is not fit to serve as a public official) we would highly appreciate [the] favor if facts were published. . . . The Chicago Tribune says: "The sin of the film is its effectiveness." We say the sin of the film is its viciousness—its distortion of history and its uncalled [for] assault on a race that was loyal when such men as Thomas Dixon opposed the North which he now cunningly seeks to win over. (Walton 1915b)

This critique of the film's misrepresentation of Reconstruction history is twofold. On a basic level, it calls attention to the film's abundant historical fictions. On a more general level, it serves as a metacritique of the nation's flawed reunification strategy, predicated on a willing "subjection to the ruling ideology" of the South's intractable antebellum-era racism.[18] Even though Chicago and the North may have been eager to exchange bitter memories of the Civil War for venal imaginings of a tyrannical black Reconstruction cunningly crafted by southern revisionist histories,[19] Walton was intent on setting the record straight and reinserting white southerners as the true culprits in the nation's nightmarish encounter with the South's white supremacist ideology. Walton reminds us that indeed it was whites, not blacks, who were the belligerents in the nation's war with itself. To this end, he reminds an amnesiac North that despite Dixon's travesty of the facts of southern history, first in *The Clansman* and then in *The Birth of a Nation* (Franklin 1989, 21), no such hoax as the film aims to perpetuate could diminish the indisputable fact that "such men as Thomas Dixon," and not African Americans, were responsible for the nation's bloodiest and costliest war to date. If it were true that America wanted a film in which "all essential episodes [are] grounded on historical fact, representing the struggles of that terrible time in the South," as the *Tribune* claims, Walton sees a major historical incongruence. What kind of historical accuracy is there in a "vicious" film that makes no reference to the treason of "the unreconstructed South," to borrow from Du Bois, but is at pains to malign African Americans, who, Walton asserts, are "a race which at this momentous period of our history should be lauded and encouraged for its loyalty and patriotism [during the Civil War], rather than unjustly maligned and unnecessarily misrepresented"? (Walton 1915b).

As the protracted battle against *The Birth of a Nation* was waged in the black press, fissures in the ranks of the black bourgeoisie became manifest. On 21 July 1915, one of the oldest black newspapers, the *Philadelphia Tribune*, signaled its break from the film's oppositional forces with this front-page headline: "Effort to Get Up a Big Sensation Proves Futile" (Walton 1915c). It becomes clear that not all black community leaders and African American newspapers were automatically in lockstep with the movement to ban Griffith's film. At issue for the *Philadelphia Tribune* were the underlying motives of "supposedly friendly white persons" who advised black leaders "to get up a protest against the film." Evidently the *Tribune* viewed this white support as an act of paternalism that the paper would not condone. Rather than have the black community manipulated in this way, apparently the *Tribune* saw this as a matter of black community autonomy in which "some of the cooler heads thought it best to go and see the play before making a kick." Instead of being outraged by the film, these "cooler heads" determined that

> there were some things about the play that are somewhat grating on the
> sensibilities, but on the whole it was not so bad, nor did they think it would
> tend to increase race hatred, because white people of the North are too
> intelligent. (Walton 1915c)

This utterance recalls Sylvester Russell's resistant reading of Dixon's plays *Sins of the Father* and *The Clansman*, but there is a marked difference in the two approaches. Inasmuch as Russell was confident in the boomerang effect of the play's racist narrative, this coterie of black spectators, made up of ministers and other community leaders, instead placed their faith in the intelligence of northern whites, though it is unclear just what this intelligence is expected to yield. As Walton cogently points out in his dismissal of the sentiment:

> Yes, white people in the North are so intelligent that in Atlantic City and in other Northern cities colored persons are refused accommodations in public places; the white people of the North are so intelligent that it is difficult for a colored person to rent a house other than in a colored settlement; the white people of the North are so intelligent that the Negro is barred from making an honest livelihood in many avenues of endeavor. The ignorant whites in the Northern cities outnumber intelligent ones; for you will find any poor white person believing he is better than a colored because his skin is white. And for that matter, there are many presumably intelligent white people in the North who are ignorant enough to believe that the color of one's skin counts for more than intelligence, wealth, culture and character. (Walton 1915c)

Obviously Walton did not share Russell's or editor Perry's faith in the transcendent powers of narrative truth or human enlightenment where America's investment in the ideology of white superiority was concerned. To Walton, nothing could persuade the majority of "ignorant whites" in the North to renounce the benefits of white skin privilege, certainly not the high ideals of racial equality. Significantly, this was the era in which Joseph de Gobineau's nineteenth-century essays on superior and inferior races were gaining increased cultural and academic currency in both Germany and the United States (Locke 1992, 15). In 1915 Alain Locke noted that it had been an Alabama physician, Joseph Nott, who helped get portions of de Gobineau's four-volume text *Essai sur l'inegalite des races humaines* (The Inequality of the Races) published in America on the eve of the Civil War (Locke 1992, 15). Following de Gobineau's theories, his supporters posited a "science of race" (15) that effectively displaced the incredibly varied social histories of different racial groups onto their distinctive physiognomies. By 1915, African American intellectuals such as W. E. B. Du Bois and Alain Locke had rebutted the de Gobineau school of scientific racism at scholarly conferences at home and abroad.[20] It is against this backdrop of eugenics, an ascendent scientific racism, and

President Woodrow Wilson's sweeping discriminatory legislation that resegregated and displaced African American workers from the national government (Null 1975, 12) that Walton's belief in the intractability of the cult of white-skin privilege seems rational. Moreover, Walton's cautionary rhetoric is consistent with Du Bois's famous 1903 prophecy that "the problem of the twentieth century is the problem of the color-line" (Du Bois 1903, 54). Unlike his brethren in Philadelphia, Walton was dubious about the integrity of northern white intelligence where matters of social justice and African Americans intersected.

In view of his unfaltering efforts to contravene public utterances of what Alain Locke has termed "ethnic fictions" (Locke 1992, 11) in popular cultural productions that serve to reify and reinforce racial prejudices, Walton's censure of the *Philadelphia Tribune* for endorsing *Birth* comes as no surprise. What is surprising about his essay "Colored Men at Atlantic City Put O.K. on Photo Play" is Walton's equally trenchant criticism of a black newspaper that refused to condemn the film. Not only does this article hint at the Du Bois–Washington ideological schism that characterized the politics of black social uplift at that time; more importantly, it attests to the antiessentialist nature of the black community's response to *The Birth of a Nation,* too often unacknowledged or unexplored in traditional film histories of this conflict. So committed, in fact, was Walton to the campaign against the film and its proponents that not even his "good friend Editor Perry" of the *Philadelphia Tribune* was spared public censure and ridicule for putting "the stamp of O.K. . . . upon 'The Birth of a Nation'" (Walton 1915c). In addition to chiding his "good friend" for being duped by the film's producers "in their efforts to get the picture in other Northern cities where strong opposition" was being waged, Walton also reprimands Perry for an even more serious infraction. He accuses Perry of undermining "the cause of the Negro" with his antagonistic rhetoric that impugned the motives of whites who opposed the film. It was inexcusable, in Walton's view, for the *Tribune* to alienate white friends of the race with such "sarcastic reference to them as 'supposedly friendly white persons.'" As if it were not enough to have to combat the influential film producers who somehow managed to "bring most of the officials in the various cities to their way of thinking" about the film, Walton also found himself in the unenviable position of having to reveal the lack of unanimity in the black community on this issue with his public rebuke of a well-respected black newspaper for lending its support to the cause of the film. Walton was at a loss to explain why the *Philadelphia Tribune* would be so shortsighted as to put its O.K. on the film and incur favor with "Negro hating" whites while alienating and ridiculing northern whites sympathetic to the cause of African Americans. This struck Walton as a highly irresponsible and self-destructive act. He was convinced that the *Tribune*'s failure to condemn *The Birth of a Nation* represented a major setback to suppression efforts. Though Walton overstates his case with the remark that "the correspondent for the *Tribune* evidently shares the opinion of Thomas Dixon and other Negro haters," he nevertheless makes the point that the *Tribune*'s public defection would "only tend to weaken [protest efforts] and strengthen the cause of the picture people" (Walton 1915c). Rather than accuse his friend Perry and the *Tribune* of betraying the race outright, Walton condescendingly proposes less malevolent rationales: "Surely, the film being shown at Atlantic City is vastly different from those presented in New York, Boston and other cities," and "Surely my good friend Editor Perry and his associates must have been asleep at the switch." Given the political stakes of this contest and that Walton views the *Tribune*'s position as a betrayal, he seems disinclined to level public accusations of graft and greed against his colleagues as he did in his criticism of the white paper one week prior.

However, confronted with the likelihood that the film was not significantly altered for the Atlantic City audiences despite the local censor's scissors (Walton 1915c), he does not ignore the devastating impact of the *Tribune*'s position. He employs a different rhetorical strategy in this case. Walton reprimands the *Tribune* editors by belittling their egoistic claims and turning their own phrases against them. Of their claims to possess "finer sensibilities," Walton writes mockingly: "The finer sensibilities of those who have put their O.K. on [the film] must be hard to prick indeed. Perhaps nothing short of a lynching or the repeal of the Fifteenth Amendment would excite their finer sensibilities." By invoking a brash comparison between such politically charged symbols of black oppression and liberation and a phrase connoting frivolous social pretenses, Walton simultaneously nullifies the *Tribune*'s objectivity claims that "cooler heads" passed decision on this crucial matter and elevates the cause of banning the film alongside these pressing social and political concerns. Moreover, he calls into question the judgment of "black leaders" who are impervious to the dangers the film poses to the safety of vulnerable black citizens. For Walton, then, the color of a paper's politics, at least on this crucial matter, superseded any consideration for the skin color of a newspaper's staff.

The *Chicago Defender* was no less vigilant in its coverage of the protest efforts. Whereas the *Age* ultimately shifted its policing of the crisis to Walton's entertainment page, the *Defender* maintained its high-profile coverage of the issue as general news worthy of front-page headlines and in-depth analysis throughout its general news sections. Because of its sustained coverage of the film controversy from early March 1915 to the decade's end, it is impossible to discuss the *Defender*'s response to the film in its entirety. However, a few of its 1915 articles are illuminating. For example, on 3 April 1915, the *Defender* ran a front-page story detailing certain questionable political machinations behind the scenes of Chicago's decision to authorize the film's exhibition in that city. The article presents a different set of problematics from those usually raised when the focus is on whites' championing of the film's artistic and technological advancements. For the first time, we are confronted with information that points directly to examples of self-serving political and racist incentives fueling the support for this film by whites not affiliated with the film's production. The headline on that date read, "Mayor's Wife O.K.'s *Birth of a Nation:* Obnoxious Movie." At the heart of this article is the *Defender*'s effort to intervene in the clandestine arrangements between the film producers and the outgoing mayor's administration to bypass official censorship channels to authorize the film's unfettered exhibition amid unprecedented public protests. To subvert this plan and publicly embarrass those involved, the paper decided on a timely disclosure of the political and personal gain that could accrue to the outgoing administration. Of concern here were political recriminations and a potential boost to the screenwriting aspirations of the lame-duck mayor's wife.

Attached to this story were three significant subheadings calculated to direct attention to the article's most damning revelations. At a glance, readers were presented with the following incriminating information: (1) "Film Based on Tom Dixon's Vile Play 'The Clansman,' and Which Tends to Increase Race Hated Is to Run in Chicago—Run Out of New York Last Week"; (2) "MRS. HARRISON CENSOR"; (3) "Promoters Enlist Her Aid and That of His Honor's Secretary—Pictures Are Viewed and Sanctioned by Them and Censor Board Is Ignored." Through this prefatory information, the editors highlighted the article's salient points for readers without the necessity of first wading through a full exegesis. From the outset, the first subheading made it clear that the rechristened film *The Birth of a Nation* was an adaptation of Thomas Dixon's infamous play *The Clansman,* a text presumably familiar to *Defender* readers. Baring this information was not only meant to erode any profit potential created by the mystique of the film's romantic and heroic-sounding title but also it intended to recall the bitter memories of violent racial confrontation engendered by the play's glorification of white supremacy and Ku Klux Klan terror.

There can be little doubt that Mrs. Carter H. Harrison's name was prominently featured (all capital letters) in the second subheading and throughout the article to imply that her status as the wife of the lame-duck mayor meant that political retaliation was motivating the reversal of the Censor Board's decision to ban the hotly contested film. This over-stepping of the Censor Board's authority marked an important development because noncompliance with the recommendations of censors was virtually nonexistent up to that point, as film producers generally deferred to censor boards in their efforts to garner respectable public opinion for the new film industry (Sklar 1976, 32). In calling attention to the precedent being set by this rejection of the Censor Board's recommendation to ban the film, the paper made a calculated decision to underscore the connection between the impotence of the Censor Board and the willful manipulation of these events by the outgoing administration. After pointing out Mrs. Harrison's appropriation of censorship powers, the editors go on to reveal the unorthodox means by which the former mayor's wife "used the high power of her nearly extinguished husband to 'sidetrack' the municipal board of film censors and herself pass upon, approvingly, the Griffith film" ("Mayor's Wife" 1915).

As suggested in the third subheading, the article goes on to reveal unflattering information detailing the power grab of the "Mayoress and 'his lordship' the [mayor's] private secretary." Not only were the usual protocols of Chicago's film exhibition practices dispensed with as the censor board was "told that the exhibition [of *Birth*] was not for their eyes," but Mrs. Harrison also usurped the power of the board by scheduling a private screening of the film at city hall and making "the final determination as to whether [the film would be presented] without censorial mutilation." As the article concludes with the unsettling news that the film was slated for "a summer run at the Illinois Theatre at two dollar prices," a final query is put to readers: "Must Chicago Bear This?" Because the summer season was still two months in the distance, it is likely that editors were hoping for a last-minute reprieve from this unwelcome eventuality. The real question implicit in the final paragraph was simply this: were the "Negro people in Chicago" and "the broad-gauged liberal citizens and leading politicians" going to permit "Mrs. Harrison, the Mayor's wife, herself a scenario writer, to close the official life of her husband" by fomenting discontent between the races?

By reminding black and white readers of their previous successes in sparing Chicago's citizens from such race-baiting "pictures and plays," it is clear that the desired response to the question of whether Chicago must bear Mrs. Harrison's political effrontery was an unequivocal no. Taking advantage of the lag time before the film's summer premiere, the *Defender* seized on any news of the hysteria caused by the film in other parts of the country. Because the issue of *Birth*'s exhibition in Chicago was still in debate, the *Defender*'s sensational front-page headlines about rioting associated with the film became a major tactical maneuver to sway undecided city officials toward the suppression movement. In *The Practice of Everyday Life,* Michel de Certeau (1984) explains the necessity and efficacy, albeit short-lived, of such guerrilla tactics when used by marginalized groups in opposition to dominant institutions of power. According to de Certeau, subordinated groups (such as the *Defender* and its black constituency) resort to these tactics to "manipulate events in order to turn them into 'opportunities'" (xix) for victory against the odds. Whereas the *Defender* and black citizens of Chicago recognized the structural impediments to their efforts to topple plans for the film's scheduled summer run, it is clear that they hoped news of the film's disastrous effects in other locales would translate into an unofficial vote for censorship outside official channels. As de Certeau observes, "When one does not have what one wants, one must want what one has" (xxiv). And what the *Defender* had was a journalistic voice with which to speak out against screenings of *The Birth of a Nation* in Chicago.

Taking its cue from the strategies of subversion deployed by the ex-mayor's wife, the *Defender* wanted to use its limited powers to effect its own subversion of official censorship protocols and have the film banned on the basis of adverse public opinion. This represents a tactic that de Certeau identifies as "making do" (29). Bearing in mind this "making do" mode of tactical cultural warfare, the *Defender*'s decision to run such

Chicago Defender front-page banner headlines regularly called attention to
the politics of race and representation in the 1915 *Birth of a Nation*
conflagration.

headline stories as "Boston Race Leaders Fight *Birth of a Nation*,"
"'Birth of a Nation' Will Not Be Shown," "Time to Fight Bad Movies Is
Before They Are Shown," "Mayor Thompson Bars 'Birth of Nation'
from Chicago," "*Birth of a Nation* Promoters after Mayor Thompson,"
"*Birth of Nation* Barred by Mayor in Cedar Rapids," and "'Birth of a
Nation' Run Out of Philadelphia" can be seen as an appropriation of
dominant "cultural techniques" (Certeau 1984, 29) to serve counterhegemonic ends. Because white newspapers helped create an audience
for the film, the *Defender* used the same technique to make journalism
"function in another register." Nonetheless, as effective as these headlines
may have been in galvanizing black audience resistance to the film, the
Defender's hope that "there will be no loophole whereby Chicago may be
disgraced by such a spectacle" ("*Birth of a Nation* Promoters" 1915) was
unavailing.

By 11 September 1915, *Birth* was being exhibited at Chicago's Colonial
Theater, and its entire summer run proceeded relatively unobstructed.
Notwithstanding the *Defender*'s valiant tactics, the powerful will of the
white majority prevailed. The *Defender*'s campaign was doomed from
the start because the black minority and its white supporters were out-
maneuvered. Though it was revealed that the new mayoral administration was able to "forestall 'Birth of a Nation'" for a time ("*Birth of a
Nation* Will Not Be Shown" 1915), the ultimate success of the film's
proponents in getting a Chicago audience for the much maligned film
speaks volumes about the difficulty faced by marginal groups attempting
to garner a progressive consensus in America's politics of race. Un-

daunted by this eventual outcome, the *Defender* maintained its high-profile coverage of the film despite the unavoidably free advertising the black press's opposition generated for the film. In its publication of Booker T. Washington's condemnation of *Birth,* the issue of free publicity for the film is highlighted.

Although written and published before Chicago officials capitulated to forces in favor of exhibiting the film, Washington's remarks in favor of suppressing the film indicate the black press's awareness of the double-edged nature of its protests. On the one hand, the *Defender* understood and accepted the risk associated with public denunciations of the film because it was painfully clear that the film's promoters "skillfully initiate[d] opposition on account of the advertising the play receives when attempts are made to stop it" ("Mayor Thompson Bars" 1915). On the other hand, it is most apparent that the *Defender* gambled on the desire of Chicagoans to avoid replicating the civic unrest found in other jurisdictions where the film was screened. In negotiating the consequences of these competing imperatives, the editors nonetheless remained optimistic that the negative publicity would ultimately galvanize public opinion against the film on moral and ethical grounds. Faced with the realization of losing its wager, the *Defender* shifted its coverage from a discourse of suppression to one of countering the film's historical inaccuracies and touting reports from other cities where the film was refused outright or ejected after riotous conflagrations.

Typical of the *Defender*'s shift in emphasis were the 11 September 1915 page 3 story "Facts about *Birth of a Nation* Play at the Colonial," and the 25 September 1915 front-page article entitled "'Birth of a Nation' Run Out of Philadelphia." Together, these articles provide a number of key reference points. In the first article, two important issues surface: the specificity of early African American reception, and the function of black popular memory in public discourse. First, this article suggests some of the sociopolitical stakes in the film's reception by the heterogeneous black community. Second, the film's status as historical document is challenged by a black community unaccepting of the film's historical representations when positioned alongside alternative histories rooted in black popular memory of historic events depicted in the film. Considering that by 1915 barely forty years had elapsed since the deinstitutionalization of Reconstruction, it is well to recall that many of the era's black survivors were available and willing to offer firsthand testimony about events in the South from 1866 to 1876 (Du Bois 1935, 717). Because the first wave of black migrants to Chicago included many of these individuals, the *Defender* was able to offer its readers not reactionary conjecture about Reconstruction but "one who has seen and knows about the early days . . . [and therefore] tells it as it was" (Bills 1915). The *Defender* found one such individual in the person of Mrs. K. J. Bills, the author of the essay with which we are presently concerned. She was not a theatrical or entertainment critic, and it is doubtful that she was a regular contributor to the paper. Bills's significance inheres in her position as repository of a specific popular historical memory. Owing to this, it seems that the *Defender*'s decision to print Bills's response to *Birth* serves double duty. First, she had seen *The Birth of a Nation,* and second, her childhood encounters with the Ku Klux Klan in the South present a perfect contradiction of the film's romantic depictions.

Beginning with black reception issues and the paradox of early black spectatorship, Bills's review produces the following concerns. Unwittingly, she makes us aware of the black informant-spectator's implication in the film's success. Even though Bills's subversive intent authorized her patronage, the two dollars she tendered at the box office still counted as a monetary vote in favor of the film. Therein lies the problem. The credibility of her film evaluation is predicated on her firsthand knowledge of the object under review. Bills, therefore, was compelled to see the film. The other problematic surrounding reception is suggested by her comment that the first half of the film contains "historical facts which hold a person almost spellbound." Now, if this is taken seriously, one might expect that other blacks would likely be as anxious to witness this spellbinding spectacle for themselves as stay away from it despite the powerful urge to uphold the boycott. To illustrate the point, C. L. R. James (1973), a renowned black Marxist intellectual and political figure, confesses his *Birth* story: "I go early in the morning to see the picture and then come in the afternoon to picket" (134). Even though James is speaking in the context of the film's 1930s reissue, the point remains. As Bills and James so aptly demonstrate, informed black critics of the film during any era found little escape from the paradox of black spectatorship. In his article titled "Black Spectatorship," Manthia Diawara (1993b) fittingly describes this paradox as "the impossible position" (217) of the black spectator, an impossibility he locates in *Birth*'s narrative and visual inscriptions of spectatorial identification necessarily aligned against blackness.

In addition to foregrounding this position of spectatorial impossibility, Bills's nonexpert film review adds an ethnographic dimension as well. It is significant that the *Defender*'s strategic deployment of Bills's personal experiences with the Ku Klux Klan functions as a historical corrective to the film's mythologizing of the terrorist organization. Bills as autobiographer-ethnographer-historian is cleverly pitted against Griffith as storyteller-filmmaker-historian. In this way, the *Defender* endows Bills's oral history with a discursive aspect (journalistic legitimacy) suited to its task of censuring Griffith's cinematic mythology. This is the meaning of the article's eye-catching subheading "One Who Has Seen and Knows about the Early Days the Author [of the film] Tries to Falsely Depict: Tells It As It Was" (Bills 1915). In her noncorroboration of the film's glorification of the Klan's terrorizing rides to the rescue of white womanhood, Bills remembers the Klan night rides differently:

> The outrages of the Ku Klux Klan were nothing like the picture shows them to be. There was no noise, no fast horseback riding, no clash between them and the Negroes. It is true they went around on horseback, but very quietly, like thieves. No one knew or heard any horses' feet. I remember well when [as] a small child the Ku Klux Klan came to my father's cabin. They knocked quietly, called him by name and made him open the door. Though they were masked, he knew their voices, for they were some of the gentlemen of his master's family. . . . They asked for his gun. He gave it to them. They left as quietly as they came. They went to every other Negro cabin and did the same thing. There was no resistance, no fighting. (Bills 1915)

Because much popular white support for the film hinged on the widespread belief that "all essential episodes [were] grounded on historical fact," at least by one white newspaper's account ("Chicago Tribune Laments"), Bills's antithetical recollections about her direct experience with the Klan provide a necessary intervention in the film's glorification of Klan terror. Against Griffith and Dixon's celluloid image of a conquering Klan charging on horseback to the rescue, Mrs. Bills positions an alternative word-image of stealthy "thieves" on horseback, quietly but forcefully terrorizing their social, political, and racial subordinates in outlaw fashion with impunity. Moreover, Bills challenges Griffith's representation by questioning the validity of the sources and assumptions on which his historic vision rests. For example, she asks: "Was there ever a congress

composed entirely of Negroes who passed laws to govern all the whites in
the South?" And more to the point is this rejoinder: "Was there ever a
time when the southern white people were at all submissive to the blacks
as this picture would have people believe" (Bills 1915)? Obviously, anyone
familiar with the South's racial chauvinism would have to respond in the
negative. But Bills and the *Defender* understood that Griffith's northern
audiences would comprise chiefly the poorly educated white working
masses and "immigrants from abroad who did not know the English language [or American history] very well" (James 1973, 134). Both Bills and
James knew that Griffith's historical facsimile would initiate and recruit
hordes of immigrant newcomers into the South's "un-Reconstructed"
(to borrow a term from Du Bois) racial order of white supremacy.

On 24 July 1915, a few months before the appearance of Bills's article,
the *Defender* ran an unusually large political cartoon in which the devil
is depicted grinning maniacally as he stands behind and stirs a huge
cauldron labeled "Chicago." Inside is a brew overwritten with the words
"Race Prejudice," which the devil stirs with a stick tagged "The Birth of a
Nation." The caption above the cartoon reads, "The Melting Pot?" The
text that appears below the illustration states, "The Hon. (?) Thomas
Dixon in proper costume. The South not satisfied with its persecution of
the race below the Mason and Dixon line, sends its imps [to] broadcast
through the land." The cartoon's allusion to the poisonous effect of the
film on northern citizens and immigrant populations is clearly pertinent.
Though published nearly two months in advance of Bills's review, the
cartoon's vivid portrayal foreshadows many of Bills's concerns.

There is a further contestation of *Birth*'s self-authenticating narrative
in Bills's analysis. She writes: "I wonder if Mr. Griffi[th] lived during
those days, and does he really remember things as they were." By calling
Griffith's fictional retelling of "those days" into question while emphasizing the fact of her own childhood reminiscences of the era, Bills clearly
aims to set the historical record straight, at least for the *Defender*'s
readers. In the process, she succeeds in temporarily deposing Griffith's
idealized Klan from its romantic perch in the public imaginary, especially
to the extent that she offers her lived experience as proof of the Klan's
more diabolical reality. As pointed as Bills's criticisms of Griffith and
Dixon were, she reserved some of her more biting judgments for her own
community. Expressing dismay at black Chicago's inability to force a
shutdown of the film, Bills laments: "No other race but this black Ameri-

The Melting Pot?

CHICAGO

The Hon. (?) Thomas Dixon in proper costume. The South not satisfied with its persecution of the race below the Mason and Dixon line, sends its imps broadcast through the land.

One *Defender* cartoon assailing *The Birth of a Nation*'s racist discourse. *Chicago Defender,* 1915.

can would stand for the exhibition of pictures which are meant to poison the mind as this picture is" (Bills 1915). This intraracial critical approach, which was common in the black press response to *Birth,* may betray an element of self-flagellation, but it points up the sense of helplessness the black community felt in the face of this latest assault on their program of social uplift.

In the second article, published on 25 September 1915, this self-flagellation aspect is reintroduced, although attenuated by the paper's desire to chasten Chicago officials for permitting the film's exhibition. The article entitled "'Birth of a Nation' Run Out of Philadelphia" commanded nearly half of the front page and was accompanied by such incendiary subtitles as "Bloody Scene Enacted in Front of Forest Theatre: Proprietor . . . Said Blacks Were Only Bluffing and Would Run like Niggers Do at a Lynching," "5000 Black and White Men and Women Fought for the Race," and "Mayor Closes House: Race Satisfied." The motivation for drawing attention to Philadelphia's reversal of its position on the film is the *Defender*'s desire to influence a similar reversal in Chicago without "a general melee." By playing up reports that black "women lead the onslaught by hurling stones in [the] theatre," and that "every race man or woman seen on the street anywhere was set upon by Irish police," the *Defender* implicitly provides a blueprint of sorts for the mobilization of black rage against the film and its white proponents, which the Irish police officers here represent. Maintaining a vigilant eye toward enlisting the support of white liberals and progressives, the *Defender* is careful to foreground the biracial makeup of Philadelphia's dissidents. It is against this background that the comment "hundreds of white friends who had tried in vain to interest the mayor and chief of police to stop the play were loyal sympathizers" can be appreciated. The article even attempts to rekindle the dying embers of the nation's bitter sectional politics. To this end, the following is remarkably telling:

> The city of Philadelphia, known as the "City of Brotherly Love," has disgraced itself and now belongs in the category of southern cities by allowing such a play to bring such disgraceful scenes as were enacted a few nights ago. Efforts are now being made by the best people of both races to see . . . that no such plays as "The Birth of a Nation" are shown here. . . . From the bravery and heroism exhibited by Philadelphia men and women and the broken bones, cut faces and gashes given the officers of the law, there is no likelihood of the play or any of its kind having a success here. ("*Birth of a Nation* Run Out" 1915)

Though this reprinted article serves to underscore for *Defender* readers the difficult but final victory of Philadelphia's black and white citizens unified against the film interests, the final paragraph of the story is addressed to Chicago's African American population. The point that Philadelphia's "melee was a lesson to the Afro-Americans of Chicago who have allowed the play to be shown with no protest whatever" is put forward explicitly. Implicitly, however, the message is that it is not too late for black Chicago to join Philadelphia in resisting race as spectacle. Perhaps the fact that Chicago was becoming a leading center of black cultural and social development left the *Defender* unprepared for the community's lack of political mobilization against the film. Subsequently, the paper expresses a profound disappointment in the black community's impotence in this high-stakes political battle for the public image of blackness with the following admonition: "Philadelphia has taught the

Chicago race leaders a lesson. The Battle cry of the Afro-American is Philadelphia, not Chicago."

A sampling of discussions about the film from the *Baltimore Afro-American* newspaper, stories printed on 25 September 1915, and October 9 of the same year, reveals the unrelenting coverage of nationwide opposition to screenings of *The Birth of a Nation*. As front-page headline stories, both articles are designed to convey the importance or the special news value of this entertainment issue.[21] In the September article, the discussion centered on the physical confrontation between five hundred African Americans protesting against the film and a number of police officers. Here the reportage was straightforward and factual, except for the editorializing located in the subhead, where the protestors are described as an "irate mob," and the film is characterized as a "vicious photo film." The October article is distinguished from this earlier piece in that it represents a more intellectual engagement with the film text and its psychosocial ramifications. In this article, bearing the headline "The Race Is Misrepresented—Rev. Grammar, Former Baltimorean, Severely Criticizes the 'Birth of a Nation,'" a letter written by the reverend for the *Philadelphia Ledger* has been reprinted, with special local interest accruing as the result of Grammar's prior residence in Baltimore. Grammar's observations are important because he considers the social costs of the film's numerous historical inaccuracies in a broader historical context. He aims to foreclose the dangers of essentializing representations by way of his well-reasoned analogy that shifts the discussion from a narrative focus on falsified black criminality as depicted in the film. After pointing out aspects of the flawed logic permeating the reasoning on both sides of the sectional divide, Grammar goes on to contest the film's characterization of rapacious black brutes preying on white virgins: "Above all, no one can understand the South who does not grasp the fact that the colored people were almost universally loyal to their old masters and protected their women and children" ("The Race" 1915). The larger issue for Grammar, however, is that stereotypical misrepresentations are dangerous no matter their objectives. As an example, he points to the sociopolitical disaster that would result from biased representations unfairly equating all whites with famous criminals such as Frank and Jesse James.

It would be an awful thing, at this day, in Ireland to enact in moving pictures the horrors perpetrated either by the conquering Saxon on the original population or by the Celts in their uprisings against the victors who confiscated their soil. ("The Race" 1915)

As we have seen, contestations of this sort appeared frequently in black newspapers across the country, but Grammar's is set apart by his parallel consideration of the impact of cinematic misrepresentations on nations rather than on races. Whereas others have made the point that the white races in America would not abide such cinematic slander as perpetrated against blacks in *Birth* (Bills 1915), Grammar points out specific historic occurrences that could as easily be exploited to pit whites against themselves as against blacks. Though he does confront the film's racism in the course of his writing, underlying Grammar's allegorical interpretation of the film's politics of divisiveness is the notion that America's modern civil society could ill afford the polarizing effects of the film's racialist discourse.

In the next year, similar denunciations of *Birth* appeared in papers on the West Coast. In yet another intellectual polemic against the film, the *California Eagle* reprinted two articles from a New York newspaper by prominent white socialist Eugene V. Debs. The first article appeared on 29 January 1916, under the title "Eugene V. Debs Flays Big Movie." Two months later, a second, revised article was printed under the headline: "Debs Flays Bad Motion Picture: Socialists' Leader Says *Birth of a Nation* Evades Southern Men's Deeds." Debs's first review article followed two stories with racially charged issues that overlapped important points in his own commentary. One article, entitled "Sowed the Wind, Reaping the Whirlwind," concerned the social upheaval surrounding the romantic liaison between a married white woman and her black lover and their flight from, and eventual return to, San Diego. The second article, "Japanese Make Strong Protest against Moving Picture before Welfare Committee of the City Council," reported on the Japanese American community's protest efforts against Cecil B. de Mille's racially inflammatory film *The Cheat*. Thus Debs's scathing review of Griffith's *Birth of a Nation* conjoins with these articles to form a triangulated discourse on the film wherein the narrative impact of each accretes exponentially to the other. For example, the article contrasting city hall's willingness to "consider" the Japanese Association's protests against *The Cheat* to its refusal to hear African Americans' protests "when The Clansman was first brought here" betrays a fundamental disparity. It also redoubles the urgency in the following statement because the adjacent article is about a consenting interracial couple: "As citizens and Americans we only ask that there be one law for all men and not a white and black man's law" ("Japanese Make Strong Protest" 1916). This appeal was directed at federal authorities and their plans to prosecute only the black man in the miscegenation case, Raymond Dodds. His white paramour would evidently face only the recrimination of her husband and ostracization of her neighbors. The article carrying news of the Japanese Americans' rejection of *The Cheat* coupled with that of African Americans' condemnation of *The Birth of a Nation* in Debs's review constructs a sort of vox populi organized around the dismantling of dangerous anti-Asian and antiblack stereotypes in America's burgeoning cinema industry. Although this mutuality of purpose can rightfully be read as a metacritique when the two articles are considered together, there is an ironic aspect of Orientalism in the story on *The Cheat*. With a subtitle that reads "Jap Protest against Film Show Considered," the *Eagle* and, by extension, its readers are inculpated in the nation's Orientalist views on Asian "otherness." On a deeper level, however, we can see how California political institutions' inconsistencies in treating different ethnic groups contributed to the strain of intergroup relations.

As for Debs's reviews, in both articles he challenges the film's portrayal of Reconstruction from the timely perspective of Indiana's very real contemporaneous election travesties. Debs effectively contrasted Terre Haute's actual Jim Crow laws of legal discrimination against blacks through the nullification of their votes ("Debs Flays" 1916) with the film's inverted disenfranchisement scenario wherein whites are depicted as being brutally victimized at polling places by newly freed slaves during Reconstruction. Another point of historical revision in the film that Debs counters is the all-important miscegenation taboo, codified often as interracial rape—if the offending couple comprises a black male and white female. Conveniently, the inverse was rarely adjudicated along the same lines.[22] The points about "intermingling of [the] races" that were central in the lead story become resonant with, and iterative of, Debs's miscegenation theme. Whereas the former article attributes black male desire for white women, as in Dodds's "elopement," to the "white man's blood coursing through his veins," Debs's latter essay refocuses attention on the true historical facts behind the baleful reality causing white blood to course through the veins of so many African Americans.

There are four million mulattoes in this country, most of whom were born out of wedlock and all of whom have a white father or grandfather, and these white gentlemen are ready to fight at the drop of the hat for "white supremacy" and against "nigger equality." ("Debs Flays" 1916)

Since Dixon broaches this subject, Debs is intent on redirecting attention to the singular shame of white males who willfully and routinely violated their own miscegenation taboos. In fact, what outraged Debs and most African Americans writing about this film was its insidious aim to erase the true history of white rapaciousness in the South by substituting in its place an insupportable fictitious construct of unbridled black male sexuality in need of violent restraint by any means necessary. It seems no exaggeration to say that the film's brazen depiction of a menacing black brute attempting to rape a virginal white girl became a lightning rod that sparked the black press's massive protest campaign against *The Birth of a Nation*. With little exception, this scene is evoked and contested in the black press articles against the film. (Incidentally, the Japanese American community objected vehemently to a similar miscegenation scene with violent overtones in *The Cheat*). Debs captures the essence of blacks' indignation on this issue:

If it be absolutely essential to the play to represent those harrowing rape scenes, then why not round them out in their historic completeness and show the dissolute son of the plantation owners ravishing the black daughter before her parents' eyes? . . . It is only the black brute that is guilty, according to this and all other stories written about the colored man by Thomas Dixon. ("Debs Flays" 1916)

In fact, such historical rewritings of southern history so outraged African Americans that Dixon's race-baiting efforts in the multimedia extravaganza of *The Clansman* in all its forms (as an immensely popular novel, as a touring play, and finally as a feature film) became the black press's clarion call and cause célèbre in its opposition to Thomas Dixon's pro-southern propaganda. Debs, for one, was willing to answer that call vociferously and publicly. In a statement that prefigures Foucaldian concepts regarding the dialectic of power and knowledge (Foucault 1979, 27), Debs's specific engagement with the nexus of historical knowledge production and regimes of power is conveyed in these terms: "Let it not be overlooked that all histories have been written by white men and that colored men had no hand in them" ("Debs Flays" 1916). It is clear that Debs is addressing American historical epistemologies. Still, his overstatement begs the question, what about the historical writings of Alexander Crummel, Frederick Douglass, and W. E. B. Du Bois, to name but three African American writers and scholars who dedicated their lives to rectifying gross misrepresentations of American history insofar as that history concerned the African American? The question of whether Debs was ignorant of these African Americans and their historical revisions is not as important as the unlikelihood that these revisionist historiographies had filtered down to the popular readership that was Debs's audience. Be that as it may, his point about the self-serving motivations of white historians on the topic of America's race history stands and is understandable given that African American historical writings critical of the nation's racism hardly counted as legitimate history in America's mainstream and public academic institutions of that era.

That two prominent black newspapers (the *New York Age* and the *California Eagle*) chose to publish Debs's critical review can be viewed as a challenge to Cripps's assertion that "blacks, though, saw no art; they only saw the retelling of Reconstruction history as a Gothic horror tale haunted by black brutes" (Cripps 1993b, 42). Significantly, the *Birth of a Nation* criticism that the black press chose to print begins by acknowledging the film's artistry. On this subject, Debs writes (in both *Eagle* versions): "There is no question that it is a wonderful production, that many of its scenes are tense and thrilling, and that there is much in the play to approve and commend," but unlike many of his white contemporaries, Debs refused to deny the centrality of the film's racist narrative or to subordinate it to *Birth*'s obvious artistic and technological innovations. The film's artistry was not at issue. Debs's point was that, artistry aside, "if the author's studied purpose was to insult the black race and to revive and intensify the bitter prejudices . . . he could not have better succeeded, and it would be passing strange if the colored people did not protest against certain shocking features of the drama as doing them and their race grossest injustice" ("Debs Flays" 1916).

It is interesting that the *Eagle*'s most prominent condemnations of *Birth* issued from reprints found at other black newspapers rather than from its own editorial staff. This is particularly noteworthy in view of the *Eagle*'s own rave review of Griffith's next film. For *Intolerance*, the paper featured a banner headline announcing the premiere in this manner:

California Eagle 1916 front-page story, striking a note of conciliation as the press tried to move beyond the pain of cinematic intolerance.

"'Intolerance' vs. 'Clansman.'" This headline accompanied a conciliatory review of *Intolerance* just eight months after the paper had published Debs's caustic reviews of *The Birth of a Nation*. Here the *Eagle* devoted its lead column on the front page to Griffith's new film, replete with a glowing review. The commentary in this instance effects a complete about-face in comparison with the two previous articles on *Birth*. This article is less politically pointed or motivated and instead critiques the artistic and thematic merits of the production. Written by C. A. S., apparently an *Eagle* staff writer, it is more akin to the traditional reviews that would be found in, say, the *New York Times, Variety,* or *Moving Picture World*. Freed from an affective response to a film rife with racist representations, this review of *Intolerance* marks one black writer's willingness to embrace Griffith's cinematic craftsmanship. Consider this: "The picture represents three distinct periods of history as it were a story told in vivid picture language. . . . The picture not only demonstrates the wonderful inventive mind of the picture producer of Thomas [Dixon's] 'Clansman,' but clearly shows that D. W. Griffith stands out above them all as the greatest humanitarian of the age" ("Intolerance" 1916). In what amounts to a complete reversal of paper's earlier stance, the article's writer all but absolves Griffith for *The Birth of a Nation:* "As a race we believe that 'Intolerance' will do much to abate the prejudicial feeling created by the 'Clansman.'" If such comments are any indication, Griffith was not alone in desiring to move beyond the damaging controversy (for the moment) and condemnation forever inscribed in the history of *The Birth of a Nation*.

By the time the May 1915 article entitled "Fighting Race Calumny: The Chronological Record of the Fight against *The Clansman* in Moving Pictures" appeared in the most widely read African American monthly magazine, *The Crisis,* an organ of the National Association for the Advancement of Colored People, the NAACP was in the throes of an unprecedented three-month battle with the mayor of New York, the National Board of Censorship, D. W. Griffith, Tom Dixon, and the film's producers to have the "race-baiting" film suppressed if not expunged of its indecency or incitement to riot. As one of many articles that constitute the germinal corpus of black film criticism, the *Crisis* magazine article "Fighting Race Calumny" (1915) was at the forefront of this watershed moment in the black press's stalwart opposition to *The Birth of a Nation.* In addition to confirming reports that the film "was produced before the President and his family at the White House," one of the *Crisis* articles also included a quote attributed to Dixon in which he declares "that the object of the film was the ultimate deportation of 10,000,000 Negroes from the United States, and the repeal of the war amendments" ("Fighting Race Calumny II" 1915). In the main, this two-part article, published in May and June of 1915, was a precise chronological summary of the association's demands and activities to suppress *Birth* and the response to those efforts by social and political institutions from both sides of the controversy.[23] It is crucial to recognize within the language of all these articles the existence of an insurgent critical consciousness that, in varying degrees, cleared the discursive terrain for black written responses to films and the film industry from this period onward. Whereas the first part of the "Race Calumny" article highlighted the association's and the community's ability to galvanize against *Birth,* the second part concluded the chronology by stressing the valiant fight being waged against the powerful forces of American cultural and political hegemony, including the film company, the courts, and the theater syndicates.

Before it was over, the NAACP, through appeals to the National Board of Censors, local censorship boards, and sympathetic politicians, succeeded in winning many concessions in its battle against the film, namely the excision of scenes in some cases and outright bans on the film in others. Ultimately, however, many of the hard-fought victories were overturned by legal injunctions favoring the financial interests of the theater owners ("Fighting Race Calumny II" 1916). In any case, the *Crisis* articles conclude by affirming the community's efforts despite the set-

backs of legal retrenchments. In part 2 of "Fighting Race Calumny,"
there is a photograph of thousands of people gathered on Boston Common to protest the exhibition of *The Birth of a Nation*. Augmenting the
power of that photograph is the last statement in the article, which
reports a heartening bit of news from Chicago: "Mayor Thompson has
unqualifiedly refused the license to the photo-play *The Birth of a Nation*"
("Fighting Race Calumny II" 1916). Of course, we have already seen that
forces favoring the film finally prevailed in Chicago and that the film
enjoyed a successful if delayed run. In spite of the black community's
efforts to the contrary, the film went on to gross unprecedented millions
in profits. The point remains, however, that the sense of purpose, community will, and collective strength instilled within African Americans
as a result of the serious challenge they mounted against the most powerful individuals and institutions of the era did result in their winning one
crucial battle, the battle over the right of a subjugated people to self-
definition and expression.

The May issue also contained two additional articles discussing Dixon
and Griffith's *The Birth of a Nation* née *The Clansman*. Most notable of
the two was commentary written by W. E. B. Du Bois, the *Crisis* editor.
Addressing the legitimate concerns of African Americans with the history of brutal lynchings and governmental indifference through his astute critique of *The Clansman,* Du Bois's article exemplifies the spirit of
this inchoate black film discourse. For Du Bois, it was important to bare
Dixon's radical motives for representing blacks and southern history. To
Du Bois, Dixon signified the embodiment of "a professional southerner"
obsessed with fomenting racial discord. With that sentiment in mind, it
is remarkable that Du Bois is still able, nevertheless, to manage some
level of critical distance in his discussion of the issue. Again Du Bois's
comments on Griffith's adroit directorial skills demonstrate black audiences' awareness and appreciation of the film's artistic merits:

> Recently this vicious play has been put into moving pictures. With great
> adroitness the real play is preceded by a number of marvelously good war
> pictures; then in the second part comes the real "Clansman" with the
> Negro represented either as an ignorant fool, a vicious rapist, a venal and
> unscrupulous politician or a faithful but doddering idiot.... Small wonder
> that a man [Dixon] who can thus brutally falsify history has never been
> able to do a single piece of literary work that has brought the slightest

attention, except when he seeks to capitalize [on] burning race antagonisms. (Du Bois, 1915)

It is telling that Du Bois acknowledges Griffith's artistic achievement
in directing the war scenes even as he underscores the real threat posed by
the film—making racial hatred artistically appealing, financially reward-
ing, and socially acceptable (Du Bois, 1915). This is an important point
because the emphasis on the film's racist discourse in the black press
forms a necessary counterbalance to the elision of that problematic in
most of the white press at the time. It is significant also that Du Bois's
legitimate protests against the promotion of "this unseemly piece of propaganda as history" (Frazier 1957, 21) did not render him blind to Griffith's cinematic talents. However, as one of African America's leading
scholars, historians, and intellectuals, Du Bois understood the new media's incomparable influence on public attitudes about race and place in
the hierarchy of American civil society. By including articles about real-
life reports on lynchings in the edition containing discussions on *Birth*,
Du Bois prompts his readers to associate these events in such a way that
support for the NAACP's protest efforts is strengthened. To illustrate the
point further, in part 2 of the "Fighting Race Calumny" article, the *Crisis*
ran a story detailing the actual lynching of a black man in Memphis just
as the edition was going into print. Thus it is not surprising that Du
Bois's and other writers' critiques stress the incendiary nature of *Birth* by
recalling the eight-year history of public disturbances and the reckless
endangerment to black lives fostered by Dixon's novel *The Clansman*.

During the first tenure of the film's volatile run (there were repeated
revival showings of *Birth* during the twenties and thirties), it was common for the black newspapers to carry reports on lynching and news of
the suppression campaign against *Birth* in the same editions. Representa-
tive stories on the terror of lynching and white mob violence were "The
Habit of Lynching" (*Defender*, 1 Jan. 1915, 8); "Stop Daily Lynchings"
(*Defender*, 18 Jan. 1915, 1); "As to Lynchings" (*Defender*, 1 May 1915, 8);
"Lynching" (*The Crisis*, June 1915, 71–73); "Lynch Two in Georgia: Mob
Spirit Again Rampant" (*Defender*, 10 July 1915, 1); "Federation of Labor
Condemns Lynching" (*Age*, 23 June 1915, 1); and "Extra! Five Burnings in
South in Five Months" (*Age*, 12 July 1915, 1). Because lynching was a real
threat to black men, women, and children, and because *Birth* legitimated
and glorified the barbaric practice, the black press was compelled to

remind the nation's cinephiles that this film more than any other demonstrated beyond a doubt that the cinema was not simply a matter of box office receipts predicated on, or delimited by, high ideals of aesthetic and artistic evolution. Considering popular reports that President Woodrow Wilson had proclaimed the film as "writing history with lightning" (Cripps 1993b, 52), African Americans writing for the black press rightly perceived that the cinema was not merely entertainment or apolitical art. At that moment, moving pictures literally signified matters of life and death for them. The failed suppression campaign prompted several African American organizations to embark on a course of counteractive filmmaking. As Cripps points out, the NAACP "opened negotiations with Carl Laemmle of Universal" to produce "*Lincoln's Dream,* a celebration of black progress" (71). The project, however, failed to materialize. Similarly, Emmet Scott, of Booker T. Washington's Tuskegee Institute, was unsuccessful in getting *The Birth of a Race* produced as an alternative or corrective to *The Birth of a Nation.* Although a film bearing that title was eventually produced, the finished film bore no resemblance to Scott's original premise, which was "an inspirational black statement with a plea for mutual respect between the races" (74). As a result of Scott's inability to retain editorial control of the film and chronic financial and legal setbacks, the project was assumed by white principals who abandoned Scott's vision altogether. In its final form, the film was crafted as a meandering biblical history of humanity and warfare from Creation to the early twentieth century. The film culminates in a theme of universal brotherhood that can be preserved only by the call to arms. Far from being an antidote to *The Birth of a Nation,* the film ends as agitprop to combat isolationism and to generate support for World War I.[24]

In the wake of the furor and recriminations over *The Birth of a Nation* and its impact, Lester Walton's reconsideration of the film in 1919 stakes out new discursive terrain. His *New York Age* article entitled "World to be 'Americanized' by Such Films as 'Birth of a Nation'" considered the film's ill effects from a globalist perspective during the final tensions of the Great War. Published on 7 June 1919, Walton's entertainment column interrogates the distorted tableaux of America that Griffith and Dixon's film portrays. As we have come to expect, Walton permits his adversaries to define the ideological terms from which he vehemently departs. In this instance, Griffith's own remarks erect an ideological platform that Walton's probing analysis deconstructs. Griffith's assertion that "the motion picture will Americanize the world. Its influence has been gradually spreading, until to-day our unconscious propaganda excites the admiration of the nations" becomes the basis of Walton's counterattack. What incensed Walton most was that Griffith, not satisfied with "spreading anti-Negro propaganda" in America, was intent on extending the reach of his "unconscious propaganda" to the very European arenas in which patriotic black soldiers were making the ultimate sacrifice. In making the point that Griffith succeeded in his racist subterfuge with the willing complicity of America's white masses, Walton remains optimistic that the seeds of *Birth*'s antiblack sentimentality would fail to take root on foreign soil. Moreover, Walton was convinced that "thanks to the thousands of colored soldiers from America who, by their gentlemanly deportment during the war, gained the respect and good will of the European people, the film's activities at 'Americanizing' will be somewhat curtailed" (Walton 1919b). This statement makes clear Walton's aim to expose Griffith's Americanizing of the world plan predicated on the uncritical adoption of America's ethos of Negrophobic white supremacy. For Walton, it is essential that African Americans be aware of the now-global reverberations of Griffith's cinematic racism. Walton well understood that the international circulation of *Birth* could affix for generations to come the binary oppositions of racial blackness and whiteness constructed by Griffith, in which "all heroes and heroines are of white complexion and . . . The Negro has a corner on ignorance and buffoonery." Most unsettling for Walton was the international perception that blacks, indeed, were not true Americans.

> But when Mr. Griffith speaks in such glowing terms of the "American man" and "American womanhood" he does not have in mind the colored American. Only white Americans are depicted on the screen as heroes and in dignified roles to command respect and admiration. The motion picture producer does not essay to make heroes out of Negroes. (Walton 1919b)

When contextualized within the Pan-Africanist discourses of Du Bois and others of that era, Walton's concern with the cultural imperialism of American cinema unquestionably represents a significant interventionist critique in the vanguard of early-twentieth-century intellectual movements.

What is important in these early responses to *The Birth of a Nation* and the influential power of the cinema is the ability of the black press network to engage issues of the politicization of cultural productions and the role of such products in the sociopolitical matrix. In the end, it is evident that the bloody fight against one controversial "birth" culminated in the remarkable afterbirth of an activist black community awakened to a new sense of racial consciousness. As seasoned cultural fighters, black press writers were intent on transforming images of racial blackness through their own cultural productions of what "black is and what black ain't," as the late Marlon Riggs would put it.

Cinephilia in the Black Renaissance

NEW NEGRO FILM CRITICISM, 1916–1930

There is a future for the race in the Motion Picture world, actively and passively.—Juli Jones, "The Moving Picture"

Long sermons against the movies, admonitions to stay away from them, seem to result in empty pews in the church and an augmented attendance at the picture show around the corner.
—Jean Voltaire Smith, "Our Need for More Films"

We need critics. Our great misfortune is that we haven't enough who understand the dignity and importance of the job. . . . Again, we frequently hear [that] there are too many critics. These complainers feel we need more boosters. True, we do need boosters—in their place. But to supplant a critic altogether with a booster would be just as grave an error as for a critic to abuse his power and become a nuisance by nagging.
—*Pittsburgh Courier,* "Part Two: Feature"

The Negro plays and acts so far to appear on the talking screen have not been all that the Negroes desired, but they are paving the way for something better.—*Pittsburgh Courier,* "The Value of the Talkies"

At the twilight of the century's second decade, African Americans' interest and participation in the cinema assumed new forms of engagement. Buoyed by the relative successes of the black press's oppositional campaign against *The Birth of a Nation,* African American elites and masses set out to redefine their relationship to the cinema beyond the bounds of protest literature and a disaffected spectatorship. That redefinition took the forms of prolific film commentary, guerrilla filmmaking, and a new black spectatorship. To challenge the antiblack bias that permeated all levels of America's ascendent film industry, African Americans established a fledgling black cinema movement of their own with the expressed purpose, in the words of the pioneering editors of the first black newspaper, *Freedom's Journal,* "to plead our own cause."[1] To plead their own cinematic cause, African Americans embarked on an audacious independent film movement replete with theaters, "race films," performers, directors, producers, distributors, and critics, all dedicated to bringing "truer ideas of the customs and aspirations" (J. Smith 1922, 8) of the diverse black community to the silver screen.

Though much of this new cinema activism can rightly be attributed to the momentum generated by the backlash against *The Birth of a Nation,* other historic developments exerted significant influences as well. Most important in this regard were such epoch-making events as the Great War, northern industrial expansion, the Great Migration, and the Garvey movement, all of which inadvertently combined to effect the phenomenal transmogrification of America's mythological plantation "darky" into the actual "New Negro." This New Negro was an existential or pure product of America's traumatic encounter with the vicissitudes of modernity, and as E. Franklin Frazier observed, he and she clearly recognized the Great Migration as a "second emancipation" (quoted in Grossman 1989, 19). The preoccupation with the demands of postwar reorganization and the sociocultural and economic flux that issued from this major geo-demographic shift apparently left white America unprepared for the emergence of this new social agent. At the same time, a forward-looking carpe diem fervor had taken hold in the black community, one that imbued them with a sense of racial consciousness, self-determination, and the resolution to seize all opportunities of the moment. By 1919, the nation may have sought normalcy through a return to the status quo, but the nearly one-half million newly transplanted African Americans in the North and the majority who remained in the southland were busily preparing themselves for the new realities of postwar life.[2] Part of the new reality was the creation of a specifically African American niche in the increasingly influential mass media, especially the popular medium of film.

Eagerly embracing the myriad benefits that accrued to them as a result of their newfound economic and social prosperity in northern factories and in other industries outside the usual constrictions of the South's white supremacist hegemony, African Americans explored novel approaches and instruments to communicate their radical self-reinvention to the nation, to the world, and above all to themselves ("Moving Pictures of Tuskegee" 1910). This imperative led to a reconsideration of the basic cinematic apparatus by certain black intellectuals, artists, and visionary entrepreneurs in the vanguard of the New Negro movement. Even politically conservative Booker T. Washington saw the advantages in motion pictures for his then-controversial Tuskegee Institute. To contain some of the "contention [surrounding the institute] among colored people, particularly in the North," Washington decided "that it would be a good thing, as well as a paying investment, to produce some pictures that would show colored people what colored people are doing" ("Moving Pictures of Tuskegee" 1910). Despite its complicity in the nation's racist regime of representation, the cinema now represented an important tool for its destabilization, especially when used to awaken a reluctant nation to the cinema's brand of incontrovertible evidence of a dawning new age in American race relations—relations now predicated on mutual economic and social prosperity, at least between white merchants and their black patrons in the North ("Why We Should Patronize" 1915).

A further inducement prompting African Americans to reevaluate the new cinema technology was the relative affordability and accessibility of motion picture technology at that time. Although the naive optimism about the cinema's emancipatory possibilities at that moment might appear callow in retrospect, it is well worth recalling the profound success African Americans made of an earlier technology of mass communication, the printing press. Given their phenomenal achievement of establishing a far-flung black press network throughout the United States during one of the nation's most racially repressive periods, African Americans' expectations for similar successes in the realm of cinema clearly were not without foundation. In fact, it was due to the black press's unwavering support that the efforts and aspirations of early black filmmakers neither died on the vine of inattention nor got strangled in a noose of newsprint by the white critical establishment, as Ralph Ellison (1972, 78) so aptly put it. Moreover, the formidable alliance between the influential black press and the evolving black cinema movement ("Moving Pictures Offer" 1915) made it increasingly difficult for the nation to delay further its day of reckoning with a multifaceted New Negro movement and its concomitant cultural revolution variously termed the black or Harlem Renaissance.

The arrival of black films featuring updated representations of black life and culture propelled other significant advancements in the overall black cinematic experience. The advent of independently produced black films allowed African American spectators new forms of image cathexis or identification.[3] Absent the need to endure a discomfited spectatorship generated by the displacement of their visual pleasure onto white cinematic heroes and heroines, black audiences could now indulge their escapist fantasies and ego gratifications through new heroic portrayals of fictional and actual black screen figures projected larger than life in the wildly successful innovation of "race films."

Celebrating the New Negro and Modernity

RACE FILMS IN NEWSPAPERS AND MAGAZINES

FROM 1916 TO 1919

Before the advent of Hollywood's studio system during that era variously dubbed the Roaring Twenties and the Jazz Age, African Americans nationwide displayed an irrepressible affinity for the cinema (Walton 1914b). However, few might anticipate that even before the furor over *The Birth of a Nation,* African Americans envisioned the cinema as a necessary corrective to America's psychosocial compulsion to "burlesque the black man," to borrow Lester Walton's acrid phrase (Walton 1912c).[4] Such black cinephilia, at first glance, seems especially misplaced because from the outset films had colluded in America's intractable racist discourse. Consider, for example, the profusion of African and African American exotica that became visual staples in newsreels, travelogues, and other actuality film representations before 1915, which film critics and historians such as Donald Bogle, Thomas Cripps, Mark Reid, Henry T. Sampson, and N. Frank Ukadike, among others, have explored in painstaking detail. Nonetheless, to better appreciate the black press's cinephilia from 1916 onward, it is useful to review salient components of this complex history so that a more nuanced analysis of the black press's reception of this first phenomenal wave of independent black filmmaking activity can emerge. The modern black press offered both a critical response to and generative mechanism for these pioneering efforts on the eve of America's post–Great War boom years.

The swell of northern, northeastern, midwestern, and western populations brought about by the Great Migration created the precondition for a new bifurcation of the African American masses. Historically, blacks in America had been defined by and split into categories of domestic servant and field-worker. The new schismatic formations later realigned into blocs of the modern working-class poor and the intellectual and cultural elites. Because America's social contract at the turn of the century necessitated the separation of the races (legally mandated by Jim Crow segregation legislation), the everyday needs of the black masses were met by a ready, albeit minuscule, corps of black leaders and entrepreneurs capable of plying their trades in all walks of life.[5] The black press network and the black cinema movement both sprang from the need to fill the information and entertainment gaps experienced by a dislocated and downtrodden population. Functioning as it did for the first generation of non-English-speaking European immigrants, the cinema quickly became one of the most expedient and pleasurable means of acculturating the first wave of African American migrants to their newfound urban existence in American industrial society,[6] particularly for the group's illiterate and semiliterate members. Even though the early cinema was significant for both groups' inculcation to the new realities of modern American life, unlike many of their first-generation European immigrant counterparts, African American migrants could rely on the well-entrenched black religious and journalistic institutional networks for additional sociocultural uplift strategies. Within this supportive kinship framework, an alliance formed between the new black cinema movement and the expanding black press network. As the cinema captured the imagination, leisure time, and limited disposable income of the post-Reconstruction era's disoriented and dislocated black masses, African American writers and journalists recognized, early on, the emancipatory potential of the basic cinematic apparatus, particularly if unmoored from the racist imperatives of white production houses. And owing to this, as early as 1913, the black press initiated a high-profile campaign to promote and celebrate the exploits of upstart black filmmakers dedicated to reinscribing cinematic images of blackness that authenticated African American progress and development. Accordingly, newspaper headlines promoting black participation in the business of filmmaking were often privileged over the more frequent reactionary headlines railing against the mainstream cinema's institutionalized racism. And when necessary, both types of film headlines and articles would be strategically juxtaposed.

A case in point is the 23 May 1914 edition of the *Chicago Defender*, in which an article about Peter P. Jones's procurement of South American capital to fund a new black-oriented film company is paired with a story condemning a white mob in Mississippi for demolishing the "No-Name" theater because it dared to show movies to segregated African American audiences ("Peter P. Jones Takes Moving Pictures" 1914). In the main, however, headlines celebrating blacks' forays into the motion picture business tended toward the following: from the *Defender*, "Foster Photoplay Company Licensed in Florida," "Peter P. Jones Heads Moving Picture Company," "Foster, the Moving Picture Man, Returns"; from the *New York Age*, "Negro Motion Pictures," "Colored Men Organize Big Theatrical Circuit"; from the *Baltimore Afro-American*, "Fisher Writes Play for Motion Picture Company," "New Theater for Wilmington: One of the Finest in the Country of Its Kind Entirely Owned and Operated by Colored People"; and from the *St. Louis Argus*, "Lincoln Motion Picture Company Making Good." The positive register of these newspaper headlines was matched by similar exuberance in such black magazines of the era as *Half-Century*. Their aim was to discredit the dehumanizing caricatures of blackness in American popular culture by submitting the works of black filmmakers as more authentic visions of black Americans' experiences and aspirations. No longer would white America's self-serving arbitration of what constituted the essential black identity be the measure and limit of African American subjectivity in modern times. Black writers thus initiated a program of de-essentializing Negroness whereby efforts "to make the public believe that the Negro of today is the Negro of forty years ago" would be unavailing (Walton 1906).

From late 1913 onward, black newspapers and magazines such as the *New York Age, Chicago Defender,* and *Half-Century Magazine* set out to rally African Americans behind the dauntless efforts of the world's first black cineasts, William Foster, aka "Juli Jones," and the enterprising photographer-turned-filmmaker Peter P. Jones. Dubbed by the *Defender* in 1914 as the "father of Afro-American Photo-Plays" ("Foster Photoplay Company" 1914), Foster was a theatrical impresario, critic, and actor before his sojourn in filmmaking. With his extensive entertainment background, Foster was virtually assured early successes. In fact, by 1914, Foster had produced such popular one-reelers as "'The Fall Guy,' 'The Butler,' 'The Grafter and the Girl,'" and "that sensational comedy, 'The Railroad Porter'" ("Foster Photoplay Company" 1914). For members of the black press, Foster's accomplishments as early as 1913 signaled an impressive intervention in dominant filmmaking practices. In 1914 the *New York Age* encouraged and congratulated Foster's moxie: "If the Foster Photo Company of Chicago has other motion pictures on the order of 'The Pullman Porter,' the firm would be conferring a favor on the colored playgoers of Harlem by sending them eastward" ("Foster Photoplay Company" 1914). This passage vividly illustrates black audiences' yearnings for new cinematic constructions of blackness rooted in the creative imaginings of their own artists.

Famed Chicago photographer Peter P. Jones's entrée to the cinema was no less heralded. The *Defender* touted Jones's venture into the motion picture arena with a front-page story covering his newsreel-style film that featured "the march of the Mystic Shriners" ("Peter P. Jones Takes Moving Pictures" 1914). The importance of this *Defender* article is its reportage on the international reach of the earliest black filmmaking enterprises. Undaunted by the exclusionary practices of America's mainstream filmmaking industry, Jones turned his attentions to international business opportunities for the realization of his filmmaking ambitions. Beginning in 1914, Jones entered into what is likely the first black venture of international film coproduction. Given this situation, it becomes apparent that Jones determined to participate in the capital-intensive but financially lucrative business of independent filmmaking by any means necessary. As the *Defender* notes:

> Mr. Jones now heads a moving picture company, made up of South American businessmen, with a capital of $100,000, organized for the purpose of making pictures showing the progress of the Afro-American in the United States. . . . The pictures are to be exhibited in Brazil and other South American countries first. ("Peter P. Jones Takes Moving Pictures" 1914)

Jones's resort to international financing reveals the limitations of business opportunities available to aspiring black filmmakers during America's Jim Crow era. It also conveys the level of commitment and determination of early black filmmakers to affix their own imprimatur on the history of early cinema despite hostile economic forces in the United

States. Notwithstanding the dearth of follow-up reports on the exhibition and reception of Jones's black actuality films in Brazil and in other South American cities, we can presume their relative success based on the *Defender*'s subsequent announcement two months later of the imminent premiere of the Peter P. Jones Company's second film project, a comedy entitled *The Troubles of Sambo and Dinah* ("Peter P. Jones Heads" 1914).

On 13 June 1914, a front-page *Defender* headline reports, "Peter P. Jones Heads Moving Picture Company." The subheading pronounces the "company a strong one." Following mainstream film practices of drawing star personnel from the stage, the Peter Jones Film Company structured its first fictional film narrative, *Sambo and Dinah*, around "the funniest man in vaudeville," Matt Marshall. As a result of his experience with the Chicago-based Pekin Stock company, one of the most successful black theatrical troupes in America, Marshall was also slated to "be the director of the humorous productions." Despite Marshall's presold star appeal, the article attributes the firm's potential success to Jones's "national reputation" as a photographer of such black luminaries as "Booker T. Washington, Henry O. Tanner, Burt Williams, Aida Overton Walker . . . Prof. Wm E. [B.] Du Bois," and others:

> Mr. Jones' work is recognized as among the very best in the country. Finishing and retouching has made his work stand out. Being an artist of the first water, a moving picture company was organized and he was selected as its president, for the purpose of making pictures showing the progress of the Afro-American in the United States. ("Peter P. Jones Heads" 1914)

By obscuring details and referring to the founding of the company in the passive voice ("a moving picture company was organized . . . he was selected"), the article's syntax calls into question the extent of Jones's power of agency in directing this filmmaking enterprise beyond his valuable name and reputation. Though Jones's ability to circumvent obstructions to black filmmaking endeavors in the United States by entering into an international venture is laudable, the progressive thrust of this arrangement appears vitiated by the suspect nature of the first coproduced film, as indicated by the demeaning terminology of the title, *The Troubles of Sambo and Dinah*.

It is difficult to explain Jones's seeming capitulation to so offensive a moniker as *The Troubles of Sambo and Dinah*. And in its rush to embrace Jones's film company, the *Defender* fails to comprehend the contradictory logic of its characterization of a film targeted at black audiences as "wholesome and refined" when one of the film's principal characters is derisively named "Sambo." Evidently Jones and the *Defender* turned a blind eye to the likely injury visited on their constituent publics when confronted with such a publicly demeaning title emblazoned across a theater marquee. Perhaps the tenor of the times subtended such ill-conceived compromises. In an era when it was acceptable even for black comedians to perform minstrel acts in burnt-cork or blackface makeup, it is not unreasonable to presume that black audiences negotiated such problematic signifiers through some form of resistant or transgressive recoding strategies. Weighed against such "disgusting" portrayals of "colored men stealing chickens" as in Lubin's *Tale of the Chicken* ("States Theater Displays" 1914), it is conceivable that *The Troubles of Sambo and Dinah* presented an advance of sorts to the *Defender* writers and their readers. In fact, the paper credits Jones's film specifically for not containing offensive material such as "chicken-stealing scenes." After all, only two weeks before its laudatory comments about *Sambo and Dinah,* the *Defender* had found it necessary to run a scathing denunciation of a Lubin comedy featuring "chicken-stealing" scenes. Under the paper's front-page banner headline decrying "States Theater Shows Colored Men Stealing Chickens," the paper's 30 May 1914 edition ran an article that reproached Lubin's *Tale of the Chicken* on the following grounds:

> A view of the pictures showed the most disgusting films witnessed on State Street. One Lubin is down as the author and the reel pictures [show] an illiterate going into a coop and stealing a chicken. . . . This illiterate uses the feathers of the stolen chicken to defeat a rival. He sneaks some feathers into the innocent man's pocket. He is arrested for rifling the hen roost and the grand climax comes in court when this evidence is taken out of his pocket. The entire chicken scene is raw and vile.

Proffered in opposition to this Lubin film, it could be argued that the *Defender*'s promotion of *Sambo and Dinah* is less compromised.

In *The Dialogic Imagination*, Mikhail Bakhtin (1981) suggests a theoretical way out of the seeming impasse created by the *Defender*'s contradictory posture vis-à-vis its tacit condoning of the racist term "Sambo" in a black film product, its castigation of a "Sambo" character and his buffoonish antics as crafted by Lubin. Bakhtin's contention that social and historic forces create "the decentralizing tendencies in the life of language" (274) presents a theory of "language stratification" in which a single national language is nuanced by the existence of "social languages" within itself (275). This view helps explain the facility of different social groups, such as African Americans, to deform and reform dominant language formations to their own in-group usages, the phenomenon that Houston Baker Jr. (1987) has addressed as virtuoso mastery of form and deformation of mastery (15). For Bakhtin, "artistic works . . . are all capable of stratifying language, in proportion to their social significance . . . [and thereby] alienating . . . words and forms from other tendencies, parties, artistic works and persons (1981, 290). In other words, the African American community's shared codes of language usage routinely imbue the dominant language with their own "semantic nuances and specific axiological overtones" (290) in such a way that traditional linguistic structures are inflected to exceed or invert mainstream expectations. We easily recognize this tendency from the late 1960s, when African Americans adapted and ultimately adopted the once-derisive term "black." By embracing the reviled term "black," African Americans re-inscribed this negative racial sign with positive meaning. This 1960s exemplar is not intended to suggest that early-twentieth-century blacks identified in similar fashion with the derisive term "Sambo." Rather, it is invoked to demonstrate the real possibility that African Americans at this historic juncture found equivalent strategic methods of semantic appropriation and subversion, especially within the ambit of a growing Du Boisian double consciousness. It is not so much, perhaps, that turn-of-the-century blacks were not offended by the utterance. Instead, the issue is that they likely took less offense when such volatile terms as "Sambo" issued from presumably well-meaning African Americans. Still, the situation does beg the question of whether the paper's attitude would be so magnanimous or forgiving had the film *Sambo and Dinah* been produced by an all-white company. Whatever the answer, there is no question that in the beginning, black filmmakers could rely on positive ink from the black press network during those crucial early years.

Black filmmaking efforts on the West Coast were also met in the black press with generosity and support. Two years later, the *California Eagle* inaugurated its promotion of the first African American film enterprise in that region, the Lincoln Motion Picture Company, which was founded by the Johnson brothers, Noble and George. Noble was an actor of bit parts in mainstream films, and his brother George was the company's business manager. Their Lincoln Motion Picture Company made its long-awaited debut on 4 July 1916. In its coverage of the event, the *California Eagle* ran a near-full-page announcement featuring the premiere of Lincoln's first feature film, a two-reel drama entitled *The Realization of a Negro's Ambition* ("Talk of the Town" 1916). One week later, an article detailing the event, "Opening of the New Angelus a Notable Success," told, among other things, of "thousands turned away on opening night":

> On Tuesday evening, July 4th, the Angelus Theatre was crowded to its utmost capacity by Colored citizens, eagerly bent upon seeing the real physiognomies of real Negroes thrown upon the canvas. "The Realization of a Negro's Ambition," is the title of the play produced by the All-Star local cast. . . . The erection of this enterprise marks another epoch in the social and economic independence of the Negroes of California. . . . The Lincoln Motion Picture Company guarantees the Colored citizens of Los Angeles that all pictures featured and delineated by this company will be of the highest order: depicting the Negro only in his natural habitat. All application and references will be true to the life and character of the Negro. . . . We are certainly proud of the work being done by this company. ("Opening" 1916)

The *Eagle*'s emphasis on the Lincoln Motion Picture Company's resolve to portray the Negro in "his natural habitat" provides insightful clues to the abiding frustrations that dimmed the spectator experience for black film fans. More important, however, is what we learn about the implacable will and determination of black filmmakers who dared to provide a pleasurable film experience for their constituency while staking their own claims to the financial windfall promised by the movie craze. Of the numerous entrants into the new "race films" market, what set Lincoln apart, especially from those in partnership with silent "white backers and exploiters" (Cripps 1993b, 85), was the company's dedication to technical merits and thematic integrity in depicting black life and culture.

As Thomas Cripps observes in his influential book *Slow Fade to Black*, Lincoln's films "had successfully incorporated every device made popular by Hollywood and yet had not compromised its emerging black aesthetic" (1993b, 86). Ultimately, Lincoln's refusal to sacrifice quality for quantity and financial expediency exacerbated its persistent financial straits. Nonetheless a commitment to serious dramas as opposed to the cheaply made ribald comedies of its competitors prompted the *Eagle* to conclude that Lincoln not only represented a significant advance for black incursions into the influential medium of film but, more importantly, symbolized a giant step in the black community's quest for building black institutions. Unfortunately Lincoln's promising beginning, marked by its impressive roster of dramatic films, *The Realization of a Negro's Ambition, The Trooper of Troop K,* and *A Man's Duty,* could not forestall its eventual demise in the face of postwar economic depression and the formidable rivalry from nonblack firms producing "race films" (84).

By printing frequent news of black filmmaking pioneers, the black press nonetheless manifested a clear understanding of its pivotal role in sustaining and extending the embryonic black film movement. As news of African Americans' lucrative patronage of the moving pictures spread (Walton 1913a), it is not surprising that expectations for the future of black filmmaking enterprises were high. Black film audiences contributed substantially to the financial success of the new film industry, an industry that was not yet dominated by the developing oligopolies of vertically integrated entertainment firms that gave rise to the indomitable Hollywood studio system of the 1920s and 1930s. Amid the unregulated business environment (in the wake of the defeated Edison Trust), the avant garde of the black independent film movement and its proponents in the black press found fertile ground on which to grow and prosper, at least for a time.

The first order of business for the earliest black film entrepreneurs was to publish and disseminate information about their interventionist representational strategies. For them, it was imperative that the black community be apprised and supportive of the filmmakers' efforts both to redefine cinematic blackness and to negate the usual stereotypes of black life and culture too often perpetrated and perpetuated by whites in blackface. Apart from "films that bore the trademark of colonial cliches" (Ukadike 1990, 30), black people were rarely if ever featured in mainstream films until the third remake of the film version of *Uncle Tom's Cabin* in 1914 (Null 1975, 9). Seizing the new medium to advance their own agenda of race pride and self-articulation, African American filmmakers joined alongside their literary counterparts to overthrow the controlling edicts of white bourgeois norms of ideological and representational blackness. Even though early black films diverged little from the narrative and formal paradigms of the dominant cinema, as they tended to imitate mainstream film style and substance, they did represent repetition with a discernible difference. Notwithstanding their hybridized constructions modeled on dominant film aesthetics and formulas, Jones's and Foster's "race films" were distinguished by undeniably African American–specific themes and cultural referents. As Mark Reid has cogently asserted in *Redefining Black Film,* it is true that

> *The Railroad Porter* is similar to the comedies turned out by the industry. Nevertheless, Foster photoplays altered the popular Rastus stereotype by using African American socio-realities as the content of his films. Some of these realities are the existence of a black middle class, employed northern blacks, and blacks who patronize black-owned restaurants.... Foster's film program retained some of the technique of vaudeville road shows, yet broke with the "coon" tradition established by Thomas Alva Edison's *Ten Pickaninnies* (1904) and *The Wooing and Wedding of a Coon* (1905) as well as Sigmund Lubin's Sambo and Rastus series (1909, 1910, and 1911). . . . Foster's films introduced a black perspective for a black audience who desired images different from the Euro-American comedies of the industry. (Reid 1993, 8)

This culturally specific strategy did not go unappreciated or unacknowledged by the press network and its loyal readers. In fact, the black press's centrality in maintaining and expanding black audiences' acceptance of these technologically lacking productions (Null 1975, 11), in marked contrast to the well-financed comedies churned out at better-equipped and -managed white film companies, is incalculable. There can be little doubt that in this era of newfound black pride and racial consciousness, the black press was essential in solidifying the all-important triangular relationship among black filmmakers, black films, and black audiences. Despite the odds, this strong and strategic triumvirate kept the vision of a new black cinema alive.

From Teshome Gabriel's theorization of the three phases of Third World film production, we can draw some useful structural and ideological parallels between later black filmmaking movements and this first wave of African American film production. Of particular relevance is Gabriel's delineation of the first and second phases of Third World film development. In his important treatise "Towards a Critical Theory of Third World Films," Gabriel (1985) describes phase one as tending toward an "unqualified assimilation" of Hollywood or Western mainstream film modalities (32). The primary characteristic of this phase, according to Gabriel, is the imperative to "create a spectacle" by aping Hollywood styles (32). In phase two, the remembrance phase, Gabriel sees the "indigenisation and control of talents, production, exhibition and distribution" as central components in the realization of oppositional films. This indigenous control is augmented by the films' preoccupation with themes and narratives celebrating the strengths, traditions, and heritage of the black community. Although Gabriel acknowledges the positive aspects of phase two, with its necessary departures from dominant filmmaking imperatives, he is rightly concerned about the dangers inherent in "the uncritical acceptance or undue romanticisation of ways of the past" (32). The problem, as Gabriel explains it, is that black filmmakers committed to recodings of the black experience in contradistinction to mainstream precepts are prone to going down a "blind alley" in which "falsification of the true nature of a culture as an act of or agent of liberation" (32) creates new, albeit well-intentioned, misrepresentations and problematics. These complaints and observations are clearly analogous to, and resonant with, early African American filmmaking and criticism as exemplified in the *Sambo and Dinah* example discussed earlier.

The tendency of early black filmmakers to redeploy the oppressive skin color caste system of meritocracy inherited from the dominant culture exemplifies an obvious aspect of this well-meaning but wrongheaded preoccupation with "aping Hollywood" aesthetics and their attendant ideology of whiteness. The films produced by Johnson's Lincoln Motion Picture Company and by Oscar Micheaux come in for special scrutiny along these lines, for both are guilty of constructing fictional black worlds characterized by fair-skinned protagonists and dark-skinned miscreants.[7] Further compromising early black filmmakers' claims to counterhegemonic and thus authentic portrayals of black life is their propensity to promote middle-class bourgeois norms over the more folk and working-class realities of the black masses who made up their target audience. To their credit, some writers for the black press did eventually challenge these misapplications of dominant film practices as the decade progressed. Still, it was the preponderance of celebratory discourses in the black press that nourished the embryonic black cinema movement from the nickelodeon phase to the film as art phenomenon. Central here was the press's successful arbitration of the often incommensurate demands of increasingly sophisticated black film audiences and the journeyman skills of upstart black filmmakers. More often than not, the black press willingly shouldered the burden of generating mass enthusiasm for the acceptance of "race films" on their own terms despite fierce competition from the more technologically advanced but racially biased films generated by the dominant industry.

Even as writers for the black newspapers heightened their celebrations of the new black cinema, they remained vigilant in their efforts to combat the relentless distortions of African American reality in mainstream American and other Western film productions. Leading this charge was the *New York Age*'s resident drama critic, the indomitable Lester A. Walton. When a film produced by the Pathe Newsreel division registered on Walton's critical radar, he immediately sounded the alarm, alerting black readers to the latest antiblack celluloid missive. Even though Walton's influence along the northeastern seaboard at that moment is difficult to quantify exactly, it is clear that film commentary occasioned by his recalcitrant gaze found an audience beyond the northeastern and southern regions of the nation.

On 7 September 1918, *Cayton's Weekly* (a black newspaper published by Horace R. Cayton Sr. in Seattle from 1919 to 1922) reprinted a Walton critique of the Hearst-Pathe newsreel series covering the activities of American soldiers in World War I entitled *Over There*. Walton's review of "The Colored Soldier on the Screen" installment is significantly longer than his usually ample columns for the *Age*. From the start, Walton's interrogatives challenge spectators' uncritical belief in newsreel verisimilitude, especially where race matters. Here he challenges one of the newsreel's most important functions, its didacticism in the propagation of white mythologies about black otherness. At the same time, he foregrounds the newsreel's racially inflected subject-object oppositions and its callous disregard for African American spectatorial displeasure. Finally, he considers the often futile attempts by liberals to intervene in or mount effective strategies of subversion against dominant filmmaking interests.

Walton's article on the Pathe newsreel mounts a frontal assault on the notion of actuality film's participation in an objective or apolitical reproduction of nature "without the creative intervention of man," as Andre Bazin (1967) put it in "The Ontology of the Photographic Image" (13). Unlike Bazin, however, Walton has an inherent suspicion of realistic representations that claim for themselves an unmotivated or transparent reproduction that unambiguously reflects some extrinsic and pure reality that the image merely captures. To foreground his understanding that indeed "all writing [including filmic writing] is a form of fabrication" (Strinati 1995, 111), Walton makes the point that "the Hearst-Pathe pictures are *supposed* [italics mine] to keep us acquainted with what our boys in khaki are doing in France . . . [b]y presenting on the screen each week the American soldier. There has been one exception to this propaganda" (Walton 1918). The exception Walton references is the newsreel's biased treatment or fabricated writing of the battlefield activities of African American soldiers. For Walton, it was clear that newsreel producers and camera operators were governed by a different reflection or mimetic theory when filming black soldiers than that directing the depiction of white soldiers. Whereas the newsreel film reflected or emphasized "white Americans in the trenches at their best," Walton noticed that on the two occasions in which black soldiers were filmed, "the colored man as a soldier [was] ridiculed on the screen." The racial and political economy served by these racially aligned "objective" portrayals signified absolutely for Walton the inadequacy of mimetic theories of representation, particularly when the subject of reflection was informed by the Euro-American racial imaginary.

Walton wanted to lay bare the newsreel's specious didactic function in reifying prevailing notions of black racial inferiority. To accomplish this act of demystification, he singled out the disparate treatment in the newsreel of black and white soldiers. To emphasize that white newsreels seemed to ignore the fact that, like their white counterparts, African American soldiers were making the ultimate sacrifice for democracy, Walton is compelled to assert that "AT NO TIME HAS THE COLORED SOLDIER BEEN SHOWN AS A MAN" (1918). Rather than provide cinematic evidence to the world that "Colored Americans" were "giving their lives, money, moral support—their ALL to help take the 'germ' out of German," Walton argues that the Franco-American film alliance had opted instead to perpetuate prevailing racist assumptions that "continue to poke fun at the colored American even when he is in the trenches 'over there.'" By exposing more than one example of newsreel imagery that camouflages the "display of generosity and loyalty" of the black soldiers through stock representations of black buffoonery, Walton negates dismissals of black responses on the grounds that blacks tend to be "too sensitive" about their images. Buttressing his assertion that "if you want to see the colored soldier misrepresented and ridiculed just go to the movies," Walton points to the existence of two separate instances of racist depictions of black soldiers abroad as suggestive of something other than innocent inadvertency or unintentionality in the derisive portrayals.

> On two different occasions last week I saw the colored man as a soldier ridiculed on the screen. The first instance was when a Hearst-Pathe picture, after showing white Americans in the trenches at their best, portrayed a colored soldier, a most dumb specimen of humanity, sitting with book in hand trying to learn French. The man who posed for the picture was scratching his head and gazing into the book in bewildered fashion. . . . The second instance in which the colored man was used it was to inject a dash of "comedy." (Walton 1918)

Because the Pathe newsreel highlighted its representation of black soldiers as inferior to their white compatriots, Walton felt duty bound to point out the overarching political and racial economies of such unfair and damaging characterizations. Demonstrating an understanding of the newsreel's unique ability to fabricate reality while the filmmaker effaces his or her artistic and ideological controls over the images presented, Walton wants to ensure that his readers are not deceived by such cinematic sleights of hand. In so doing, Walton makes it clear that the indexical nature of newsreel footage can guarantee nothing, least of all a direct and unmediated experience with its referent. He is insistent that readers recall the political function of comedy in earlier American narratives of racial difference that authorize and legitimize the nation's belief in the myth of black inferiority. According to this logic, Walton recognized how easily whites could be expected to accept the proposition that blacks need not be taken seriously in any endeavor requiring intellectual skills. This ethos, Walton suggests, is at the heart of de rigueur cinematic deployments of white-inflected "black dialect" in filmic representations of blackness. Because blacks, in America's popular imaginary, had not adequately mastered the English language, they could hardly be expected to master the difficulties of a foreign language, and for them to conquer or master the lingua franca of civilized societies was unfathomable. Given such assumptions, Walton knew that few whites would challenge the newsreel's depiction of a black soldier scratching his head when confronted with such a demanding intellectual task as learning to speak French. Walton understood the ideological function of comedy that attaches to a scene in which an inferior black soldier has the audacity to attempt even linguistic parity with the genetically superior foreign whites he was sworn to protect. Not even the objectified black soldier performing the humorous antics is spared in Walton's scathing commentary: "Evidently he was as dumb as he looked for no intelligent, self-respecting colored soldier would permit himself to be used as a clown" (Walton 1918).

Questioning the verisimilitude of the newsreels as well as their ideological imperatives was not Walton's only concern. His critique also raises the issues of black spectatorship and reception. In describing his own and a black war worker's spectatorial positioning in the newsreels' texts, Walton gives us a glimpse into an early instance of resistant reading or transgressive decoding strategies available to early-twentieth-century black film audiences. Walton astutely identifies the duplicity involved in the cinematic construction of black and white war character ideals. Blacks, he noticed, were expected to cheer on the heroic portrayals of white soldiers in battle at the same time that black soldiers were maliciously characterized in the same texts as buffoonish comic relief:

> I was in company with a colored war worker, and we applauded without stint pictures showing white troops engaged in fighting the Hun. Then a "joke" was flashed in which one colored man called another "niggah" in controversy as to whether it would be safer to enlist in the army or navy. The implication behind this "piece of humor" was that two badly frightened Negroes were figuring on the less dangerous way to serve their country. "That isn't funny to me," stated the war worker after he had read the "joke," and I, very much abashed, concurred. (Walton 1918)

Aside from his castigation of the fundamental unfairness in the treatment of black soldiers and, by extension, black spectators, Walton's recalcitrant gaze betrays an even greater insight into some unanticipated connections that spectators draw between their socially constructed everyday existence and certain cinematic images. Using Walton as a barometer of their resistant spectatorship, we can trace instances of the concept of cinematic excess at work. Following Stephen Heath, Kristin Thompson's thought-provoking essay "The Concept of Cinematic Excess" explains how cinematic narratives often contain seeds of their own cognitive and perceptual subversions and thereby invite spectators, especially nonprivileged ones, to consider "those aspects of the work which are not contained by its unifying forces" (K. Thompson 1986, 130). In other words, Thompson enables us to see the ways in which black spectators particularly may refuse to be bound by a film's use of conventions and stylistics to resolve or unify the inherent tensions existing among image, text, and discourse (141). Although Thompson's formalist view does not take issues of race in its purview, her observations nevertheless suggest pertinent means by which Walton and the war worker were able to resist the arbitrariness of the black soldier's image as "joke," and in the process question the "canons of verisimilitude" (141) throughout this otherwise reverential cinematic tribute to American soldiers making the ultimate sacrifice for the high ideals of democracy.

One aspect of cinematic excess seeping through the newsreel image of the colored soldier as "joke" that Walton and the war worker perceive has to do with an encoding of "insidious propaganda." Evidently the filmmakers thought they were adding levity to the serious war text by injecting a bit of racist humor. Walton and his war worker companion, however, produced a different reading: "Both of us agreed that no more insidious propaganda could be used to humiliate and dampen the martial spirit of the colored American" (Walton 1918). Although we may safely presume a disinterest in, or insensitivity to, black audiences' and black soldiers' adverse reactions to such gratuitous racist imagery on the part of Hearst-Pathe filmmakers, even in the face of traditional and long-standing black protests, it is doubtful that the filmmakers paused to consider the case Walton makes about the alienating effects such debased images exerted on African American patriotism. When Walton comments, "And yet now and then you hear absurd talk about attempts to create dissatisfaction among Negroes of this country by German Agents!" it is clear that he rejects attempts by white authorities to displace African Americans' disaffection with America's incessant racist practices conveniently onto external or foreign forces. In Walton's view, responsibility for any "dissatisfaction" among African Americans must be placed where it rightfully belonged, at the feet of racist enemies at home. "As long as our motion picture people and many of the daily newspapers insist in carrying on a propaganda of misrepresentation," Walton asserts, "just so long will there be a race problem" (1918).

Walton concludes his investigation of the celluloid Negro soldier by discussing the centrifugal forces of racism radiating throughout early American cinema that make the intractable racial discourse virtually impossible to eradicate. To make his point, Walton sets up a sort of case study in which he reports on the unsuccessful interventionist efforts of a well-meaning young white performer who wanted to "write a motion picture play with the hope of bringing about a better understanding between the races" (Walton 1918). After touring the South in Broadway productions, the young woman was so distressed by lynchings that she resolved to write a screenplay advocating better treatment of African Americans. As expected, her efforts were to no avail.

> She soon found that fair play and right meant nothing to motion picture producers when the Negro question was at issue. It was not very long before it dawned on her that a photo play dealing with facts in advocacy of better treatment for the colored American had no commercial value. (Walton 1918)

Walton was not surprised by the woman's disappointing experiences with mainstream film producers. In fact, for him the woman's experiences confirmed African Americans' belief that powerful and influential southern sympathizers were convenient rationalizations for cinematic perpetuations of the nation's race problem. Thus it was not news when Walton learned that a film producer had informed the young woman "that he was a Southerner and for years had a colored cook." Walton knew that among whites such credentials possessed by a white producer were the guarantor of expert status insofar as the so-called Negro problem was concerned. His rejoinder reveals, however, that these essentialist sentiments exposed the height of white arrogance and racial chauvinism: "Here was another case of a white man having the audacity to assume to know twelve millions of people of all walks of life by his cook." Ultimately, the issue for Walton, speaking on behalf of his wounded constituency, was simply one of fair and necessary adjudication of these matters by responsible authorities and legislators during this most important time of national and personal sacrifice:

We the colored people of the United States are tired of being maligned; we resent being misrepresented. . . . Whether this policy is put into execution either by sins of omission or commission, it is dangerous, it is unjust, it is un-American. . . . As for the failure of the Hearst-Pathe and other film companies to show the colored soldier in France as warriors bold fighting proudly and valiantly for democracy and the general tendency to make him a Sambo, I respectfully refer this matter to Mr. George Creel, head of the Committee on Public Information, Washington, D.C., with the request that it be regarded as important and worthy of immediate consideration. (Walton 1918)

In keeping with sound journalistic principles, Walton is mindful of his rhetorical posture as it pertains to libelous accusations that often turn on the issue of intent (Hyde 1926, 201). He wisely holds the issue of intentionality at bay. Rather than accuse the filmmakers of intentionally misrepresenting African American soldiers outright, he situates his contestations within the context of established patterns of racist behaviors whereby the inference of culpability can stand on its own owing to a lack of evidence to the contrary. At the same time, Walton offers Creel's Committee on Public Information an opportunity to negate such charges and prove him wrong by rectifying gross miscarriages of power and influence by advocating fair and unbiased portrayals of the black soldier in officially sanctioned pro-war newsreel and actuality films. A retrospective consideration of Walton's demand for fair cinematic treatment of the black soldier's contribution to the war, especially in light of reports about the lynchings of returning veterans, demonstrates the foresight and necessity of his interventionist criticism and protestations.[8] Although we will never know if accurate representations of African American soldiers in the mainstream media would have helped quell the upsurge in lynchings after the armistice, perhaps they could have assisted in the creation of a national climate of outrage and intolerance for such wanton displays of white supremacist terror at that crucial historical juncture.

Cinema Criticism in *The Half-Century Magazine*

As the black magazines took up the crusade for an independent black cinema movement, their discussions precipitated new discursive approaches. In addition to the boosterism that typified much of the news-papers' engagement with the issue, magazines extended the pro-cinema discourse to include historical and philosophical investigations of the cinema, prescriptives for filmmaking successes, film criticisms and re-views, and sociological considerations of the cinema's impact on the African American community in the face of the Great Migration, among other social changes. To better appreciate the function of the black maga-zines in charting and formulating the preprofessional and institutional contours of the first black cinema movement, Carolyn Marvin's (1988) study of the essential nature of professional literature in the invention of the electrical expert is instructive. Writing in *When Old Technologies Were New,* Marvin demonstrates how vital and essential the production of professional literature was in transforming electrical tinkerers and hob-byists into the professional class of electrical engineers in the mid– to late nineteenth century. To a significant extent, this argument is applicable to the earliest independent black filmmakers as well. As Marvin notes, "Before 1900 . . . The electrical work force comprised a motley crew from machine tenders to motor designers and from physicists to telegraph operators, all sharing in some fashion the title electrician." Through their professional literatures, Marvin adds, electrical workers convinced readers that these "experts were entitled to greater social position and respect, a quest officially framed as the pursuit of proper standards and career experiences or training future electrical workers" (11). A similar tendency to self-promotion is exhibited by black filmmakers William Foster ("Juli Jones") and Oscar Micheaux in their use of the various black press outlets to reorient the black masses' perception of the benefits and advantages posed by the cinema and themselves in the quest for social change. In the process, Jones and Micheaux, much like the electrical pioneers before them, availed themselves of the power of journalistic discourse in their important task of self-repositioning as uniquely quali-fied "experts." Unlike the electrician's use of a specialized literature, as described by Marvin, to exclude laypeople or the "unlettered audience" from their newly forged "textual community" of the electrical "priest-hood" (10), Micheaux and Foster saw the black press's (particularly black magazines) textual community as an inclusively populist forum encom-passing both film insiders (filmmakers) and outsiders (audiences) alike. What these black film visionaries shared with their electrician counterparts of an earlier epoch was their ability to use the press to promote their own group professionalization (15).

In the vanguard of black magazine film criticism and commentary at this time was *Half-Century Magazine,* published monthly in Chicago. Founded in 1916, *Half-Century* (1916–1925) envisioned itself as African Americans' "home magazine." This shrewd use of "home" did not signify exclusive devotion to the cult of domesticity. On the contrary, a text box appearing on the front cover, which reads "A Colored Monthly for the Business Man and the Home Maker," clearly reveals the magazine's aim to target both male and female readers. In fact, the text box's ordering of the terms indicates that the male reader is the slightly more privileged of the magazine's readership. (Not surprisingly, women are the targets of most of the advertisements.) "Home" in this instance is used to argue that the magazine belonged in the homes of all African Americans. In its May 1918 editorial entitled "The Black Vanguard," which functions as a manifesto of sorts, the editors set forth the following mission statement, and here we get a more precise understanding of the use of the term "home." It is good to remember that *Half-Century* wanted to embody the concept of "home" to a newly displaced mass of black migrants from the South who were in dire need of the psychological benefits this concept represented:

> The *Half-Century* is hostile only to evil. It aspires to become the home mouth-piece, the instructor in every home; to carry into the dark places of ignorance, the beacon light of truth, the perfumed aroma of God's Love and the sweet paradoxes of a consistent and gracious ideality, where the symptomatic ignorance and gossip and the foul-tongued marauding of character may need its purifying influence and teachings. Such a magazine, with intellectual healing would ever act as a ray of God's sunshine. . . . We want to be longed for, and looked for each month, to be desired with an appreciative heart. Then we want you to take your magazine and show it to your neighbor, and get him to become interested. ("Black Vanguard" 1918)

Centered as it was at the heart of the burgeoning migrant community of transplanted black southerners in Chicago's black metropolis, *Half-Century* comprehended well the special literary needs of its niche market.[9] Taking advantage of the literacy demands precipitated by the war effort (which required prospective black conscripts to complete questionnaires), and the desire of African Americans to keep abreast of "the intricacies of the draft" and news of black soldiers and nurses in battle "over there," *Half-Century* stepped up its proselytizing for widespread literacy among the black masses. Significantly, the spiritual inflection of the magazine's mission statement at once attests to the wide net it aspired to cast over the religious and secular members of the heterogeneous black community. At the same time, it foregrounds its ability to provide the much-needed "intellectual healing" for the "symptomatic" ills of an oppressed community in dire need of spiritual as well as social, economic, and political uplift. In keeping with its adherence to the embourgeoisement thesis of middle-class assimilation, *Half-Century*'s altruistic appeal is tempered by the demands of its own self-sustaining consumerist pragmatism. By encouraging its readers to "take your magazine and show it to your neighbor, and get him to become interested" ("Black Vanguard" 1918), the editors demonstrate their familiarity with the reading practices of the largely semiliterate masses comprising the new arrivals from the South.[10] Knowing, however, that one of the primary reasons that blacks made the arduous trek to northern industrial centers was to pursue literacy and education, *Half-Century* also knew that its own growth and prosperity were inextricably bound to those of its black audience base. Attuned to the latest means by which the community might elevate itself, *Half-Century* followed the newspapers in recognizing the potential of the cinema in African Americans' program of self-sufficiency and social upward mobility. On its January 1918 "General Race News" page, *Half-Century* ran an item about the cinema as both a public service outlet and a public relations emissary: "The National Colored Soldiers' Comfort Committee . . . in their effort to raise $2,000,000 for the dependents of Colored soldiers will show a series of motion pictures. These pictures will serve two purposes, to help raise money for a good cause, and to create a better sentiment between the races, for they will show progress and development of the Colored people." This cinema news appeared in the magazine's edition saluting black patriotism during the Great War. On the cover of this issue was a photo of a domestic scene in which a black woman is pictured in profile, knitting. The caption under it reads "Knitting for the Sammies" ("Sammies" was a term of endearment coined by the black community for its soldiers).

Another interesting feature in this edition is an ambivalent editorial, "What Will the New Year Bring," which comments on black patriotism

Knitting For The Sammies

Half-Century January 1918 cover, Celebrating black ideal
womanhood and black patriotism, since mainstream films
fail to do so.

and valor in World War I. While granting that "war is terrible," the
magazine emphasizes African Americans' sincere belief that the war
represented a unique opportunity for the race to "show the world that the
Colored is willing—nay, anxious to help make the world safe for democracy, even though in so doing he has to sacrifice all that he holds dear" (3).
It is important to understand that African Americans' seemingly anoma-
lous patriotism becomes less contradictory in the face of racial persecution when contextualized in the framework of the black community's
ardent belief that victory "over there" would result ultimately in victory
against racial oppression at home (Buchanan 1968, 12). The "Double V"
campaign waged in the black press during World War II resuscitates this
aspect of black patriotism decades later.

Supplementing its editorial discussions of the cinema, in 1919 the magazine carried several feature articles on film by filmmakers and theatrical critics. Because the magazine's monthly publication dates and format tended to be conducive to lengthier exegetical contemplations, its film articles represent a departure from weekly newspaper articles. Also, unbound by newspaper journalism's ostensible demand for the rigid separation between subjective and objective reportage, black film critics writing in the magazines freely and routinely condensed and unified the two narrative modes. Undoubtedly, this literary freedom is what attracted early black filmmakers and freelance critics to the black magazines.

When Oscar Micheaux sought a platform for discoursing on black cinema in 1919, he found a suitable environment in the pages of *Half-Century*. In his "Negro and the Photo-Play" article for the "World of Amusements" department of the magazine, Micheaux drew on his individual experiences to set out his now-expert prescriptives for successful black filmmaking. Framing his May 1919 article as a response to the perennial query "How can I break into the movies?" (9), Micheaux develops his critical argument by shifting the focus of this rhetorical question to what he describes as "a more essential point." More essential for Micheaux is the pressing concern "How is the Negro to break into the movies?" (9). For Micheaux, "the author and producer of the popular film-play 'The Homesteader,'" among others, it was crucial that *Half-Century* readers achieve a clear understanding of the structural and cultural impediments to black success in the cinema and thereby commit to their reversal. In his view, it was the often unintentional yet counter-productive attitudes and actions of well-meaning black and white sociocultural elites that most curtailed black progress in cinema. Equally debilitating in his estimation was what Micheaux perceived as the dismaying ignorance of basic cinematic production principles exhibited by novice black filmmakers.

To illustrate the self-sabotage of some myopic black leaders, Micheaux (1919) begins his essay by recalling the demand for censorship brought by those often self-appointed leaders who failed to appreciate the artistic choices he made in his film *The Homesteader*. Micheaux's argument with his critics erupted over their uncompromising press for only positive black film images. He was clearly frustrated by the controversy spurred by "race men" to prevent the showing of *The Homesteader* because the film's depiction of a "hypocritical" black minister held the race up to ridicule. As the article progresses, however, Micheaux seems less concerned with the "race men's" cultural policing, because he finds an even larger concern with the attitudes of his white liberal supporters. While Micheaux obviously was not new to racist attitudes, he appears unnerved by them when they are expressed by a liberal-minded female member of the State of Kansas Board of Censors, whom he describes as an otherwise "kindly disposed northern [white] woman" (9). The painful realization that white liberals were similarly predisposed to racist sentiments and presumptions came after his official meeting with the censorship board. At the conclusion of their business, Micheaux was approached by this female member of the board, who entreated him to consider producing her "scenario concerning Colored people." In explanation of his dismay after having read her treatment, Micheaux writes, "She then gave me a synopsis of it, ending with the statement, 'And you cannot imagine what a perfectly lovely and original title I have given it!' I admitted that I couldn't. 'A Good Old Darky,' she replied, sweetly, and looked kindly up into my face for approval" (9).

As expected, Micheaux does not approve of the racist affront, no matter the good intentions. Though he appreciates the woman's solicitude, Micheaux nevertheless recognizes the larger significance of this evidence pointing to the limits of white liberal sentiments in race matters. For him, the situation makes explicit society's de facto prohibitions against even fictional considerations of black equality. Now Micheaux seems committed to an evangelical approach to black cinema because without it, "the white race will never come to look upon us in a serious light, which perhaps explains why we are always caricatured in almost all the photoplays we have even the smallest and most insignificant part in" (9). For Micheaux, it is clear that such patronizing attitudes, even among liberal-minded whites who considered themselves friends of the race, when aided by the incredible sway of the cinema could only exacerbate the nation's already chronic racism. To undermine the calcification of the African American image as "always the 'good old darky'" in the increasingly influential new cinematic medium, Micheaux expostulates the necessity of well-conceived scenarios written by "men of the race" to plead their own case in the silent film drama (9).

Always the "good old darky," our present environments and desires seem under a cover to them, and as the time is here when the black man is rightfully tired of being looked upon only as a "good darky," my statement that the race will only be brought seriously into the silent drama when men of the race, through whose veins course the blood of sympathy and understanding of our peculiar position in our Great American Society, puts him in [*sic*]. (9)

Since the dominant society's apparent blindness to the reality of the New Negro was yoked to its fixation on the "good old darky" (mythologized in Stowe's *Uncle Tom's Cabin*), and since white liberals proved a disappointment as the good-intentioned white woman from the censor board attests, Micheaux was convinced that only self-interested "men of the race" were capable of, and willing to, bring counterhegemonic representations of black life to the silent drama. And without benefit of a well-crafted scenario or script to convey this dynamic reality, Micheaux feared the black cinema movement was destined to remain moribund or doomed to failure altogether. Micheaux then expounds on the essential nature of competent screenwriting:

The first thing to be considered in the production of a photo-play is the story. Unfortunately, in so far as the race efforts along this line have been concerned, this appears to have been regarded as a negligible part. I personally know that a large share of the few plays featuring Negroes and produced by Colored people have been made without a scenario. Fancy it! An interesting theme, is after all, only a careful regard to a mass of detail concerning some particular something with an intense appeal. Without detail there would be no art, and the very irony of attempting to produce a photo-play without a scenario is foolish. Such an attempt is doomed to get no where as motion pictures go, before it is even started. (11)

Micheaux's adherence to Aristotelian principles and aesthetics is apparent here. To the extent that he wishes to enlist art in a revolutionary program of sociopolitical transformation, his remarks foreshadow, in some ways, the volatile debates about the best approach to efficacious agitprop films for social reorganization that polarized Sergei Eisenstein and Dziga Vertov in revolutionary Russia nearly a decade later. Even though Micheaux's commitment to the scripted scenario is opposed to Vertov's antiscript stance, and is more aligned with Eisenstein's embrace of scripted film narratives, Micheaux's pro-script comments nevertheless resonate with the spirit of Vertov's desire for a cinema uniquely suited to the political agenda of an oppressed constituency. And although the differences in approach to filmmaking between Micheaux and Vertov pivot on the advisability of scripted films, the ultimate ends of the two positions nevertheless are in sync. As Vertov wrote in 1928, "We have come to serve a particular class, the worker and peasants not yet caught in the sweet web of art-dramas" (Vertov, quoted in Michelson 1984, 73). Clearly, this ideal is compatible with Micheaux's belief that "the race will only be brought seriously into the silent drama when men of the race, through whose veins course the blood, sympathy and understanding of our peculiar position in our Great American Society, [put] him in" appropriate film vehicles (9).

Although it is true that the motivations of these two national groups have significant political differences (many revolutionary Russians wanted to overthrow bourgeois society entirely, whereas many politicized African Americans wanted to reform American capitalism),[11] it is more the case that they shared a desire and will to use cinema as an important tool in the escape from proletarian misery caused by class and, for African Americans, race subordination. This comparative example returns us to Teshome Gabriel's observation about the dangers inherent in oppositional cinema's fixation on "aping Hollywood stylistics" with their nested ideological imperatives. And while Gabriel's point about the inherent dangers that attend Third World nations' uncritical "aping of Hollywood" is well taken, it is also important to recall an important distinction. It is the case that when African American filmmakers ape Hollywood, like their Third World counterparts, they become uncritical agents serving Hollywood's racist regime of representation. However, unlike their Third World counterparts, African American filmmakers are pure products of and share the national, historical, political, cultural, and ideological milieu from which the Hollywood model springs. As with minstrelsy and popular music, American mainstream entertainment institutions owe much to African American folk idioms, so that black filmmakers' appropriations of the classic Hollywood model do not suggest the same illegitimacy or exact dangers that Gabriel identifies for Third World filmmakers. Yet Micheaux's eventual full-scale capitulation to mainstream norms of representational blackness in later years makes the comparison between the two seem fair after all. Still, Micheaux's desire to see black films "written to fit the people who appear" as well as reflect "their particular condition" is commendable (Micheaux 1919, 11).

Moreover, his contention that "before we expect to see ourselves featured on the silver screen as we live, hope, act and think today, men and women must write original stories of Negro life" continues to resonate powerfully even today.

Micheaux's filmmaking predecessor William Foster (aka "Juli Jones") also found *Half-Century* a fitting forum for his film commentary and historiography. His June 1919 article entitled "The Moving Picture: Their Good to the General Public and to the Colored Race in Particular" constructs the earliest black history of the motion pictures for a popular black reading audience. The article, penned under Foster's "Jones" pseudonym, outlines the world cinema's rise and America's ultimate domination of the new art form. From his remarkable observations of the cinema's intriguing past, he moves on to proffer ideas about a prospective "future for the race in the Motion Picture world, actively and passively." Jones begins by informing readers of the 1901 Empire Theater premiere of *The Empire State Express Train in Action* that left New York audiences proclaiming the film marvel "the greatest invention of the age" (J. Jones 1919b, 9). From his detailed discussion of that event, Jones moves on to consider European and American national approaches to the new medium. Considering that it was written in 1919, Jones's critique, which encompasses a brief survey of the specificities of certain national cinemas, must be regarded as remarkable indeed.

After discussing America's failure at first to "see the future possibilities [of the cinema] at that time," he turns his attention to the European cinema and America's subsequent rediscovery of its power and profit potential.

> That was all for a while. This fifty-foot reel soon ceased to be a novelty and it looked as if the idea would die a natural death. That was in this country. But Brain and Capital got together elsewhere and when these two forces are combined, there is no failure or decline. France and Germany caught the inspiration and lead America by a large margin. The French made really good pictures based largely on French comedy which was never accepted in this country. Germany's pictures were out of the question for any one but themselves and after showing in Germany and Holland, the producers cared nothing about the outside world. The French had a different idea and the Pathe gave America the finest pictures she has ever seen. The "Passion Play" was the greatest financial success the world had

ever seen up to the time of the recent "Birth of a Nation." America awoke and took this great world invention seriously. (9)

Contained within this lengthy excerpt from Jones are prescient intimations of later theoretical and historical engagements with the epistemologies and ontologies of national cinema studies. It is notable that Jones's critique takes within its purview such important, albeit brief, considerations as the financial determinants, industrial history, specific nationalist preoccupations, dominant aesthetic and thematic forms, and regimentation of spectator tastes in the phenomenal rise and development of world cinemas.

In his evaluation of the global impact and influence of European films, Jones compares France's and Germany's abilities early on to "lead America [in the realm of cinematic ingenuity] by a large margin." Although Jones was greatly impressed by France's use of the traditions of the commedia dell'arte, he reveals an ardent disregard for the strides being made in contemporaneous German cinema. It is difficult to know if Jones's diminution of German cinema was predicated on the pervasiveness of postwar anti-German sentiments or on a rejection of the emerging "highbrow" expressionist tendencies taking root in German cinema from the prewar years on into the Weimar period (D. Cook 1990, 111). Regardless of the motivating principle, Jones's observation of German cinema's insular quality at that moment ("Germany's pictures were out of the question for anyone but themselves. . . . The producers cared nothing about the outside world") is echoed by later critics, most notably Siegfried Kracauer (1947) in *From Caligari to Hitler*. Kracauer's symptomatic reading of the German character as conveyed through the film *The Cabinet of Dr. Caligari* registers striking similarities to Jones's evaluation: "If it holds true that during the postwar years most Germans eagerly tended to withdraw from a harsh outer world . . . Wiene's film does suggest that during their retreat into themselves the Germans were stirred to reconsider their traditional belief in authority" (Kracauer 1947, 67).

As does Jones, Kracauer unfavorably compares German film motifs to those of French film in the prewar years. Comparing the works of Georges Méliès and Paul Wegener, leading filmmakers from France and Germany respectively, Kracauer writes: "But while the amiable French artist enchanted all childlike souls with his bright conjuring tricks, the German actor [turned filmmaker] proved a sinister magician calling up

the demoniac forces of human nature" (28). Although Kracauer's theoretical assumptions have come under attack in the wake of postmodern
theories and cultural studies paradigms for what many charge are over-
simplifications of irreducibly complex issues, his astute investigation of
issues surrounding national identity and the early cinema remains an
important precursor to contemporary national cinema discourses. And
to the extent that Jones's essay marks an impressive premonitory utterance in this direction as early as 1919, it must be regarded as an important
contribution to early discussions of national cinematic constructions of
identity.

If Jones was unimpressed with the characteristics of German cinema,
he was absolutely effusive about the spectacular film product coming out
of France. Though Jones does not envision Charles Pathe as "the Napo-
leon of the cinema" in the same sense as does film historian Georges
Sadoul (D. Cook 1990, 49), it is evident that he recognizes the imperial
scope of the Pathe Freres film company with such remarks as "Pathe gave
America the finest pictures she has ever seen. 'The Passion Play' was the
greatest financial success the world had ever seen" (J. Jones 1919b, 9), and
this before Griffith's *Birth of a Nation*. Whereas Jones locates the German cinema's failure to generate international interest in the films themselves, in contrast, he inculpates the audiences, not the French films, for
any failure of, or unresponsiveness to, France's "really good pictures."
Moreover, he contends, "The French made really good pictures based
largely on *French comedy which was never really accepted in this country*"
(italics mine). This comparative view of French and German cinema
illustrates Jones's ability to analyze, distinguish between, and pass judgments on important identifying traits of different national cinemas, and
to synthesize and situate the information in broader global contexts.

As the essay progresses, Jones's observations about national cinemas in
general give way to a more detailed and particularized consideration of
one national cinema—the early American cinema. In his consideration of
the formative years of American cinema, Jones explores such variegated
topics as the nation's industrial film history, American cinema's rise to
prominence, cinema versus stage melodrama, cinema's influence on society, spectatorship, and finally the cinema and African Americans. By
engaging so many aspects of the cinema, Jones clearly wants to provide
Half-Century readers with a necessary crash course in American (and
world) film history up to 1919 so that, perhaps, they might understand

and ultimately share his enthusiasm for the cinema and come to appreciate it as a powerful tool for social progress and racial equality.

The first point of emphasis for Jones's survey of American cinema's past concerns setting the record straight on America's relative latecomer status in the early global development of narrative cinema. He thus makes it clear that only after following France's lead, "America awoke and took this great world invention seriously." From that point he moves on to a discussion of the seminal importance of Edwin S. Porter's 1903 breakthrough film, *The Great Train Robbery*. As Jones saw it:

> Some producer conceived the idea of making a picture on the James Boys of Missouri and "the Great Train Robbery" set the country wild. Many a boy can recall the real thrill he received when he first witnessed the picture of the famous Train Robbery and that picture seemed to dictate the tenor of the American taste for movies for years. (J. Jones 1919b)

Whether *The Great Train Robbery* was based directly on the adventures of the infamous Frank and Jesse James is uncertain. Yet Charles Musser's (1991) assertion in *Before the Nickelodeon* that the film was inspired by "Scott Marble's play *The Great Train Robbery,* Wild West shows, and newspaper accounts of train holdups" does not serve to rule out Jones's attribution.[12] In fact, since the exploits of the "James Boys of Missouri" were fodder for newspapers, Musser's remarks about the film suggest more of a corroboration than a refutation of Jones's claim. In any case, Jones augments the film's import by aligning it with historical events. What is interesting here is that Jones makes only a perfunctory mention of *The Birth of a Nation,* and conversely a full paragraph is devoted to *The Great Train Robbery*. Perhaps this can be explained by the historicist aims of Jones's article. But his situating of *The Great Train Robbery* at the center of a young boy's spectatorial coming-of-age or initiation, and his contention that this film and not Griffith's directed spectator tastes for years, does not seem insignificant. It is significant, however, that Jones takes note of this film's centrality in inculcating and directing spectator tastes and future expectations of film narratives.

Next Jones assesses the industrial practices, strategies, and historical contingencies that helped push American cinema to international prominence immediately following the Great War. Jones notes that "the first great set back" to America's rise in the international film competition "came about when Thomas A. Edison and other big men got together and incorporated every known camera that could make a moving picture and cut all the independent producers out of the game" (J. Jones 1919b, 9). As an independent filmmaker directly affected by the Edison cartel, Jones had firsthand knowledge of its destructive reach, especially the threat it posed to the embryonic black cinema movement. By calling attention to Carl Lemmle's successful legal challenge to the Edison Trust, Jones informs his readers that indeed there was room enough for the independents (including black independents) in the highly influential and lucrative film enterprise. His consistent focus on the economic determinants in the myriad phases of the business of cinema creates a necessary corollary to the psychological, aesthetic, and formalist critiques that dominated mainstream writers' debates about the cinema during that era (the criticisms and theories of Hugo Munsterberg and Vachel Lindsey immediately come to mind). To his credit, Jones does not separate the financial and creative imperatives, nor does he privilege one set of determinants in his analyses of the early cinema's modern formation. Of the Lemmle case and its far-reaching ramifications, Jones writes:

> This brought about a tremendous legal fight and one Carl Lemuel [sic] of Milwaukee started the fight to the finish, taking it to the Supreme Court, and he won. The whole country was in sympathy with him. The publicity given the industry could not have been bought at a million dollars and the industry flourished from that time forth. That fight gave America her start and today she leads in the great industry which ranks seventh in the scale of importance, commercially. (James 1919b)

By foregrounding economic considerations in this way, Jones gives his readers a more balanced view of the industry that they assiduously supported, and often at inflated prices for black spectators. The *New York Age* printed a damning exposé on this very matter. On 29 August 1912, the *Age* ran a front-page story revealing discriminatory pricing schemes at area theaters. The article entitled "Negroes Charged 20: White Patrons 10 Cts: Scale of Prices in Force at Moving House in Harlem" uncovered the existence of racially motivated policies when "a very light [complexioned] colored woman" attempted to purchase movie tickets and was charged double the amount whites were expected to pay. In light of these and other routine racial indignities suffered by African American movie patrons, it is notable that Jones elected to underscore the fact that "the whole country was in sympathy" with Lemmle and his cause because of what the case signified for all independents. Jones knew that blacks could feel vindicated and inspired by this legal contest of David and Goliath proportions. It also affirmed that the black community was not alone in its grievances against the large film cabals.

In the course of charting America's rapid ascent to the top of the world film production heap, Jones focuses on one of the major spoils of the Great War that few of his readers were likely to conceive, that being the reapportionment of America's share of worldwide film audiences.

> During the great world war, she was practically the only big country pro-
> ducing anything except war scenes and she will continue to reign for the
> reason that American pictures can be understood the world over. The title
> need but to be changed to the language of the country. The stories are as
> real in one land as another wherever civilization has touched. (J. Jones
> 1919b)

Here Jones's insights into silent cinema's propensity to undermine the formidable national boundaries existing between countries as a result of language barriers round out his earlier discussions of specific national cinemas and the general and universalizing tendencies of cinema's iconic significations. Jones recognizes the representational economy inherent in silent films owing to their detachment from the limitations of national linguistic differences, and how that visual economy, conjoined with the exigencies of the wartime economy (Sklar 1976, 46), became the conduit to American cinema's usurpation of the universal or global film standard in the postwar years. In this area, Jones implicitly states his understanding of Western norms in the production and consumption of cinematic narratives. American "stories," the conventional generic films that gave birth to America's classical system of film narratology, are what Jones alludes to in his remarks about the global comprehensibility of American films. When considered in tandem, then, Jones's and Micheaux's magazine essays point the way to an impressive critical legacy of interventionist film writings by black filmmakers that recall the later canonical writings of Russian filmmakers similarly engaged in critical discussions of filmmaking theory and praxis during the formative years of the cinema arts explosion.

In the March 1919 edition of *Half-Century*, critic Howe Alexander contributed his essay "Colored Motion Picture Drama" to the magazine's collection of film articles. The object of Alexander's critical inquiry

Still from *Shadowed by the Devil*, a film produced in the first wave of independent black filmmaking. Film reviewed by Howe Alexander for *Half-Century*, 1919.

was the motion picture *Shadowed by the Devil*, produced by the Unique Film Company. Most striking in Alexander's article is his contribution to the end of innocence in black criticism of specific "race films." Unlike Micheaux's general castigation of inexperienced black filmmakers, Alexander critiques a specific film product and engages with the problematics of this particular film's high-tone narrative. Although complimentary of the film's general structural and performance features, Alexander is nevertheless troubled by its bourgeois emphasis:

> The photo grips one as it unfolds; the climaxes are well placed; the acting commendable. . . . We saw many things to criticize and we consider it no more than just that we speak of the weaknesses as well as the merits. We believe that less attention should be given to high life drama. The race has not risen sufficiently in the world of finance to digest easily too much parading of servants, too many limousines, and too much finery. (Alexander 1919)

Like many of his contemporaries engaged in the business of theatrical entertainment, Alexander was a proponent of the representational schools of realism and naturalism. For him, the film's retreat to an escapist world of the upper classes was at least untenable or at most unsuitable for a mass black audience composed mainly of the working poor. What use did such a group have for fetishized depictions of a nonexistent black aristocracy? If the black film drama was to posit a more authentic view of African American existence than the popular comedies and slapstick varieties, Alexander insisted that the dramas be less fanciful and unrealistic. "The movie has great educational and technical values as well as comical possibilities," writes Alexander, and thus he fears the squandering of such an asset if the likes of *Shadowed by the Devil* were to become a model for black dramatic films.

Film Criticism in the Jazz Age of the Roaring Twenties

As the 1920s dawned, American postwar society became engrossed in its program of reintegrating servicemen from the Great War into the ranks of American civil society. After fighting against imperialism for the ideals of American capitalism abroad, returning black soldiers and their supportive communities in America expected an abatement of Jim Crow laws that heretofore had relegated them to a state of de facto slavery in postemancipation America. Instead, most returning vets were greeted with chronic unemployment, and for those who managed to get work, they were "offered only the menial and the lowest paid positions" ("General Race News" 1919). Black veterans' hopes for an appreciation of their patriotism were thus dashed as heartbreaking news of "lynchings of returning African American soldiers and the expulsion of African American workers from unions abounded. . . . Twenty six race riots in towns, cities and counties swept across the nation all the way to Nebraska. The 'race problem' became definitively an American dilemma. . . . And no longer a remote complexity in the exotic South" (Lewis 1994, xxiv). Exacerbating this dire turn of events during the post–World War I years was the phenomenal upsurge in the numbers of black migrants from the South searching for basic human rights, economic opportunities, and constitutional protections. Many quickly learned that the commonplace lynchings, employment discrimination, and voting-rights violations endemic to the southern political terrain were becoming more frequent in other regions of the nation.

In Harold Cruse's *The Crisis of the Negro Intellectual,* we get some indication of the extent of this massive influx of southern blacks into the northern industrial centers. He notes that "in 1914, the Negro population of Harlem was estimated at just under 50,000; by 1920 it approached 80,000" (1967, 71). *Half-Century* frequently published its tally of the northern population explosion.[13] David Levering Lewis's observations underscore the fact that when southern African Americans arrived in the northern cities and presumably were unshackled from the racist regimes of what Du Bois termed the "unreconstructed South," they found, often to their dismay, that they had not reached the promised land exactly. What they found was a disappointing, hostile political and geographic environment bursting at the seams with the wretched of the earth, for they were not alone in seeking better economic opportunities on America's northern shores. These displaced migrants from the South met with the discomfiting realization that they would have to compete for jobs and housing with already established northern blacks and the hordes of West Indian immigrants to the region seeking a better lot.[14] Nevertheless, this mass of southern black migrants and West Indian immigrants created in the North a means of tolerance and peaceful if tenuous coexistence.

Miraculously, this confluence of cultures resulted not in an embittered cultural clash but rather in the cultural flowering known variously as the "Harlem Renaissance" and the "Jazz Age" (Library of Congress 1993, 175). Orchestrating this new sociocultural reality was a select cadre of black activists and intellectuals who emerged from within these two groups and who were regarded reverently as "race men." It is important to note that these were the black communities' organic intellectuals, many of whom personified Du Bois's notion of the "talented tenth." Typically, these were individuals who by virtue of their privileged educational and socioeconomic backgrounds were deemed uniquely qualified to lead and direct the strivings of an oppressed people, and hailing as they did from disparate class, caste, and national backgrounds, they could hardly be expected to constitute a monolithic bloc. Far from it. Frequently espousing diametrically opposed political viewpoints, these black leaders splintered off into fractious camps because of their competing philosophies about how best to effect meaningful change and advancement in the predicament of this new mass of black diasporic citizens. Yet despite or perhaps because of these socioeconomic, political, and cultural vicissitudes, the black press maintained its progression of black film literary output.

Placing the Harlem Renaissance in the context of American culture's self-exploration in the "larger independence project of the 1920s," Ann Douglas (1995) has argued that "the black past yielded treasures as rich as the classic American literature excavated by Lawrence and others from the white past, and it did so at least as suddenly and unexpectedly" (344). But the pages of James Weldon Johnson's (1968) *Black Manhattan* that Douglas draws on here make a distinction worth bearing in mind. Johnson asserts that this was a "seeming" suddenness, as "America at large" became aware that "there are Negro authors with something interesting to say and the skill to say it." It was, then, for white America that the appearance of aesthetic treasure from the black past was unexpected, and in Johnson's view, "It was the quickness with which this awareness was brought about that gave the movement the aspect of a phenomenon" (263). The phenomenon of black writing about cinema had already been in evidence for readers of the African American press for some years before the Harlem Renaissance. What was phenomenal during this period was the rapid evolution and circulation of debates about film within the communities of black America as they proceeded on the larger independence projects of their own.

Film criticism in the press during this tumultuous period began generally to reflect a less parochial view of the nexus of cinematic discursivity and the African American experience. Black magazines continued their less truncated feature-oriented essays, and black newspapers in turn expanded their traditional coverage of film news and commentary to include star discourse and fan culture reportage. Because the twenties brought a panoply of critically acclaimed black-cast theatrical shows, particularly in the northeast, such as *Shuffle Along* (1921), *Chocolate Dandies* (1924–1925), *Dixie to Broadway* (1924), *Blackbirds* (1928), *Hot Chocolates* (1929), and many more (Hughes and Meltzer 1967, 97–105), entertainment pages of black publications rekindled their interest in stage news, now sometimes overshadowed by the rush to exploit news of the cinema. Once news spread that northern black stage shows were enjoying an unprecedented success at the box office ("double lines formed on the sidewalk for tickets, motor car and taxi jam[s]" [101]), even the staunchly segregated mainstream film industry saw the benefits of capitalizing on the talents of such black performers as Lincoln Perry (Stepin Fetchit), Clarence Muse, Rex Ingram, Mildred Washington, Nina Mae McKinney, Daniel Haynes, Allen Clayton Hoskins (Farina of *Our Gang*), and others (Null 1975, 16–38). The postwar boom in Hollywood resulted in the replacement of Griffith's black villains with the "high-stepping and high-falutin' and crazy as all get-out" (Bogle 1989, 19) black jester figure that Stepin Fetchit epitomized. Coupled with Hollywood's self-serving postwar discovery of select black performers was the ascendancy of independent black filmmaker and entrepreneur extraordinaire Oscar Micheaux. Surviving the financial calamities that forced the dissolution of his predecessors and rivals, the Lincoln Motion Picture Company and the William Foster Film Company, and the entry of many whites into the black film market, Micheaux's entrepreneurial resilience made him the singular independent voice for black filmmaking throughout the twenties.[15]

To keep their readership apprised of all these theatrical developments, black newspapers especially revamped their publications to encompass the trend. A case in point is the *Pittsburgh Courier*. By the mid to late twenties, this weekly newspaper featured a special section—section 2— formatted with two full pages of entertainment news and commentary. Whereas page 1 in the dyad carried feature stories of celebrity, gossip, and fan-oriented coverage, the second page contained theater schedules and offerings and brief film and stage reviews and commentaries. Occasionally film news surfaced on the front and editorial pages. Significantly, the *New York Age*'s vigilance in monitoring cinema news remained constant throughout the early twenties. And consistently the *Chicago Defender* carried theatrical news. During the late twenties, the *Baltimore Afro-American* stepped up its film news coverage as well. Joining the magazine field in 1920 (a field dominated since 1910 by the NAACP's organ *The Crisis* and Chicago's 1916 entrant *Half-Century*, and to a lesser extent the 1917 socialist New York publication *Messenger*) was Robert L. Vann's short-lived *Competitor*, published in Pittsburgh, Pennsylvania. And in 1923, the National Urban League's house organ, *Opportunity: A Journal of Negro Life*, entered the fray.

Micheaux's incredible successes in the face of Hollywood's "postwar spirit of artistic aggressiveness and programmed levity" alone could not sustain the crush of black press interest in the cinema (Bogle 1989, 19). The press's shrewd focus on mainstream cinema's opportunistic turn to black performers and black-inflected themes was financially astute and hardly unexpected. After its unavailing attempts to marshal forces to undergird the embattled and underfunded nascent black film movement (the tenacious Micheaux Film Company was one of the few to survive for any length of time; see Cripps 1993b, 88–89), the press network rededicated itself as the African American community's watchdog over Hollywood efforts to commodify and fetishize the black cinematic image.

In the early 1920s, black magazines were still caught up in the euphoria generated by the black independents. Even though the depressed postwar economy, monopolistic practices of Hollywood, and chronic financial setbacks of these maverick filmmakers finally obliterated the self-sufficiency of the black cinema movement (Cripps 1993b, 88–89), the black press and its readers remained cautiously optimistic that mainstream film companies' interest in African American performers signaled a long-awaited improvement or rapprochement in American attitudes toward its black citizenry. Owing to this misplaced optimism and the harsh reality of rigid segregation in America's film oligopolies, black press coverage adopted a schizophrenic critical discourse that simultaneously celebrated the marginal achievements of black performers circumscribed by new stereotypes, and denounced those stereotypes and the institutional racism in Hollywood responsible for crafting and disseminating them. At the same time, black editors and journalists continued to press the black bourgeoisie into service for the resuscitation of the rapidly fading black cinema movement, being driven to near extinction under the crush of twin burdens.[16] Pressing down on one side was the growing incursion of whites into the "race film" market through silent and not so silent partnerships with black company figureheads. On the other was Hollywood, dedicated to cornering the lucrative "race films" market for itself, especially during those difficult economic times. But if the twenties witnessed the destruction of fledgling black cinema companies, they also saw the maturation and increasing proliferation of black film literature and other cultural writings.

Competitor Magazine (1920–1921)

The Competitor magazine helped to usher in the black cultural criticism of the twenties with three features on stage and film drama. In its January

1920 premiere volume, the magazine carried "Progress of the Drama," a thesis on the timeliness of black stage drama, by Romeo L. Daugherty; "The Colored Thespian," by Salem Tutt Whitney, who profiled leading black actors; and staff writer Rose Atwood's "novelized" version of the Lincoln Motion Picture Company's film *A Man's Duty.* Of the three, Daugherty's provides the most pertinent information for our investigation with its insightful look at African Americans' desire to break the representational bind of "old-line vaudeville" comedy, the mutual benefits arising from theatrical productions and black press partnerships, African American and Jewish American theatrical alliances, and the pitfalls of actor typecasting. Even Atwood's "novelized" treatment of Lincoln's film script is significant to the extent that it exemplifies the magazine's ability to construct an intertextual discourse between film and literary productions while acquainting its northern readership with Lincoln's respectable, family-oriented films being produced in California.

Mark Reid (1993) has written in *Redefining Black Film* that before Lincoln's arrival on the black filmmaking scene, the other black film companies relied on "the use of humor, sex and violence" to sell their comedic shorts or one-reelers (10). With the black magazines' emphasis on bourgeois cultural norms and assimilationist ideology, Lincoln's new film dramas of black middle-class life espousing the American "puritan work ethic" were highly endorsed (10), because they represented the caliber of theatrical entertainment that was consistent with *Competitor*'s cultural agenda. That Atwood's adaptation also served a promotional function for the film is another obvious motivation that must be granted absent any prefatory comments or prologue to the lengthy treatment.

In Atwood's "novelized" rendering of the film script for *A Man's Duty,* there is an implicit grasp of the meaning-producing distinctions inherent in such oppositional narrative modes that Genette describes as showing versus telling or mimesis versus diegesis. As it appears in the *Half-Century,* Atwood's "novelized" adaptation of the film lacks references to visual cues such as camera positioning and spatial and temporal settings (except for one film still and datelines on personal letters that figure in the film text), and thereby it creates a separate narrative experience from the film itself. However, the subtitle to her piece, "This Story Has Been Filmed by the Lincoln Motion Picture Company and Is Now showing throughout the United States," reaffirms the idea that despite the specific narrative distinctions and demands, the basic "story" of both the film and her "novelized" treatment remains constant. In terms of the ranges of literary and filmic intertexts forged by African American writers and filmmakers, Atwood's treatment must be viewed as making a meaningful contribution at this developmental stage of early black cinema discourse.

In comparison, Daugherty's portentous probings sketch the preliminary contours of the literature's movement toward a more philosophical approach to the issue of race and representation by black film critics that becomes more pronounced in later years. For example, Daugherty begins by asking, "Are we different in our emotions from the white man or any other race? . . . I have never believed that we are different, and I have always argued that what is good will be accepted by the intelligent people of any race" (Daugherty 1920, 53). This appeal to a universal humanist appreciation of all things "good," which Daugherty makes clear includes African Americans, opposes familiar white paternalist assumptions that the mass black audience would only support "slap-sticks and the most vulgar form of suggestive stuff 'put over' by so-called colored comedians" (53).

Since the cinema was now twenty-five years old and black participation in stage musicals, minstrels, and vaudeville shows preceded films by decades, Daugherty suggests that African American audiences were indeed capable of appreciating and performing in the classic tragedies and other dramatic offerings. After all, the first semiprofessional African American drama group, the African Company, performed "Shakespeare" and other classics in Manhattan regularly during the 1820s (Hughes and Meltzer 1967, 41–43). Further, Ira Aldridge, the great African American tragedian, toured Europe and Russia playing Othello, Macbeth, Shylock, and King Lear, among other parts, for thirty years in the mid– to late nineteenth century (43), and the press network regaled the masses for decades with news of his European acclaim and accomplishments. This history is important because it clearly shows that although the African American performers of classical drama and music were welcomed onto white stages abroad, such was not the case in the United States. Despite this rich history, it was not until the late teens and through the twenties that American general audiences could witness the dramatic talents of black performers.

To break with this tradition and usher in "a new day in theatricals," Daugherty asserts, "it took the ever-ready and far-seeing Jews to give us our first real chance at a 'flyer' in the drama" (53). In applauding the

interethnic cooperation between African Americans and Jewish American impresarios, led by Robert Levy's takeover of New York's Lafayette
Theater in Harlem, Daugherty comments:

> Mr. Levy took the step which afterwards proved timely. High-class drama
> was the result and packed houses greeted our players . . . and it was only
> when mediocre shows were brought to Harlem did the people refuse to
> patronize the Harlem house. Like all other peoples, the Negro in New
> York demanded the best, and when given what he demanded fine houses
> were always on hand. Washington and Chicago responded in the same
> spirit as New York, where the drama is concerned. . . . This form of
> amusement has undoubtedly lent tone to this great community in which
> dwell almost one hundred and forty thousand Negroes, and although we
> will from time to time be regaled with musical comedy, I firmly believe the
> drama on a high plane is here to stay. (54)

Daugherty stresses the point that black urban audiences, like other
groups, appreciated good dramas, and they demonstrated that appreciation through their enthusiastic patronage of the better shows. Moreover,
Daugherty refutes the notion that the mass urban audience was somehow indifferent to, or disinterested in, dramatic presentations by drawing attention to factors besides mediocrity that plagued the progress of
black dramas, particularly the lack of suitable venues. "Colored people,"
Daugherty writes, "are the same all over and cannot be asked to travel an
unreasonable distance even to support such a laudable venture as the
drama." With the prospect of "a chain of theaters" to showcase "our own
authors" on the horizon, Daugherty seems convinced that the black
"drama on a high plane is here to stay" (54).

Even though Daugherty is gratified by the progressive steps made by
Levy and other white producers of black dramas, he still agitates for "the
race play." Like Micheaux, Daugherty is certain that talented black authors could "do much in fostering the writing of a real, thrilling drama
built along race lines, for be it pathos or humor, I think we have enough
of both in the race to make a play along this line something that would
draw thousands wherever shown" (54). For Daugherty, it would only take
the stellar talents of such prominent men of the theater as Bert A. Williams, Lester A. Walton, James Weldon Johnson, and Alexander Rogers
to coproduce a double-edged, "thrilling" drama that would serve, as he
put it, to "carry its propaganda of race pride right home to the people and

help along the work of the colored magazine and newspaper" (54). Conjoined with Daugherty's desire to exploit the pedagogical possibilities of the affinities existing between the theater and the real world for black social and cultural uplift was his awareness of the theater's economic potential for black press newspapers and magazines.

Also contained within Daugherty's prescriptive are comments about vaudeville star Bert Williams that raise considerations of star discourse and the unfortunate limitations of typecasting. Believing as he does in the merits of Bert Williams's star persona and his unquestionable box office appeal, Daugherty is yet besieged by doubts. Personally, he knows Williams to be "one of the most serious-minded men of the race, although the most prominent laugh-producer in the world." Daugherty fears "that any attempt by him (Williams) at this time to assume a heavy role in the serious art would not be received in serious veins by theatergoers" (54). Daugherty's concern with the traditionally strict boundaries demarcating comedy and drama, as well as audience reception, does not render him blind to Williams's usefulness in other dramatic forms. Alternatively, Daugherty recognizes the benefits of Williams's "ideas being put into practical form through the medium of writing" (54). Additionally, Daugherty considers the "amateur societies in the churches" to be a reservoir of talent from which to "develop artists to assume [important] roles" in his program of raising black theater to a higher plane. Clearly, Daugherty is advancing a philosophy of community-based theater that encompasses all institutional sectors of the African American community. Unfortunately his dream of a community-based theater for black dramas to replicate the successes already afoot in the black comedies and musicals would be deferred until the 1940s and 1950s.[17]

George M. Bell wrote "Social Value of the Contemporary Drama" for *Competitor*'s April 1920 edition. In this essay, Bell attempts to theorize the role of dramatic performance as oppositional cultural production and its utility in the program of black social and political elevation. "If the drama is to be any social value to our race," he writes, "our audiences must be taught to analyze the plays produced, and our young playwrights must be encouraged to write the play that will benefit us socially." Most important is Bell's desire to equip his readers with a basic comprehension of, and appreciation for, the effective representational approaches advanced by modernist techniques of drama and literature. His aim is to point his more literate readers toward important modernist texts while acquainting the rest with the basic contours of the dramatic arts. Bell explains the drama's specific requirements, structures, elements, and leading authors:

> The drama must contain one or more of the following qualities: Realism, that is, there must be a touch of reality, of truth, it must contain phases of life, the things that we see must be real and the characters must be real people not Punch and Judies. Naturalism; revealing the ugly, the sinister side of life, seen to a great extent in the writings of Zola, and De Maupassant. The Subjectivist tries to bring out character, assuming a mental instead of a physical attitude. Symbolism; is represented by a concrete thing standing for an abstract idea. (Bell 1920, 71)

What Bell offers in his essay is a primer. After explaining what the drama is ("the play with a purpose, not the musical comedy, nor review, but the Thesis play, . . . tries to uncover some sore spot in our social structure and call our attention to it"), Bell illustrates his points by analyzing an unlikely but popular play of the moment, selected "because its content is racial." The play in question is *Pride of Race*. Bell says that it is "antagonistic to our race." Having briefly discussed its Negrophobic content (the psychological dementia and social stigma engendered when a white person bears a trace of Negro blood), Bell adds, "we used this play merely because of its racial content, but not as a model for future playwrights who would hope to benefit the race" (71). Bell moves on to a brief consideration of dramatic technique, unfortunately abridged because of spatial limitations. His main point of illumination concerns modern texts' use of dialogue. "Another necessity of this type of drama is the simple dialogue . . . people no longer speak in poetry but in prose, so the dialogue must be in prose," he asserts. In his conclusion, Bell mentions plans for an ongoing series of essays on the value of the drama. "In order to follow me in this work," Bell writes, "I should suggest the reading of the following plays: *Ghosts, A Doll's House, An Enemy of the People,* and *Wild Duck* by Ibsen. *Sunken Bell,* and *The Weavers* by Hauptmann, *Magda* by Suderman, all of Shaw's works if possible. *The Red Robe* by Brieux, *Hindle Wakes* by Houghton, *John Ferguson* by Ervine, and if possible, *The Nigger* by Edward Sheldon" (71).

Bell might be charged with elitism by some, but it is important to recall that one of the central tenets of American and Russian modernism was making the best that was thought and produced available and accessible to the masses. Bell is merely following this line of reasoning. Also, he

THEATRICALS

MORAL AND MOVIES

IN the handling of a subject of this sort—the "moral" end of the movies—there are many things which have to be considered. Not that there is anything particularly "deep" in the idea, but of the diversified offerings, all of which are practically silent preachments of the deepest kind. While it is a fact that in the production of moving features, "interest" is apparently the main idea, it is also true that everyone of the stories handled is graded according to the moral lesson taught somewhere between the introductory and the finale.

Tony Langston
Dramatic Critic Chicago Defender

It is but a short time since a prominent and cultured lady approached the writer in the lobby of Chicago's most popular theatres and put forth this question:

"Do you consider a moving picture theatre the proper place for a mother to send her children for amusement? I have a boy and girl, 13 and 10 years of age respectively. A teacher in one of the Sunday Schools told them that it was wicked to attend "shows." I had never before given the idea a thought and am not ashamed to admit that for years I have been an ardent "movie fan," and I will thank you for your honest opinion in the matter."

It didn't take but a few minutes to tell the lady what my personal idea was and when we parted I had her promise that she would not keep her children from attending their neighborhood theatre reasonably often.

Every state in the Union and every city in each state has it's own censor board. These boards are usually composed of men and women who are experienced in "up-lift" and moral work. In reviewing a picture prior to the issuing of a license for the same, it is not a personal proposition, the entire membership of the board acting as a whole. This does away with any chance of "reaching" or pull and guarantees a faithful carrying out of the work for which the board has been organized. It is seldom, therefore, that even a too strongly worded sub-title "gets by," and never

a scene or series that might displease the most fastidi... the case of certain productions built around stories," they are permitted to show only by speci... which accounts for the appearance, from time to ti... "Adults Only" sign, and at such times only is danger of polluting young minds by sordid display, pictures coming through on special permits are the last degree.

One phase of censorship which is known t... should here be mentioned: No matter what sort

A. A. Hasten
Whose Performances in Europe Have Been Highly
to London Critics. Mr. Hasten Has Bee
Abroad for Many Years

Defender critic Tony Langston (on loan) promoted film fandom to *Competitor* magazine readers because early film codes required morality lessons. *Competitor,* 1920.

represents a continuation of the Ira Aldridge school of classical drama. It is a shame that the magazine produced only three volumes before its untimely demise. Bell's ambitious program would have been interesting to follow, and it demonstrates the cultural strivings and great social potential of such writers at this stage of the black press network's development.

Returning to the magazines' incipient film criticism and commentary, Tony Langston, the drama critic on loan from the *Chicago Defender,* wrote an article for *Competitor* that explores the nexus of film content and the black spectator. Langston's advice-style article "Moral and Movies" centered on the cinema's propensity toward educating and edifying the young. In the essay, Langston responds to a parent expressing concern about the adverse affects of films on her adolescent and teenage children, ages thirteen and ten. As both Langston and the mother in question admitted a partiality to movies, he instructed her to ignore the church's prohibition on films. He assured her that frequent visits to the movies were indeed beneficial to impressionable children because boards of censors were charged with, and were vigilant in, passing only those films espousing unambiguous messages where good triumphed and evil was punished (Langston 1920, 75). Langston confesses to making the parent "promise that she would not keep her children from attending the neighborhood theatre reasonably often" (75). He was of the opinion that the moral instruction contained in films passed by national censor boards benefited urban youths and posed no threat to the community. Additionally, Langston believed, as did many other emerging cultural activists, that the community had outgrown the religious dogmas of those unenlightened and self-interested members of the traditional religious establishment bent on preserving their religious and political sway. In fact, Langston's disagreement with the church on the value of the cinema leads us to the next two articles that take up this very issue, but in greater detail.

Half-Century Magazine in the Twenties

One of the few film criticism articles written by an African American woman during the twenties comes from Jean Voltaire Smith. Her essay entitled "Our Need for More Films," published in April 1922 by *Half-Century Magazine,* takes up the conflicted relationship between the cinema and the black church. Serving both as a prescriptive for the advancement of independent black filmmaking and as an admonition against the church's self-defeating anticinema platform, Smith's article proposes a pragmatic program of cooperation between proponents of the church and the increasingly influential cinema. At issue for Smith is the community's need to come to terms with the cinema as a formidable power capable of advancing the cause of black political, social, cultural, and moral progress. Smith begins her critique by discussing how the African American religious establishment's attacks on the cinema at once manifest and exacerbate preexisting tensions in black community relations.

> Moving pictures hold the center of the stage in America for both races. There is probably no other form of recreation in which the masses of people are more interested than in motion pictures. Like many other forms of amusement, the cinema had been condemned by many of our religious leaders for various reasons. In many sections the war between the church and motion picture theater has been a very bitter one. . . . Indeed a canvass of the school in one of the large cities brought out the fact that some of the students as well as the teachers attended as many as nine shows a week. This means that an enormous amount of money is spent in the motion picture theaters, much of which would reach the church, if the movies were less popular. (J. Smith 1922, 8)

From the outset, Smith stresses the incomparable power and allure of the cinema for all Americans, which she feels the church and other black civic leaders would be well served to understand rather than condemn. Its unparalleled popularity, particularly among African Americans, represented for Smith a phenomenal opportunity for the realization of black dreams of self-determination and self-definition.

This passage leaves little doubt that Smith wanted to defuse the counterproductive and bitter war between cinema lovers and detractors, which hinged on the not so surprising element of patronage. Smith's analysis of the internecine battles between pro- and anticinema factions within the African American community of that era illustrates only one of many black intragroup factionalisms that often go unnoticed when subsumed under such reductive ideas as the concept of a black monolith. Lest readers presume that the arrival of the cinema represents the originary moment of discord between the contesting groups battling for the hearts, minds, and fiscal loyalties of the black masses, Smith reminds us of the long-standing pattern of church opposition to other amusements that threatened to usurp its influence and income. Although Smith does not identify them specifically, her inference that the stage, secular music enterprises, juke joints, and cabarets were earlier targets of the church's moral crusades and intolerance seems clear.

Undaunted by the church elites' self-serving prohibitions, Smith was attracted by the cinema's ability to bridge the gap between the black majority and the black elites who "were often divided by language, politics, economic interests, education and religion" (Marable 1983, 24–25). In addition, she was quick to notice the intergenerational appeal of the cinema, as indicated in her comments about the increase in black movie fandom among both teachers and students. In fact, by contrasting the offerings of the church with those of the local movie theater, Smith suggests just how far removed the black church had become from its newly urbanized flock. Despite the "long sermons against the movies, [and] admonitions to stay away from them," Smith holds that such protectionist strategies or "cultural estrangement," to borrow a phrase from Frantz Fanon (1963, 210), seemed only to "result in empty pews in the church and an augmented attendance at the picture show around the corner" (J. Smith 1922, 8). Whereas the contest between the church and the cinema has created a situation in which a dour minister is forced to face "his tiny audience in despair," Smith is convinced that "long lines wait patiently for their opportunity to purchase a ticket from the pretty cashier at the nearby film theatre" (8). Even rain, which must surely have eroded church attendance, had no discernible "effect on the movie crowd," according to Smith.

She attributes this radical shift in black popular taste and allegiance from religious compulsion to secular indulgence to "the entrance of so many Colored people into film work." This same development, in Smith's view, "gives added anxiety on the part of Colored ministers. For many of our people who would not attend an ordinary show will go when they know a Colored star is to be featured" (8). Even though Smith does not specify the Micheaux film company or other firms producing "race films" explicitly in her discussion, her statement that African American audiences are lured to the movies whenever "a Colored star is to be featured" certainly implies the films produced by these "race film" companies. That Smith was a staunch supporter of films seems evident. However, she was discriminating and conservative in her endorsements. She notes that "figures show that school children who attend the moving picture shows from one to four times a week are brighter than those who do not attend at all." Regarding the educational merits of films, she remarks:

> Educational films are explaining the oddities of nature and the methods employed by natural forces more perfectly than mere books can. A child

may read about fission fungi or the pteridophytes and their method of reproduction and get a vague idea of the subject, but when he sees a magnified thallophyte, in natural colors on the screen, sees the cells split and form new ones, or sees the fern frond unroll, his ideas are clear on the subject and he can explain the matter intelligently. (8)

She also finds educational lessons in popular fiction films.

Likewise the average child may read of the Sahara desert or the ice fields of the North and have no interest in them whatever beyond getting a mark in "exam" but having seen his favorite film hero lost in a sandstorm on the desert or the hardships of his heroine in the land of half-year twilights, he manifests an unusual interest in geography and has a more intelligent understanding of the matter. (8)

Historical and biblical films have educational value in Smith's estimation as well. She even promotes the weekly newsreel as an excellent source of news and information about current events, especially for "those who are too busy to read the papers carefully" (8). Though she concedes that crime dramas "of the underworld are perhaps not the best form of entertainment for young boys and girls," she quickly credits them with imparting edifying social lessons "warning against certain evils cloaked in pretty guise." Recognizing the cinema's apparent permanence as a feature of modern society, Smith wants to help religious leaders reconsider its potential and advantages for the race, though she understands the church's fear of this formidable rival. Nevertheless she warns religious leaders of their hasty propensity to condemn the cinema and all stage folks. And her analogy that the church's "prejudice against stage folks is like the prejudice of most white people against Colored—they judge the whole race by a few miscreants" is an astute one indeed. For Smith, it is better that the black community as a whole put aside any cinephobia and instead harness the cinema's power for its own benefit. "Would it not be better then, to encourage more of our people to produce pictures—films of the clean, helpful sort, that will uplift; urge them to build class moving picture theaters, rather than discourage them from attending picture shows?" she asks. Smith sees this alternative as a more fiscally sound policy, "This would help to keep within the race at least a portion of the millions spent each year by Colored movie fans" (8).

Before Smith's cogent analysis of the fundamental issues at the heart of the church's antagonism toward the cinema, a writer for *Half-Century,* known as "the Investigator," wrote an article exploring the dynamics of the church and the cinema in the June 1920 issue. Like Smith, the Investigator observed the disparity existing between audiences for the church and the cinema. In an article entitled "Is the Church Losing Its Hold on the People?" the Investigator asks some probing questions:

> Why is it that relatively few young people attend church with any degree of regularity? Why does the average school child know more about Bill Hart, Mary Pickford, Nazimova, the Talmadge sisters, the Griffith stars, Doug Fairbanks and Charlie Chaplin than he does about Peter, Paul, Job and the Apocalypse? Is it that the people on the whole, especially the younger generation are growing more wicked, are they straying away from Christianity, are they finding religion unnecessary in their lives, or is the church at fault? (Investigator 1920, 14)

The Investigator holds the church responsible for its diminishing flock. Citing numerous abuses of its authority, this critic goes beyond Smith in condemning the motives of the church where the cinema is concerned. In addition to dissuading its obedient members from the cinema, the Investigator charges, the church has condemned its members for participating in any leisure time activities that would siphon off its all-important revenue (14). Even procuring clothes or grooming items, according to the Investigator, was deemed wicked by the church because it meant spending money outside the church. Such blind obedience could no longer be expected of the younger, better-educated generation:

> The young people of today are capable of reasoning for themselves and refuse to be bound by the preacher and his right hand man. They take nothing for granted. They are not less religiously inclined, but they are not given to blind worship. When you tell them they will burn in hell for a certain offense, they demand proof that there is a hell and that an eternity in hell is the punishment for that offense. They insist on knowing why the Omnipotent God could permit them to be so situated that they are obliged to break one of the commandments almost hourly and then punish them with an eternity of torture. (14)

As the Investigator makes clear, the arrival of the New Negro not only represented a challenge to the status quo of society's white racist regime of power but also posed significant challenges to black church establishments out of step with the times. From this discussion of ecumenical inconsistencies, the Investigator extends his query to some ministers' hypocrisy on the matter of theatrical entertainment. For the Investigator, it is difficult to condone certain ministers' protestations against the movies when these same clerics "offer to present a play in the church as a means of raising funds for the church work." Without a doubt, the double standard at work here turns on the desire to preserve the church's dwindling money supply and not on the ethics or morality of members' souls. For this reason, the Investigator prefers the less-ambiguous moral instruction contained in many films.

> It is generally conceded that the moving picture shows, through showing the evils of whisky, have done more to bring about prohibition than any other medium. Picture fans know that almost invariably the villain in the play is one who is under the influence of liquor and if he reforms in the last act, as he often does, it is because he has stopped drinking. In the same manner gaming and its dangers are shown on the screen. . . . Don't such plays deter our young people from such evils as much as a long "Holy Glory" sermon to which they do not listen? (14)

Although such effusions overlook the complexities of spectatorial decoding strategies and options, the Investigator's final point is still an important one. If the church had hopes of recapturing the loyalty of its forward-thinking constituency, the Investigator makes the case for a complete reformation of its anachronistic and often contradictory catechisms.

These articles on the church and the cinema reveal an interesting by-product of the press's incipient cinematic discourse. By critically examining the ramifications of the cinema's penetration in the African American community and its didactic uses, these writers were emboldened to reevaluate and make strong recommendations for many of their own sociocultural institutions.

Newspaper Criticism and Hollywood's "Discovery" of Blackness

Film criticism in the newspapers was far more prolific than in the magazines. Although the weekly circulation for the newspapers, versus the monthly schedule of magazines, necessarily created this disparity, other factors distinguished this mode of cinematic discourse as well. The primary producers and consumers of the magazines were of course the black bourgeoisie.[18] In contrast, the newspapers' textual community of readers comprised mainly the working-class poor and the semiliterate classes (although the editors tended to be members of the black elite), who together formed the overwhelming mass of the African American population during the earliest years of the twenties. To attract their audience, newspapers' headlines often shifted between the grave, the sensational, the hyperbolic, the mundane, and the trivial. This was particularly true of many film articles. This does not suggest that more sober, thought-provoking, and trenchant critiques were absent from many of these papers. On the contrary.

In the case of the *New York Age,* for example, Lester A. Walton regularly wrote some of the most insightful and thorough critiques of the cinema during the early twenties. Even literary giant James Weldon Johnson, who wrote a feature editorial column for the *Age* entitled "Views and Reviews," contributed film criticism. In their advocacy mode, the newspapers often turned out compelling articles on the cinema and racial matters. Because Lester A. Walton and the *New York Age* have been covered extensively in the preceding chapters, only brief mention will be made of this paper's twenties film commentary. Film criticism also appeared in the *Pittsburgh Courier,* the *New York Amsterdam News,* the *Chicago Defender,* and the *Baltimore Afro-American,* among others. Our consideration of the newspapers will focus on those elements of their criticisms that helped forge a black film culture in the midst of the so-called Harlem or Black Renaissance.[19] Within the pages of these newspapers, we can discern the earliest formations of star analysis and the cult of personality, image criticism in mainstream and "race films," critiques of industry trends and practices affecting African Americans, and promotional discourses around individual or specific film texts.

Consistent with its trailblazing film criticism and commentary during the 1910s, the *New York Age* and Lester A. Walton set the tone and agenda for the newspapers' evolving film criticism during the 1920s. In his 10 April 1920 column, Walton wrote "To Sue Company for Altering Race Film." The article concerns a $50,000 legal suit for damages brought by "a motion picture firm composed of colored promoters against the L.KO Comedy Company" on grounds that a film "formerly entitled 'Injustice'" had been "radically" altered to such an extent that "colored managers throughout the East, in particular, refused to book it." After screening the film, Walton supported its cancellation. Driving the controversy was the fact that the original seven-reel film had been reduced to five reels, with the most positive aspects of black life and culture left on the cutting-room floor. Most outrageous was news that "Negro dialect and many other objectionable features had been added to many scenes and lines calculated to put the Negro in a favorable light had been eliminated." Most important in Walton's consideration of the film is his broaching of what would ultimately become a cornerstone of black film criticism (and continues even today), the issue of an abusive and insidious use of dialect as a marker of black intellectual and social inferiority. Again, it is Walton who initiates some of the earliest concerns with specific points of image criticism.

It is important to recognize that Walton was equally disparaging of negative image portrayals in black-produced films. In "Sam Langford's Wallop Makes 'The Brute' a Screen Success," he takes Oscar Micheaux to task on this very issue in a mixed review of the film *The Brute*, published on 16 September 1920.

> So far as the story which "The Brute" unfolds, it is neither original nor any too pleasing to those of us who desire to see the better of Negro life portrayed. A dive where colored men and women congregate to gamble, the susceptibility of a devoted aunt who takes money from a dive-keeper seeking the hand of a niece, a detailed exhibition of a crap game in which a woman is the central figure, are included in some of the important scenes. As I looked at the picture, I was reminded of the attitude of the daily [white] press, which magnifies our vices and minimizes our virtues. (Walton 1920b)

Here Walton denounces Micheaux's emphasis on the "vices" of the black underworld. Because the white press can be counted on to magnify the vices of the African American, Walton insists that black filmmakers not only become superior technicians "of photography and stage direction, but [that] a determined effort must be made so that in the thematic construction of plays the Negro is given high ideals and types which he can emulate and of which he can feel justly proud. The screen not only is functioning as a great entertainer, but a great educator as well" (6). Having dispensed with these criticisms, Walton adds, "There is much to commend Oscar Micheaux's latest photoplay. It is a very creditable endeavor in many respects." Then Walton praises Micheaux for the boxing scene, and he reserves his most complimentary remarks for the performances of the actors.

Star Discourse

After enduring decades of white signifiers of celluloid blackness—the white performer in blackface, the loyal but infantile old darky, et cetera— it is not surprising that actual African American screen performers were enthusiastically received in the black press, at least during the early twenties. Contemporaneous articles make it clear that black writers and spectators delighted in the experience of watching authentic black bodies on the screen and that they exhibited "an interest in players as 'real persons.'"[20] These tendencies are in evidence in front-page star news from both the *Pittsburgh Courier* and the *New York Age*. In the former, a two-column-wide photo of actress Edna Morton, dubbed "Our 'Mary Pickford,'" graces page 1 of the *Courier*'s 11 August 1923 edition. Although there is no story to speak of accompanying this glamorous yet demure photo, her visage and autograph tell a larger story of accessibility and mystique, dignity, and above all promise, the promise of a future for the race in mainstream films, for along with her photo, a credit list of her films is provided. But the news that occasioned her front-page coverage is that she broke through the color barrier and achieved a "first" for the race as a performer in Jesse Lasky's Famous Players film *Beyond the Salt Frontier*. Her photo is meant to signify the beautiful black female body long hidden from America's general film audiences.

Rising star Shinzie Howard of the Micheaux Film Company receives front-page coverage on 31 March 1923 in the *Age*. Her star discourse serves a different function, the negation of the widespread assumption that stage performers are a morally bankrupt lot. There is no photo accompanying the article entitled "Race Screen Star Becomes Popular New York Favorite," but there is a full essay detailing Howard's numerous virtues. Covering the actress's personal appearance before a capacity crowd at a New York theater to promote her latest star vehicle, the paper describes Howard thus: "The dainty little star of Micheaux's vital drama of Negro life, 'The Virgin of Seminole' . . . is a graduate of the Steelton High School, and she took an extension course at the University of Pennsylvania branch at Harrisburg. She is an accomplished little body, for in addition to being a competent stenographer, she is a musician of parts, having graduated in piano from the Pennsylvania Conservatory of Music at Harrisburg, and she speaks French and Spanish with considerable facility" ("Race Screen Star" 1923). Howard's solidly middle-class family background is incorporated into the article. Her address is even published, perhaps to aid admirers in directing their fan mail. Indeed, the article constructs her as the community's sweetheart and group asset. The moral guardians of the community, with their misgivings about actors, have nothing to disparage in this young model of true womanhood.[21]

By the decade's end, the *Courier* expanded its star discourse in a combination of image and text to broader considerations of performance technique and the dialectical dimensions of performer and star personae. For example, on the 6 July 1929 cover page of its special entertainment section, the paper carried a feature story about Lincoln Perry as himself and as Stepin Fetchit. The article, "When Stepin Fetchit Stepped into Fame," is an interview text written by Ruby Berkley Goodwin that contains a trio of photographs depicting three separate Perry personae. The largest photo features Perry in aviator garb, replete with cap, goggles, and bomber jacket, behind the wheel of one of his expensive automobiles; the second-largest presents Perry as "the Smooth Cultured Gentleman" wearing a three-piece suit, tie, and a sporty cap (interestingly, the caption under the photo of Perry as himself identifies him as "Stepin," and not Perry or Lincoln); positioned between these is a photo of Perry in a familiar pose as the lethargic and befuddled character, Stepin Fetchit. Whether by design or by serendipity, it is interesting that the distinction between the real and the actorly is maintained. In *Acting in the Cinema*, James Naremore's consideration of the techniques and craftmanship of acting yields important insights for our look at this series of Lincoln Perry/Stepin Fetchit photos. For example, in the two photos of Perry as himself, Perry addresses the camera directly, but as Fetchit he is figured in character, with downcast eyes as an "object to be looked at" providing "evidence of role-playing" (1988, 15). This difference in looks overrides the article's conflation of the two personae in the photo captions. This rags-to-riches narrative promises that Perry will answer his critics and divulge "in his own words . . . Where he got his name; why he was forbidden to drive his three stunning Cadillacs, and many other things about his interesting and unique career" (Goodwin 1920).

The *Pittsburgh Courier*'s 1929 star discourse: Actor Lincoln Perry, a.k.a. Stepin Fetchit, reveals the New Negro behind the coon performance. Reprinted by permission of GRM Associates, Inc., agents for the *Pittsburgh Courier*.

In her role as interlocutor and surrogate fan, Goodwin sets out to discover "a hidden essence of personality," a supposed "true-self" (Naremore 1988, 19) behind the eccentric and discomfiting icon known to the world as Stepin Fetchit. As with Shinzie Howard, Perry is constructed as a virtuous real-life person, someone in whom the community can take great pride. The article reports on his sober home life with his sister and emphasizes that he "never misses church." Goodwin describes Perry as the consummate businessman, who has even written "an original scenario" for Fox.

Dame Rumor has it that he does many foolish things. But don't worry. Stepin Fetchit knows his public and he is artist enough to be the Stepin Fetchit they expect him to be; but underneath all this the real Stepin

Fetchit (Lincoln Perry) is as intelligent and shrewd as the twentieth century business man. (Goodwin 1920)

Expressing perhaps the most salient yet frustrating sentiment pertaining to the perennial conflict between black actors and their often ambivalent black critics, Charles Gilpin, in defense of his participation in Eugene O'Neill's *Emperor Jones,* unrepentently asserts: "We actors don't
care whether we portray heroes or villains" (quoted in L. White 1922b, 6).
Goodwin delivers a similar treatment of performer Nina Mae McKinney
before the release of King Vidor's 1920s black-cast film *Hallelujah* in the
*Courier'*s 8 June 1929 edition. Appearing in the caption above a large still
of McKinney in character from the film is a promising "At Last! 16-Year-
Old Nina Mae McKinney's Own Story of Her Meteoric Rise to Talkie
Fame!" (Goodwin 1929, 6). Again, the confluence of star persona and real
person serves at once to blur and to capitalize on the lines separating
McKinney's personal and theatrical roles. Moreover, such newspaper
production of star discourse plays a vital role in "the 'manufacture of
female iconography'" so central to getting "the spectator into the theater
in the first place" (Waldman 1984, 39). Diane Waldman has observed the
specific function of the inquiring reporter in fostering a sense of "self-
identification" and "projection" with female spectators in the lucrative
film "tie-in" campaigns (47).

Waldman's analysis can be extended to our consideration of similar
propensities where the black spectator is concerned. For the black spectators starved for true cinematic role models of their own, we can easily
see how such strategies would have an even more powerfully suasive effect "in shaping the context of [a favorable] film reception" (48). As noted
earlier, much of the favorable opinion for the film rests on the favorable
reception of the stars themselves. Thus Goodwin's own complimentary
commentary, coupled with McKinney's positive, self-mythologizing utterances, endows this process with a seamless flow direct to the audience's
hearts. For her part, McKinney endears herself to her ever-widening
audiences with such quotable phrases as "The phenomenal success of
Florence Mills and Josephine Baker stimulated me. I longed to hold a
place in the hearts of the world as they did" (quoted in Goodwin 1929).
The article spreads three separate photos of McKinney over three pages.
One photo depicts McKinney in costume from her theatrical days as a
chorus girl with Lew Leslie's play *Blackbirds.* In this way, her theatrical

credibility and popularity spill over to benefit the promotional efforts of the new film. As with Perry, McKinney's real-life image is played against the film characters she portrays. Instead of the conniving, man-eating vamp character, Chick, that McKinney creates for *Hallelujah*, Goodwin posits her as a charming adolescent who, in reality, reflects well on her family and the race.

> Miss McKinney's success came at an age when most girls are dreaming. She is only 16 years of age and for all her sophistication, is still a child who wants the admiration of the world. She is not haughty. She is modest and despite her phenomenal success carries no air of affectation. . . . I turned to Miss McKinney's mother and said to her, "I know you are proud of your daughter." (6)

Goodwin's flattering portrait of McKinney not only makes a mother proud but ensures the pride of the race as well.

McKinney does her part for black cinephilia when she responds to the query about her preference for the screen over the stage. Answering affirmatively, McKinney replies, "I think the screen offers a greater chance for originality than the stage. The screen is ever on the outlook for something new and original. Everything is experimental" (6). Capitalizing on the youthful star's beauty, the layout team for the paper astutely surrounded the McKinney article with illustrated advertisements for hair and skin care products. Clearly, the paper's editors understand the ideology of consumption that its star discourse afforded in the selling of the paper itself and its advertisers' myriad consumer products. The cartoon illustration of a black woman enjoying the aroma of a hair pomade strategically placed under the McKinney story and photograph bears a striking resemblance to the young star. Thus selling the star helps sell the products that help sell the newspapers to both readers and advertisers.

Industry Practices

The newspapers also kept close tabs on film industry practices, especially to the extent that they infringed on or advanced the goals of African American progress. In 1921 Lester Walton once again explored developments pertaining to global cinema and matters of cultural imperialism. Technological innovations in the cinema made by African American

Peter Jones were discussed in a 1922 *New York Age* article. The *Baltimore Afro-American* and the *Pittsburgh Courier* examined the phenomenon of sound pictures in 1928 and 1929, respectively. And most papers carried news of legal issues surrounding the cinema and black empowerment.

Following from his routine practice of surveying the international press for news of interest to his constituency, Walton discovered some racialist imperatives motivating Britain's film censorship practices. The essay, "Bar Photo Plays in India Which Lower Prestige of White Races," published in his *Age* column on 24 September 1921, consists of an excerpt reprinted from the *Times* of London and Walton's critique of it. Of concern to Walton is the express aim of the British to suppress in India all cinematic portrayals of whites thought to compromise white supremacy and colonial rule. Walton's quote from the *Times* illustrates the point:

> It must be remembered that in 99 percent of the films shown in India the characters are all white people. There is a white hero, a white heroine, a white evil woman and a white villain. This is obviously unfortunate for India, but quite irremediable. In most films, the villain and the evil woman are shown carrying on successfully through the greater part of the film, and this does not tend to uplift the prestige of the British race in India.... Such scenes shown to an illiterate Indian audience can have no other effect than to lower the prestige of the white woman and the white races in general. The board have accordingly been compelled to be somewhat strict on this point. (Walton 1921)

Of course, Walton remembers only too well the international export of *The Birth of a Nation,* and the derisive newsreel depictions of African American soldiers during the Great War, and the countless travel actualities that demeaned African diasporic peoples that were permitted global circulation. For him, then, this latest censorship ploy attests to the desperate measures white authorities take to foist their mythologies of supremacy on dominated and oppressed peoples. Moreover, Walton demystifies yet another apparatus of white hegemony and racial reification for his readers. But Walton is of the opinion that such patent "moral whitewashing" is destined to fail.

> This moral whitewashing—this attempt to hide the truth and cause East Indians to believe all Caucasians are "angels robed in spotless white," is

merely wasted energy. Neither the white nor colored races can rightfully claim sole ownership to Puritanical virtue, the propaganda subtly spread far and wide by the former in their behalf, notwithstanding. (Walton 1921)

Although one might wonder about Walton's characterization of "truth" here, we can accept the notion that the kinds of censorship proposed by the British authorities do violate and hide the narrative truth of films subjected to such purgings. Walton implicates nonfiction films as well when he moves on to considerations of the Fatty Arbuckle tragedy that destroyed the famed comedian's bright film career. Certain that newsreel footage of this incident would not pass British censors in India, given their criteria for acceptability, Walton makes the point with the following analogy:

> The unfairness of it all is, of course, patent. For instance, had the principals to the recent tragedy in San Francisco in which motion picture stars figured been Negroes, today the white press would be stricken with horror and disgust over the immorality of a race whose faults for years have been held up to the glare of pitiless publicity while their virtues have been kept in eclipse. (Walton 1921)

By reminding his readers of the white press's unrelenting campaign to overemphasize any instance of black vice while ignoring its virtues, Walton demonstrates how the tendency of British whites to invert this scenario was nothing more than the flip side of the common coin of racist propaganda. Walton suggests that the failure of the British scheme inheres in the East Indians' firsthand encounters with the tyranny of colonial rule. That is the precondition that Walton believes predisposes the illiterate masses of India to easily reject this subtle form of film propaganda, much like the illiterate African American masses' rejection of the more blatant variety. For Walton, though, the goal was to provide for his readers uncontrovertible evidence of the deliberate and systematic methodology of white structures of ideological domination. Through his strategy of reproducing an article from the *Times*, Walton suggests the importance of letting the whites' own utterances indict them and thereby delegitimate their claims to superiority.

If Walton apprises us of a film industry development that African Americans found abhorrent, the effusive news that Peter P. Jones, a former black filmmaker, was then head organization photographer with the Selznick film laboratories is indicative of the community's excitement about the promises of technological innovations for black cinephiles. Lifting quotes from the Selznick house journal, *The Brain Exchange,* the *Age* ran a 17 June 1922 story detailing Jones's unorthodox career at Selznick and his successful experiments with "color photography" for the movies.

> If you mention the name "Selznick" in the presence of motion picture "fans," it is at once recognized as that of the head of one of the biggest companies in America engaged in the making of films for the "movie." But not even the most ardent movie fan would know that the man who for five years, up to about the first of May, just past, had full and complete charge of the Selznick photographic laboratories was a colored photographer, or that his name is Peter Jones. (L. White 1922a)

After touting the *Exchange*'s laudatory remarks about Jones's superior work on lobby display photos for the Ince film *A Man's Home,* the *Age* delivers more flattering news about Jones from yet another *Exchange* edition.

> There is in the Selznick laboratories a man who is energetically, practically, making a dream come true—and that dream is color photography. Peter Jones is the man. . . . there is only one Selznick Peter Jones. . . . Jones has been working at photography for thirty-three years. He is, perhaps, the most skillful "still" man in the industry—ask exhibitors. "Stills," as everyone in the motion picture business knows, are actual photographs of situations—the most dramatic and vital situations in a photo-play. Their importance as a lobby display cannot be overestimated. A weak, imperfectly developed "still" means death at the box office. The people will not come if the "stills" do not hold their attention. And it is in this particular niche of the business that Peter Jones has won and established a real fame. (5)

That this news of Jones's trailblazing in the area of film promotion for a major film company was a revelation for the *Age*'s readers comes as no surprise. But what is surprising is that it is still news today. Few contemporary revisionist histories of this aspect of the cinema's past consider African American participation, apart from consumerism, in the behind-the-scenes life of important film concerns. At any rate, the *Exchange* reprint continues in this complimentary vein with a bit of biography on Jones thrown in. Even as the Selznick company had high hopes for Jones's continued successes with the company, we learn from the *Age* that Jones decided not to follow the Selznick photographic labs when they moved their operations to Hollywood in May of that year. Instead, Jones remained behind to open his own Service Film Laboratory in Fort Lee, New Jersey. Jones set up his new company in the two-story edifice that had formerly been home to the Eclair Film company (L. White 1922a). The *Age* was not only hopefully optimistic about Jones's decision to continue with his innovative color film photography; it was equally heartened by the company's potential benefits for the black economy. In addition to detailed reports on the facilities' industrial apparatuses, the article carried information about the employment plans of the new firm headed by one of its own.

The *Courier* brought news of Thomas Edison's claim that movies would supersede books as a superior learning tool. In its straight reportorial style, it is difficult to ascertain the paper's stance on this latest hype of the new medium. "The Children of the future will get their education at schools in which the movie screen will supplant the blackboard and the motion picture film will take the place of textbooks" is how the lead paragraph begins on the cover page of the *Courier*'s 2 June 1923 entertainment section. The item, "Movies to Replace Books in Schools, Inventor States," attributes such boasts to Edison during hearings about the racketeering of his trust before the Federal Trade Commission.

The *Courier* even makes early strides in the direction of genre criticism. An unattributed article dated 13 October 1923 delves into the finer points of slapstick comedy and the more subtle humor of farce, expressing a distinct preference for the latter. The headline and subhead, "Gone Are Hey-Days of Slapstick Comedy: Harold Lloyd Has Pioneered the Way to Comedies That Have Set a High Plane for Funny Films—'Why Worry' His First Serious Attempt at Farce," set the tone and aesthetic agenda for this consideration of one of Hollywood's generic mainstays, the comedic film. This essay is striking for its focus on the structural oppositions posed by these differing modes of film comedy. Among the chief complaints made against slapstick by the writer of this article is the copycat syndrome that afflicts too many comedians of the genre.

> When a comedian sees a gag he likes, he takes it! On that principle the motion picture has developed since the beginning. One comedian threw a meringue pie! It splashed! We laughed! So another comedian did likewise,

and another and still another. . . . Some developed the bathing beauty—or rather she developed herself and someone brought her to the camera—and soon every film mill in Hollywood had the title over the door: "What is fun without a cutie?" Such was the case with the Keystone Kop, the skidding automobile, slow crank chase . . . and all the other breakaway props . . . it gets silly and monotonous. ("Gone" 1923)

According to the critic, this tendency of repetition without much difference was killing the very art of comedy. The critic is of the opinion that "the trend today is away from the Slapstick, with its easy sighted gags, which are imitated by a dozen other comics as soon as one displays a new gag!" Harold Lloyd's new film *Why Worry* is held out as representative of this new approach to comedy that the writer encourages. "Comedy with a situation is the latest form of film entertainment," in the writer's estimation. Lloyd's vision is applauded because "it depends on none of the old slapstick hokum." What separates *Why Worry* from its inferior slapstick counterparts, for the writer, is its ability to sustain a story "often better than the feature picture, and the fun lies in humorous, life-like situations that are funny because they are so human and ridiculous." Clearly, the writer is fed up with Hollywood comedies' tendencies towards perpetuating what Andrew Sarris (1976) terms "vulgar illusionism" (239). Lloyd's adherence to a more naturalist and realist aesthetic is what the writer considers as his (Lloyd's) major contribution.

> Harold Lloyd's introduction of this type of comedy . . . created a sensation among the public and critics who were weary of the set-em-up-and-knock-em-down type of film. . . . "Why Worry" is straight farce. It can be likened best to the high-class musical comedy, with its slightly overdrawn plot, yet with the characters kept virtually true to life and true to the atmosphere in which they are set. . . . Lloyd crams it with laughable situations, all of which are inextricably a part of the plot, and to keep a sustained plot moving and still maintain a staccato laugh effect is an achievement worthy of any comedian. . . . Slapstick is dead! Long live humor! Lloyd's laughs last! ("Gone" 1923)

Among the numerous accolades for Lloyd, the writer also engages in a bit of auteur critique. In noting Lloyd's unique style in several of the comedian's films, *Grandma's Boy, Safety Last,* and *Why Worry,* the writer effectively raises issues of the comedian's idiosyncratic style and authorial predisposition, which we now regard as central markers of the director, actor, or writer as auteur.

Another film industry innovation that caught the imagination of the newspapers was the coming of sound technology. In its 3 November 1928 issue, the *Baltimore Afro-American* reviewed one of the first all-talkies on its entertainment page. "All-Talking Film Heads Regent Bill" is the headline of this brief review, although it is substantially longer than the other billboarding announcements highlighting the remaining film fare to be found at the other neighborhood theaters advertised on this page. *Lights of New York* is described in this way:

> Brilliant scenes of Broadway, the crowds, glittering night clubs, mystery, the police—these and many more combine to make a pulsating drama of "Lights of New York," the first of the all-talking pictures. . . . The voice of New York's "Roaring Forties" has at last found its way to the screen in this picture, all of the myriad conglomerate sounds being in addition to the spoken dialogue that eliminates entirely any printed subtitles . . . and gives the audience a chance to hear the talkative tonsorial artist on the screen for the first time. ("All-Talking" 1928)

Whereas the *Afro-American* only hints at the aesthetic appeal of sound and its practical value for illiterate film lovers (it "eliminates entirely any printed subtitles"), the *Pittsburgh Courier* sees larger implications. In an editorial statement entitled "The Value of the Talkies," published on 6 July 1929, the position taken is as follows:

> The Talking Pictures ought to contribute considerably toward bettering race relations in the United States. Not only have two very sympathetic Negro plays been produced, one of which has received wide acclaim, even in the South, but a number of Negro acts, singing and dancing, have gone into the most remote sections. In "Hearts in Dixie," a Negro is shown going to a white man's front door. The South is shocked but stays through the picture; the story of the sacrifices of an old man to send his little boy NORTH to school. Then comes "Show Boat" with Jules Bledsoe, the famous singer, being introduced from the screen as "Mister Jules Bledsoe!" The South is doubly shocked. What heresy is this? For years they have been addressing Negroes as Doctor, Reverend, Professor, Gal, Boy, Auntie, Uncle, Chief, George and about everything else except Mister. Now it is shouted at them from the silver screen. ("The Value" 1915)

The "deepi-talkie," which is an African-inspired turn of phrase that approximates the concept of subtext or deep structural meaning (Tolson 1953, 62–63), occurring in this passage is overdetermined in its sociocultural critique of white racist practices and black responses to it. The condensation at work here involves one of many rationales for the great black migration "NORTH," the denial of black manhood and womanhood status by the larger white society, the critique of Jim Crow segregation, the valuation of black cultural forms—namely, folk music and dance and the seditious nature of more authentic portrayals of blackness, especially in the "solid South" and other "remote sections." These comments about the South have particular significance when viewed against the background of the papers' resistance to the South's campaign to lure African Americans back to its depopulated and economically depressed agricultural plantations.[22] Although a surface reading of this pro-talkie statement might suggest, for some critics of the black press,[23] an overinvestment in a couple of racially problematic films, the hyperbole is tempered by a point made at the statement's conclusion: "The Negro plays and acts so far to appear on the talking screen have not been all that the Negroes desired, but they are paving the way for something better" ("The Value" 1915). As we later learn from the case of *Hallelujah*, not released at the time of this statement, the press had high expectations for an improved climate of racial representations in Hollywood with the coming of sound.

Regular reviews of "race" and mainstream films became another staple of the newspapers' entertainment coverage. These reviews ranged in format from the more familiar style incorporating cast lists and commentary to film analysis and social criticism combinations. Again typifying this aspect is the *Courier*'s special two-page entertainment section. The *New York Amsterdam News* featured a similar separate entertainment section with three full pages of amusement news.[24] Often the reviews were unattributed, but there were many cases when a byline did accompany a specific review. An unusually lengthy disquisition on Pola Negri's film *Bella Donna* is one example of an unattributed film review article that focuses on the film and its southern detractors. Published on 2 June 1923, the essay carried the headline "Southern Editor Flays Movie That Depicts White Woman in Love with a Dark-Skinned Man," and a related news item about the racial epithets leveled at the film's producers also appeared under that headline. A sizable photo of Negri was situated between the two stories with a bold caption, "Criticized!"

In response to a Colonel Mayfield's vitriolic denunciations of the film's interracial theme, and especially the intertitle "white skinned ladies will flirt with browned skin men when their husbands are away" (9), the article provides a capsule review of the film and then takes delight in the southerner's pain of misrecognition in this text about a white woman and an Egyptian prince. Recognizing the irrationality of the southerner's rabid racism, a racism that blinds him to the film's non-American text and foreign context, the article responds accordingly:

Just why these lines irritated the southern editor may be found in those time-worn sayings, "if the shoe fits, etc.," and "it is the hit dog who hollers." The Colonel calls the Egyptian prince such pet names as "coon" and goes so far to refer to the promoters as "depraved Jews" and "kikes." Why the wrath? Is it possible that in the sneaking, sensual way in which Bella Donna follows the Egyptian prince, the Colonel sees the ghost of similar conditions in his own southland: Doesn't the play bring home to the white south the treatment of colored slaves by white masters? Isn't there something in the veiled meaning of the drama that lays bare the truth about the most common cause of lynching? Does the Colonel so doubt the chastity of his southern white women that he fears the play will "break down the moral life of this country with its subtle and convincing propaganda?" Has the Colonel forgotten "The Birth of a Nation"? ("Southern Editor" 1923)

The Colonel's antiblack and anti-Semitic rantings have been reprinted in the article, and a few of the comments deserve attention. Take for example, these blood-curdling statements:

The South has never been safe from the Negro rape fiend. We have hung them by their necks, we have burned them at the stake, and still no woman is safe beyond the range of her husband's rifle. Conditions have ever been deplorable in the South, watch as we would, along this line, and now comes the Jewish propaganda that "White skinned ladies will flirt with brown skinned men when their husbands are away." That brutal lie and that dirty play will lead more Negroes to the funeral pyre than all of the other influences that ever combined to lure the black man to death for ravishing. That dirty lie will play upon the lips of ten million Negroes now dreaming of social equality; that dirty play will stir up more turmoil and strife than all the influences of rabid Negro papers ever published in the history of America.

That these are the statements of one southerner is granted. Nonetheless it must be viewed as exemplary of a southern mentality that seizes on any pretext to foment and rationalize the horror of lynching blacks, given the weekly reports of commonplace lynchings in the newspapers, both white and black. It is also important to see the lengths to which southerners of the era would go to find a pretext for the displacement of the economic motives as well as so-called moral impetus for lynchings. In this regard, the article's mention of *The Birth of a Nation* is salient. For in reality the offense of interracial rape has nearly always rested with the southern white male and his rapaciousness toward the black female, the inverse of the mythology, as alluded to rightly in the article.

A *Courier* review of *The Flaming Crisis,* a film produced by the African American film company Monarch, is notable for what it contributes to our knowledge of the way in which black film companies experimented with generic forms and technical aesthetics. In the review, "'Flaming Crisis' Most Powerful Drama Screened: Melodrama with Colored Artists, Teeming with Action and Sensational Scenes," we learn that the Western genre is enriched by black stunt riders performing "death-defying, thrilling rodeo feats," and by the incorporation of early scenes "laid in Eastern society circles" with "beautiful romance." Adding to the "powerful, smashing melodrama, commencing with [a] mysterious murder" is the technical experimentation with form: "For the first time on the colored screen there is employed double and triple exposure, one of the most difficult and expensive feats in motion picture photoplay, in the production of the climatic ending of 'The Flaming Crisis.'" The acting is said to have been handled masterfully.

The *Courier*'s 7 September 1929 rave review of King Vidor's all-black-cast film *Hallelujah* provides some interesting insights into this film's initial reception among black and white audiences, and the critics' own conflicted admiration of the film. "'Hallelujah'—One of Year's Big Screen Hits: Well-Known Critic Lauds New Film in Pointed Review" is the banner headline announcing Maurice Dancer's review of the "long expected Metro-Goldwyn and Mayer saga of the colored race." Dancer's review also reveals that this film occasioned a break with established booking practices. Rather than the separate and staggered premiere at white and black theaters that typically defined the pattern for screenings of mainstream films, there were simultaneous premieres in both communities. We also are apprised of the different audiences' responses to the film.

At the Lafayette theatre [black trade], a good sized audience applauded
loudly, and did not react when certain scenes called for it. Profuse laughter
was prevalent all through the theatre, while the audience at the Embassy
sniffed [white trade] and were awed. (Dancer 1929, 8)

As Dancer describes them, the white audience interpreted the film
along tragic and sentimental lines, but the black audience viewed the film
primarily in the comedic vein. Perhaps James Weldon Johnson's criticism
of the bourgeois sensibility of "some [in] Harlem's sophisticated audiences" can help shed light on this difference in reception. Johnson
attributes the fixation by many in the audience on "the shiftless type of
Negro" in the film to a lack of appreciation for film producers' desire to
cast according to "types that lent themselves to dramatic representation"
(J. Johnson 1929). The black audiences, however, apparently preferred to
resist these stock stereotypes no matter how dramatically or nobly motivated. What Dancer appreciates most about the film is Vidor's construction of characters who possess some complexity, especially the lead
character, Zeke. Dancer applauds the fact that Zeke's story allows for the
impartial probing of "his virtues and his vices, his strengths and weak-
nesses" (Dancer 1929, 8). Even though Dancer finds the dialogue unsatisfactory, that point is vitiated "because here is a story that is better
told with the eyes, dance and brood [*sic*], restless feet and menacing
fingers." In sum, Dancer is of the opinion that "'Hallelujah' was well
worth waiting for" (8).

In the following month, the *Courier* exposed the racism motivating the
simultaneous premieres in the de facto segregated black and white theaters. Although the laws forbade Jim Crow policies in New York theaters, the owners found methods of subverting these protections for
black theatergoers. Perhaps to save themselves embarrassment and box
office receipts if caught deliberately restricting black spectators from obtaining seats to an all-black cast film, theater bookers opted to break with
established distribution patterns by sponsoring a dual premiere. Some
African Americans were not so easily misled. On the front page of its
31 August 1929 edition, the *Courier* carried a big story of a legal suit
brought against the film's producers. The story is entitled "Three Suits
for Discrimination Filed against Producers of King Vidor's Movietone,
'Hallelujah': Harlem Business Men Refused Tickets for the Embassy
Theatre Performance Are Told the House Is Sold Out: Others Refused,

Too." Seeing through the subterfuge, the article contends: "That 'Hallelujah' is being presented at the Lafayette Theatre in Harlem to keep Negro patrons from going to the Broadway showing is the charge made last week by three young Harlem businessmen in a suit filed under the Civil Rights Law against Loews's, Inc." As was the usual custom when African Americans wanted to demonstrate willful discrimination based on race, the businessmen enlisted individuals who could exercise their white-skinned privilege and bade them attempt to buy tickets, and then they waited to see the expected results. Here is how the situation unfolded: "The ticket seller informed them that the house was sold out for two weeks. They got out of line and for fifteen minutes watched white patrons buy tickets for the performance which they had been told there were no more tickets" ("Three Suits" 1929). Whereas the article reports this as the first suit filed in connection with the film, it suggests that many more were in the offing as "a number of complaints have been heard from Harlem residents who sought tickets at the Embassy and were informed that the house was sold out but tickets could be secured at The Lafayette" ("Three Suits" 1929).

From the strict bounds of film protest literature of earlier years, the writers for the black press network in the late teens and through the twenties first configure a celebratory discourse on the new independent black cinema movement and second advance toward more historical, philosophical, and self-reflexive examinations of the cinema and its utility in the "New Negro" ideology of racial and sociocultural transformation. As we have seen, the discourses of cinephilia in the newspapers and magazines developed specific topologies. The weekly newspapers, which appealed primarily to a popular or mass audience, often, but not exclusively, approached film news from a fan culture perspective. They tended to foreground star discourse or celebrity hagiographies of black performers who managed to break the color line in mainstream films, approving reviews of black-produced film texts, general film fandom, and the unending advocacy for equitable treatment by the dominant film industry of loyal African American spectator-patrons.

The magazines, by contrast, stressed middle to highbrow aesthetics in much of the film literature they fashioned. Film criticism in the magazines lays bare its pedagogical intent, an intent designed to raise the community's collective consciousness to an appreciation of the medium's economic, historical, philosophical, sociological, and aesthetic import.

For the magazines, it was necessary to impart a greater critical awareness of the cinema's growing influence if the apparatus was to be enlisted successfully in the community's struggle for a new politics of identity and sociocultural liberation. Together, the newspaper and magazine film discourses served to prepare and acclimate their heterogeneous readerships to the evolving conditions and possibilities of constructive engagement with the nation's newest mass cultural form. In all its eclecticism, this twenties-era discourse created an intellectual conduit to the next critical phase of African American film literature.

4

Black Modernist Dialectics
and the New Deal

ACCOMMODATIONIST AND RADICAL FILM

CRITICISM, 1930–1940

Naturally, there are sequences in the film [*Imitation of Life*] that will grieve my people, but I beg them to be tolerant . . . in their thinking and grow into the industry that aims to erase the color-line. Don't spoil your economic advantages and possibilities in the movies by intolerant criticism.
—Bernice Patton, "Critics Weep"

Uncle Tom has dropped his hat; Aunt Jemima has removed her bandanna; Pickaninnies are wearing shoes and slowly but surely, Hollywood films are growing up.—Fay M. Jackson, "Fredi Washington Strikes New Note"

In all class societies, the dominating class rules by controlling the instruments of culture, along with economic and political power. To talk of pure and unbiased art under such circumstances is sheer rot and nonsense. Art is a weapon in the hands of the white ruling class.
—Cyril Briggs, "Art Is a Weapon"

Black film criticism of the 1930s is prolific, complex, and deeply imbricated in the political, social, and economic upheavals of the Great Depression era, retrospectively dubbed by some critics "the Red Decade."[1] The preponderance of the literature bifurcates along familiar lines in

African American political thought, that duality of accommodation and radicalism. Along the accommodationist axis are criticism and commentary concerned with effecting a progressive reform of Hollywood in matters of race and representation; along the radical line are those critiques defined by a politics of opposition to dominant filmmaking practices and their attendant bourgeois ideologies. Whereas the former is marked by an integrationist strategy to increase black participation in the Hollywood mainstream, the latter often mobilizes radical political ideologies, such as Marxism, socialism, and proletarian art aesthetics to redirect black spectators away from the lure of false consciousness transmitted through Hollywood's escapist and too often racist cinematic productions.[2]

Another discernible characteristic of this thirties film criticism is its intellectual evolution from the amorphous and often truncated film discussions of previous decades. Unlike the earlier, more fragmented modes of criticism that dispersed into separate analyses of the dominant cinema's deleterious effects on the moral authority of the church, racial uplift programs, sociocultural attitudes, and black performers' right-to-work campaigns,[3] this later discourse developed these and other concerns in more focused and cohesive ways. Additionally, criticism in this period absorbed much from those radical movements responsible for earning the thirties era its "red" character (Holman and Harmon 1992, 350). As the depression plunged the already financially strapped black communities further into economic destitution and despair, the radical ideologies of socialism, communism, Garveyite nationalism, and the African Blood Brotherhood's paramilitarism, among others, began to take root in overpopulated urban centers with large, disenfranchised African American and West Indian populations.[4] Although the black press carried ruminations about African Americans' involvement with alternative political regimes as early as 1923,[5] this political dimension, for the most part, remained extrinsic to the entertainment news at that time. By contrast, the critical shift that occurred in the film literature of the thirties is marked by discussions more politically pointed and attuned to these radical undulations as they spread throughout the nation's cultural life. As a consequence, there is a greater emphasis on, and engagement with, the political economy of race and class issues in film. This newly politicized thrust is especially evident in the radical film critiques appearing in liberal and far-Left newspapers and journals.

Repercussions deriving from the innovation of sound technology in 1927 also played an important role in shaping the film literature of the thirties. With the coming of sound, Hollywood developed a new interest in black talent associated with the successful wave of such black stage musicals as Lew Leslie's phenomenally popular *Blackbirds,* among others produced in northern theaters. In fact, Hollywood's cinematic adaptations of the black-cast stage hits *The Emperor Jones, The Green Pastures,* and *Porgy* are exemplary. Thus Hollywood's co-optation of black musical idioms for its sound films led white and black critics to presume that a new era in black cinematic representations had finally arrived (McPherson 1929, 90).[6] As the studios scrambled to retrofit their lots to the new sound technology, African American performers, critics, and activists anticipated the opening of greater opportunities for blacks in Hollywood ("A New Departure" 1934). For African American performer Geraldyn Dismond, the advent of "talkies" signified a necessary and long-overdue reevaluation and reformulation of the black screen image. In 1929 the British journal *Close Up* dedicated the August edition entirely to the issue of blackness in the cinema. In her contribution to that edition, Dismond observes that "it is significant that with the coming of talkies, the first all-Negro feature pictures were attempted by the big companies. . . . The movie of yesterday, to be sure, let him dance, but his greatest charm was lost by silence. With the talkie, the Negro is at his best. Now he can be heard in song and speech" (Dismond 1929, 119).

With the relative thaw in America's racial climate during the postwar prosperity of the twenties, other white liberal and radical magazines began writing about race in the cinema and publishing criticism produced by black writers as well. The *New Masses,* the *Daily Worker, Sight and Sound,* and *New Theater* were among those Left-oriented publications that protested against Hollywood's penchant for churning out racist depictions of black life and culture as a matter of course. During the late 1920s and early 1930s, white writers at these magazines penned blistering reviews and commentary about racism in Hollywood,[7] even though some betrayed their own primitivist viewpoints in the process. Indicative of the "noble savage" assumptions that permeated some of the writing is this curious commentary by Harry Potamkin as it appears in *Close Up*'s special issue on race in the cinema:

As for me, I shall be assured of the white man's sincerity when he gives me a blue nigger. . . . I want cinema and I want cinema at its source. To be at its source, cinema must get at the source of its content. The Negro is plastically interesting when he is most negroid. In the films he will be plastically interesting only when the makers of the film know thoroughly the treatment of the negro structure in the African plastic, when they know the treatment of his movements in the ritual dances, like the dance of the circumcision, the Ganza. (Potamkin 1929, 109)

The repugnant and racist essentialism of these remarks by Potamkin is inescapable and arguably symptomatic of the writer's contradictory racial attitudes. Nevertheless, it is important to point out that despite his highly objectionable rhetoric, Potamkin's overall argument is affirmative in its impassioned call for new and more credible cinematic depictions of blackness. Even as modernist perspectives were effectively destabilizing and transforming traditional art aesthetics and values across the board, it is significant that this special 1929 edition of *Close Up*, with its multiracial perspective, contributes one of the earliest serious critical engagements with the issue of race in the now legendary debates over sound technology and its implications for the cinema as an art form. A comment by Dismond provides the best summary of *Close Up*'s position on the potentially revolutionary impact of sound technology beyond the heated debates around cinematic aesthetics. Regarding the limitations of, and possibilities for, new cinematic articulations of race and representations of blackness, Dismond writes: "And the talkie, which is being despised in certain artistic circles, is giving [the African American] the great opportunity to prove his right to a place on the screen" (97).

As this new critical literary flurry was occasioned by Hollywood's 1929 releases of not one but two all-black-cast films, MGM's *Hallelujah* and Fox's *Hearts in Dixie*, we can appreciate the critics' guarded optimism that despite these films' perpetuation of "the way down South in the land of cotton idea" (Herring 1929, 101), "The present vogue for negro films was inevitable" (Potamkin 1929, 108). As for some critics in the black press who sought to capitalize on the big studios' "inevitable" demand for novel approaches to the special requirements of sound technology, the moment had indeed arrived to press for a wider integration of African Americans in Hollywood and, by extension, in the larger mainstream of American civil society.

The Rise of the Accommodationist Discourse
and the Case of the 1934 Film Sensation *Imitation of Life*

Although it would be easy to presume that the black accommodationist texts on film constituted a monolith, a close scrutiny of the accumulated literature around this tendency reveals a more polysemous scenario. Moreover, the competitive black newspapers and magazines frequently contained contradictory or wide-ranging points of view often serving diverse ends even within their respective folds (it is important to bear in mind that white mainstream journalism itself is marked by an intrinsic polyphony of voices and positionalities—to say nothing of the cacophony existing within the nation's various regionalisms). In the black press, it was not unusual to encounter significant political and cultural diversity in the structural order of one specific newspaper or journal. For example, the *New York Age*'s political conservatism closely reflected Booker T. Washington's accommodationist philosophy of black economic advance-ment (although the paper's resident film critic Lester Walton espoused more radical cultural views), and the liberal NAACP tolerated, for a time, the radicalism contained in its literary organ *The Crisis* under the aus-pices of its often embattled editor in chief W. E. B. Du Bois. It is interesting to note, however, that Du Bois rejected the notion that *The Crisis*, in its earlier incarnation, was the association's organ. And his resignation from the organization in 1933 lends credence to Du Bois's assertion. Significantly, between 1915 and 1925, Du Bois's relationship with the association "was filled with quarrels" fueled in large part by the "continued growth and development" of *The Crisis* (Graham-Du Bois 1978, 43). Du Bois later remarked on the persistently tenuous nature of the relationship, and clearly his comments have broader implications for later aspects of our discussion:

> I began to realize that something was going wrong with our [America's] economic organization. The income of *The Crisis* began to fall off and I began to see that Negroes were losing their jobs, the opposition to them in the trade union ranks was still strong, and it was clear that *The Crisis*, as the depression went on, was not going to pay for itself—it was not going to be self-supporting. Now that brought an inevitable change. So long as *The Crisis* was self-supporting, I could be practically independent within cer-tain wide limits in what I was saying to the public. But if the National

Association had to support *The Crisis,* then of course the National Association had a right to have the last word as to what was to be said and it would become an organ. Organs are never interesting. They have to say whatever the Board of Trustees vote. I made up my mind that my job in propaganda was over. (quoted in Graham Du Bois 1978, 67)

Deprived of his editorial autonomy in the depression years, the beleaguered Du Bois tendered his resignation from the association and the magazine in 1933. As the *Crisis* example indicates, the black press network, despite its often incongruous economic and political imperatives, did strive for a sort of unified front in the liberation struggle against the intransigence of American racial oppression. Of particular interest here, however, are the manifestations of these ideological ruptures and convergences as they arise in the black press's complex engagement with American cultural institutions and their by-products during the volatile depression era.

A *Baltimore Afro-American* article featuring Zora Neale Hurston's denunciations of certain black intellectuals for what she perceives as their self-serving complicity in popularizing the distorted white depictions of black folk culture further illustrates this schism. Consider the following commentary attributed to Hurston in the 1930 *Afro-American* article "Too Much Pampering of White Writers by Negro Leaders: Zora Neal Hurston Raps Harlem's Literati Who Praise All Nordic Creations on Negroes":

> Whenever a hungry Nordic is suddenly bitten by Negrophobia and sets out to scribble a "true" picture of his darker brother at so much per word, he just takes his brain child to such people as James Weldon Johnson, Dr. W. E. B. Du Bois, Charles S. Johnson and others and submits it for their approval, which is generally forthcoming. . . . The truth is . . . the Negro leaders who champion the Negro's cause at so much per champ, don't know the Negro themselves. This was evidenced in the profuse and lavish praise that attended the success of "The Green Pastures." Supposed leaders rushed to print with a waste basket full of adjectives and the authors and producers were so flattered that they actually believed that they were authorities on Negro religion. ("Too Much Pampering" 1930, 8).

Although Hurston's repudiation, as reported in the *Afro-American,* does not sufficiently take into account Du Bois's or others' particular

radical leanings at this point, the uncompromising indictment of black
leaders' culpability in this instance has some merit. While it is true
that Johnson, Du Bois, and others found value in such white imaginings
of blackness as *The Green Pastures, The Emperor Jones,* and *Hallelujah,* the charge fails to consider what Hurston's colleagues'—whom she
dubbed elsewhere "the Niggerati"—found most compelling in these
flawed works.[8] As problematic as these productions were, for Johnson
and these other scions of the black literati, they nonetheless represented
measurable improvements over previous white renderings of black life
and culture. In actuality, these films and plays were not uncritically endorsed by black leaders, as is suggested in Hurston's remarks. Johnson's
observations about *Hallelujah* that appeared in his *Age* column of 4 January 1930 reveal a bemused and qualified reception of that film, and we
may reasonably expect that this qualified attitude attaches to the other
films and plays in question as well. As Johnson puts it in "A Director's
Dilemma":

> King Vidor is the name of the director who was responsible for the produc-
> tion of the all-Negro film, "Hallelujah." Mr. Vidor patted himself on the
> back after the production of this vocal and pictorial representation of what
> he considered Negro life, regardless of what Negro audiences may think of
> it, and considered he had done a good job. By comparison with previous
> films depicting the darker race, he was not without reason. (J. Johnson
> 1930, 4).

When we consider the *Afro-American* article's description of Hurston's critical approach to this issue (Hurston was, after all, a trained
anthropologist-ethnographer concerned with authenticating and valu-
ing actual black folkways and culture, "which she both lived and studied"),[9] the polemic against this white simulacrum is not surprising or
without credibility. James W. Johnson, author of such seminal texts as
The Autobiography of an Ex-Colored Man and *God's Trombones,* texts that
helped form the cornerstone of the so-called Harlem Renaissance, presents an attitude of critical distance to these white narratives of black life
that suggests his willingness to allow for the creative tensions and fundamental differences existing between art and reality. Perhaps this explains
why Johnson and others were more tolerant of these white southerners'
fixation on antebellum conceptions of blackness. Hurston, like Johnson,
was a respected and "full fledged member of the Harlem Renaissance"

(Barksdale and Kinnamon 1972, 612), and as such her lack of compunction or reservation about calling her intellectual progenitors on what she considers their ethical and philosophical betrayals is indicative of the generational split that existed between the older and younger proponents of this movement. Charles Johnson, renounced by Hurston, published one of her first influential works, "Drenched in Light," in a 1924 issue of *Opportunity Magazine.* Hurston also won a second prize in that magazine's competition for both a short story ("Spunk") and a play ("Color Struck"). As a result of these publications, she also served for a time as secretary to Fannie Hurst, author of *Imitation of Life,* and on a scholarship at Barnard College, she became a protégée to famed anthropologist Franz Boas (Barksdale and Kinnamon 1972, 612). Despite this indebtedness to Charles Johnson as her editor and mentor, Hurston would not compromise her position on this important issue. After all, by this time Hurston brought her own impressive literary and academic credentials to this early debate over the commodification of black culture. Hurston's boldness, then, in confronting black leaders publicly in the press on the issue of accurate depictions of African American folk culture points to the many antinomies that both define and complicate the accommodationist body of work.

Because the sound revolution gave particular impetus to the dominance of the integrationist logic in the literature of accommodation, it is necessary to consider its direct effects. The advent of sound on the eve of the Great Depression brought with it mixed results for the film industry in general, and untold catastrophe for the black film independents in particular. On the one hand, it created a means by which blacks could wedge limited entry into what had been Hollywood's racially closed shop. On the other hand, the prohibitive costs associated with the conversion to sound in the wake of the stock market crash of 1929 proved insurmountable for the fledgling independent black film companies. Many historians have considered the widespread devastation wrought by the technology on the continued viability of both the white independents and the major and minor Hollywood film studios,[10] although Roosevelt's New Deal legislation insulated some of the majors from total demise in the depression years. Even in the wake of revisionist historiographies of that period, sound's total decimation of the black independents has yet to receive adequate scrutiny.

Despite this lacuna, we can deduce the deleterious and the far-reaching consequences of sound technology on the black independents by their coterminous disappearance. Some telling comments appear in a 1931 *New York Age* article. "Sidelights on New Picture, 'The Exile'" is a brief discussion of Oscar Micheaux's first sound film, *The Exile,* which was produced in that same year. While a cursory reference to Micheaux's "lack of funds" that resulted in a partnership arrangement with white theatrical manager Frank Schiffman is telling. Micheaux's particular case ultimately becomes synecdochical for the entire independent black film industry: "The difficulties of creating talking pictures were so great, however, that he [Micheaux] was hardly able to get started." As the article progresses, it stresses some of the costly sound production elements that increased the financial expenditures associated with the effort to harness the technology for the race films market. Formidable obstacles plagued the financially vulnerable film concerns specializing in low-grade "B films" that once thrived during the less capital-intensive era of silent-film production. Unfortunately, most black independents, such as the Lincoln Motion Picture Company, were not as resilient as Micheaux. Consequently they failed to make the expensive transition to sound. However, Micheaux's interracial alliance with Schiffman was double-edged in that it saved the mercurial company from bankruptcy, but that salvation had a Faustian dimension:

> When he began to make "The Exile," there was placed at his disposal an up-to-date modern studio with crews of trained cameramen, electricians, stagehands, scenic artists, lighting experts, make-up artist, assistant director, etc. Donald Heywood and a little staff of music writers wrote a special musical score: Leonard Harper organized a complete revue for the cabaret scenes. Five weeks of intensive rehearsal were put in by the cast. No such period of preparation had ever been allowed before. ("Sidelights" 1931)

The trade-off, then, for Micheaux's survival during the sound era, as Mark Reid describes it in *Redefining Black Film* (1993), was that "even though Micheaux retained his name in the Micheaux Film Corporation, the corporation was financed and controlled by two whites" (18). This transfer of power in the Micheaux case was symbolic of an even greater transformation impelled by the advent of sound. The successes of the "Schiffman-Brecher-Micheaux union" "presaged later interracial [film-making] collaborations" (18), but most importantly, the flood of white-controlled film companies into the lucrative race films market, conjoined with the sound revolution and the economics of the depression, engulfed and ultimately supplanted the last vestiges of the black-owned and -operated independent film companies.

Ironically, George Johnson, a co-owner of the defunct Lincoln Motion Picture Company, itself a casualty of these forces, has left us one of the most detailed documents of the various black and white film companies that survived the sound revolution and grew to dominate America's segregated race films market. Among the surviving white-dominated interracial film concerns producing black-cast films during the thirties and forties, Johnson lists (1) Million Dollar Productions and their films *Am I Guilty?, While Thousands Cheer, Four Shall Die, Bargain with Bullets, Life Goes On, The Duke Is Tops, Smashers, Reform School*, and *House Rent Party*; (2) George Randol Productions, *Mystery in Swing* and *Broken Strings*; (3) Hollywood Productions, *Two Gun Man from Harlem, The Bronze Buckaroo, Harlem Rides the Range*, and *Son of Ingagi*; (4) Gateway Productions, *Bad Boy*; (5) Dixie National Pictures, *Mr. Washington Goes to Town* and *Harlem on the Prairie*; (6) Herald Pictures, Inc., *Boy What a Girl, Sepia Cinderella*, and *Miracle in Harlem*; (7) Grand National, *Spirit of Youth*; (8) Toddy Pictures, *Lucky Ghost, Up Jumped the Devil*, and *Brown Venus*; and (9) Sack Amusement Co., *One Dark Night* (G. Johnson 1940, 6–7). As expected, the newly reconfigured race films industry had specific ramifications for the careers of black performers as well. After Hollywood temporarily abandoned its experiment with all-black-cast films, established black stars such as Nina Mae McKinny and Rex Ingram could only gain acceptable roles in these interracial film combines. Later black performers, such as Lena Horne and Mantan Moreland, got their starts with these race film outfits before moving on to bigger successes in the mainstream film establishment.

With this new white colonization of the black cinematic image by Hollywood and the white-controlled race film independents, the black press network's popular entertainment pages became an unacknowledged and unwitting extension of the white film industry's massive publicity machinery. So that if the press expected to benefit at all from the black audiences' increasing demand for film-related news and information about popular black and white films and star personalities, and the much-needed advertising revenue from film exhibitors, clearly it was compromisingly tethered to the mass-produced films originating from Hollywood's vertically integrated studios and their endless parade of cinematic mammies, coons, toms, and tragic mulattoes, and the formula films produced by white independents, with their emphases on a simulacra black underworld. With the industry's timely turn to escapist narratives and the social problem films that addressed variously the new economic realities of a depressed economy and the social disintegration they engendered, the counterhegemonic film images produced by the black independents that proffered different conceptions and perspectives of the black American experience were unceremoniously sacrificed on the altar of profiteering. These important developments served to delimit and redirect the film discussions of the thirties. The accommodationist discourse reflects this painful and turbulent encounter with the era of sound.

This turn of events even precipitated a strong accommodationist ethos among certain black intellectuals interested in the cinema. Sterling Brown, a professor at Howard University, is representative in this regard. Although he produced later writings more compatible with the radical mode, Brown's first film essay adheres to the accommodationist line. His initial contribution to the accommodationist literature is a coauthored essay, "Folk Values in a New Medium." Here Brown and Alain Locke, the founding father of the "Renaissance" literary movement, found much to celebrate in Hollywood's 1929 production of *Hearts in Dixie* and *Hallelujah*. Written in 1930, the essay endorses aspects of those films that Hurston would surely have found anathema to authentic portrayals of black cultural norms. But for Locke and Brown, the element of sound had brought something truly new to the fore—"the first all-Negro talkie" (Locke and Brown 1930, 25). Locke and Brown view sound as an appropriate vehicle for the long-awaited cinematic exploration of traditional black folk values. Of primary interest to them are the films' expressions of the "vibrancy of the race through acting and singing," and they place much stress on the mellifluous black voice in film. As they put it, "the Negro voice achieves an artistic triumph and becomes a more purely Negro thing, for once—a true peasant gem in a genuine setting" (27). Although they elaborate further on these films' capacity to display positively the inimitable attributes of the black voice and performance style, Brown and Locke's essay continues the attenuated sanction of white-produced works initiated by James Weldon Johnson.

"Folk Values in a New Medium" begins with a qualification: "From the traditional sentimentalities of the moving-picture version of *Uncle Tom's*

Cabin to anything approaching true folk values is a far way—not to be reached without at least one turning. That they should have been notably attained in the next Hollywood venture in the portrayal of Negro life, *Hearts in Dixie,* is, after all, something of a modern miracle" (25). The authors continue with a cautious and rationalized discussion of Hollywood's limited progression from the first employment of an actual African American actor in Carl Lemmle's 1926 *Uncle Tom's Cabin* to the 1929 breakthrough films *Hallelujah* and *Hearts in Dixie,* featuring all-black casts. Citing the "sobering risk of large financial outlay," based in large part on an acceptance of the now disqualified myth of the southern box office, Locke and Brown commend these later films that owe their existence to Hollywood's "sincere experiment and [its] determination to overdo rather than miss the truly genuine." Locke and Brown favorably contrast what they view as the less distorted constructions of black characters in *Hallelujah* and *Hearts in Dixie* to the "oversentimental and overrealistic" formula in *Uncle Tom's Cabin.* For them:

> *Hearts in Dixie* caught Negro life at a level angle without much distortion, and in spite of some sporadic tinting from the plantation tradition and occasional intrusion of slapstick comedy, projected a really moving folk idyll on the peasant level. The usual types are there—the Daddy, Uncle, the Mammy, and the inevitable pickaninnies, but in this group they are real flesh and blood Negroes evoking a spontaneous and genuine human interest. In fact they have real individuality. . . . The story is sketchy; too often a slender skeleton for heavy coatings of "human interest" and "local Color"; but nevertheless, *Hearts in Dixie* is the truest picturization of Negro life to date. It is to the credit of both the story and the production that, while they do not fully exhaust the full depths of Negro life and character, they do not perpetuate the old libels and the hackneyed caricatures. (26)

These conciliatory utterances are exactly the type that Hurston is at pains to contest. Hurston is of the opinion that the black "literati who praise all Nordic creations on Negroes" do so out of their own inexcusable and unconfessed ignorance of the black masses, particularly those from the rural South. This point vividly illustrates the incommensurable class positions that often divided the vocal black elite from their silenced mass counterparts. Hurston's "truth" of the matter, as the *Afro-American* reports it, is that "Negro leaders who champion the Negro's cause at so much per champ don't know the Negro themselves. . . . the Harlem literati did not know anything about the religion of the deep South themselves, but rather than reveal their ignorance they climbed upon the band wagon and blew their horns" ("Too Much Pampering" 1930). Locke and Brown's assertions that Stepin Fetchit's character in *Hearts in Dixie* "is as true as instinct itself, a vital projection of the folk manner, a real child of the folk spirit" (26) voice an essentialist view that could easily have emanated from bigoted white writers and thus lends added weight to Hurston's concern over black intellectuals' endorsement of white writers' ventriloquizing of blackness. The issue that Hurston raises and that Locke and Brown unwittingly authorize is the unstated power dynamic of this racial ventriloquism that functions at once to perpetuate the unequal and inferior position of blacks and to reify blacks as objects of white dramatists' "privileged discourse on race" (hooks 1984, 12).

Still, Locke and Brown's desire to find redeeming qualities in these problematic texts must be seen as an earnest effort to account for the films' enormous popularity among black audiences, both the masses and the elites. More important is the authors' ability to identify sites of specular pleasure for black audiences in their yearnings for attractive screen images with which to identify. Locke and Brown locate such points of pleasurable suture in the performance styles and vitality of the black actors rather than in the narratives that flow from the creative imagination of the white writers and producers. This privileging of performance over textuality is clearly communicated in their statement that "unfortunately *Hallelujah* relies heavily on the usual claptrap. . . . As this comes from Hollywood, we should probably be resigned to the trick plotting; to the coincidences such as the accidental death of the brother, the clouds at the right moment in Zeke's conversion; to the silliness of waiting for a husband to come home before eloping noisily out a back window, although the husband has been away at work all day. . . . To the Elmer Gantryism crudely overlaid with a poorly popularized Freud. We resign ourselves to a great deal, hoping that the milieu will be permitted to show, without too drastic an alteration" (27–28). As they hold up *Hallelujah*'s obvious narrative flaws to rigorous scrutiny, we see that Locke and Brown have not sublimated their critical faculties to a one-dimensional celebratory discourse aimed at vaunting black performers' achievements above all other considerations. When we compare such measured praise as this to the lack of critical reflection by most white critics toward *The Birth of a Nation,* we can better appreciate the spirit of integrity motivating this enunciation of black accommodationist film discourse. It is important also to note that Locke and Brown did not engage in blanket statements of praise for all the black actors involved in these films. For instance, they did not see transcendent portrayals in the acting of Nina Mae McKinney and William Fountaine. As for these performers' contributions, Locke and Brown state: "The more obvious type acting of Miss McKinney as Chick and of William Fountaine as Hotshot, siren and villain respectively in the piece, furnishes no such folk values as the nuances of some of the other characters. . . . Chick is too consciously arch, Zeke seems too determined to speak dialect as the years have mistaught us that it should be spoken" (28). Even with these complaints, Brown and Locke find recuperative elements in the work. Of *Hallelujah,* they conclude: "Even so, *Hallelujah* is important. Its pioneering, its very failures, promises a great deal" (29). For *Hearts in Dixie,* they claim that it "is the truest pictorialization of Negro life to date" (26). As we shall discover, however, in 1934, Brown's searing critique of *Imitation of Life* demonstrates an unwillingness to condone the ventriloquizing discourse of one prominent white writer's view of black subjectivity. Nonetheless "Folk Values in a New Medium" marks an important intellectual contribution to the corpus of film criticism in the thirties.

From a survey of the accommodationist tracts, it becomes apparent that most lack the scope and nuanced discussions that we find in Locke and Brown's essay. This does not mean that most were devoid of critical appraisals. On the contrary. The main difference is that many are journalistic in nature and often one-dimensional in scope, typified by a singularity of emphasis on either negative or positive responses to a specific film issue. Mostly, the overriding theme is that of assimilation to the Hollywood mainstream. It is necessary at this point to emphasize the important role of journalistic muckraking in this program of cultural integration. Alongside the discourses of celebrity fandom and film promotion are exposé and muckraking aimed at revealing the unfair obstacles and deterrents to wider black participation in mainstream cultural productions. In addition, this accommodationist commentary devotes considerable ink to covering the race films produced by the interracial independents and their willingness to depart from the all-black musical ghetto of Hollywood's black-cast films.

The Promotional Discourse and the Interracial Independents

Notwithstanding the critical acclaim that *Hallelujah* and *Hearts in Dixie* met with in the black press in 1929 and 1930, African Americans still constituted a phantom audience for Hollywood's czars. That the black press was routinely refused advance screening privileges ("Race Press Ignored" 1934) attests to this de facto invisibility. With the necessary application of public pressure by the black press, there were exceptions to this rule. The clear message, nonetheless, is that for the "big film interests," it was enough that black performers—Stepin Fetchit, Louise Beavers, Hattie McDaniel, and Bill "Bojangles" Robinson—could draw black audiences through the lure of their bit parts as servants and comic relief in white-cast films. Until the 1934 premiere of *Imitation of Life*, Hollywood virtually ignored this large segment of its filmgoing public. Responding to this, the black press consciously focused a pragmatic gaze on Hollywood's mainstream films, with or without black performers, and in so doing, the press by and large became a shadow auxiliary of Hollywood's promotional machine. In fact, the newspaper reviews and commentary fashioned a hybrid discourse marked by a bricolage of individual critics' remarks and information lifted from Hollywood press releases (Miller 1934b).[11]

While a retrospective view of the black press's promotional boosterism finds much to question, especially regarding issues of black celebrity, it must be recalled that the black press was founded on a principle of protecting and promoting its vested interest in the accomplishments of African Americans (Buchanan 1968, 7). This tactic was necessary in view of the mainstream white media's historical practice of demonizing and ridiculing the African American community.[12] Boosterism thus became a counternarrative strategy in the press's enthusiastic coverage of black actors who succeeded in crossing the color line in Hollywood, no matter the demeaning and straitjacketed character of the stereotypical roles. Typical of the often tortured logic that failed sufficiently to problematize Hollywood's plethora of black stereotypes is the 12 March 1938 *New-Age Dispatch* article "Sign Noted L.A. Screen Artist for MGM Picture." From a Negro Press Bureau byline comes the following:

> The scene of studio activity this week of a necessity, shifts to the gigantic film making city, called Metro-Goldwyn-Mayer studios. Observe, how-

ever, the scene shifter is concerned only with that activity that shows films
using sepia artists, bit players or extras. . . . No mention was given at the
time of news of the signing of Lillian Yarbo, Clinton Rosemond, Clarence
Muse or Libby Taylor as to what the story was all about. However, the
Negro Press Bureau correspondent learned that it was to be produced from
story material based almost on the same idea as the much discussed and
never produced "Gone With The Wind" tale. . . . The signing of Miss
Yarbo . . . followed a long search for a capable colored girl . . . to play the
exciting and difficult role of the "Topsy"-like character in the story. . . .
Libby Taylor . . . was signed for the important "mammy" role. ("Sign
Noted" 1938, 3)

In prefacing, with a positive slant, news that the black actors would be
repeating the old stereotypes, the author—the "scene shifter"—praises
them for securing enviable contracts with MGM. At the same time, the
"scene shifter" primes his readers for a positive reception of this untitled
southern-sympathizing film. Further, by characterizing the formulaic
roles as "difficult" and "important," the writer assists in foreclosing critical avenues of receptivity that might otherwise diminish the individual
stars' credibility with their adoring fans.

A 1935 *Pittsburgh Courier* review of Fox's *The Little Colonel* performs a
similar apologist or damage control function for Bill "Bojangles" Robinson and other black cast members in that plantation drama. Representing a slight departure from the foregoing example is Bernice Patton's
"Bojangles Teamed Up with Shirley" article. Published by the *Courier* on
16 February 1935, this article does manage to interject a bit of critical, if
unintended, distance: "The picturesque filmization portraying the characteristics and mannerisms of Dixie, in her historic seventies, revived the
ironic memories of the staid, old Confederacy, and the Union causing the
audience to be lavish in its tumult of applause." Only Patton's use of
the term "ironic" gives her review a tinge of critical awareness. As she
develops the review further, however, we see that she is equally as compromised in her acceptance of these portrayals as is the Negro Press
Bureau's writer "the scene shifter." Patton's assessments of the individual
performers and their respective roles all but undermine any previous urge
to complicate the film's racist narrative. Rather, Patton's uncritical celebration of the stars and matters of performance betrays her own starstruck blinders.

Lionel Barrymore, versatile artist of the cinema gives a grand characterization of the aristocratic, old confederate Colonel Lloyd, who hates his Yankee son-in-law Jack Sherman. . . . To this union comes pretty, little Shirley Temple, whose laughing eyes and bouncing curls tends to temper the increditable [*sic*] scorn of her grandfather Colonel Lloyd. . . . Bill Robinson, known as Walker, the high class man of all chores in Barrymore's mansion, gives a fine performance. . . . The lovable Mom Beck role is that of the screen's most famous mammy character, Hattie McDaniel, who is the hilarious comedienne of the film . . . and makes her big hit with the novel "Pink Story," which is followed by Shirley's elaborate pink party in technicolor. (Patton 1935a, 9)

Although it was the *Courier* that gave headline news coverage to Hollywood studios' systematic denial of advance screening privileges to the black press months earlier, perhaps the fact that Patton was granted this privilege after the paper's exposé accounts for her glowing review. That she opens her article with an ingratiating genuflection to Hollywood suggests this compromise. "Courtesying my paper, The Pittsburgh Courier," she writes, "I was invited at the initial showing: in order to watch the dramatic unfolding of Annie Fellows Johnson's famous classic." It seems that Hollywood rightly perceived that the best way to circumvent the *Courier*'s negative publicity of its discriminatory promotional practices was simply to grant that "squeaky wheel" a token oiling. Following Hollywood's strategic retreat before the *Courier*'s public pressure, the paper's subsequent film reviews characteristically include some reference to its advance screening privilege in the body of its review texts. In addition, Patton's reviews uniformly adopt a treacly tone of praise and solicitude for the Hollywood product, as evidenced in her concluding assessment of a frenzied baptismal scene in *The Little Colonel:* "The public," Patton continues, "will appreciate this scene because it is void of false interpretation. Sincerity reigns throughout the sequence: therefore, 12,000,000 Negroes will be pleased." Understatement, as we can see, is not Patton's particular forte.

Two weeks later, the *Courier* deployed a prominent subheading to emphasize its newfound chumminess with Hollywood's publicity departments. In a review of the Edward G. Robinson film vehicle *The Whole Town's Talking*, the subhead reads, "Courier's Hollywood Correspondent Invited to Glamorous Preview of New Cinema Triumph."

Remarkably, in this review, headlined "Edward G. Robinson's 'Tops' in Columbia's Latest Film, 'The Whole Town's Talking,'" the potential black audience for this mainstream film has miraculously expanded to thirteen million. Again, Patton is the reviewer, and she writes: "Inasmuch as thirteen million Edward G. Robinson fans of African descent clamor to see his spectacular 'hits,' the Columbia Studio invited me to review the picture for America's best weekly, The Pittsburgh Courier." Even without the cause of a black performer to champion, Patton's and the *Courier*'s desire to cement their friendly rapport with Hollywood while celebrating the paper is stark. More to the point is Patton's eagerness to exchange honest appraisal for self-censorship to protect her honorary inclusion in this arena of white privilege. Underscoring this tendency are her disingenuous remarks to black performers, critics, and spectators. On the release of *Imitation of Life,* she admonished the black community: "Don't spoil your economic advantages and possibilities in the movies by intolerant criticism" (Patton 1934). Having accepted the compromising terms of its insider status, the *Courier* appears determined not to jeopardize it with "intolerant criticism." The *Courier*'s new position as Hollywood's publicity auxiliary is revealed further by the number of promotional film stills it features in its regular two-page "Stage, Screen, Drama, Music" section. The edition containing the review of the Edward G. Robinson film features among its many film stills one of Shirley Temple and Bill "Bojangles" Robinson, locked arm in arm, performing a can't-miss audience pleaser, "the famous Bo's steps" (10).

By 1937, the *Courier* flaunted its insider status with Hollywood by making its ability to secure advance previews fodder for its entertainment news headlines. In its entertainment section, rechristened "Stage and Screen," the banner headline for 28 August 1937 reads, "Courier Critic Pre-views Mixed Cast Film: Lautier Says 'One Mile from Heaven' Opens New Field." This article by Louis Lautier is a review of Twentieth Century Fox's mixed-race film *One Mile from Heaven,* and it presents a familiar refrain of the accommodationist dicta—Hollywood's changing attitude toward blacks in the cinema. The film is a melodramatic tale of a white reporter's involvement in the affairs of a black woman who attempts to raise a white child.[13] Absent the need to amplify the importance of black performers' bit parts, this review can legitimately tout the performances of the film's black supporting cast members, Fredi Washington and Bill "Bojangles" Robinson. The prominence of these black actors in this mainstream film emboldens Lautier to lead off his review with an optimistic prelude: "Hollywood is beginning to catch on, if 'One Mile From Heaven,' the Twentieth Century-Fox production is any criterion. It is the first American made picture with a mixed cast in which there is not only no objectionable dialogue from the viewpoint of the colored movie-goer [but] the colored actors are decent, upstanding people" (Lautier 1937, 8).

> The picture presents a sociological drama. It may be described as a forthright account of actual cases which find their way to the juvenile courts. The narrative is simple. Bill Robinson and Fredi Washington give performances deserving commendation. The story describes a colored seamstress, who is rearing a white child. Quite accidentally the child becomes an object of curiosity when three male newspaper reporters play a trick on a girl who is assigned to cover the courts. (8)

As Hollywood attempted to ensure its "universal" relevance and protect its profitability during the political and economic upheavals of the depression era, it clearly turned to more socially relevant topics. As a consequence, the films spanned the representational spectrum from Capraesque populism to the "urban nightmare" social issue movies typified by Warner Brothers' crime and gangster films (P. Cook 1992, 85).[14] Thus Lautier's commentary responds to Hollywood's furtive engagement with the pressing social issues of the day via its new urban crime genres. That Lautier finds much to commend in the fact that the usual white-inflected black dialect has been omitted, and that the black characters are permitted an atypical level of human dignity in a Hollywood film, is revealing of black spectators' yearnings and frustration regarding their cinematic images. For Lautier, who seems to be taking note of what might be considered the studios' "symbiotic relation to contemporary events as circulated in a sensational press" (Cook 1992, 85), *One Mile from Heaven*, as "a sociological drama," finally signals a redirection of Hollywood's attitude about race. Clearly, he hopes that Hollywood possesses the will to treat matters of race as sympathetically or realistically as it treated class issues in the new sociological approach to cinema.

In the main, the review is heavy on plot summary with perfunctory accolades for the black cast at its end. In a bit of semiotic condensation, Lautier's review is accompanied by a still of black actor Clinton Rosemond, looking terrified as three sets of white hands are clasped to his shirt and suspenders as if to drag him off to a lynching. The photo is a promotional still for the Warner Brothers' film *They Won't Forget.* The caption below the photo reads, "Clinton Rosemond, veteran actor, whose performance in the sensational new Deep South anti-lynching film, 'They Won't Forget,' produced by Warner Brothers has skyrocketed him to stardom" ("Stardom" 1937). Here is another mixed-cast film in which a black performer, Rosemond, plays more than a bit part. Though his character is a stock menial type, his centrality to, and high visibility in, the narrative represents a significant departure from most establishment films featuring African American characters. Hollywood's production of these socially conscious dramas is what drives Lautier's hope that "Hollywood is beginning to catch on." With Lautier's review and the Rosemond still, one can imagine that the *Courier*'s readers could share in that optimistic view.

As the accommodationist black press's ties to Hollywood strengthened, promoting and reviewing films were not the limit of the papers' service to the industry. They also helped the studios condition audiences' expectations and acceptance of Hollywood's latest trends. One clear example of this phenomenon can be seen in a 9 April 1933 *California New-Age Dispatch* article wherein readers are primed for a diminution of the famed happy-ending fade-out kiss. No doubt Hollywood saw this convention as losing some of its cachet with Depression-era audiences less inclined to such anachronistic narrative closures. The article "No More Kiss! Hero Loses Reward" reports on "a survey completed in Hollywood" that discloses news "that screen kisses have gone out of fashion." We learn from an inside source, "veteran director" Alfred E. Green, that "a new cinema trend is in the making." Green is quoted as saying, "not long ago ... Every picture with a happy ending closed with the hero kissing the heroine. But now we have the audience do it—in its imagination. That seems to be what the public wants." Frank Capra is named as the force behind this development. Audiences are encouraged to look for this new trend in such films as *Lost Horizon, Swing High, Swing Low,* and *Love on the Run.* Later that year, the *Dispatch* says that "big stories" over big budgets are the latest studio trend ("Big Pictures Now Built on Great Stories" 1937). This November article also prepares audience-readers for lower-budget films, citing insiders as the source of this privileged information, which lucky *Dispatch* readers are receiving in advance:

Producers juggling million-dollar budgets have ceased attempting to out-
shine one another with lavish sets and multitudes of extras, and are insisting instead that their big pictures have strong, dramatic story value. . . .
"Wells Fargo," which Producer-Director Frank Lloyd is making for Paramount . . . [has] big sets, big scenes, but because Lloyd is emphasizing the
gripping story of his subject, the picture is hailed as the greatest the director of "Calvacade" and "Mutiny on the Bounty" has produced. ("Big Pictures" 1937)

Other studio films adopting this more cost-effective yet quality-
conscious production design are specified in the article as well, namely,
The Buccaneer, Ebb Tide, Robin Hood, and *Marco Polo.* What is interesting is that the Depression-era economy driving this financial scale-back
is not even hinted at in these articles. As a consequence, the industry's
obvious capitulation to the nation's new downward-spiraling economy
gets effaced, and instead Hollywood is portrayed as altruistically responding to audience demand as opposed to depressed market forces.
The black press willingly assists Hollywood in recasting itself as a cultural benefactor giving the public what it wants, as in the no-more-kisses
"trend," and in giving the public what it needs, as in "big stories" often
based on great literature. Clearly, the *Dispatch*'s and the *Courier*'s promotional methods of currying favor with Hollywood and the film exhibitors provide us with choice examples of the compromising and self-
serving aspects of the accommodationist discourse.

The white-dominated independents who produced black cast films for
the "race" market benefited even more from promotional liaisons with
the black press because the press's readership constituted the independents' niche market. This operational symbiosis is predicated on a mutuality of benefit. The press's promotional discourse for the race market
films was effective and complete. The race films industry benefited from
the black press's extensive coverage of its products from preproduction on
through exhibition bookings. And the counter or alternative programming imperatives of the race market industry benefited black audiences
because they satisfied black spectators' desires for black-themed dramas
overshadowed by a glut of big-budget, high-profile musicals and comedies. This is the context for the black press's largely favorable predisposition to these B-level films. Another indication of the independents' fer-

vent pursuit of black critical endorsement for their films can be ascertained in correspondence circulated among Dudley Murphy, director of the film *The Emperor Jones*, NAACP executive secretary Walter White, and *Courier* critic Louise Lautier. Actually, it is important to acknowledge that black press endorsements of race films were not always automatic. In October 1933 Murphy sought White's help "to overcome the film's adverse publicity" in most of the black press. What is particularly interesting in Murphy's letter is that he requests, and evidently expects, White's cooperation even though he, Murphy, was uncertain as to whether White had seen the film. Murphy attempts to rationalize his own failure to provide a screening of the film for White (or other African Americans) in this less-than-convincing manner:

> Due to the necessity of finishing the picture quickly and an advancement of the showing date, I was unable to contact you before we released the film, which I *should liked* to have done [italics mine]. But I would appreciate it if you saw fit to recommend the film as a sincere work of art and help us overcome some adverse criticism we have received from some of the editors of colored papers. (Murphy 1933)

It is doubtful that such a request, sight unseen, would be made of white film critics or ethnic community leaders responsible for scrutinizing and recommending films containing questionable images of their groups. This suggests either that Murphy was aware of White's favorable disposition toward the play version or that he took black support for granted. In any case, it is true that White liked and supported *The Emperor Jones* in both play and film forms. In fact, before Murphy's letter, White had received a request from the film's producer, John Krimsky, asking for the NAACP's help in getting the film into southern film theaters. In communicating this request to the NAACP's executive director Roy Wilkins, White seems amenable to the idea. The correspondence indicates that White is willing to embark on a letter-writing campaign to urge local theaters in the South to book the film, and apparently the NAACP created a press release or news story surrounding this issue. In deferring the final word to Wilkins, White writes: "I don't know whether we can get that in the story, but I leave it to your judgement. Will you send a marked copy of the story to Mr. Krimsky, 509 Madison Avenue?" (W. White 1933b). When writer Louis Lautier sought guidance from White as to what the appropriate response to the film's frequent use of the word "nigger" should be, White's reply, by telegraph, was this: "Have not seen film of Emperor Jones yet. Saw play several times—Use of nigger was logical as that is precisely language which characters in those circumstances would have used—Prefer not being quoted until I have opportunity see film" (W. White 1933a).

Although Lautier's communiqué to White suggests a monolithic black party line on the issue of black cinematic representations, the fact that Murphy seeks to subvert negative black press coverage of the film demonstrates otherwise. And White's desire not to be quoted immediately suggests his own reservations about the organization's ability to achieve black consensus on this controversial film as well. However, these letters do demonstrate how black civil rights organizations and black press writers attempted to work together to foster what they considered acceptable images of the black cinematic subject. More to the point is that through these communiqués, we can better understand how the white independents perceived the crucial mediating function of these "captains of black consciousness" between their product and the black film audiences.[15]

Although few of these so-called "race films" received outright bad reviews or recommendations of boycotts, it would be a mistake to presume that they all enjoyed unqualified endorsements, as is revealed by the necessity for the studio to lobby black support for the *Emperor Jones* film. Frequently these films' technical problems and narrative limitations were pointed out to readers who had become quite sophisticated film consumers after decades of habituation to Hollywood's high technical and narrative production values. Characteristic of the frequent mixed reviews of independent white-controlled films appearing in the black press are Lawrence La Mar's reviews of Dixie National's film *Harlem on the Prairie* and Million Dollar Productions' *Life Goes On,* published in the 4 December 1937 edition of the *Dispatch.* Even though La Mar decides that *Harlem on the Prairie* "happily escapes the usual run of all-Negro cast films" and that the "production triumphs in that it presents a Western horse opera in an altogether different manner," he nonetheless criticizes the fact that "there is not much story. . . . And, likewise there was an insufficiency of settings" (La Mar 1937, 1). Regardless of these shortcomings, La Mar states: "Where these narrative necessities were obviously missing, the novelty of the story settings and the portrayals turned in by superb Negro screen players, hardly made it matter. Fine singing, rollicksome comedy and old-fashioned villainy and nick-of-time heroic rescuings" were sufficiently handled that La Mar did deliver an overall favorable recommendation for this film.

Life Goes On, the other film reviewed by La Mar, receives special accolades because it presents one of the few dramatic renderings of a black-themed narrative. After saluting the production team for assembling a fine cast (most notably the film's star, Louise Beavers, who was now a bona fide star after her appearance in the acclaimed mainstream film *Imitation of Life*), La Mar discusses the film's most consequential features:

> Phil Dunham developed a remarkable vehicle to bring to the screen and a doubting public that Negro actors were less capable of playing highly dramatic roles with any degree of artistic ease. The screen story concerns itself about a widowed mother and her two small sons, which she is compelled to rear without a helpmeet. The problems recounted in the film story are definitely true to life. Any of a number of Negro mothers will easily recognize the heartrending problems encountered by this heroic, self-sacrificing mother for her 2 sons. . . . Of course, there is some stealing, some gambling and a slaying in the picture, it wouldn't be real life drama without it. (1)

For La Mar, the single most impressive aspect that elevates *Life Goes On* from "the usual run of all-Negro films" is a fealty to dramatic realism or urban naturalism. He commends the white filmmakers for eschewing the "superfluous tear jerking scenes," which otherwise would have relegated the film to an unsatisfactory parodic version of an overwrought Hollywood melodrama. That "a number of Negro mothers" could easily identify with Beavers's character and her situation imparted to the film a vital sense of verisimilitude, at least in La Mar's estimation. In anticipation of the adverse reaction to the film's black-on-black violence, La Mar maintains that the underworld elements that enliven the otherwise uneventful saga are not gratuitous but necessary to the narrative's internal logic. As he describes it: "Make no mistake, this film production does not go to the other extreme of satisfying the Negro theatre public by merely inserting scenes and action which might appear pleasing to it" (1). La Mar refuses to assume the role of moralizing censor against the film's violence or its depictions of life's seamier sides. More to the point is his conviction that the film is meritorious precisely because it refuses to pander to audiences' expectation of gratuitous violence and unmotivated action scenes. His goal is to acclimatize readers to a new form of black cinematic expression so as to advance the cause of a quiet drama like *Life Goes On,* and in the process to encourage similar works in the future.

Indicative of the black press's affirmative stance toward the race films produced during this era are articles in the *New York Age,* the *Dispatch,* and the *Courier.* W. E. Clark's 23 May 1931 *New York Age* review of *The Exile* states: "Oscar Micheaux's first talking picture, 'The Exile,' was presented to a capacity audience at the Lafayette Theatre last Saturday. While it has many obvious faults, it is by far the best picture Mr. Micheaux ever turned out" (Clark 1931, 6). The *Dispatch* carried a preproduction review of the 1937 black-cast film *Bargain with Bullets,* published on 23 July 1937. It also refers to Ralph Cooper's and Million Dollar Production's previous hit film, *Dark Manhattan.* Another *Dispatch* article, entitled "Begins Work on New All Colored Cast Picture," promotes Million Dollar's ambitious plans to produce "twelve pictures a year." It was particularly important that the firm promised to produce other films outside the gangster genre. The *Dispatch* reports, "Musicals, comedies and adventure films will also be produced, not only giving the Negro fan a new type of show fare but furnishing more regular employment to hundreds of colored players. In the course of time, technicians, artisans, mechanics, modistes, hair-dressers and many other classes will be benefitted by this new pioneering into the business world by Negroes" ("Begins Work" 1937, 4). In the following month, the *Dispatch* reported, "'Bargain with Bullets' Finished." On 11 September 1937 the *Dispatch* ran "'Bargain with Bullets' to Premiere at Lincoln Theatre" (4). This headline view delineates the *Dispatch*'s complete coverage of Million Dollar's *Bargain with Bullets* and is exemplary of the black press's full promotional cycle at work, from the film's announcement, to completion, to exhibition and beyond.

As it happens, *Bargain with Bullets* was a successful film. Andy Razaf, one of the most popular and prolific African American songsmiths of the twenties and thirties,[16] who also was a frequent entertainment critic for the *Pittsburgh Courier,* reviewed the film. Razaf found broader demythologizing potential in *Bargain.* The film was special for Razaf because it contravened Hollywood's depictions of Prohibition's and the numbers rackets' underworld as the singular domain of white gangsters. He notes that "the Million Dollar Production, Inc., has, at last, given the public something new—a real honest-to-goodness-big shot-colored gangster, killer and hi-jacker! We had always thought that our group was a flop in this particular field, but evidently, we haven't been reading the papers. What's more the production reveals that the New York police department is all colored and even when this dusky public enemy number one walks his last mile, nary a pale face guard, turn-key nor official can be seen! There are other innovations, but why spoil it by telling you" (Razaf 1937, 8). While Razaf's jocularity regarding the film's creative license in depicting the racial character of New York's police department is understood, it is true that black bootleggers and racketeers were operating in Harlem at the height of the Prohibition era. In fact, New York's black papers routinely ran editorials denouncing this criminal element and even spearheaded clean-up campaigns with community leaders in an attempt to rid the city of that particular scourge.[17] Razaf is clearly taking an impish delight in the broadening out of black character archetypes in Million Dollar's cinematic treatment of this all too unfortunate reality. In the context of Warner Brothers' successful exploitation of actual newspaper coverage of white organized crime for its wildly popular crime and gangster genre, Razaf's humor is grounded in the ethos of the times.

Another *Courier* article that celebrates the black crime film genre is Faye Jackson's flattering review-interview with Edna Harris, the female lead in Grand National's 1937 film *Spirit of Youth,* costarring the young heavyweight boxing champion Joe Louis. The popular actor Clarence Muse was one of the film's black producers. As with the promotional pieces for Hollywood, these articles on the activities of the independents were accompanied by stills from the black-cast films, publicity shots of contract signings with black performers and white company heads, and promotional photos depicting these interracial partnerships. It is important that we consider the signification of these photographs because they are historical documentation revealing that black audiences were apprised of the fact that white principals were the controlling forces behind these race films.[18] In view of the black audiences' position of dependence on white Hollywood products for most of their specular pleasures, their acceptance of the white power structure behind the race films industry is wholly consistent. Any resentment associated with the problem of the white independents' control over black film images had to be weighed against the realization that this particular white-dominated film sector was after all catering to the black community's demand for black cinematic heroes and heroines in leading roles. That the films were little

Principals of black-cast film *Life Goes On*, which typified the race film industry's interracial collaboration between white producers and black talent. *California New Age Dispatch*, 1938.

more than poor imitations of Hollywood films was apparently a trade-off that the accommodationist critics and black audiences could accept, especially when contrasted with mainstream films' more demeaning, one-dimensional black representations. As one black critic put it: "We're just like every other group, we like to see our friends and neighbors on the [screen]. We feel they're our own" (Camera Eye 1934c). And with the support of the black press, the relationship between the race films producers and black spectators sufficed for years.

Muckraking and Exposé in the Accommodationist Discourse

As the black press's accommodationist discourse emerged through the thirties, the writers' tenuous rapproachment with Hollywood was not restricted to a docile acceptance of the industry's status quo on the race question. This era, we must recall, is defined by race and class antagonisms that permeated all strata of American civil society.[19] Tensions erupted into lethal worker strikes, racial confrontations, and cultural standoffs.[20] While the bulk of the radical and militant literature and pamphleteering issued from the Communist front organizations allied with the black working classes, the fiscally conservative black press mainstream also engaged in journalistic muckraking and negative exposés when the need arose. It is to the black press's accommodationist mainstream and their particular brand of investigative critiques that we now turn. Characteristic of this mode are muckraking revelations about specific episodes of the dominant film industry's discriminatory practices. Whereas they may not exactly constitute probing analyses of endemic or structural racism, inferences along these lines can certainly be adduced from the articles when the individual criticisms are juxtaposed. In addition, the exposés that center on individual star personalities function to complicate the usual star discourse inasmuch as damaging news comes to supplant, for the most part, the usual hagiographic slant.

Taking the lead in this regard is the *Pittsburgh Courier,* with an array of these negative publicity stories. The paper's 15 December 1934 exposé of the "big film interests'" blatant exclusions of black reporters from standard media preview screenings of new film releases is one of the earliest and most trenchant. The eye-catching headline story that led the edition's "Stage and Screen" entertainment section was entitled "Race Press Ignored by Big Film Interests." An earlier report appearing in the *New York Age* provides some necessary insight and background information that helps bring the later *Courier* coverage into sharper relief. The *Age* article "'Green Pastures' Not Liked by Negroes" reveals the financial motivations behind white producer-promoters' callous disregard for black audiences, who rejected the demeaning portrayals of their group by staying away from the performances. In view of the play's enormous popularity with white audiences, which resulted in the production being held over for an entire year's run, the theater owners concluded that black patronage was inconsequential.

All the financial results have been achieved without the aid of colored patronage, says J. Robie, general publicity agent for Laurence Rivers, the producer. Mr. Robie stated to a representative of The Age that colored people did not like the show, and that there [was] an average of not more than half a dozen colored persons at each performance. . . . This experience

caused him to conclude that the show was unpopular in Harlem, and that
the patronage did not warrant the continuance of the advertising. (" 'Green
Pastures' Not Liked" 1931)

There is an obvious absence in this discussion. At no time does the
article account for black audiences' justified refusal to patronize the film
because of discriminatory seating practices that segregated the black patrons in the least-desirable seating areas; neither does it mention the
defamatory nature of the production. In a straight reportorial style that
hews to certain facts while omitting others, the article does manage to
indicate the loss of advertising revenues sustained by New York's black
newspapers. At *Green Pasture*'s opening, play producers spent fifty dollars per week for thirty-nine weeks in ads with the black press (6). Because black patronage failed to produce adequate returns on the investment, the ads were dropped. It is difficult to ascertain the paper's attitude
toward this issue. Does it assess blame in this case, and if so, is blame
directed toward the audience or the producers? Because the *Age* emphasizes the loss of advertising revenues associated with *Green Pastures* while
omitting any explanation that might account for the lack of black patronage, it is fair to surmise that the article's main purpose was to underscore the unanticipated financial havoc the boycott was wreaking on the
black press. Despite this glaring lack, the article does relay essential
information, further evidence pointing to the conflictual nature of the
class interests among the black elites who produced the newspapers and
the masses who consumed them. Regardless of the play's qualified endorsement by members of the black literati, as we have already seen, we
are apprised here that the masses, for whatever reason, did not share that
view and stayed away from the production in droves. Again, it could be
that in balancing the high prices of theater seats against white theater's
segregated seating practices, black audiences opted to forgo the certain
humiliation that awaited them only to experience a play that ridiculed
and insulted them. But we get no sense of these complicating factors in
the *Age* article, factors that could shed light on why *Green Pastures* was
"not liked by Negroes."

Returning now to the *Courier*'s exposé of big film interests' flagrant
bias against the black press regarding courtesy film screenings for newspapers, there are resonances in the two situations that have to do with
white production companies' practice of denying the black press a cut of

their advertising revenues. What complicates a one-to-one correspondence in the two episodes, however, is the fact that film screenings do not present the same problems in terms of seating practices. Films, unlike live stage shows, eliminate this racially charged aspect of accommodating racially mixed audiences. The difference is that multiple prints of films mean that simultaneous screenings can occur in both the black and white communities. Yet we learn that the major film studios and exhibitors still excluded this lucrative audience and its press representatives from this important stage of a film's overall market potential. Decrying this act of discrimination in its 15 December 1934 article entitled "Race Press Ignored by Big Film Interests," the *Courier* reveals:

> Universal Studios' publicity department was exceedingly negative this week toward the Negro press agents as an attempt was made to secure press courtesies for the world's premiere of "Imitation of Life" featuring Louise Beavers, Fredi Washington, Little Sebe Hendricks, Dorothy Black and a host of colored players. "We have nothing for the Negro press on the first night," director John Leroy Johnson relayed from his office when a request was made of him for tickets to the show. "The Negro Press means nothing to us," came the illuminating reply from Hollywood Pantages theatre publicity officials. We're not interested, the studio ought to be. (9)

That this incident occurred at the height of the depression era, with the obvious economic implications, is telling indeed. The arrogance of the white firms' representatives testifies to the primacy of white chauvinists' attitudes in Hollywood that were not even restrained or tempered to ensure better box office potential in the midst of a depressed economy.

On a different register, it is notable that the article delivers less than is suggested by its headline, "Race Press Ignored by Big Film Interests." Though this headline hints at industry-wide practices, the article limits its damaging probe to incidents involving one film, a film of obvious and immediate interest because of its sizable black cast. Nonetheless the article's import obtains synecdochically, especially when we factor in the follow-the-leader mentality of the film industry in general, and on race matters in particular. Rather than pursue a full-scale investigation of Hollywood's institutional racist practices, this article turns a questioning eye toward one of the leading black performers in the film, popular actress Louise Beavers.

In its efforts to seek an alternative means of sharing in this film's promotional budget, doubtless expected to be significant because of its obvious crossover appeal (among white and black audiences), the *Courier* expressed its feeling of being doubly injured by the starring black performer's rebuff of its desire for a special promotional arrangement. It presents Beavers as a female Machiavellian lout whose self-centered actions and ingratitude toward her supportive black fans in this matter revealed her lack of race consciousness and solidarity. At the same time, the paper strikes out against other black performers viewed as placing their individual interests above the group's aspirations. Though accepting that "the motion picture industry on the West Coast is a source of livelihood for scores of Negroes," the *Courier* abhors performers' apparent ingratitude concerning the black press's enormous contribution to their stardom. Exacerbating this situation is the press's convenient distaste for the performers' perpetuation of anachronistic characterizations of black reality. It is suggested that Beavers is guilty on both fronts. In addition, the article impugns her as complicit with the big film interests:

> Echoing the same policy with alarming candor, Miss Louise Beavers . . . a black performer said: "I'm getting a lot of publicity and I'm not worried about it." . . . Negro players, after being subjected to the usual exigencies of the profession (which is certainly not confined to them as a group and is likewise endured by all who hope for an "upward" climb, one way or another)—often through caricature of their race—reach a modicum of success and find themselves in demand as a "type." ("Race Press Ignored" 1934)

The gist of this complaint is that racial sellouts are not an anomaly confined to the entertainment business. But most repugnant to the *Courier*, in this particular instance, is the fact that Beavers and others fail to acknowledge or appreciate how much of their success is purchased by the efforts of the black press.

> With very few exceptions, the performer never receives mention in the white press, and almost without exception he [or she] is portrayed as a "Mammy" or as an "uncle Tom," cutting the ante-bellum antics with which Negroes have for so long been associated. Consequently, [the] only plugging of any degree of dignity or self-respect is done by his own reporters and published in his own race papers that are not in the least considered by the agent or the studio or the theater in the so-called "pub-

licity budget." Despite these facts, however, the self-effacing race reporter, fully aware of the public interest in Negroes in motion pictures, and knowing the box office appeal they have in the theatres . . . to the tune of several million dollars a year, must by force of duty supply the necessary information his reading public demands. ("Race Press Ignored" 1934)

More than simply putting forward the case that black "stars" owed much of their celebrity to the black press, the article also sets out to save face with readers by deflecting criticism first from the paper, for not prevailing against the Hollywood blackout, and second from the paper's own cupidity in helping to popularize such undeserving actors as Beavers. In this connection, the article implicitly shifts blame for the stalemate onto readers themselves by explicitly chastising the readers for their seemingly insatiable demand for celebrity news and gossip that the press, against its better judgment, is obliged to meet. Although this approach does serve to illustrate the dilemma of the press, it also comports with Walter White's (1948) finding that the black press "of necessity remained more responsive to its readers' wishes than has any other." White attributes this necessity to the fact that the black press's revenue "from advertising has been microscopic. The result has been the perpetuation in the Negro press of personal journalism, with its advantages and disadvantages. . . . The Negro Press has been and is today the only large segment of American journalism whose major support comes from its readers rather than its advertisers" (209). In its exposé, the *Courier* emerges as stalwart defender of its readers' rights to know how Universal, Beavers, and others take the black audience for granted. More important, the article seems to take pride in divulging Beavers's pro-studio outspokenness, her failure to be accessible to her black audience, and her role in detracting from the community's goal of racial uplift. Although the press is right to remind forgetful performers that most are duly indebted to the black press for their cult of celebrity, the press fails to acknowledge its own culpability in the larger situation. They could have adequately criticized these actors for their eager acceptance of such demeaning roles from the beginning and been consistent about it. Instead, the press opted for its own brand of self-serving racial compromise that is at one with the charges it levels against Beavers and other race actors—that is, the securing of advertising revenues tainted by an implied acceptance and endorsement of films' damaging black stereotypes.

Another damning exposé of Louise Beavers appeared in a *New-Age Dispatch* article dated 12 February 1937. The article, "Louise Beavers Says Company Makes Movie, Trends Writer Says No," castigates the actress for her character's pro-slavery utterances in a Reconstruction-era film entitled *Rainbow on the River.* This article provides striking insights into issues of black reception via direct quotes from black spectators who routinely communicated their feelings to the press through letters to editors.

The article begins with editorial commentary from an unnamed press writer, but it draws much of its narrative impetus and rhetorical strength from comments submitted by a reader who voices objections to Beavers and her film from the vantage point of a noncritic. The reader identifies herself as a member of the community's elite, a college teacher, and as such she represents a top-down versus a bottom-up perspective on popular black spectatorship. Because she is a teacher, we can presume that she is intimately familiar with the viewing habits and preferences of black youth, which she alludes to in her letter. The letter thus provides a firsthand ethnographic account of the ambivalence black spectators experienced because of their divided loyalties between beloved black performers and the discomfiture caused by the bind of stereotypical performances. On the one hand, the article does object to Beavers's expected acquiescence to the racist demands of her profession. But on the other, like the *Courier* article mentioned earlier, the *Dispatch* article draws the line at Beavers's outspoken rationalizations. For the *Dispatch* editors, the issue turns on this incommensurability:

> We do not object to Miss Beavers' viewpoint, for we would naturally expect that to be colored by the fact that she is directly concerned because of her livelihood. . . . We have not yet seen Miss Beavers in her latest picture, "Rainbow on the River," but members of our family have, and we can tell Miss Beavers right here that while her acting is said to be excellent, the role she plays is certainly not appreciated by our modern, high school colored girls and boys. We understand that she pleads in the picture that she wants to remain a slave, and that she shows every solicitation for the education of a little white boy, while she lets a little colored boy grow up in ignorance. Of course that is the script, and Miss Beavers is paid to do the acting, but we are mentioning it to show our well-liked star just how her roles register with her public. ("Louise Beavers" 1937)

The editors, like the schoolteacher they quote, clearly want to give Beavers the benefit of the doubt as to her own race loyalty. But both stress the difficulty they have in turning a blind eye to such an anachronistic and scandalous role. There is the suggestion that "modern" high school students are more critically aware of the mass media's growing influence and less easily manipulated by its sway. In trying to appeal to the actress's sense of racial duty, the article evokes an analogous circumstance involving the implied actor-audience contract, namely, that "white stars are very anxious to know how their public takes their roles." Obviously Beavers is being encouraged to be as solicitous of black public opinion. To that end, the article's tone shifts, "and if Miss Beavers is to remain popular, she must be like the white stars in this respect." And though the article does not begrudge Beavers her popularity with the white audiences to whom she caters, it takes the position that the actress would be well served to display a modicum of interest in or concern for the attitudes and desires of "her own race as well." At this point, the article gives way to excerpts from "a letter [by] Mrs. Carrie Pembrook, head of the Department of English of Lane College, Jackson Tennessee." As part of its "Changing the Movies" campaign, the *Dispatch* conducted a survey on the movies among its readership. Mrs. Pembrook responded:

> I believe that I speak for the race when I say that we feel personally affronted every time we see the coon hunting, dice-throwing scenes. We feel ashamed and disgusted when we see any stalwart man playing a frightened, cringing role. It is insulting to the race to show only the mammy type of woman. This type of woman is rarely given anything to do except hang clothes on a line in some rich lady's back yard, or chase small boys away from a dice game. . . . Will the general public ever get an idea of the "Souls of Black Folk" by the roles Negroes play in the movies? . . . We believe the present interpretation is faulty. ("Louise Beavers Says" 1937)

Pembrook's remarks convey well the sense of unending frustration that challenges and confounds black spectators seeking sites of identification or resistance (Diawara 1993b, 211), especially in Hollywood films of the thirties. Pembrook's castigation of the mammy stereotype is particularly salient here as Beavers is credited along with the studios with crafting the mammy prototype (Bogle 1989, 62).[21] Pembrook's call for cinematic reinscriptions of the "Souls of Black Folk," emphasizing the negated "higher aspirations or sensibilities of the race," leads her to proffer *Sanders of the River*, with Paul Robeson and Nina Mae McKinney, as a cinematic work that leans in the right direction. "I think that we generally appreciated the role given to Mr. Paul Robeson," Pembrook says. And while black spectators have found alternative sites of entry into mass-cultural products such as films, even through intentional misreadings of film narratives or through the circumscribed agency of the black screen performer, Pembrook informs us that this was hardly satisfactory.[22] As she puts it, "There is talent in the race, and we should like to see it used more fully. We believe that the present interpretation is faulty" ("Louise Beavers Says" 1937, 2). Ultimately, the attitude here is one of compromise. Beavers and other actors of stock black stereotypes are deemed entitled to earn a livelihood in Hollywood so long as they manifest their racial pride and solidarity off-screen when called on to do so. According to this logic, Beavers had failed miserably to separate the requirements of her public persona as film star from her private responsibility as member of an oppressed minority community. Adding further to Beavers's temporary ostracism in the black press was her dismissive attitude toward her black constituency, as reflected in the numerous unflattering quotes attributed to her that launched a good many black press missives against her.

In comparison, Earl J. Morris reveals in an "Exclusive to The Courier" that Bill "Bojangles" Robinson, another black film actor and purveyor of stereotypes, is indeed a "race man." The 31 July 1937 *Courier* article, "Morris Interviews 'Bojangles': Learns He Is Real Race Man," permits Robinson to negotiate a middle ground for himself that effectively deflects criticism of his Uncle Tom roles by "many who innocently feel," as Robinson explains it, "that I haven't my race at heart" (Morris 1937, 9). Robinson, cognizant of the immense chasm separating his Uncle Tom star persona from his self-presentation as a race man, refutes the conflation of the exigencies of his screen image with his personal racial politics. To charges of "Tomism," Robinson responds: "This is not true. I am a race man" (9). Morris, the writer-interviewer of the article, understands the need for some authenticating information if his exposé is to succeed in recasting the nation's foremost "Cool-Eyed Tom" into the potent image of a fearless race man. How does one transform "the Robinson figure . . . obviously the familiar contented slave, distinguished, however, because he was congenial, confident and very, very *cool*" (Bogle 1989, 46–50), into an emblem of New Negro achievement? For Morris, the matter was resolved easily enough:

> The great artist showed this writer . . . sufficient proof that he was a race man. Last year, Bill Robinson gave more than $16,000 to Negroes who were unfortunate. He is the man who established a signal light at a dangerous intersection in Richmond (his home town) in the Negro district. It was his money that provided a playground in Harlem which bears his name. These things alone should prove to the entire world that Bill Robinson instead of just being mayor of Harlem, should be the unofficial sepia President of the United States. (Morris 1937, 9)

As Robinson's philanthropy is set against the background of the depression era, Morris's desire to exchange a favorable discussion of Robinson's checkbook consciousness for a sincere look at Robinson's compromised screen images represents an understandable but truly missed opportunity. Robinson is not pressed on certain statements that would be fruitful to pursue insofar as issues relating to his screen work. For instance, when pressed on his frequent pairings with Shirley Temple, Robinson quips, "I was wrongly taken to task about employing a white girl to work with me. That situation was unavoidable." There is no follow-up to these remarks by Morris. Rather, he moves on to cite Robinson's many civic and humanitarian awards, which Morris credits with demonstrating the high regard with which Robinson is esteemed by "our white brothers." Finally, Robinson concludes by taking the opportunity to set the record straight about rumors that he is illiterate. Unlike Beavers, Robinson, who likewise held the race up to ridicule in his screen roles, is recuperated by the *Courier* as a "race man" worthy of the community's respect, admiration, and continued support at the box office.

High-profile white performers did not escape scrutiny from the black press if their actions impinged on the interests of the community. The *New-Age Dispatch* published an exposé on Al Jolson's involvement in a restrictive residential covenant designed to discriminate against African Americans. A second story, also appearing in the *Dispatch*, reports on the protest efforts of prominent white actors against the Scottsboro boys' convictions. The Al Jolson case is noteworthy because it threatened to divide Los Angeles's black presses against themselves. On 1 April 1938, the *Dispatch* ran the front-page story "Al Jolson Heads Petition Seeking

THE NEW AGE

VOLUME 31—NUMBER 41   LOS ANGELES, CALIF.,   Friday, April 1, 1938   5 CENTS

Al Jolson Heads Petition Seeking Racial and Other Restrictive Enactments Before City Body

Front-page film news: *California New Age Dispatch* exposes the real-life racism in Hollywood that films often naturalize. *California New Age Dispatch*, 1938.

Racial and Other Restrictive Enactments before City Body," which detailed the failure of Al Jolson, Francis X. Bushman Jr., and a host of other Universal City, Encino, and Cahuenga Park residents to secure a restrictive covenant that would bar "non-Caucasians" from these neighborhoods. On its unanimous denial of the petition, the city council reportedly stated that "the area mentioned already enjoys zoning privileges in all save that affecting the races of people." The Negro Press Bureau reports the black community was "aghast" at the news. Apparently they were shocked to learn that "the famous 'black face' comedian and singer of 'mammy' songs headed such a list of ardent race baiters." Two weeks later, on 15 April 1938, the *Dispatch* ran a follow-up front-page story, "Jolson Denial Divides Negro Press." At the center of the controversy was the fact that "several other local newspapers [who] likewise ran the story" were issued a subsequent denial from Jolson. However, for some reason, Jolson refused that press courtesy to the *Dispatch* and its supplier news service. As the controversy expanded, the *Dispatch* found itself at the epicenter of a credibility crisis: "Mr. Jolson's denials taken as they are suggest that this paper has erred and published an untruth. . . . However, the New-Age Dispatch merely passes along to its readers the facts in the case, that they themselves may judge the truth or error."

The *Dispatch* then reiterates its charge and assures its readers that the "information was gleaned from the files on the case kept in the City

Clerk's Office," despite apologias on Jolson's behalf issued in other black papers or the granting of "a clean slate" by "a group of alleged 'leading colored citizens.'" The next week on 22 April 1938, the *Dispatch* printed a rebuttal letter on the Jolson matter by *Sentinel* publisher Leon H. Washington Jr. This front-page reply reveals the internecine battles that arose over the fierce competition for highly lucrative celebrity news. Washington remarked to *Dispatch* editor and Negro Press Bureau director Lawrence La Mar that

> There seems to be some doubt in your mind as to our position in the Jolson matter. . . . In the first place, I did not represent the Negro citizens of Los Angeles, I merely represented the Sentinel, and at no time have I ever made any statement that I was satisfied that Mr. Jolson did not sign the petition in question. . . . As you further remember, you and I discussed ways and means by which we [might] get in touch with Mr. Jolson. . . . I believe you too would have felt the same way had you been invited on the interview. . . . The facts are that I had the privilege of being the first paper to print Mr. Jolson's statement. It was not my statement, but a signed statement by Jolson. ("The Sentinel's Letter" 1938)

That Jolson was not African Americans' favorite film celebrity as he rose to film stardom through pernicious blackface masquerades is hardly news, but the *Dispatch* reports that Jolson's professional alliance with black featherweight boxing champion Henry Armstrong had contributed to a significant transformation in blacks' attitudes toward Jolson ("Al Jolson" 1938). According to the *Dispatch*, "Since he became identified with this wonderful little colored fighter, Jolson has been popular with colored citizens the world over." The *Dispatch* adds, "he was definitely down, in some quarters as an ardent friend of the Negro." If Jolson's standing in the black community had indeed improved, then the newsworthiness of the restrictive covenant issue would have been of immense importance to black readers, to say nothing of the circulation advantages a newspaper could gain for "scooping" all others with the latest information. Clearly, the contest between the various black press outlets in Los Angeles created by this scandal became further complicated and intensified by such irreconcilable aims as racial solidarity in the information-gathering stage, and financial competitiveness in the news dissemination stage.

White screen stars who participated in a cause to benefit the community's quest for fair treatment could count on positive press coverage. One of the most controversial and highly publicized legal cases in America at that time was that of the Scottsboro boys. This case initially concerned a complaint taken out against nine black youths, ages thirteen to twenty-one, charged with throwing several white boys from boxcars the groups had been riding together. Once it was discovered that two white girls were traveling with the group, the black youths were charged with rape. News of this development quickly spread across the nation and became a lightning rod for social outrage and protest. According to Mark Naison (1983), "the case became synonymous with Southern racism, repression and injustice" (57). In the cultural and political ferment of the times, this case fired the imagination of the entire country and became a cause célèbre for people across the nation's ideological, racial, economic, and political divides. On 21 August 1937, the *Dispatch* focused special attention on the Hollywood Scottsboro Committee. This article, "Hollywood Screen Stars Protest Scottsboro Convictions," excerpts key passages from a letter penned by the committee addressed to President Roosevelt seeking to overturn the convictions of the defendants. Among the points stressed in the petition was this one: "Together with all other progressive Americans, we pledge ourselves to continue this struggle until all these victims of prejudice and hatred are freed." Among the ninety-six signatories to the petition listed here were Robert Benchley (the force behind the committee), Fredric March, Robert Montgomery, Jimmy Cagney, Boris Karloff, Dorothy Parker, W. S. Van Dyke, Lionel Stander, Oscar Hammerstein, and numerous others ("Hollywood Screen Stars" 1937). We can be reasonably certain that this favorable publicity further endeared these white leftist and liberal Hollywood celebrities to their black fans.

More typical, however, was the accommodationists' muckraking concerned with shaming Hollywood into doing fairly by its loyal black audience. Take as an example a 1935 *Courier* exposé that tells of Louise Beavers's exclusion from Academy Award consideration for *Imitation of Life* ("Color Bars" 1935), or news that same year of a black-owned theater group that was forced to sue Paramount Pictures for failing to honor its contract to furnish first-run films to the black exhibitors, resulting in the concern's bankruptcy ("St. Louis Theatre" 1935). The independents' "race movies" were repudiated in a 1937 *Dispatch* article along with Hollywood fiction films and newsreels for repeating the "same roles endlessly" ("Complains" 1937). And for some stars, like Rex Ingram, the star of *Green Pastures,* the press revealed the fate of black actors who failed to endlessly repeat the stereotypical roles responsible for their fame. That fate typically resulted in financial ruin and career obscurity, in Ingram's case by age forty ("Rex Ingram" 1937). Ingram did, however, find smaller successes in later years as a character actor in such 1940s films as *Sahara.*

Significantly, such advocacy journalism did produce results, as we saw in the *Courier*'s ability to turn adverse publicity about Universal's and Pantages' discrimination against the black press in advance film screenings to its advantage. Neither did the black press's muckraking exposés go unnoticed by white writers of the mainstream press. On 23 April 1937, the *New-Age Dispatch* reprinted comments from *New York Post* staff writer Arthur Winsten's article "The Negro Stereotype in American Pictures," which Winsten said was "inspired by recent critical articles in the Negro press" ("Complains" 1937). Moreover, the muckraking impetus found in the accommodationist mode of film criticism produced results apparently because it championed reform over radicalism. As Walter White once asserted about the black press network, "Its function as a watchdog of Negro interests has given it power and influence which will continue and increase as long as prejudice and proscription plague the Negro" (1948, 210).

One of the most remarkable elements of the accommodationist discourse was that it achieved a functional, although not always seamless, balance between its advocacy and promotional literature. The press successfully navigated the choppy economic waters between agitating for black performers' rights to work in Hollywood and critical appraisals of films casting black actors in stereotypical roles. The papers were cognizant of the risks associated with alienating Hollywood, especially where the matter often pivoted on calls for access to studio publicity departments or strident insistence on black performers' employment opportunities. The press understood as well the unlikelihood of meaningful change without the demand for it.

Imitation of Life in the Accommodationist Discourse

When Universal Pictures released its cinematic adaptation of Fannie Hurst's best-selling novel *Imitation of Life* at the end of 1934, the general consensus in the black press mainstream was that the film portended "A New Departure in Movies." At least this is the sentiment expressed in a *Pittsburgh Courier* editorial of 22 December 1934. As a film that centered on the enduring friendship and professional partnership between two widowed single mothers, one black and one white, this highly successful social problem film did represent a departure from the usual Hollywood films featuring black characters. But as one of the first Hollywood films to explore in depth the depression's impact across race and class lines, it departed from the usual conventions on a number of significant levels. In terms of casting alone, this film broke new ground, and on several fronts. First of all, it is the first interracial buddy film featuring a black actor in a central role outside the strict narrative economy of the slavocracy. Second, it is the first to feature a representation of "the modern black woman." And though she was "still a servant," Donald Bogle (1989) reminds us that this particular celluloid servant was figured as a modern black woman "imbued with dignity and a character that were an integral part of the American way of life" (57). Third, in casting Fredi Washington and giving her narrative range and agency as the mulatta Peola, the film is the first to treat sympathetically the psychosocial dynamics of the mulatto question from the perspective of the mulatto character. Last, on this subject, this is one of the first interracial Hollywood films to permit the white and black characters to occupy positions of relative parity insofar as the narrative emplotment was concerned. In terms of locale and setting, it should be noted that this is the first mainstream film with an integral black storyline not confined spatially to a romanticized southern plantation. At the same time, it is important not to overlook the southern antebellum ethos that drives this melodramatic plot of race, lies, and pancake fortune.

The *Courier* assessed the film's impact in succinct and unambiguous terms: "For these United States 'Imitation of Life' is a daring moving picture, because it plays with what is considered dynamite: The race question. And it is playing to capacity audiences" ("New Departure" 1934). What the *Courier* finds so explosive in this essentially reactionary film is the departure in its treatment of the black characters. Beavers's character, Delilah, and Washington's character, Peola, were hardly realistic cinematic constructions of modern black womanhood, although they occupied a modern diegetic universe. Yet the film's apparent value for black audiences of the thirties is summed up best by the *Courier*:

When before has any screen or stage drama for general attraction pondered the pertinent question of the "colored" girl who can pass for white? . . . When also has the question of the proper relations between a white and colored person in a business partnership been propounded? . . . When before have colored people appeared as dignified, intelligent, well-dressed human beings and not as jovial cretins on the silver screen? Here are Negroes who go to college, have beautiful churches and dignified religious services quite contrary to the libelous nonsense of "The Green Pastures." . . . Imagine! A moving picture with Negro actors, and yet no hoofing, no blues singing, no vociferous horselaughs, no razor wielding, no barnyard amours! There is much in "Imitation of Life" which is dreadfully superficial and needlessly sentimental and far-fetched, but it will really set America to thinking furiously. It is dynamite. ("New Departure" 1934)

While the tragic mulatta is a staple of southern literary fiction, her appearance as a sympathetic character in the mainstream cinema had not been attempted before *Imitation of Life*,[23] so that this film's engagement with the complexities of racial passing marked an innovation indeed. Whereas the *Courier* found the mere suggestion of a black and white business partnership in this film as propounding a step forward for race relations, its failure to see the Delilah character's rejection of her fair claim to financial compensation in the business venture as the equivalent of two steps backward and as an insidious narrative redeployment of the antebellum master-slave relationship is curious. Perhaps this is one of the "far-fetched" elements alluded to at the essay's conclusion. Within the context of the times, it is obvious that this film struck a responsive chord among both its white and black audiences. In fact, Earl J. Morris (1935), staff correspondent for the *Courier,* reports that the black response to the film in Chicago was so overwhelming that it was "held over for a second week at the Metropolitan Theatre." He reports the manager of the theater as saying, "We have done more business with the motion picture 'Imitation of Life' and Fredi Washington, one of the stars making a personal appearance with the film, than any other week in the history of Warner Brothers Metropolitan Theatre. So eager were the people to see the picture with their own stars that hundreds paid for standing room." Morris relays news from entertainment critic Chappy Gardner that this situation was duplicated in New York.

To account for the immense popularity of this film among African

Americans, it is useful to examine some of the specific issues that bear on the film's allure for 1930s black spectators. That the film is among the first to set its tale of interracial cooperation against the backdrop of the depression must have resonated forcefully with this financially weary audience. But that surely was not enough to motivate them to part with their meager resources for standing-room-only accommodations to see this film. However, we get an indication of just what depression-era black audiences found so compelling in *Imitation of Life* from *Courier* critic Fay M. Jackson. Writing on 15 December 1934, shortly after the release of the film, Jackson uncovered the one element in the film that triggered the black audiences' affective response. In two words, it was Fredi Washington. Washington's powerful performance in the film made her "the great black hope" (Bogle 1989, 60). Far beyond the limits of the tragic mulatta icon, Washington's Peola generated a signifying chain of highly complex social, historical, economic, racial, and psychical meanings for black spectators. In her review, "Fredi Washington Strikes New Note in Hollywood Film," Jackson describes many of these coordinates as they converge to produce what I term "the Peola discourse":

> In "Imitation of Life," Fredi Washington . . . utters a cry. "I want the same things other people enjoy[.]" [T]hat found an echo in the hearts of 12 million smoldering Negroes throughout the United States and probably has been since their so-called emancipation from chattel slavery. Actress though she be, Fredi Washington expresses the desire for freedom and equal justice in this picture that is more convincing than any mere performer could have voiced. True to her own life, the injustices of color and race prejudice have retarded and prohibited a fuller life and freedom of expression. . . . You feel some of the weight of the bars of race prejudice in this country when you see, probably for the first time, the true symbol of the American Negro struggling against these bars as Fredi Washington portrays the role of "Peola" in "Imitation of Life." (Jackson 1934, 8).

As Jackson patently illustrates, black audiences responded so favorably to the fair-skinned Washington because the actress's own racial identity imbued the character with an authenticating aura unavailable to a caucasian actress attempting to pass for a black attempting to pass for white. It was precisely Washington's degree zero of representational whiteness that allowed "Peola's" performance to be read as the cry "I want the same things other people enjoy."[24] Black audiences understood this subtext and the yearning at its core. If an African American could possess all that America holds dear, education, good looks, youth, vitality, and, above all, luminous white skin and still be denied the "same things other people enjoy," then the question the film poses for the nation is, what chance has the darker African American? Such an utterance interjected in the mass consciousness of a racist nation was tantamount to an act of sedition. The subversiveness of Peola's pathos and impatience is nonetheless confined within the tragic mulatta problematic. And thus Washington becomes the cinema's first reluctant black antihero. Her private yearning was the public demand for an acknowledgment of black humanity. Jackson and Bogle concur on the point that Washington's "Peola" absolutely symbolized the "New Negro demanding a New Deal" (Bogle 1989, 60). In 1934, at the height of the depression, one can imagine that Washington's performance alone was worth standing room only.

Even before the film's release, Washington's own outspokenness against Jim Crow practices in Hollywood made headlines in the black press to rival any of her fictional character's. In a 21 April 1934 *New York Amsterdam News* article, Fred Daniel warns that "Fredye [*sic*] Washington may talk herself out of the movies" if reports are true that she charged Hollywood with a failure to "see ability when it chose to pick its stars." Moreover, she is reputed to have said that "producers did not smile with favor on pretty Race girls." Clearly, Daniel's fears were unfounded, as Washington was cast as Peola, to the delight of white theater owners and black audiences alike.

When we consider the implications of one particular test of the film's allure in the black community, one episode is especially revealing: " 'Imitation' faced strong [competition] from Duke Ellington at the Regal Theater, half a block away, when it opened [in Chicago], but toward the end of the week 'Imitation' was still jamming them in with plenty of vacant seats at the Regal" (" 'Imitation' Sets" 1935). This cultural contest for the leisure time and money of Chicago's "Black Belt" gives us some index of how powerful the Peola discourse must have been.

While Beavers's breakout performance in the film undoubtedly warmed the hearts of black audiences as well, it is unlikely that 1930s black spectators found Beavers's modern "mammy" compelling in its own right. However, if Beavers's modern mammy, defined by a self-sacrificing acceptance of her position of inferiority, can be viewed as a strategic narrative device that ensures white audience patronage, then it is not unreasonable to view Washington's rebellious tragic mulatta type as being sufficiently overdetermined that both white and black audiences could find her appealing and for reasons that are diametrically opposed and racially bound. Of course, what we get from Jackson's review is evidence of black spectators' transgressive readings of the film and particularly of the "Peola" character. It is further doubtful that Hurst, Universal, or Stahl (the film's director) imagined "Peola" as a subversive element, a "rebel against the system" (Bogle 1989, 60), to the extent that Jackson and the legions of black fans suggest. Donald Bogle points out fundamental differences between the black and white interpretations of the Peola discourse. "The explanation for Peola's rebellion," in the white imaginary, "is that she wants to be white," whereas the black interpretive community understand "that she wants white opportunities" (60). It matters little whether either interpretation accords with an idea of narrative intent in the character's construction as a literary or cinematic object. What is certain about racialized interpretive contests in the social meaning of texts, as Stanley Fish (1987) points out, is that "one cannot appeal to the text, because the text has become an extension of the interpretive disagreement that divides them [*sic*] and, in fact, the text as it is variously characterized is a consequence of the interpretation for which it is supposedly evidence" (348). Put more plainly, we cannot successfully arbitrate between these two perspectives on the grounds of textual "fact" because, ultimately, black and white audiences saw in the film's mulatta character "facts" or evidence that corresponded to the dictates of their 1930s racially and socially constructed outlooks. We can, however, credit the production of the film and its sympathetic portrayals of Beavers's and Washington's characters to the nation's new spirit of liberalism, impelled in large part by the realities of the depression economy.

If *Imitation of Life* was teaching blacks and whites a vulgarized class solidarity in the "fight for better living conditions,"[25] in the words of Arthur Draper (1936), it was likewise undermining the cause of racial equality by reconstituting white supremacist ideology in the black and white characters' domestic relations. Apparently *Courier* critic Bernice Patton recognized that this flawed logic constituted a bitter pill for black audiences. But Patton, as representative of the accommodationist press, opted for the most conciliatory gloss in her film review titled "Critics Weep at the Preview of 'Imitation of Life.'" Even though she concedes that "naturally there are sequences in the film that will grieve my people"

Pittsburgh Courier 1934 entertainment features page: *Courier* critic Bernice Patton gets a black press exclusive when permitted at advance screening of *Imitation of Life*. Reprinted by permission of GRM Associates, Inc., agents for the *Pittsburgh Courier*.

(1934, 8), Patton goes on to articulate a position of acquiescence that one would expect from *Imitation of Life*'s modern mammy, Delilah. Eschewing the more critical stance, Patton continues:

> Don't spoil your economic advantages and possibilities in the movies by intolerant criticism. You must remember that this film gave you your first real star, Louise Beavers, fabulous financial gains to the race and opens the way for other Negro artists in the films. I think the epic really serves its

purpose, inasmuch as it proves to white people that they have been unkind and unjust to their American brother of African descent. The picture gives them a more human understanding and love for the Negro. (8)

It is interesting that after admonishing black critics and spectators against expressing their just dissatisfactions, Patton would hold up Beavers—the new and improved modern mammy—as evidence of good faith from "the industry that aims to erase the color-line." To justify her untenable position, Patton advances this appeasement: "The making of the picture has been a delicate task, because the plot involves the social and economic problem of the Negro. The kind, sympathetic Stahl was a mighty brave man to produce the stirring, daring drama. He took every precaution not to offend either race. . . . Throughout the screen version, he struck out the word 'nigger'" (8). Patton either conveniently neglects to mention or is unaware that the excision of the epithet was the result of pressure from the NAACP that was brought about at the behest of Louise Beavers (Bogle 1989, 64). Patton's subtitle revealing her singular presence as the black press representative allowed at the screening suggests a powerful motive for her compromised point of view.

Significantly, Patton's and Jackson's differing perspectives on the film's meaning as conveyed through the two black performers almost reenact the philosophical split separating the film's characters Delilah and Peola. Whereas Jackson's review foregrounds the latent subversiveness contained in Washington's portrayal of a would-be modern black woman, impatient with the slow pace of racial justice, Patton's preaches patience and acquiescence to the status quo in terms consistent with Delilah's acceptance of "her place." Although Jackson and Patton assess the film's merits differently, both endorse it. Still, the recognition that each woman approaches the film from opposing critical positions leads us to a more nuanced appreciation of the often unruly and multifarious nature of the seemingly unified accommodationist film literature.

The Crisis criticism of *Imitation of Life* is instructive on this point as well. In the June 1935 edition, Howard University professor Mercer Cook wrote a review of the film from Paris, France. Cook's critique is fascinating because his reception of the film is conditioned by the zeitgeist, if you will, of a foreign national culture. More important, Cook's exposition is not confined to issues of the profilmic or the narrative diegesis. His review is enlarged by its anthropological function. In addition to communicating his feelings about the film, Cook relays and interprets the French audience's response to the film for his American readers back home.[26] To this end, Cook opens the discussion with the following observation: "The reaction of the spectators at last night's performance was one of perplexity rather than of enthusiasm. Nevertheless, from the Negro's point of view, the showing of the film in France is significant and deserving of passing comment" (M. Cook 1935, 182). Having said that, Cook then explains the perplexing cultural and linguistic factors that in all probability would prevent the film from enjoying "great popularity in Europe." For one thing, Cook notes that "the subject is too foreign." He adds, "The action drags at times," and "the French subtitles are in several instances extremely unsatisfactory."

The cultural barriers Cook finds most significant have to do with "the difference between the American and French conceptions of race relations" (182). This explains much in the way of accounting for the insufficiencies in the French subtitles. For as Cook points out: "There is, for example, no French equivalent for the word *Mammy.*" The translator, therefore, was "unable to render the idea intelligible to French audiences." As confounding as that example is, Cook relates an even more glaring cultural meconnaisance or misconstrual revealed by the French subtitles concerning the peculiarly American racial problematic, known as "passing."

> Less excusable, perhaps, is the error in the scene in which Delilah visits Peola's school. The latter, ashamed to let her comrades know she is colored, hides her face so that her mother will not recognize her. Delilah, seeing her, asks the teacher: "Has she been passing?" The translator, confused at this point, misconstrues this meaning of the verb *to pass*, with that which indicates success in one's studies. . . . In like manner, when Delilah explains, on reaching home: "Peola was passing, and I spoiled everything," here again the subtitle reads: "She was studying well, and I spoiled everything." (182)

Cook finds similar hermeneutic difficulties with "the rendition of Delilah's dialect." Despite these "exceptions," Cook is relieved that "the version is reasonably exact, and the French spectator is able to follow the story." It could have been much worse, he assures us. The film could have been dubbed with French voices. The only time French was audible at the screening was during the film's introduction, in which a benshi-like discussant "states in a few words the situation of the Negro in the United States, explaining how discrimination, segregation and prejudice often made his life unbearable." (A benshi is a Japanese figure responsible for interpreting and explaining the narrative in silent films to the theater audiences. They were often as famous as movie stars.) Cook found this explanatory element, and the fact that it was deemed necessary, proof of French society's more enlightened attitudes on matters of race and difference. Cook reports that the French journal reviews were, for the most part, positive. But he was not willing to assume that these "flattering" assessments represented the attitudes of the general French audience. After surveying a few glowing reviews of the performers, Cook found the French reviewer's renunciations of "American race prejudice" to have even "greater significance." He gives several examples: "One deplores the 'redoubtable and cruel problems created in the United States by the tragic condition of Negroes.' Another remarks: 'Yes, Peola, who finally understands, has been criminal, but how much more criminal yet are those atrocious prejudices!'" Given such antiracist attitudes expressed by the French intelligentsia, one can easily comprehend what Cook and several African American expatriates found so affirming about life in France at that time.[27]

In discussing his own reactions to the film, Cook is quite abbreviated, which suggests that his main focus was a cross-cultural reception study of the film and its implications for evaluating African Americans as global cinematic subjects. But he does make the following comments relative to his own spectatorship:

> I do not know how the Negro press reacted to this film when it was shown in the United States; there were in all probability, objections concerning the segregation of the daughter at her mother's funeral. Nevertheless, as propaganda favoring the American Negro in his struggle for recognition as a human being, no picture has been as effective. (182)

It is unclear if Cook knew that his colleague and fellow Howard University professor Sterling Brown led the charge in denouncing the film in America. Brown's critique of *Imitation of Life* ran two months earlier in the National Urban League's *Opportunity Magazine* in March of 1935. Whereas Cook liked the film, if for no other reason than what he considers its pro-black propaganda value, Brown took the dissenting view.

It takes no searching analysis to see in Imitation of Life the old stereotype of the contented Mammy, and the tragic mulatto; the ancient ideas about the mixture of the races. Delilah is straight out of Southern fiction. . . . The director would not even let Delilah die in peace. She must speak . . . I have heard dialect all my life, but I have yet to hear such a line as "She am an angel." . . . The music of the quartet is stirring, although it is unfortunately synchronized with Delilah's dying, and is another instance of Hollywood's poor imitation of life. . . . It hardly seems anything to cheer about. (Brown 1935, 88)

In juxtaposing Cook's and Brown's opposing views on the same film, we can see the range of opinions held by these black intellectuals, and by extension the larger black community, regarding cinematic depictions of blackness during the interwar and depression years. Brown's review is more structural in its concern with various levels of signification, script, music, performance, and dialogue. Cook's project, in comparison, is more journalistic and sociological. When conjoined with the literature produced by female journalist critics Jackson and Patton, Cook's and Brown's responses to the film render glimpses of historical black spectatorial engagement that clearly dispel the notion of an essential black viewing subject, at least as one might be theorized in 1934. Moreover, these writers problematize any conception of black spectatorship that does not theorize effectively what I term "the recalcitrant gaze," rendered unruly by a historically racialized subjectivity always impossibly multiple, always shapeshifting, and always in constant self-redefinition that *is* the negotiation of what W. E. B. Du Bois calls "double consciousness."

Brown's review, *"Imitation of Life:* Once a Pancake," however, is set apart from the rest because unlike the others, his is a comparative analysis of Hurst's literary text and Hollywood's cinematic adaptation that points the way to one of the most important features of the radical discourse—a disruption and rejection of the accommodationist compromise—that we consider in the next section. The review appears in the *Opportunity*'s book review section, "The Literary Scene: Chronicle and Comment." Brown was a frequent contributor to this department of the journal. His disruption of the accommodationist discourse is a refusal to recommend the film—"it hardly seems anything to cheer about." However, Brown's recuperative impulse toward the performances of Beavers and Washington is the one element that tethers him to the discourse of accommodation. Beavers's cinematic portrayal of Delilah is less objectionable for Brown than is Hurst's literary characterization (perhaps the "intrinsic dignity of Louise Beavers kept down the clowning").

Brown sees symbolic importance in the fact that the bandanna has been exchanged for a white chef's cap (87). He surmises that if given the opportunity to speak dialogue consistent with Hurst's more complex mulatta character, "Miss Washington could have risen to heights in its delivery" (88). Regarding the most significant distinction between film and book, Brown apprises us that in the literary universe, Peola is successful in her "passing" quest, which is not the case in the film. After giving us the necessary background story informing the novel but not the film, Brown ultimately reminds us that "the [fundamental] characterization and ideas, however, are little changed" (87). Owing to this thematic consistency between film and literary texts, Brown is incredulous at the promotional hype touting the film's "novelty": "Remembering the book, I was unprepared to believe the theatregoers and critics who urged the novelty, the breaking away from old patterns of the picture. Of course they had reasons." He then catalogs some of these "reasons." At the same time, he convincingly discredits the film on its own "realist" terms, and here Brown's interrogation is trenchant. For example, in disclosing some specifics of Delilah's character and speech that betray many deep-seated racial fantasms of the period, Brown demonstrates the racial economy that this central character's speech and actions serve, namely, the reification and naturalization of black inferiority and subordination.

> Delilah is straight out of Southern fiction. Less abject than in the novel, she is still more concerned with the white Jessie than with Peola. She has little faith in Peola's capacities: "We all starts out smart; we don't get dumb till later on." Resignation to injustice is her creed. . . . When she refuses her twenty percent (not because it was too little) she is the old slave refusing freedom: "My own house? You gonna send me away? Don't do that to me[!] . . . I's yo'cook. You kin have it; I make you a present of it." . . . She is canny about the ways of men and women where Miss Bea is concerned; but when her daughter is yearning for music and parties, she says, "Come on, honey, I'll dance with you." (88)

Brown is on to something here. What he captures in his analysis is the black character's internalized panopticism.[28] In other words, Delilah and Peola behave in such a way that the white masters do not have to exert their white privilege, because the black characters police their own racial boundaries and act accordingly. But Brown does not stop at pointing out the logical fallacies governing the construction of the black characters. He also presents an astute semiotic analysis of the film's expressionistic spatial dimensions. Brown has noticed the racialized nature of the characters' spatial environments and how they convey the nation's race and class hierarchies.

> There is one scene where Miss Bea [the white heroine] goes upstairs while Delilah goes down. It is symbolic of many things. One is, that in *Imitation of Life* where Claudette Colbert has a role to bring out all that there is in her, both Miss Beavers and Miss Washington have, so to speak, to go downstairs; Miss Beavers to a much greater childishness, and Miss Washington a much greater bewilderment. (88)

Upstairs, for Brown, symbolizes an attainable upward social and economic mobility that is unavailable to the black characters, whereas the downstairs domain signifies black social and economic stasis, which is attributed not to endemic racism but to the black characters' personal limitations, hence Delilah's infantilization and Peola's delusions. Brown's analyses are incisive because they clearly engage with the text's manifest and latent meanings, meanings heavily sedimented with American racial mythemes.

Brown observes that even though the manifest content of the film's racial discourse purports to evacuate "ancient ideas about the mixture of the races," they nonetheless are smuggled back in through the film's latent significations of racial difference and separation. As Brown observes: "The bandanna has been exchanged for a white chef's cap," and "Cabins and cottonfields are a long way from the suite (downstairs) of Delilah. Both Delilah and Peola can dress up, after a fashion" (87–88). While "all of these things are undoubtedly gladdening to our bourgeois hearts," Brown reminds us, "that doesn't make them new." For all the film's pretense to racial equality, Brown aptly demonstrates how it still preserves the primacy of racial separation, especially through the latent economy of space (the upstairs and downstairs suites, the fact that black and white characters do "not ride side by side in the same automobile"), and in the psychodynamics of the characters, especially Delilah's self-sacrificing volunteer servitude signified by her refusal to accept even a paltry 20 percent of the pancake business built entirely on her own "rec-

ipe and skill." According to Brown, these deep-structural elements provide unexpected truths about "the ways of America." But for Brown,
"they hardly seem anything to cheer about" (87).

Given *Imitation of Life*'s immense popularity, it is hardly surprising
that the African American journals of the day would publish responses to
the film by its readers who weighed in with their own critiques. In the
same month that *Opportunity* published Sterling Brown's learned evaluation of the film, *The Crisis* included in its "Letters from Readers" department commentary from a Pauline Flora Byrd. Six months later, *The
Crisis* included a reader's letter on the film from a Frank T. Wood Jr.
What is notable in these lay readers' responses is that one concurs with
Brown's assessment whereas the other departs significantly. The opposed
view comes from Frank T. Wood Jr. of Baltimore, Maryland, and Pauline
Flora Byrd of Kalamazoo, Michigan, and shares much with Brown's
perspective. Most interesting here is that these readers' commentaries are
apparently regionally conditioned. Ms. Byrd of Kalamazoo finds that
"from beginning to end this picture is full of vicious anti-Negro propaganda . . . that deadens the discriminatory faculties of those who see it"
(Byrd 1935, 91). Picking up on the film's claims to verisimilitude, which
she reproves, Byrd continues: "The pity of it is that great care is taken not
to present this picture as an imitation of life but as the real thing" (92).
"These are not real Negroes, Delilah and Peola," Byrd insists, "They are
what white people want us to be" (91).

Mr. Wood of Baltimore disagrees. He finds Byrd's "criticisms . . .
unfair to the picture and the stars" (Wood 1935, 283). In a direct challenge
to Byrd's point of view, Wood expresses a counter view. He believes that
the film mirrors some difficult and unflattering realities of the black
American experience that reasonably account for the characters' nar-
ratological function. Specifically, he finds that Delilah and Peola are
symbolic of a black existentialism tied to historical and contemporary
conditions of survival. For example, he does not see Delilah as a dis-
simulating racial construct that serves only to reinforce negative black
stereotypes. Rather, he finds Delilah to be the "old-fashioned Negro
type" representative of a cunning or trickster ancestor who intuitively
adopts the tactics of docility and self-deprecation as a necessary survival
strategy in a racially oppressive society. Moreover, he credits Delilah's
brand of racial passivity with positively influencing the improved predicament of blacks in thirties America, whereby "our Nordic friends" were

motivated to found and fund "high schools, colleges, and universities which now open wide their doors to us." In addition, Wood believes that Peola's character exhibits characteristics consistent with those featured in George Schuyler's important novel about passing, *Black No More*. As Woods expresses it, Fredi Washington personified a Schuylerian archetype who embraced her physiological whiteness out of tactical necessity, not out of a self-negating rejection of her ancestral blackness. In a challenge to Byrd, Wood writes: "I would like to take the lady from Michigan on a tour through the East and South, where the bulk of the Negro population is, and if she were to . . . hear and see the thought and actions of the Negro, I believe then her criticism of the picture would be greatly changed" (283).

Regardless of the interpretive chasm separating these readers on the issue of the film's treatment of black identity politics, even Byrd tries to find an escape hatch to avoid denouncing Beavers and Washington outright for their participation in such a "vicious film." The alibi for Byrd is what she calls the "present equivocal position which the Negro holds in Hollywood" (91). More than anything, Byrd's concession reinforces earlier observations about black spectatorial ambivalence toward mainstream films featuring black players. As we see in the case of *Imitation of Life*, often the one element of thematic consistency in the accommodationist discourse is a glaring absence, an absence of censure where black performers of these demeaning stereotypes are concerned. On one level, this inconsistency regarding black stereotypical performativity might be explained as a paradoxical instinct of cultural self-preservation in that it ensures at least a minimal amount of specular pleasure, no matter how compromised, for black film audiences weary of lily-white-hero films. The rationale, then, seems to be that some visual pleasure is better than none at all. On another level, one cannot overlook the imperative to inhibit intraracial, intragroup strife and discord among African Americans during this crucial time of national insolvency.

Although the majority of the black press's mainstream film discourse of accommodation is symptomatic of the arrested development of the black independent cinema movement owing in large measure to the impact of sound technology, and to the devastation of the Great Depression, the radical critiques are more indicative of the black community's evolving political fragmentation and receptivity to revolutionary ideologies of class resistance and social change.

The Radical Imagination in Black Film Criticism

The general currents of radical and grassroots political activism that swept through black America during the depression-era thirties included a wave of highly politicized cultural criticism produced by a contingent of leftist writers who turned a radical gaze toward the cinema. This turning resulted in a proliferation of radical film literature decidedly anti-Hollywood and anticapitalist in nature. Among these writers are such New Negro intellectuals and artists as poet and writer Langston Hughes, actor Wayland Rudd, newspaper editor Louise Thompson, lawyer and journalist Loren Miller, and political activist Cyril Briggs. As a result of their varied intellectual backgrounds, cultural pursuits, and individual agendas, the literature is naturally characterized by a pronounced diversity that achieves its moments of coherence at the intersection of radical political ideology and rebukes of the classic Hollywood product. The articles under discussion here are culled primarily from two sources, the *Negro Liberator* (later changed to the *Harlem Liberator*) and *The Crisis.* The existence of the radical *Liberator* newspaper and the moderate *The Crisis* magazine testifies to the ideological complexity that characterized the black community's responses both to the far-reaching depression-era conditions and to Hollywood's polarizing discourse of whiteness that further threatened the fragile glue uniting civil society in 1930s America. Even though black membership in radical movements such as Communism was negligible,[29] it nevertheless had a powerful impact on the lives of the urban black masses because the few black intellectuals who joined the party or who were considered "fellow travelers" wielded a tremendous sociocultural influence. They helped to popularize the American Communist Party's (CPUSA) political and cultural agendas for a time. At this point, it is necessary to give a brief historical overview of the conditions that led to Communism's allure for an influential segment of black America's literati.

When the economic prosperity promised by the Great War's military economy failed to materialize concretely for the masses of southern black migrants and the West Indian immigrants who had jammed the nation's northern industrial centers, this newly transformed industrial working class was ripe for the cultivation of radical political ideologies and movements. Seizing on the discontent and alienation of the urban black masses, West Indian émigrés Marcus Garvey and Cyril Briggs estab-

lished rival nationalist organizations that attracted large segments of this
newly formed industrial proletariat (C. Robinson 1983, 298). Marcus
Garvey was the force behind the much larger and more influential of the
two, the Universal Negro Improvement Association (UNIA), with a
membership that Cedric Robinson numbers in the hundreds of thousands to millions (297). Cyril Briggs's African Blood Brotherhood (ABB)
was significantly smaller, with a membership ceiling at about three to five
thousand members, most of whom were veterans of the Great War (298).
The important thing about the UNIA and the ABB is that the organizations were spearheaded by an organizational cadre "of West Indians and
Afro-Americans who had developed professionally as social agitators
and journalist-propagandists" (298). Through their respective magazine
and journal publications, both groups gained a powerful influence at this
juncture over an impressive throng of black factory workers, artists, and
intellectuals. This tradition of producing radical public literature since
1919 (298) led directly to the radical film discourse of the thirties. Briggs's
and Garvey's black nationalist movements, however, were not the only
new ideas to exert influence on the black collective imagination.

According to Mark Naison (1983), World War I had created a global
backlash of anticapitalist sentiment that included an intellectual strata of
black Americans who until that moment "had no tradition of mass socialist activism" (4). Since the bond of international socialist organizations was the concept of class solidarity predicated on worker unity and
organized unionism, its appeal to the black American masses was under-
standably limited, given that white American unions were rigidly segregated and, most important, that "white workers participated in lynch
mobs and race riots." When American socialist organizations refused to
reject the system of Jim Crow discrimination practiced by unions against
blacks, they willfully closed off the possibility of a viable mass workers
movement extending across America, although some black intellectuals,
such as A. Philip Randolph and Du Bois, were attracted to socialism's
philosophical progressivism. As the national government embarked on
its postwar anti-Bolshevism measures in the early twenties, socialism as
a potential mass phenomenon in America was aborted without ever
having made significant inroads with the black community (4–5). Naturally, the federal authorities' orchestrated raids on socialist organizations
throughout the twenties had a chilling effect on the black radical movements, namely, the UNIA, the ABB, and even the NAACP. By the late
twenties, the UNIA had essentially collapsed under the pressures exerted

from both internal and external forces. Following this, the ABB dissolved, and the NAACP moved away from its radical origins to a more liberal approach to social transformation.

Cyril Briggs and the *Liberator*

FORGING A RADICAL CRITIQUE OF AMERICA'S
CULTURE INDUSTRIES

With the dissolution of his paramilitary organization, the ABB, Briggs was one of the first black intellectuals to join the Communist Party (Naison 1983, 3). On the strength of their antilynching platform and general community activism to fight for black rights, the "Communists improved their standing with black intellectuals of the Renaissance generation," and the Harlem Communists formed a party front organization called the League of Struggle for Negro Rights (LSNR) in 1930 (42). Three years later, the organization began publishing a weekly newspaper organ, the *Harlem Liberator,* later the *Negro Liberator* with Briggs as editor in chief. Briggs assembled an impressive roster of contributors and editors around the *Liberator* that included Harlem social worker Louise Thompson (former wife of Renaissance novelist Wallace Thurman), Langston Hughes, lawyer and journalist Loren Miller, and other leading black intellectuals. The *Liberator* was supported by the party but was fundamentally a black newspaper with a black editorial staff, although as with most leftist presses, literary contributions from other races were routinely published. Like most black urban newspapers, the *Liberator* included an entertainment page devoted to covering the arts. It featured two columns devoted to the stage and screen. "Screenings" was one column written by an African American critic operating under the nom de plume of Camera Eye, a name perhaps deployed in homage to Dziga Vertov's concept of Kino-Eye, or "film truth." The other was called "Drama—Movie: Snapshots," edited by the white socialist writer Dave Platt, who also was among the founders of the Film and Photo League. Before we move on to an analysis of the film discourse produced in these columns between 1933 and 1935, an examination of Briggs's 1932 essay "Art Is a Weapon" is necessary, as it explicitly sets forth the *Liberator*'s cultural mission statement, or its "Variant of a Manifesto," to borrow a phrase from Vertov (1984, 5).

"Art Is a Weapon" is Briggs's articulation of the economic imperative behind the social construction of "the Negro" and the international class war in cultural terms that are comprehensible to average working-class black Americans. Cedric Robinson (1983) has described Briggs as a master of agitprop literature (298), and Briggs's rhetorical acumen is on vivid display throughout this article, which is suffused with premonitory utterances that run through and unify the entire corpus of radical literature under discussion here. "Art Is a Weapon" is a project of cultural demystification that aims to mobilize a disaffected black citizenry into a formidable Jacobin army cognizant of its historical role and responsibility in effecting an American cultural revolution. To this end, Briggs presents his argument in the nomenclature of militarism. In this way Briggs at once recodes complex Marxist theories of class analysis to make them accessible to the uninitiated and untutored black masses, and he makes manifest the political economy served by mass culture's timely entry into America's class struggle. Briggs's deployment of military tropes in an address to blacks, already suffering actual bloody confrontations with white supremacist institutions and citizen groups, is an astutely effective rhetorical strategy, especially in view of the depression economy's exacerbation of black oppression and victimization. Consider the following from his opening paragraph:

> Today with the acute crisis of world capitalism and the sharpening terror against the Negro People, all the cultural weapons in the hands of the white ruling class are being turned against the Negro. . . . The press, the radio, the theatre, all are increasingly utilized to slander us and to justify and condone the growing legal lynchings in the courts and lynch murders by landlord and police gangs. (Briggs 1933, 2)

The class war for blacks, then, was not mere metaphor, for the depression crisis of American capitalism was the unrelenting material reality that conditioned the wretched African American experience naturalized by the nation's fetishized race relations. In other words, Briggs knew that to inhabit a black body in America was to exist in a perpetual state of social repression with economic depression and physical endangerment as its material consequences. So Briggs's project was to demonstrate the social and political function of art as a potent weapon of capitalist domination and, more importantly, to propound ways of appropriating art as a weapon for the development of race and class consciousness.

Briggs's critique is impressive because, in addition to paraphrasing some key Marxist aphorisms and maxims, his interpolation of race matters into Marxist class analysis makes the theories more responsive and pertinent to the specificity of black oppression,[30] as Cornel West would term it. For example, Briggs looks at the culture industries and the co-optation of "Negro culture," the schools, New Deal legislation such as the National Recovery Act (NRA), science, films, and, as mentioned above, the press, theater, and radio as ideological state apparatuses that function with "especial virulence against the Negro masses." In his exegesis of these forces, Briggs clearly borrows from Marx's comments in "The German Ideology."

> In all class societies, the dominating class rules by controlling the instruments of culture, along with economics and political power. To talk of pure and unbiased art under such circumstances is sheer rot and nonsense. Art is a weapon in the hands of the white ruling class. Art can be, and must be made a weapon in the hands of the toiling masses and the oppressed Negro People in their struggles for bread and freedom. (2)

Briggs informs his readers that despite this seeming balkanization of political, economic, and cultural power, there is hope and a way out. Here he gives the example of the revolution that occurred in Russia. He wants blacks to reclaim "the revolutionary traditions of the Negro People," such as the slave insurrections, and to be inspired by the revolution that created the Soviet Union. "The example of the Russian toilers offers to the black and white toilers and the Negro people of this country the only way out of the capitalist morass of permanent unemployment, mass misery and imperialist war." "Negro artists and intellectuals have a great role to play in the liberation struggles of the Negro People," Briggs asserts. He points to "those Negro artists now grouping themselves around the Liberator" as leaders in the struggle for black liberation and as beacons of light for redirecting the black masses back to their authentic cultural traditions. These artists and intellectuals working in concert with the *Liberator* represent, for Briggs, a vanguard who have already begun laying the foundation for a black proletarian cultural revolution through the establishment of a "Liberator Chorus, a Liberator Theatre Group, Liberator League of Struggle for Negro Rights (LSNR) Forum, Liberator Children's drawing classes, etc.," with other programs in development. For Briggs, only this level of political and cultural intervention and commitment could forestall the New Deal's National Recovery Act (NRA) and its programmatic assault on the black masses carried out through the institutions of American culture.

> Under the NRA program of lower living standards for the toiling masses and starvation level for the Negro toilers, art and science, the radio, movies, press, etc. are all fully mobilized to carry through the attacks of the New Deal against the workers, directed with especial virulence against the Negro masses. (2)

Briggs recognized that even after blacks had endured centuries of ridicule and abuse, the depression economy of the thirties signified a more dangerous turn in the history of American race relations:

> The white ruling class finds it more than ever necessary to turn its propaganda guns against the Negro People. The white ruling class not only utilizes against us the instruments of culture at its disposal, but seeks to disarm the Negro People culturally as well as economically and politically. It has suppressed the revolutionary traditions of the Negro People. It has prostituted Negro culture to suit its dictum of Negro inferiority, holding Negro Art to the level of black face clowning. (2)

Rather than acquiesce to the degradation of black culture put in the service of American racism and classism, Briggs proposes that the masses return to "genuine Negro culture with its proletarian content, work songs, songs of revolt, etc." Along that path, he suggests, lies true black emancipation and self-determination. To undergird his bold plan for a black cultural revolution based on the Soviet model, Briggs holds up "the life of Alexander Pushkin, famous Russian Negro poet." He obviates any resistance to replicating the Russian example on the basis that blacks may not know that Russia was not a homogeneous society by insisting that Pushkin presents a worthy model for emulation. It was Pushkin's political activism coupled with artistic genius that, Briggs contends, endeared him to the Russian masses. But more central to the point at hand is Briggs's reminder that Pushkin "has left a heroic heritage to the Negro People and an example to the Negro intellectuals," which black masses and intellectuals should neither ignore nor dishonor.

Briggs's interjection of the race question into the economic determinism of traditional Marxist class analysis marks an important intervention because it suggests a real motive for black investment in the concept of the "dictatorship of the proletariat." It is important to remember that absent such an overt address to, or consideration of, the particularities of black racial oppression in Marxist theoretical formulations on working-class victimization, the black masses were not easily convinced that their economic or human lot could be cast with that of the white working-class masses who had been their historical enemies, enemies whose participation in lynchings and race riots made them as vicious and formidable as the capitalist ruling classes. To this end, Briggs's contemplations that include associating Pushkin with the general Russian proletarian group can be seen as astute, even if tangential.

"Art Is a Weapon" clearly serves as an important introductory text in our examination of black radical film criticism because it provides a cogent overview of some of the most pressing microstructural and macrostructural concerns that recur throughout these radical critical analyses of race in the cinema. In effect, Briggs's title points to the intent of this article and of this radical discourse, which is to have the literature itself become potent weaponry pointed directly at Hollywood and its consciousness industry.[31]

The *Liberator* begins its demythologizing of celluloid blackness with a critique of blacks in Hollywood films in an article entitled "The Role Assigned the Negro in American Films." This article accompanies Briggs's "Art Is a Weapon" and continues in a similar vein by addressing the special predicament of black performers in Hollywood. Written under the byline JCL (1933), the essay opens with a discussion of the acute exploitation of black performers in American films. From a mention of the obvious fact that blacks come in for special ridicule in cinematic narratives, JCL's content analysis focuses on the treatment of other nonwhite groups in Hollywood and the response by them to such caricatures, which he contrasts to the black situation. As JCL sees it, "Mexicans were villains, Japanese were spies and Chinese with long pig-tails were kicked around by cowboys. Now the Negro, if he is not represented as being of the lowest mentality, is shown as completely gripped by the voodooism of camp-meetings." JCL finds effective the strategies of resistance that Mexicans, Japanese, Chinese, and other groups brought to bear on the studios that forced them to desist from this "easy writing" of such stereotypical representations. He contends that protest letters, "telegrams and a general and well-organized boycott" must be adopted by blacks. In the absence of this kind of organized resistance, intervention, and pressure,

JCL makes the case that "a story dealing with the Negro as a normal being would be as taboo in Hollywood as one having a Marxist viewpoint." Further, the suggestion for a way out of this representational bracketing of blacks into the cinema's ideological ghetto of comedy and minstrelsy is that blacks must become more active in progressive workers film collectives like "the Workers Films and Photo League and other class-consciousness groups" (2). Only through the propagation of such corrective measures, JCL concludes, will a solution to the problem of cinematic misrepresentations in mainstream film productions be found.

As this *Liberator* writer sees it, only black- and worker-produced counterhegemonic films and newsreels will effectively contest mainstream films that persist in portraying workers and other oppressed groups as militant and undeserving malcontents. Steven J. Ross (1990) has written of a similar tendency in "Cinema and Class Conflict," his study of the Workers' Film and Photo League and its white working-class constituency. Ross notes that mainstream filmmakers of the period routinely portrayed disaffected white workers aligned with the labor movement as "lazy and greedy individuals . . . who resorted to unnecessary violence against essentially kind bosses" (71). He credits the league with attempting to produce more accurate and positive depictions of the everyday lives and struggles of working-class Americans (71), whereby a balance of the representational scales in favor of the nation's underclasses could be achieved. It is no wonder that JCL argues for collaboration between blacks and the league. His hope, clearly, is that honest films depicting the oppressed in the "proper light [will] give the lie to the vicious caricatures sponsored by the princes of exploitation in Hollywood" (JCL 1933, 2). As with other articles in this radical mode of critique, "The Role Assigned the Negro in American Films" also considers aspects of the dominant cinema's mode of production responsible for the unique economic exploitation of the black performers as film industry workers. For JCL, the fact of Hollywood's racially motivated salary differential and abusive employment tactics is a further indictment of capitalism's mass-culture apparatus that profits enormously from the creation of a subsurplus labor among aspiring black actors:

> Even the Negroes working on the lots in Hollywood are treated as menials, shabbily indeed. They are called as extras, they appear for work many times before they are actually put on the job. That job will scarcely ever last more

than a day, and the pay will be so much less than that of the white worker on the same job, that he will absorb all the day's pay in carfare consumed in getting to and from the lot. . . . A group of 350 Negroes was called to a certain location in Hollywood ten days in succession. When the job was finally ready for them, they worked only two days, and received $2.50 per day. (JCL 1933, 2)

Compounding these economic hardships imposed by the studios is the complicity of the American Federation of Labor's (AFL) biased union practices, which JCL terms "the worst offender in matters of discrimination." The union is cited for undercutting black musicians employed in musical films. Whereas the black musicians were paid at a rate of $12.50 per day, JCL reports that the more lucrative synchronization work, "the $10.00 per hour jobs that will follow are given to white orchestras by the leaders of the Musicians Union." What JCL demonstrates is that the on-screen distortion corresponds to the off-screen reality in the Hollywood colony. The point is that to expect sympathetic and accurate cinematic depictions of blacks under conditions determined by this racist mode of production is to misunderstand the economic and ideological imperatives of the mainstream film industry.

The *Liberator*'s Camera Eye

A RADICALIZED GAZE

It is not difficult to detect in this literature the influence of the Russian cultural revolution (specifically its development of a new Marxist-oriented cinema founded on a principled rejection of the bourgeois cinema of the West) encoded in the film critiques of the *Liberator*'s entertainment pages as well as in articles of contributing writers sympathetic to the paper's black Marxist ideology.[32] After all, many of the individuals linked to the *Liberator* had firsthand experience with the Communist Party's state-run film and political institutions. Mark Naison (1983) points out that the Comintern made it a common practice for blacks identified as future leaders of the U.S. Communist Party to be trained in the Soviet Union (16). In 1933 Langston Hughes, Louise Thompson, and other black artists were invited to the Soviet Union and commissioned to work on a Soviet-German film coproduction about the African American experience. In that connection, the pro-Marxist film discourse produced within the pages of the *Liberator* is less unanticipated. The paper's two film columns, David Platt's "Drama—Movies," and "Screenings," written by "Camera Eye," are characterized by a decidedly Marxist viewpoint in discussions of Hollywood films' ideological imperatives and general industry praxis. Significantly, there is little engagement with issues of style and form in the films under review. Perhaps this can be attributed to the fact that these writers' exposure to Russian art aesthetics coincided with the rise of the socialist realism film aesthetic in the 1930s that supplanted the 1920s formalist experimentation model of Soviet filmmaking in the wake of Stalin's rise to power. In any event, when we consider the articles' emphasis on the lack of thematic realism where black subjectivity and class distinction are at issue, it appears that the formal aesthetic of socialist realism is the preferred artistic mode for the *Liberator*'s film critics.

In the main, these critiques center on such issues as the uses and abuses of Hollywood's Production Code, the political economy of racial blackness in the cinematic text, commodity fetishism in the cult of star personalities, critical consciousness and spectatorship, and the need for establishing alternative, worker-based cinema programs. These discussions over the three-year run of the *Liberator*'s entertainment page were accompanied by film stills, advertisements for and capsule descriptions of Hollywood films on display at the Lowe's theaters in Harlem, advertisements for stage productions at New York area theaters, and promotional copy for cultural programs sponsored by the League of Struggle for Negro Rights (LSNR) and other worker-based organizations. This dialectic of mainstream film promotion and ideological castigation reflects a unique double-consciousness orbit around which Briggs's black Marxist editors circulated that deviates from the Du Boisian conception of the African American's split subjectivity in terms of an avowed patriotic Americanness and a heightened racial consciousness. By contrast, the Briggs group's black Marxian double consciousness inheres in that identity split between adherence to an interracial Bolshevist ideology and Briggs's fierce and vocal black nationalism.[33] Perhaps it is more efficacious to speak of Briggs's *Liberator* as operating from a tripartite dynamic: the urge for interracial Bolshevism, the pull of black nationalism, and the capitulation to the demands of advertising revenues. Whatever the case, the idea is that the *Liberator*'s radical film discourse is a forced bricolage trying to negotiate its anticapitalistic ideology with capitalistic business practices driven by the need to advertise the very mainstream cultural productions it seeks to discredit. And although the *Liberator*'s entertainment page bears some structural similarities to its competitors in the black press mainstream (theater ads, stills, capsule reviews, etc.), its foregrounding of Marxist nostrums in the film discussions unquestionably sets the two poles apart.

On the Uses and Abuses of the Production Code

In voicing concerns about the hegemonic function of Hollywood's self-policing agency, Will Hays's Production Code Administration (PCA), the *Liberator*'s film columns routinely presented scenarios that confirmed suspicions that the PCA's inconsistent deployment of the Production Code was being used unfairly against films espousing anticapitalist messages. David Cook (1990) finds that the institutionalization of the Code among other things became a strategic move to curtail the possible spread of Bolshevism in America in the wake of the destabilizing effects of the Great Depression and the increasingly influential organized labor movement (296–97). Reacting to the pressures from the public and civic organizations such as the Catholic Church's "Legion of Decency" and others to clean up the immorality and excessive violence in films prompted by the innovation of sound, the studios reluctantly initiated a self-censorship program to avoid government regulation and to stave off threatened consumer boycotts (298). From 1934 onward, the Code became law, and as the *Liberator* observes, exceptions to the rule of the PCA were not uncommon, especially if box office receipts indicated public demand for anti-Code material, particularly anti-Code material that did not undermine or disparage capitalism's profits.

The *Liberator* writer pseudonymously called Camera Eye presents one clear example of the Code's double standard where nudity and sexuality are at issue. Writing in the column "Screenings," Camera Eye demonstrates the hypocrisy of the Hays Office in its approach to censorship on the grounds of nudity. Supposedly "nudity of all sorts" was absolutely prohibited (D. Cook 1990, 299). Camera Eye illustrates, in the 27 January 1934 column, that this decency taboo is elastic indeed when race enters into the equation. How else to account for the nonapplicability of the nudity taboo to the black female body? The issue for Camera Eye is this: "Will Hays's boys are on the rampage again with blasts against too-naked women. But it's Okay when African women appear with the proverbial G string. Morals are funny things" (Camera Eye 1934c, 6). Camera Eye's point is well taken, though understated. Presumably American spectators understood that nudity was disallowed in films at all times; but with the exception to the rule allowing black nudity, the Hays Office and the studios found yet another way to construct racial binary oppositions in representations that privileged whiteness. On one hand, the Code's morality clause shielded nude white bodies from the prurient gaze, while on the other, the fetishized "native" black body, positioned outside the code of human morality and decency, was at once made an acceptable site for sexual titillation and sanctioned racial degradation. Whereas Camera Eye takes aim at mainstream films' diegetic manifestations of the Code's duplicitous uses, Dave Platt takes on Will Hays directly in a parodic utterance designed to reveal Hays's actual function as the studios' rubber stamp instead of as guardian of the public morals.

In his 31 March 1934 column "Drama—Movie: Movie Snapshots," Platt opens with a reference to the recent release of a Universal Studio's horror film, expected to be a major hit because it features Hollywood's most famous monster icons, Bela Lugosi's Dracula, Boris Karloff's Frankenstein, and Lionel Atwill's Doctor X, together in one film, *The Suicide Club*. After framing his main discussion in terms of the upcoming cinematic monster fest, Platt shifts his focus to a consideration of what he terms the nation's true monstrosity.

> But the biggest monstrosity of them all is not manufactured by make-up men in Hollywood, but is right here in our midst doing some real blood sucking and bone breaking. I mean that gigantic monstrosity called Capitalism. Will Hays believes that Walt Disney's "Three Little Pigs" put an end to the Big Bad Wolf of the Depression. Hays sees signs of prosperity all around his palatial residence in Beverly Hills. According to Mr. Hays the Depression which put fifteen million honest workers out of work was started by Miss Betty Boop singing "The Sun Is Going Down." That's upper class ideology for you. (Platt 1934f, 6)

Platt's wicked humor is effective here because it successfully recodes Hollywood's fictitious monster discourse to make it symbolize the economic bloodletting visited upon real victims of the economic depression.

In this way, Platt forces readers and spectators to refocus their attention onto their own actual pain and suffering caused by the special capitalist interest that men like Hays represent. Platt's aim is to make film audiences understand the different lenses through which the unemployed, presumably themselves, and the overemployed, individuals such as Hays, see the realities of the depression. Of course, Platt insists, Hays and his class cannot see accurately the depths of the depression from their "palatial" residences in Beverly Hills, and he, Platt, is more insistent that the suffering masses begin to see how ridiculously inadequate Hollywood's escapist film fare is for a nation caught up in this crisis of capitalism.

In his column published a week earlier, on 24 March 1934, Platt considered Will Hays and his official duties more directly:

> Will Hays once again says the movie companies must keep the moral code or suffer severe penalties. . . . Hays has been saying this for many years now and the movie companies have been paying him handsomely for it . . . but still we get the same old pictures day after day. . . . It's just a game of tag with them. . . . Hays knows too well that if he steps out of bounds just once, he's through. . . . That is [why] this "moral code" business is such a big joke. (Platt 1934e, 6)

Platt is intent on revealing the chief "moral code" enforcer's own lack of morality. By reminding readers that Hays is not an independent agent but wholly beholden to the powerful film moguls, Platt, like Camera Eye, bares the economic and ideological motives behind the Hays Office's highly selective use of its immense powers of censorship. This is an important emphasis that takes on added significance when viewed in the context of both columns' critiques of specific instances where films were censored for political reasons. For example, on 23 December 1933, Platt criticizes the Hays Office for banning a film exposing the conditions of a squatters' camp known as "Hooverville." Officially the film was banned for a violation of the morals code because it depicted a common-law relationship between an unmarried couple. But Platt contends that this was a mere pretext used to foreclose the circulation of cinematic interrogations of the crisis of unemployment (Platt 1933d, 6). To illustrate the hypocrisy of this instance of censorship, Platt states that "Mae West and her whole tribe are permitted all kinds of salacious liberties in their films without encountering any trouble whatsoever from Mr. Will Hays." (Although Platt fails to acknowledge the extent to which Hays and West actually collided, the fact that West's films were permitted wide distribution makes Platt's comparison valid nonetheless.) Platt observes, along with his black colleagues and readers, a similar tendency on the part of the censors when the subject of lynchings appears in films. This leads us to the next thematic concern that traversed many of the *Liberator*'s film articles.

On the Political Economy of Racial Blackness in the Cinematic Text

The *Liberator* critics, black and white, found mainstream films to be particularly resolute in their commitment to portrayals of antiblack stereotypes, and they were equally intent on revealing the subtle and overt means by which racial bias was encoded in the films. In one critique, Camera Eye takes up this issue in terms that prefigure Roland Barthes's (1972) structural analysis of a photograph depicting a colonized black Senegalese soldier whose very image is adeptly mythologized to function as an alibi for French imperialism (122–23). Camera Eye likewise interrogates American cinema's deployment of the image of the happy, inferior darky to expunge the nation's racism of its odiousness.

> Run over in your own mind the characterizations of Negroes you have seen in the films. . . . Universally, they show us as grinning, cringing Uncle Toms or as helpless and happy little children—In short, as definite inferiors. Hardly a word appears about lynching, peonage, share cropping or chain gangs. And when these subjects are treated they are glossed over. Don't get it into your mind that this treatment is accidental. It's part and parcel of Hollywood's code. Remember that these pictures go to the uttermost ends of the earth. And it is good business for Wall Street to play down exploitation of Negroes in the United States. Exploitation is best played down by repeating these endless lies about our inferiority *and our happiness in the face of oppression* [italics mine]. (1933, 6)

This cogent account of the political and racial exigencies served by Hollywood's black stereotypes, especially the happy coon and the loyal Uncle Tom and mammy, certainly helps to account for the fact that Stepin Fetchit, Clarence Muse, and Louise Beavers were the most frequently employed black actors during the early thirties. Unstated, but clearly suggested by Camera Eye, is the notion that the ubiquity of these exaggerated images constructs such mythic signifiers of blackness that it becomes nearly impossible to dislodge them from the social imaginary, and the further implication is that since this representational strategy serves the needs of Wall Street, there is no impetus to dislodge them.

Ultimately, then, the fear expressed by Camera Eye is that "endless lies" replace the lived realities that they purport to represent, and in the absence of films' truer depictions of black lives on the screen, the corrective process of mythological disarticulation becomes increasingly remote. Camera Eye is rightfully concerned that with this breach, Hollywood's international film circulation threatens to effect a global contagion of American racism, and this concern is reflected in the statement that "unfortunately, we haven't got ambassadors, consuls, and diplomatic representatives to protest the treatment of Negroes in films. Whatever action is to be taken by way of protest must be taken by ourselves" (6). Camera Eye adds, therefore, that "it is imperative that we fight on this front just as we do on all other fronts in our battle against exploitation and oppression." By frequently making connections between biased films and the persistence of racist attitudes, Camera Eye and Platt strive to make readers aware of mass culture's growing importance in the black community's overall liberation struggle, hence Camera Eye's admonition, "Don't get it into your mind that this treatment [of the black image] is accidental." Through their discussions of specific Hollywood film texts, Camera Eye and Platt set out to uncover what they consider persistent and deliberate manipulations of the black image that can in no way be construed as accidental.

In his 18 November 1933 column reviewing *Laughter in Hell*, Platt describes how this "Southern chain-gang film" demonstrates well Hollywood's use of censorship to manipulate images that could otherwise present a powerful indictment of the rampant lynchings that occurred in thirties America. Instead, Platt finds that the censors sanitize the horror of lynchings by excising "all scenes of preparations for the execution of Negro prisoners and all views of feet and bodies hanging after execution." He points to a similar exigency at work in the censors' elimination of an important foreword in Warner Brothers' 1932 crime drama *I Am a Fugitive from the Chain Gang*. Platt is convinced that the film's foreword was censored because it contained a powerful utterance from the actual brother of the convict whose prison experience inspired the docudrama:

> My brother, Robert E. Burns, is now a fugitive from a chain gang and he has been branded a convict and that makes him a hunted thing on earth. The scenes in "I Am a Fugitive" which depict life in a chain gang are true and authentic being based upon my brother's experiences. (Platt 1933b, 6)

Without this important authenticating statement, Platt contends, the film's most powerful elements are terribly compromised: "By the time the censors had finished their scissors work this film had lost most of its original authenticity." Certainly, its critical thrust against capitalist repression, as manifested in the abuses of the penitentiary chain gang system, had been blunted significantly by the censors.

These critics approach films featuring black performers or explicitly racial themes from a different critical angle. Although the critique of class is a definite subtext, the primary goal is to reveal the racist logic in the films that supports the nation's white supremacist attitudes. Camera Eye's column of 20 January 1934 is exemplary. The article begins by considering the scandalous debacle wrought by the Hays Office's hasty ban of the film *Ingagi* after a pay dispute prompted the film's producer to reveal that the film was a hoax. Even its claims to being shot in Africa were proven false. As Camera Eye describes it, the film "supposedly photographed in Africa depicted a gigantic ape who carried off white and native women. Of course, the Hero—yep, a white man—rushed to the rescue. The big ape's name was Ingagi." Upon disclosure, Camera Eye reveals, Hollywood spokesmen were forced to recant earlier assurances that the film was genuine, claiming "that the [law] suit was the first notice of the fake character of the production." Camera Eye's rejoinder was "Of course, that wasn't true. The damage [however] had been done. Thousands of people still believe that they saw an authentic picture" (6). The significance of this episode for Camera Eye was its analogous relationship to Hollywood's treatment of blacks in films. But here was a rare instance when the subterfuge was publicly disclosed:

> What, in principle, is the difference between Hollywood's entirely false picturization of Negro life and the fakery of Ingagi: Negro life a la movies bears about the same relationship to reality as did the ape picture to biological facts. And the same "critics" who sigh and sniffle over the perfectly

darling picturization of simple, happy Negroes strumming banjoes while they accept peonage and Jim Crow threw ink all over their papers when they gazed on Hilton Phillips pretending to be a savage. "Really, it's so artistic." (6)

Just four years earlier, the *Chicago Defender* threw ink all over its pages to reveal a near mirror image of the *Ingagi* hoax. With the *Defender's* headline story "Wild Cannibal Turns Out to be Ex-Janitor: Salary Suit Reveals Harlem as Scene of Fake Movie,"[34] it seems that Hollywood's cinematic hoaxes about Africa were not only "so artistic," as Platt intones, but not at all unusual. The Tarzan film series is presented as an extension of the racial problematic suggested in *Ingagi*. But there are no claims to anthropological truths here, as with *Ingagi*. Like *Ingagi*, however, the Tarzan films posit an essentially heroic white subject who triumphs over an essentially savage black object, the African native. Most disturbing in this genre for Camera Eye is the implicit message of an immutable white superiority that is genetically programmed. Writing on 27 January 1934, Camera Eye comments that "the epidemic [of] Tarzan plays is still raging with their obvious moral about white boys raised-in-the-bush-reverting-to-innate-superiority bunkum" (1934c). The critique here is that notwithstanding environmental and cultural determinants that would naturally obliterate intellectual distinctions between a Tarzan and his native adversaries (leaving out any discussion of Tarzan's rearing by apes), the myth poses the idea that Tarzan's innate superiority is inescapable and emerges despite himself or his nonexposure to white civilizing influences. And for spectators already interpellated and hailed by the nation's racial discourse, the myth of Tarzan set against the backdrop of an unknown and exotic Africa becomes powerfully seductive and difficult to disaggregate from related myths constructed around blacks in America.

Black-cast films such as *Hallelujah* (MGM, 1929) and *The Emperor Jones* (United Artists, 1933) are criticized by the *Liberator's* critics for a parallel representational bent, but these critics understand well that critiques of black-cast films targeted at a black readership require yet another rhetorical approach. Like the critics in the black press mainstream, the *Liberator's* writers attempt to negotiate the thorny problem of condemning damaging black stereotypes without pillorying black performers of them. Unlike the accommodationist discourse, however, the radical critiques are less concerned with the use value of these films for black audiences, a use value that hinges strategically on the cult of star personalities. This is not to suggest that the radical critiques are characterized by a totalizing discourse that dismisses or condemns all black performers. Rather, the emphasis here is on the particular commodification of black stars and their insidious exchange value in Hollywood's general star discourse.

Commodity Fetishism in the Cult of Star Personalities

The image of the Hollywood star provides the radical critics a rich discursive field in which a host of economic and political concerns can be raised. Through their particular take on the star discourse, these critics seek to expose the veiled reality of America's class society, the breakdown of racial solidarity under capitalism, and the use of stars in the government's and the studio's program to undermine the labor movement and to rally support around the New Deal's National Recovery Act (NRA) programs. Whereas both the mainstream white and black presses helped forge a fan culture around specific film stars through a celebratory discourse, the radical approach wants to minimize the allure of stars by emphasizing, in the case of white performers, their selfishness and greed, and as for black actors, their complicity in Hollywood's racist regime of representation.

In his 16 December 1933 column, Platt highlights what he considers the depravity of Jean Harlow's exorbitant salary during the height of the depression. He suggests that it is obscene for one person to be paid so lavishly "while thousands starve." He writes: "Jean Harlow's salary has just been raised from $1500 to $3500 per week, a slight increase of $2000 a week in the midst of the worst depression in history—Only a system of society as insane as this could ever hand out so much money to one single person while thousands starve." He adds, "$3500 would temporarily feed over two hundred families every week" (1933c, 6). Directly adjacent to this scathing commentary is a still of Myrna Loy smiling in profile. Because there is no other apparent reason for this photograph, the juxtaposition implies that Loy is similarly overcompensated for her work in films. A few months later, on 17 March 1933, Platt reiterates the news of Harlow's pay increase, but this time he comments directly on the absurdity of the raise, which he sarcastically claims will enable her to "afford that nice new hat and shoes she has been wanting to buy but couldn't on her previous meager wages." Platt's motivation for divulging Harlow's enormous salary increase is to force a reckoning with the class structure of Hollywood celebrity that is rendered opaque because it is not associated with the traditional aristocracy of entitlements based on bloodlines. The point is that America's capitalist aristocracy constitutes a rarefied class just the same. For his dubious readers, Platt presents as evidence the aristocratic trappings of Douglas Fairbanks in his 24 March 1934 column:

> Douglas Fairbanks is opening a pheasant rabbit, deer, etc., private hunting ground near Beverly Hills that is expected to rival the Romanoff's before 1917. The hunting orgies will begin in the spring with a royal housewarming for a few selected friends says this title-mad actor. [I]n the meantime, just outside this hunting lodge, at the gates of movie studios, tens of thousands of extras, technicians, office workers, are clamoring for jobs to enable them to eat not pheasant or deer but coffee and rolls. (1934e, 6)

As with his Harlow example, Platt is careful to follow news of this excessive wealth immediately with information about the grim realities of the depressed working classes. Pointing out Hollywood's own oppressed working class, however, gives the Fairbanks story added potency. In addition to pointing out the stars' habits of conspicuous consumption in the depression economy, Platt also aims to diminish their stature by calling attention to their fallabilities and childish antics. On 25 November 1933 he reports on Buster Keaton's unfortunate fall "into a small volcano while vacationing in Mexico." In noting that two Mexican workers rescued the actor, Platt installs the workers as the true stars of the story. In the same article, actress Constance Collier's distress at not being allowed to take her dog from Paris to London is reported so as to illustrate that even the most trivial of the stars' concerns will be circulated as public-interest news for mass consumption, whereas information about the grinding poverty of workers is routinely censored. We can clearly see the imperative of dimming the luster of Hollywood stars in this discourse.

Similarly, Camera Eye shines a spotlight on the dross that tarnishes black performers' star image. In calling attention to a questionable film project involving the popular actor Clarence Muse, Camera Eye illustrates how readily black performers volunteer their talents for "Hollywood's shameful treatment of Negroes" (23 December 1933, 6). Their complicity is not only attributed to a sycophantic acceptance of stereotypical roles, but to the propensity to compound the problem by offering apologies for them. Writing on 23 December 1933, Camera Eye suggests that Muse's capitulation to this arrangement is primarily responsible for the actor's prolific career. His on-screen presence in numerous films is calculated at approximately fifty films in only eighteen months (6). The suggestion here is that film success for minority actors usually accrues in direct proportion to their disavowal of race and class loyalties. In support of this hypothesis, Camera Eye details the circumstances surrounding a highly promoted film project slated to dramatize the sensational Scottsboro case. The specifics are these: Clarence Muse would sponsor the film, and the black community at large was asked to make financial contributions to ensure its production. Camera Eye further describes the unorthodox scheme in his 6 January 1934 column:

> When the Scottsboro case was hot copy last spring, Clarence Muse permitted his press agent to send out a press release with the claim that Muse was sponsoring a gigantic Scottsboro film. The film would be financed, it was said, by inducing every American Negro to contribute the "small sum of five cents." It was claimed [that] a studio would be placed at the disposal of the company, also cameramen would contribute free . . . but not another word has been said about this grandiloquent Scottsboro film . . . and Muse certainly deserves censure for permitting the case to be used as a publicity gag. (1934a, 6)

Evidently the project was abandoned as public fervor around the Scottsboro case subsided. As an observer of Hollywood, Camera Eye surely was no stranger to the exploitative promotional tactics of the industry, but this particular incident posed more serious problems because the Scottsboro case had become much more than "hot copy" arising out of a high-profile legal issue. Scottsboro had become an important referendum on ethics with broader implications for the nation's legal, political, and social institutions. That Muse would manipulate public sentiment around such an important social cause for personal gain and career enhancement (6) was prima facie evidence, for Camera Eye, of Hollywood's corrupting and disrupting influence even on historical constituencies such as homogeneous racial minorities. In fact, Camera Eye found Muse's claim that certain Jewish studio heads were committed to the project because of their overall rejection of fascism disingenuous on the following grounds:

There are many rich Hollywood film executives, but it is significant that Hollywood has not produced an anti-Hitler film. In fact, these same rich Jews squelched one that was projected. Hollywood's rich Jews won't make an anti-Hitler film because it is bad for business. Fascism is a rich man's racket, to keep the poor in check and the rich—Jewish, Negro, or white— never let their racial loyalties or feelings crimp their profits. (6)

The irony and test of this situation for Camera Eye is the fact that if many working-class and immigrant Jews could expect little in the way of anti-Hitler films from their constituent groups in Hollywood, certainly producers could not be expected to act against their financial interests by producing antiracist films on the behalf of African Americans. For Camera Eye, the kinds of progressive interracial alliances Muse spoke of are impossible, given that Hollywood's blacks and Jews too frequently abnegate their responsibilities to the oppressed members of their respective ethnic blocs as a condition of personal success. Subsequently they consent to the industry's hegemonic position that equates honest depictions of black and working-class concerns with the evils of "propaganda" (6). Following this qualified view of propaganda, Muse's press release states: "This feature . . . is not planned as propaganda. It will be a saga of the American Negro, depicting his love of home, religious ecstasies, revival meetings, and other typical phases of Negro life" (6).

Hollywood's familiar insistence on a specified separation of art and propaganda (read, race and class issues) leads Camera Eye to a sobering interrogation of what Hollywood means by "propaganda":

> And that brings up the question of what propaganda is. The quotation is a perfect example of Hollywood's hocus pocus. Showing the Negro as a religious child spending his time at camp meetings, songfests, etc., etc., and that is typical. And more it's art. But show the truth behind Scottsboro, peonage, share cropping, exploitation and that's propaganda. (6)

This attempt to assert and preserve the "Noble Lie" of racial difference by legitimating the nation's racist assumptions and divisions through these hackneyed depictions of black alterity is effectively challenged as Camera Eye rightly divulges the inverted logic of Hollywood's concept of propaganda.[35] In effect, Hollywood is shown attempting to turn the concept of propaganda on its head by reinscribing its own doctrinal black stereotypes as true representations of "typical phases of Negro Life" while dismissing the demands for more accurate portrayals of black life and culture as political propaganda.

The *Liberator* critics take every opportunity to expose Hollywood's self-serving contradictions on this point. In fact, debunking Hollywood's recourse to the propaganda trope is a recurring emphasis in the radical critiques of Hollywood and the race question. Take as an example a 27 January 1934 *Liberator* front-page editorial on famed tenor Roland Hayes's failed efforts to get his life story made into a feature film. Once again, the irreconcilable issue is Hollywood producers' estimation of what constitutes propaganda. The article, "Hayes Refuses to Insult Race in Negro Movie," reports that Hayes was approached by Hollywood producers to make a film of his life. Hayes reportedly turned the offer down because the producers "refused to include the most significant parts of the story." Moreover, the article continues, "they branded Mr. Hayes's efforts to portray Negroes as they are and not the happy go lucky clowns and buffoons that the stage makes them, as propaganda" (1). This, however, was one of the few instances in which the *Liberator* endorsed the actions of a mainstream black celebrity in Hollywood. In fact, in his 3 February 1934 column, Camera Eye chastises Hayes for being a latecomer to such expressions of racial consciousness. More commonly, however, performers such as Stepin Fetchit and the Mills Brothers, to name only a few, are discussed in the film critiques as manifestations of an essentialized black subject that by now had become a privileged and ubiquitous icon in classical Hollywood cinema.[36]

To further deprogram adherents to Hollywood's cult of personality and to problematize spectators' star fetishes, the *Liberator* critics name names of individual celebrities who lend their star status to the government's unpopular campaigns of militarism and antiunionism. In Platt's 23 January 1934 column, Actors Marie Dressler and Charlie Chaplin are singled out as government coconspirators:

> Marie Dressler and Charlie Chaplin both spoke over the radio in the last two months to the people of America asking them to support the NRA at a time when the people of the country particularly the workers and poor farmers are beginning to feel and see acutely that the NRA is benefitting only Wall Street. Dressler and Chaplin utilized their popularity as entertainers to [sway] the minds of their admirers in a manner that no one directly connected with the government could. (6)

Platt maintains that the stars' effectivity inheres in the public's belief that somehow movie stars are apolitical and thereby not "connected with any definite political views." The consequence, as Platt sees it, is that the public is apt to be less skeptical of these pro-government positions when espoused by stars rather than by government "spokesmen in Washington" (6). A year earlier, on 11 November 1933, Platt discussed Chaplin's radio appearance in connection with the NRA program, making a similar point about the popular actor's function in helping "to sell Liberty Bonds back in 1918." In this article, however, a Chaplin film is called into question as well. Since Chaplin was slated to portray "a factory hand in a big American city," Platt aims to discredit the work in advance by asking, "I wonder if this will be more New Deal propaganda." Platt's larger goal is to challenge Chaplin's revered "everyman" star persona by pointing to the actor's compromising relationship with "Roosevelt and his raw deal cabinet" (6). By repositioning Hollywood's stars and mainstream films on the side of the capitalist oppressors to shift readers' attention away from the stars' fabricated celebrity and onto their actual politics, the *Liberator* attempts to radicalize the spectatorial gaze of its readers.

Radicalizing Spectatorship and the Establishment of a Proletarian Cinema

One of the most important aspects of the radical film critiques was the push to reinvent spectatorship. To counteract the dominant cinema's narcotizing effect during the turbulent thirties, radical film critics set out to mobilize black filmgoers into a ready force of critical consumers forever on the alert for Hollywood films' "ingenuity in aesthetisizing oppression" (C. Taylor 1993, 184). Camera Eye, and especially Platt, frequently made direct appeals to readers enlisting their support in identifying and criticizing films containing reactionary, or more specifically antiblack and antiworker, messages. Typical of this stratagem is Platt's 9 September 1933 column where he invites readers to become spectator-informants for his weekly reviews: "Readers of this column are invited to send notes, comments and criticisms of films they have seen, liked and disliked. Keep a sharp lookout for bits in movies that misrepresent the lives of Negro and white workers and send them to me" (6).

This approach by Platt has a twofold imperative. First it makes readers cowriters of the column and encourages them to forgo passive spectatorship by encouraging a more active viewing experience. In his 30 December 1934 column, he gives them a primer on how to decode films laden with submerged antiworker, pro-government content.

> Here is a list of Hollywood films which have appeared almost simultaneously with the New Deal and NRA program of the Roosevelt Administration and which bear unmistakably the stamp of collaboration between the State Department and the Hollywood film industry. It is significant that nearly every one of these films is intimately bound with some current issue in which the Wall Street Government, through the Hollywood films, attempts to either pacify the unrest and discontent of the masses or prepare their minds to accept some new NRA trickery being hatched against them. (6)

He follows this overview by listing several films, along with his particular interpretation of their embedded or deep structural meanings. For example, he views the film *Washington Merry Go Round* as little more than an attempt to rationalize the government's violent dispersal of workers who actually gathered in Washington to protest the nonpayment of their overdue back wages. And, in his view, *Gabriel over the White House* "prepares the way for the militarization of the unemployed in labor camps, increased armaments for war and the growing fascization of government as a measure against the masses." *Hell Below* is described as "a recruiting picture for the U.S. Navy as well as propaganda for bigger armaments" (6). Platt wants to make it clear that such films are not innocuous escapist fare but rather propaganda tracts embedded with questionable content aimed at redirecting and refashioning public sentiment against depression conditions to the benefit of the "Janus-faced backers of Munitions Manufacturers" who claim that 'the next war can be averted in one of two ways only—thru preparedness or thru universal disarmament,' and then frankly add that 'since there is no immediate prospect of the latter, America must be in such a state of preparedness that no nation or combination of nations dare attack her'" (6).

In the March columns of that year, Platt follows up on earlier promises to reveal big business's interests in the government's "Preparedness Week" campaign. To this end, Platt discusses the partnership of the film industry and other public institutions in fomenting mass acceptance of government policies that ultimately work to the disadvantage of op-

pressed minority groups and the working poor. Newsreels and war films
come in for special scrutiny along these lines because of what Platt considers their special function in legitimating government-sanctioned propaganda campaigns: "Fox Newsreel No. 10," he writes, "has been de-
clared by the Hitler government to be 'state-politically valuable.' In
recent months Fox Films has been spreading fascist propaganda right
and left in features as well as newsreels" (24 March 1934). Platt's conflation of Hollywood's and Germany's use of film in state-licensed movie
propagandizing is clearly meant to dislodge the perception that newsreels are uniquely objective, disinterested reportage of historical events,
and thereby disconnected from any particular political or ideological
regime. "Hitler's government," he warns, "has begun the use of the film
on a grand scale for Nazi propaganda purposes. Says Goebbels, Hitler's
partner in murder, 'we are convinced that the film is one of the most
modern and far reaching means for influencing the masses, a government
can therefore not possibly leave the film world to itself.' Roosevelt, not
to be outdone, is characterizing the same course which leads to open
government control of the medium in the interest of war and fascism"
(14 March 1934).

By invoking the notion of governmental control over cinematic representations, Platt wants to foreground the "impression of reality"[37] that
films construct to displace and replace the true reality that they claim to
present. The message here, then, is that mainstream films cannot be
trusted by groups positioned outside the protective fold of Wall Street
interests. Platt is equally dubious about Hollywood films in the social
realist vein, as his comment about King Vidor's production of *Our Daily
Bread* attests. After reminding readers that "Vidor's petit-Bourgeois
conception of life among Negroes down south" made a mockery of *Hallelujah*, he dismisses *Our Daily Bread* with an offhand remark: "But don't
take him [Vidor] seriously, because he most certainly is not going to tell
us in this picture how and where to get this daily bread of ours."[38]

As early as 13 January 1934, Platt pointed to "the deepening reactionary
character of the church, university and other social organizations who
have acclaimed 'Cavalcade' as an inspiring film worthy of emulation" as
proof that these civic organizations are but ideological state apparatuses
conjoined with the "Janus-faced" munitions manufacturers and Hollywood to promote the nation's "jingo 'preparedness week' campaign" (6).
He considered this pro-military boosterism as rationalizations for "why

the more courageous and adventurous youth should leave the ranks of the unemployed and join the army with its 'unlimited' opportunities for learning trades while training and fighting" (10 February 1934). But workers and other members of the nation's disenfranchised, he insists, must be prepared to resist these seductive cinematic images and hegemonic discourses. Whereas Platt seeks to advance this critical preparedness by utilizing a solicitous tone to "invite" readers to become spectatorial conscripts in the war against Hollywood's onslaught, Camera Eye is more forceful in his approach. Consider this direct appeal issued in Camera Eye's "Screenings" column dated 27 January 1934: "And won't some industrious reader (if any) write me a letter some time telling what in hell is the matter with this column. I'm trying to get out something you want and if you do, or if you don't let me know. Thanks" (6). From this we can gather that Camera Eye is not entirely certain that the column is reaching readers with the desired effects. The tone of frustration that informs this utterance suggests a larger concern. The concern is that the *Liberator*'s oppositional discourse may not be achieving its consciousness-raising objectives outside its constituency of the already initiated. It is certain, however, that Camera Eye envisions and insists on a two-way communication flow of the paper's readerly directed radical journalism. He seeks to spur reader involvement by welcoming their criticism of his own writings as a first step in this interactive criticism.

In addition to disseminating their own demystifying discourse, Camera Eye and Platt encourage readers to become even better critics of Hollywood by enrolling in film courses sponsored by the Workers Film and Photo League (9 September 1933). Platt wants his readers to be able to recognize the political economy of Hollywood's ghettoizing of immigrant groups and blacks in "comic relief" roles, especially if they are marked as "others" to the constructed "self" of normative American whiteness. As examples of this propensity, he gives these character types:

> The Polish maid in "Three Cornered Moon," the Negro chauffeur in "The Wrecker," the German radical in "Heroes For Sale," the Chinese cook in nine out of ten Westerns, Eskimos in "S.O.S. Iceberg," Negroes in "Emperor Jones." Italians, Jews, Japanese, Cubans, Mexicans, Spaniards, Greeks, are all represented on the screen in such ways as to arouse laughter from unsuspecting movie goers. (6)

This excerpt is from Platt's 27 January 1935 column. When we consider that European and Soviet immigrant groups were prominent in the nation's alternative political movements in the twenties and thirties, such as in communism and socialism (Naison 1983, 5), one can sense immediately Hollywood's desire to neutralize these groups and their radical political ideas by making them the butt of American film humor during the depression era. While Platt is confident of his own demythologizing discourse, he pushes readers to become their own critical interpreters of such films. Thus he urges them to get involved with the Film and Photo League: "One of the purposes of the new Film School of the Film and Photo League of New York is to provide courses that will train workers to better analyze and expose films such as these" (6).

For Platt and Camera Eye, the job is not completed once readers become more critically conscious of mass culture's often reactionary character. Readers are encouraged to act on their newfound critical awareness by demonstrating against and boycotting films deemed hostile to social change movements and progressive ideologies. By encouraging readers to join in the Film and Photo League's demonstration against "the distorted version of Eisenstein's 'Thunder Over Mexico,' now playing in various parts of the city," Platt makes it clear that they are being offered a sanitized version of the great Soviet director's work. This is important because Russian films enjoyed a privileged position on the cultural Left. The possibility that mainstream distributors might foist censored versions off on the public as the authentic work was a disturbing prospect indeed. Because the Soviet films represented a real political alternative to Hollywood, the *Liberator* critics were determined to help readers recognize the authentic products so that their emancipatory discourses might proceed unimpeded. In this connection, Platt's 25 November 1933 column is revealing. Here Platt again tries to maintain the separation between the socialist realism aesthetic of the Soviet Union and America's adaptation and co-optation of it, as in the case of Warner Brothers' "socially conscious" films. Platt tries to ensure that spectators are not deceived by Hollywood's simulacra.

> Recognition of the Soviet Union has had an immediate effect upon Hollywood film studios. Several films dealing with life in the first Workers' and Peasants' Republic are in the process of production. "Red Square" (Columbia), "Chocolate" (Paramount), "Soviet" (MGM) [and] "Ural" (Universal).

Whether these films will deal sympathetically with the problems of the
workers and peasants in the Soviet Union remains to be seen. In our opinion, if the current distortions in Hollywood films of the struggles of the
workers and farmers of America are any indication of the nature of this new
batch of films, we can most certainly expect equal if not more misrepresentations and slander of Soviet workers and peasants. Wait and see. (6)

While reviews of these specified films have not appeared in the *Liberator*'s film columns, films with related themes such as *Our Daily Bread,
The Good Earth, The Oval Portraits,* and *Shanghai Madness,* among others,[39] are reviewed and bear out Platt's prognostication. None fares well
in the pages of the *Liberator.* Obviously, Platt's negative predisposition
toward the films must be taken into account when assessing his interpretative approach. Platt found *Shanghai Madness* to be "one of the most
vicious attacks on the Chinese people" he had ever seen. As he puts it,
"No doubt the others too will spread thick their particular brand of
propaganda for American imperialism in China" (15 January 1933). Contrast this to his views on films that he considers more sympathetic and
honest in their depictions of workers and issues of class. Writing on
29 April 1933 of the German worker's film *Kuhle Wampe,* Platt states:
"'Kuhle Wampe' (Whither Germany) . . . is a picture made by united
working class organizations of that country. It depicts the conditions of
the unemployed and their struggles against starvation and misery. But
throughout the picture there is a fine spirit of determination to fight.
Many of the people who took part in the production are now in Fascist
prison camps and dungeons" (6). Platt finds the Russian film *The Return
of Nathan Beck* also exemplary in its humane treatment of race and class:

> In this Soviet movie we have for the first time in the history of films a
> portrait of an American Negro worker, a bricklayer, in the Soviet Union—
> an honest, living, breathing conscious human being, depicted as a true
> equal with his white brethren, who are building a new world, where segre-
> gation, jimcrow, and racial superiority does not and cannot exist. (6)

These comments are about as close as we get to an indication of Platt's
preference for the Lukácsian aesthetic principle of narrative realism that
focuses on typical heroes to address larger sociopolitical issues. Again,
Russian films and directors were regularly discussed in the *Liberator*
because the critics wanted to assure readers and film lovers that progres-

sive films were out there and that they were the models on which a new ideal of film production and spectatorship could and should be based. Platt suggested that indeed American spectators were impoverished by the fact that American film screenings did not have the interactive dimension available to film audiences in the Soviet Union, where directors and cameramen met to discuss the films with their audiences (9 September 1934).

Through the *Liberator*, black spectators were introduced to the philosophies of Eisenstein and the innovative color film experiments in Nicolai Eck's film *Road to Life* (Platt, 23 December 1933), Russian films such as *Enemies of Progress*, one of the first sound films from Russia to make it to America (Platt, 11 November 1933), and others. It is clear that the *Liberator* functioned as a progressive film school of sorts for its readers. *Liberator* readers were exposed to alternative filmmaking praxis, both in America and abroad, and in the process new vistas of spectatorship opened up before them that in turn obliged them to share their new ways of seeing films with the community at large. Platt's and Camera Eye's affirmation of the Film and Photo League and imported Soviet films becomes the flip side of the mainstream black press's promotional discourse for dominant cinema productions.

Transgressing the Boundaries

RADICAL FILM CRITIQUES IN *THE CRISIS*

Before W. E. B. Du Bois terminated his quarter-century official relationship with the NAACP, ending his reign as the editor in chief of its *The Crisis* magazine (Graham-Du Bois 1978, 68), he brought a discourse of radicalism before the African American mainstream. Prior to his 1933 departure, Du Bois's *Crisis* published an article that surveyed the attitudes of fourteen leading African American newspaper editors on the issue of Communism and "the Negro question." The article, entitled "Negro Editors on Communism: A Symposium of the American Negro Press," is an important historical document of black attitudes toward Communism because it reflects the views of black captains of consciousness who arbitrated and disseminated news and information about Communism to America's black masses. As one might expect, there is no monolith or consensus of views on the matter, although W. P. Dabney of the Ohio *Union* best articulates the primary reason for black interest in Communism. He asked, "What matters motive? When a man is drowning does he demand reasons for the helping hand?" The issue is that by 1932 *The Crisis* and other mainstream black press outlets could ill afford to ignore or fail to take a stand on this phenomenal political development. For its part, *The Crisis* met the challenge head-on by occasioning the black press symposium and producing its own share of radical literature, beginning with Du Bois's own efforts to acquaint black Americans with the fundamentals of Marxist ideology as applicable to African American liberation struggles. In the March 1933 edition, Du Bois wrote an essay entitled "Karl Marx and the Negro," which was followed in May by his "Marxism and the Negro Problem" article. The former is a historical overview of Karl Marx's interest in the issue of American slavery and his epistolary writings on the subject, and the latter is Du Bois's attempt to adapt Marxist philosophy to the specificities of African American oppression, to use Cornel West's phrase. It is interesting that even the post–Du Bois *The Crisis* continued a discursive engagement with the issue well into the decade. One such example is an article published in the May 1935 edition, entitled "Which Way Out for the Negro?" This question effectively sums up the black intelligentsia's dilemma over black America's flirtation with Communism in the thirties. This, then, is the context of *The Crisis*'s publication of radical film critiques.

Louise Thompson's February 1933 article "The Soviet Film" is the initial offering of the four *The Crisis* essays in the radical mode that will be discussed briefly. The others are Langston Hughes's "Going South in Russia" (June 1934) and Loren Miller's two entries, "Uncle Tom in Hollywood" (November 1934) and "Hollywood's New Negro Films" (June 1938). What is most important here is that *The Crisis,* through its publication of these four articles, makes it possible for the radical perspective on the cinema to be extended beyond its traditional boundaries of influence in the pages of Communist front literary organs like the *Liberator,* the *New Masses,* and the *Daily Worker.* At the same time, however, it is important to note that although the "jargons of authenticity" that became discursive markers of, say, the *Liberator*'s film criticism are less pronounced in *The Crisis* essays, they do surface and with enough force to announce their Marxist-inflected critical imperatives.[40]

Though they were published months apart, it is important that we consider Thompson's and Hughes's articles in tandem, since both deal with the unrealized film project *Black and White,* which was to be a collaborative venture among Russian filmmakers and black artists to portray African American workers and their struggles with racial prejudice in the United States. Although Louise Thompson and Langston Hughes, like all the other black film critics under consideration here, might be considered members of the "black bourgeoisie," in E. Franklin Frazier's terms, their well-known contacts with the Communist Party U.S.A. (CPUSA) reposition them, ideologically at least, as bourgeois class outsiders. Significantly, it was Thompson who assembled the twenty-one black artists, including Hughes, for the Russian expedition (Naison 1983, 67). To defuse mounting public criticism of the failed project, Thompson and Hughes defended their participation in the project, which Thompson contends was grossly and strategically misrepresented by "the white capitalist press of America" (37).

In "The Soviet Film," Thompson addresses the film issue directly, whereas Hughes's "Going South in Russia" presents an ethnographic comparative analysis of Russian and American racial politics. For Thompson, the controversy surrounding the "postponed" film project was little more than an orchestrated campaign of misinformation employed by the white press "to discredit in the eyes of American Negroes the one country in the whole world which gives them complete equality" (Thompson 1933, 37). To corroborate this position, she cites political motivations behind United Press correspondent Eugene Lyons's decision to publicize the statements of four disgruntled members of the black entourage while suppressing the signed statement commending the project issued by herself and thirteen other members of the group. Thompson believed that the "white capitalist press" used the "postponement" of this film to disparage blacks and the Soviet Union in one easy motion. For Thompson, the issue hinges on the white press's specious attempts to transform *Black and White*'s not uncommon production problems and difficulties into a scenario of international intrigue:

> The matter of postponement of a film is something which occurs daily in Hollywood or other film centers. Scenario and technical difficulties are not mysterious, political intrigues in any place but the Soviet Union. In the case of this film, the facts of its postponement are very simple to understand, once one divorces them from the entanglement of bourgeois propaganda against the Soviet Union. (37)

Thompson explains the problem as simply a matter of premature planning on the part of the film producers, who sent for the group "before the necessary preparations for the production of the picture had been completed in the Soviet Union." Because the group could not agree on the final script before the winter season, she says that it was mutually agreed that a postponement was wise. Thompson insists that the film was not abandoned, only postponed until August 1933. Ultimately Thompson wants to remind the black community that given the white press's history of disinformation where black issues were concerned, the mainstream press's accounts of this unique experience could not be accepted at face value. For her, the true betrayal, at that point, was perpetrated not by Meschrabpom-Film but by the four members of the African American entourage who as a result of their public recriminations provided their historical oppressors with new ammunition to be used against them.

Hughes's "Going South in Russia" is a Dickensian tale of two nations' different approaches to the issue of racial difference. The article is an autobiographical travelogue of his experiences while traveling by train to the southern regions of the new Soviet Union. By contrasting the treatment of racial and national minorities residing in the southernmost regions of that continent to the plight of African Americans in the American South's "Black Belt" region, Hughes delivers an indirect rationale for black intellectuals' favorable predisposition toward Communism. At the same time, he deflects attention and criticism away from charges that "the few intellectuals espousing the cause are no closer to the movement than the average ballyhoo man is to the circus he advertises," as *Pittsburgh Courier* editor R. L. Vann (1932, 154) derisively contends. Because Hughes had already discussed the film project in detail in the *Liberator,* this essay can be seen as a companion piece that defends the experience in more humanistic terms. Hughes constructs the essay around painful memories, flashbacks if you will, of his Jim Crow experiences riding American trains and the lack of racial discrimination experienced by himself and other black members of the group on the Soviet trains.

You can never travel anywhere [in America] without being reminded of your color, and oft-times suffering great inconveniences. Now I am riding South from Moscow and am not Jim-Crowed. . . . so I make a happy mental note in the back of my mind to write home to the Negro papers: "There is no Jim Crow on the trains of the Soviet Union." . . . I learned that there were many cities in Central Asia where dark men and women are in control of the government. And I thought about Mississippi where . . . Negroes cannot even vote. And you will never meet them riding the sleeping car. Truly a land of Before and After. . . . Before, no theatres, no movies, no modern culture. Now, national art encouraged and developed everywhere. (Hughes 1934, 162)

It is true that the film *Black and White* never materialized. (And since there seems to be no follow-up information detailing Hughes's and Thompson's reactions to this missed opportunity, it is difficult to speculate about their final views on this matter.) Nonetheless these articles by Hughes and Thompson illustrate unequivocally black radical intellectuals' resolve to go literally to the ends of the earth on the slightest chance that they might intervene in Hollywood's intractable racist film discourse. Because the Russian filmmakers' global influence was legendary, it is easy to imagine that Hughes and Thompson envisioned *Black and White* as a means by which the American film industry might begin to rethink its proscription against black writers, which, in turn, could contribute to redefinitions of the black cinematic image.[41]

Loren Miller's (1934, 1938) film criticism that appeared in *The Crisis* signaled yet another developmental phase of thirties film criticism. First, his are among the lengthiest of film discussions designed for a general magazine readership, which not surprisingly allows for a more thorough examination of the issues at hand. Second, Miller's articles advance beyond mere content analysis and positive and negative image criticism to considerations of how Hollywood's triangulated production processes involving audience response, film texts, and production teams mutually interact and react upon themselves and ultimately on the larger socioeconomic structure of American society. By considering these multifaceted aspects in one essay, Miller initiates some of the earliest black metacritiques of mass culture's hegemonizing effects, which later critics develop more fully.

For example, in his essay "Uncle Tom in Hollywood," which appeared in the November 1934 *Crisis,* Miller considers the manifestations of racial politics that radiate throughout the Hollywood mode of production, better known as the studio system, from a materialist perspective. He considers the racial economy at work in the Production Code, on both explicit and implicit levels. The "unwritten, but iron clad rules in the movie industry," as set forth by the Code, require films with interracial casts to depict white characters as victors, or "overlords." In this way, Miller sees the Code functioning as a self-fulfilling prophecy that demands nothing in the way of intellectual imagination, since black actors are relegated to "either buffoons or ubiquitous Uncle Toms" (Miller 1934b, 329). He thus credits the written codes against miscegenation with legitimating such vicious screen types as were originated by *The Birth of a Nation*. The "cumulative effect" of such representational strategies as newsreels' caricatures of "Negro revivals or baptisings," while avoiding the legal and economic roots of African American emiseration, Miller holds, "is tremendously effective in shaping racial attitudes" locally and globally. As a particularly poignant example, Miller's consideration of issues surrounding black reception of the MGM film *Trader Horn* reveals the triumph of Hollywood's racial hegemony, wherein the oppressed are recruited to applaud their own victimization. His analysis of the dilemma of black reception bears quoting at length:

> A few years ago I attended a showing of Trader Horn . . . at a Negro theater. One scene depicts the "beautiful"—of course, blond—heroine in the clutches of "savage" Africans. In typical Hollywood thriller style the girl is saved just as all hope is ebbing away. At this particular showing the audience burst into wild applause when the rescue scene flashed on the screen. I looked around. Those who were applauding were ordinary Negro working people, and middle class folk. Hollywood's movie makers had made the theme so commonplace and glorious that it seemed quite natural that white virtue should triumph over black vice. Obviously these spectators were quite unconscious of the fact that they were giving their stamp of approval to a definite pattern of racial relationships in which they are always depicted as the lesser breed. (Miller 1938, 329)

Miller's psychosocial critique attempts to demonstrate how spectators internalize Hollywood's antiblack codifications and significations as a result of years of inculcation to this way of viewing cinematic articulations of racial difference. To his credit, Miller rightfully points out the disingenuousness of Hollywood's attempts to excuse these practices "on the grounds that it is merely supplying the audiences with what they want" while concealing the fact that it often induces audiences to want the images it produces, as happened, he recalls, in World War I. Miller's prescriptive to counter such acts of black spectatorial conditioning is as follows: "They [audiences] must be taught to recognize and resent anti-Negro sentiment in such a manner [that] their feelings can reach the box office. . . . They must stop applauding for such imperialistic jingoism as Trader Horn." Moreover, he observes that "the Negro masses will adopt a critical attitude only if organs of opinion and Negro leadership establish an adequate critique for their guidance." As with the *Liberator*'s discourse, Miller's advocacy of a Leninist vanguardism in film criticism is evident.

Miller also demystifies the studio system and the moguls' gatekeeping function by making it clear that Hollywood, controlled still by those same powerful individuals interlocked with other monopolies and oligopolies, was driven by economic and not artistic imperatives. He makes this point by revealing the capitalist interests behind the studio system. He names the Chase National Bank and the Rockefellers as major Hollywood players, and he reveals that Louis B. Mayer had personal ties to the Republican Party machine. Miller also calls attention to Jack Warner's reputation as the Roosevelt spokesman in Hollywood (1938, 329). Such powerful businessmen and politicians as these, Miller says,

> direct the destinies of the film world. The pictures they produce accord roughly yet firmly with their politico-economic outlook. Certainly, these men . . . realize that the movies are valuable aids in preserving the status on which their own welfare and profits depend. An important factor in the preservation of the status quo is the continued subordination of the Negro people. White superiority has cash value. (Miller 1938, 329)

If we accept Miller's explanation of the studio moguls' gatekeeping function, then the scapegoating myth of the southern box office becomes easier to put in perspective. According to this view, it is not that the South dictates racist representations against the objections of more enlightened Hollywood executives, as most were led to believe. More accurately, Hollywood and its Wall Street backers used the South's rabid racism as a cover for their own needs to legitimate a racially divided social polity.

Miller brooks no compromise. He criticizes the black press for its failures and complicity in this situation: "Criticism of the movies is in a deplorable state at the present time." For Miller, black film criticism in the black press "is worse than useless. . . . It is acceptance of 'our place.'" Black spectators are not absolved, either. "The people who can change that attitude are the theater-goers themselves. . . . Armed with an intelligently critical spirit," black spectators can "demand pictures that reflect their own lives and aspirations. So long as we sit acquiescent and give either passive or active support to the Hollywood bilge of the present we are guilty of teaching ourselves, our own children and millions of white, yellow and brown movie-goers the world over that the Negro is an inferior" (Miller 1938, 336). Miller asserts that the reform movement instigated by the Catholic Legion of Decency and other activist groups has created an opportune moment to force Hollywood to change its representational practices. But he insists that these reform campaigns will not make race an issue in their "'clean' films" reform, because "these moralists themselves define 'cleanliness' in traditional terms. The Catholics, for example, list the showing of miscegenation as objectionable along with perversion and sexual intercourse" (329). If reform of Hollywood's attitudes on race is to be achieved, Miller insists, "the Negro will have to fend for himself" (329).

Miller's essay "Hollywood's New Negro Films" critiques the black-cast films produced by the interracial independent film producers. This article, written in June 1938, reiterates many of the same charges leveled at Hollywood. In the intervening four years, Miller finds "little to cheer about" in this counterprogramming strategy (1938, 8). He suggests that these be produced in accordance with a niche versus a mass audience appeal. In that way, the so-called "race" films would better reflect and respond more accurately to the specific needs of the black audience they purport to serve. Miller rightfully recognizes that films unencumbered by the racial and thematic narrative demands of the nation's white masses could address black issues in a more straightforward manner. As a result, Miller believes, films targeted at a black audience would survive and thrive even after the initial lure of the novelty of black-cast films had run its predictable course. "There is no reason why producers should be permitted to hide behind either popular taste or difficulties of distribution. It must be remembered," Miller adds, "that movie makers help dictate public taste as well as cater to it" (9). He opposes such black-cast films as *Bargain with Bullets, Dark Manhattan,* and *Harlem on the Prairie* to such Hollywood socially conscious films as *Dead End, Fury,* and *They Won't Forget,* and he finds the former lacking in comparison. Miller suggests that if Hollywood can broach such serious social concerns as lynching, then the independents' race films should go even further in their cinematic engagements with "the complexities of Negro life in America" (8).

> What is required for the job is the simple honesty necessary to turn the camera around and focus it in such a manner that it will catch the phases of our lives deliberately neglected for cash and carry considerations. . . . The conflicts that arise out of the Negro's necessary attempts to cope with these [Jim Crow] problems provide the richest mine of dramatic material available. (Miller 1934a, 9)

The biggest complaint Miller has with the race films is that they replicate and perpetuate Hollywood's distortions of black life. Although he is sensitive to the race film industry's comparative lack of financial and technical resources, he finds these limitations no justification for the films' failures to represent black issues more honestly and adequately, especially given the social responsibility that attaches to the production and diffusion of such a powerfully influential public medium. For Miller, the desire for less of an emphasis on "lavish cafe and cabaret scenes" (1934a, 8), for example, "is not a plea for heavy-footed problem or propaganda films. All that can be asked is that the pictures tell the truth. Truth on the screen will pose its own problems and suggest answers and those answers will be the best possible 'propaganda'" (9). Miller's argument, then, is that if the independent's black-cast films would forgo their present "crass commercialism," they could become substantive alternatives to the Hollywood product, because they would "fulfill the real function of any art: help [people] understand the world in which [they] live and cope with the problems inherent in that world" (9). Miller is correct to point out the problems inherent in the black community's un-selfconscious embrace of black-cast films owing to a misdirected sense of "race-pride" (9). And though he does not dismiss or disparage the efforts of black and white independent film producers in absolute terms, he does call for a rethinking of the industry's cultural agenda as well as the black audiences' rededication to the cause of improved black cinematic representations.

As improved social conditions at the decade's end and Roosevelt's New Deal politics helped rein in much of the nation's radicalism, with its attendant mass agitations for social, economic, and political transformation, most of black America's radical activity was driven underground, if not obliterated altogether. In the face of this retrenchment, the cultural Left lost much of its appeal to the politically weary and economically besieged black community. Harold Cruse's (1967) description of this sociopolitical shift and its effect on black artists and intellectuals is instructive. Though he centers his discussion on Paul Robeson, whose career suffered tremendously as a result of his political beliefs and actions, the points that Cruse raises bear directly on the issue at hand.

> In joining the left wing in the 1930s, Robeson, as artist, encountered the old, unsolved problem of art versus politics. This problem had not even been solved in the 1920s for the white creative intellectuals such as John Dos Passos who broke with Communism in refusing their art [*sic*]. . . . The first issue of New Masses (May 1926), the literary and cultural magazine of the Communist movement, listed fifty-eight artists and writers as editors and contributors [including African Americans Claude McKay, Jean Toomer, and even Walter White]. (71)

By the end of the thirties, Cruse continues, "most of these leading writers moved and severed their relations with the Communist-influenced political left" (71). The resulting marginalization of black radical intellectuals created a leadership void in the black cultural arena that was rapidly filled by the more moderate black intelligentsia, now led in large part by Walter White, the executive secretary for the NAACP. As the 1940s dawned, White and the NAACP resumed their ideological dominance of black cultural politics and succeeded in forging a rapprochement of sorts with some of Hollywood's major studios. Thomas Cripps has described a starstruck Walter White, who nearly turned the venerable civil rights organization into an apologist organization for Hollywood (1993a, 48–62). It is certainly true that by the forties, the mainstream black press, including *The Crisis*, was less strident in its opposition to Hollywood. In the words of black press editor Roscoe Dunjee, "The radical of today is the conservative of tomorrow. Ten years ago the N.A.A.C.P. was classified by many as dangerous to American institutions" (156). Clearly, the times had changed.

Even though the failure of the cultural Left in the face of mounting anti-Communist sentiments nationwide ensured the primacy of the accommodationist hegemony, the strategies and tactics of resistance initiated by the radicals were not abandoned entirely. Quite the contrary; in fact, the next generation of black critics of film, particularly Melvin B. Tolson and C. L. R. James, continued to walk in the *Liberator* critics' "ideological footsteps," to borrow a phrase from Manthia Diawara (1993a, 14). Thus the black press's dialectical engagement with the Hollywood cinema during the thirties became the discursive precondition out of which subsequent oppositional black film literary formations emerged.

5

The Recalcitrant Gaze

CRITIQUING HOLLYWOOD IN THE 1940S

Between me and the other world there is ever an unasked question . . .
How does it feel to be a problem?"
—W. E. B. Du Bois, *The Souls of Black Folk*

During the war years Hollywood reached a new low in hiring Negro
talent. . . . "you don't need maids and porters when you're making mostly
war pictures."—Carlton Moss, "Your Future in Hollywood"

The Southern Box Office excuse is all washed up and the movie industry
as a whole stands exposed as the real culprit in the prejudice against
Negroes.—Robert Jones, "How Hollywood Feels about Negroes"

The anti-Negro image is thus a ritual object of which Hollywood is not
the creator, but the manipulator. . . . Obviously these films are not *about*
Negroes at all; they are about what whites think and feel about Negroes.
—Ralph Ellison, *Shadow and Act*

The decade of the 1940s presented black intellectuals and cultural leaders
with new sociocultural concerns that became important subtexts in the
film criticism of this era. Although the coming of World War II effectively "put an end to the radicalism of the thirties," which was replaced by
a national mood of reaction, conformity, and conservatism (Holman and
Harman 1992, 351), the legacy of radical discursive practices and the
prospect of black conscription in the war imbued the black press's accommodationist literature with a renewed sense of urgency to push forward
its program of racial and social justice. This period also saw the expan-

sion of the black press with such new publications as the academic quarterly journal *Phylon: The Atlanta Review of Race and Culture,* published
by the Atlanta University (and edited for a time by W. E. B. Du Bois),
and the mass-market monthlies *Our World, Negro Digest,* and many
others.

These new press outlets quickly became important forums for discussing and disseminating the increasing production of black film criticism
and commentary along with other general cultural criticism as well. In
fact, this flurry of literary activity is indicative of African Americans'
growing impatience with the stagnation of black racial and social justice
in America, and it reflects the community's concerted efforts to place
black civil rights at the center of the nation's renewed call for protecting
democracy in the face of global fascism. Black intellectuals and community leaders once again sought to enlist the cinema in their new plans for
effecting social change. This rededicated interest in the cinema led to
newer, more sophisticated paradigmatic formations of black film analysis
and commentary that ultimately fulfill the intellectual promise held out
by the film discourses of earlier decades.

It is important to stress that though the cinema literature of this period
is less politically polarized or fractured than its immediate predecessors
in the depression-era thirties, it nevertheless issues from a contested
discursive terrain that makes manifest African Americans' intragroup
struggles to redefine black subjectivity for a nation seemingly ready to
confront its historical and traditional racial assumptions. Reflecting this
new tenor of the times was the University of North Carolina Press's
publication of Rayford Logan's controversial but highly influential critical anthology *What the Negro Wants* for a white mainstream audience
(Janken 1993, 147). Publication of the book was envisioned by white
liberals and black intellectuals involved with the project as an important
first step toward ushering in a new era of American racial understanding
and cooperation. The philosophical differences that gave rise to the
book's fractious production and reception created many of the conditions
that brought about new critical approaches to the cinema in the forties.
Consequently, it is necessary to consider briefly the case of *What the
Negro Wants* before proceeding to our discussion of black film criticism
during this pivotal era.

In 1944 the University of North Carolina Press published *What the
Negro Wants* after much unanticipated wrangling and recrimination

Cover photo of Rayford Logan's *What the Negro Wants,* the groundbreaking post–World War II anthology on race and culture in America. Courtesy of the University of North Carolina Press.

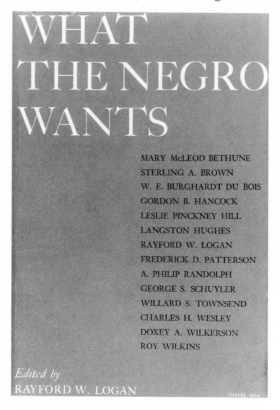

WHAT THE NEGRO WANTS

MARY McLEOD BETHUNE
STERLING A. BROWN
W. E. BURGHARDT DU BOIS
GORDON B. HANCOCK
LESLIE PINCKNEY HILL
LANGSTON HUGHES
RAYFORD W. LOGAN
FREDERICK D. PATTERSON
A. PHILIP RANDOLPH
GEORGE S. SCHUYLER
WILLARD S. TOWNSEND
CHARLES H. WESLEY
DOXEY A. WILKERSON
ROY WILKINS

Edited by
RAYFORD W. LOGAN

CHAPEL HILL

among the press, Logan, and his contributors (Janken 1993, 161). The text, a critical anthology about American race relations, was written by leading black intellectuals and activists and was intended to be incontrovertible evidence of white liberals' sincere efforts "to solve the American race problem." According to one of the book's editors, "this ably written book published by a Southern press" was to be "an outstanding example of the frontal approach" in the battle against racial prejudice (Janken 1993, 163). Though conceived in 1941 by Logan as his own single-author monograph on "the 'Negro in post-war society,'" *What the Negro Wants,* produced three years later, is a compromise text intended to satisfy the press's demand for "a book which represents the personal creed of 10 or 15 prominent Negroes" (147). Logan, a staunch integrationist, made every effort to produce a manuscript that "would be palatable to the southern liberals and the white mainstream generally that was the target audience" (147), going so far as to inquire of William Terry Couch, the editor and instigator of the project, if "such men as Richard Wright, Paul Robeson,

Langston Hughes and Max Yergan, whose affiliations are said to be euphemistically extreme left," should be deliberately excluded. Couch advised: "It seems to me the book will be most interesting if it represents all the more important views now current among negroes, whether these views are radical or conservative or in between" (147). However, the fact that Logan's conservative, radical, and moderate contributors were consistent in the call for "complete equality and the discontinuance of Jim Crow" (148) prompted Couch and the press to reject the final manuscript, claiming that such thematic unity "made the articles redundant" (148–49), when the real obstacle was simply Couch's fear that "publication of the book would have 'extremely unfortunate' consequences for southern race relations" (155). Moreover, Couch's final explanation of why he felt obliged to abandon the project not only provides rare insight into the fundamental problem of American race relations at that moment but also conveys a recrudescence of white paternalism that militates against solving America's race problem even today.

> The things Negroes are represented as wanting seem to me far removed from those they *ought* to want [italics mine]. Most of the things they are represented as wanting can be summarized in the phrase: complete abolition of segregation. If this is what the Negro wants, nothing could be clearer than that what he needs, and needs most urgently, is to revise his wants. (quoted in Janken 1993, 155)

This statement, more than any other, is ample testimony to the limits of white liberals' ability even to perceive, let alone to accept, unconditional racial equality. This is certainly true for many southern white liberals in the forties. And given the frequency of race riots in northern urban areas at that historical juncture (Janken 1993, 150), Couch's remarks cannot be viewed as reflecting only southern attitudes. Whereas Couch and other white liberals believed that wartime conditions signaled America's willingness to address the race problem, so long as blacks did not expect full racial equality, the June 1943 "violence in Harlem, along with the riot in Detroit that same month, were graphic signs that blacks were increasingly unwilling to participate in the defense of the United States so long as it refused to grant them full democratic rights" (150). This is the background of Logan's embattled efforts to get *What the Negro Wants* published. Ultimately it was Logan's threat to sue Couch and the University of North Carolina Press that forced the latter to relent and publish the unrevised manuscript. Despite the press's deep reservations about the book's marketability, *What the Negro Wants* sold well and went through three printings during its first year of publication (162).

Even though the book was well received by both black and white presses, some leading black intellectuals felt the book had not gone far enough in conveying to the nation what the "Negro" truly wanted. Following publication of Logan's *What the Negro Wants,* a group of intellectuals associated with Richard Wright proposed in late November of 1944 a more radical response to the book (Fabre 1973, 267). The working title for the Wright volume was *The Meaning of Negro Experience in America* (267). Michel Fabre reports that Wright had

> refused, the year before, to contribute to Rayford Logan's book *What the Negro Wants* because of a disagreement between the white liberals and the Blacks assigned to write it. . . . In the spring of 1944, Wright had even thought of organizing what he called a "thinking coterie" and of assuring the collaboration of certain friends and acquaintances [Including] . . . Horace Cayton, Melvin B. Tolson . . . Lawrence D. Reddick, C. L. R. James . . . All accredited writers. (Fabre 1973, 268)

When plans for this book failed, Wright pursued the possibility of an alternative work with the same group of intellectuals. The idea was to produce a popular magazine entitled *American Pages* (Fabre 1973, 580). Wright biographer Constance Webb (1968) quotes Wright describing *American Pages* as "a magazine reflecting a minority mood and point of view. Nonpartisan, nonpolitical, espousing no current creed, ideology or organization" (220). Webb asserts that Wright wanted to produce "a popular publication" targeted at the American white mainstream that would "be a means of 'psychoanalyzing' the American middle class reader . . . and would attempt, without telling him so, to resolve his conflicts, rendering him conscious of his false illusions about race and subject peoples, about individual lives, and about America's happiness and success formula" (219). Webb describes Wright's formula for ensuring the magazines' popular appeal across such traditional boundaries as race, class, politics, and literary tastes:

> More specifically, there would be fiction, articles, essays, poetry, cartoons, profiles of individuals who lived the "American way" such as Frank Sinatra, Gene Krupa, Frances Farmer; surveys on race tension's [*sic*] popularly

written, excerpts of novels that revealed the American scene, studies of crime and criminals, black and white. (Webb 1968, 220)

According to Webb, Wright believed that by "using the Negro as an abstract and concrete frame of reference to reflect a constructive criticism upon the culture of the nation as a whole" (219), the aims of better racial understanding could be achieved indirectly, without didacticism. This project failed because Wright could not procure the financial backing necessary for such an ambitious undertaking.[1] Wright, Cayton, and James later tried to revise these plans for a popular cultural journal, but the plan was abandoned when Wright moved to Paris (Fabre 1973, 268). Although these myriad plans for a more radical but popular forum for critical discussion of American cultural life were never realized, each of the authors in the group continued to write and publish cultural criticism. We will consider some of the film literature produced by this "thinking coterie" of black intellectuals.

Our purpose in reviewing these literary struggles over who gets to articulate "what the Negro wants" and how the desiring black American subject is to be represented for mainstream consumption is twofold. First of all, Logan's *What the Negro Wants* is a seminal cultural text in the history of African American intellectual thought on the eve of World War II, and the controversy it sparked in both white and black literary circles is emblematic of the struggle for representational control of the black image between many of these same intellectuals and the Hollywood film establishment. Second, Wright's ill-fated attempt to contest publicly *What the Negro Wants* bespeaks, once again, the conflictual nature of leading black intellectuals' positions on what constitutes authentic "blackness." Additionally, it is by members of Wright's veritable black brain trust that some of the most sophisticated and indispensable film literature is produced, such as the works of Lawrence Reddick, Melvin B. Tolson, and Ralph Ellison. Film criticism written by Reddick, Tolson, and Ellison will be of special interest here. It is important to emphasize that these three prominent leftist intellectuals often espoused political ideologies and discursive positions that represent a continuity with, and evolution of, the thirties-era radical film criticism. Similarly, Logan and other mainstream black writers author film criticism that reactivates the earlier accommodationist approach even as they reflect the general sociocultural agenda of the times.

What the Negro Wants

HOLLYWOOD, THE WAR YEARS, AND THE NEW BLACK

CRITICAL PARADIGMS

We begin our analysis with Rayford Logan's (1940) contribution to the forties-era film discourse, which concerns, among other things, "the influence of the movies on American Negro youth" (431), and selected film discussions published in *Opportunity, Our World, Negro Digest,* and *Phylon.* We will also consider commentary from the black newspapers that bears directly on the issue at hand. Since the works produced in the magazines exhibit certain thematic and ideological consistencies, they yield new paradigmatic formations of critical engagement with such issues as mass media effects, cinema history and the racial discourse, exhibition and the myth of the southern box office, and spectatorship and subjectivity. The one issue that transects each of these critical categories is American anxiety about World War II. Rayford Logan's 1940 essay "Negro Youth and the Influence of the Press, Radio, and Cinema" inaugurates these critical discussions.

Mass Media Effects and the Case of Black Youths

Prior to his involvement with, and publication of, *What the Negro Wants,* Logan, a professor of history at Howard University, put his academic training to work on a project considering the effects of popular culture on African American youths. Logan's essay, published in the July 1940 edition of the *Journal of Negro Education,* is a study of mass media effects on black youths that is in dialogue with a host of mass communications surveys that attempted to explain some of the root causes of youthful delinquency in America.[2] For the most part, these studies attempted to gauge what was perceived as the deleterious effects of "the industrialization and commercialization of popular culture" on children (Strinati 1995, 11). In many ways, Logan's critique, which questions many of the epistemological assumptions about mass media's technological determinism, is prescient indeed. For example, in his opening remarks, Logan challenges the cultural bias that informs certain anthropological positions and interpretations.

One problem, however, that gives me concern is this—even when we know how youth act, can we be sure of our interpretation of their acts? For example, many missionaries are unable correctly to explain native customs because they interpret them in the light of their own experience. A classic illustration is "bride purchase," denounced by almost every missionary who has been to Africa. . . . One might add that an American heiress who, by a pre-nuptial agreement, confers a sum of money on her titled prospective bridegroom, would certainly be insulted if any one accused her of buying her husband. (Logan 1940, 425)

Logan's astute observation that Western missionaries' biased interpretations of African cultural practices result from their own misdirected ideological impositions recalls Dominick LaCapra's (1987) caution against the problem of "transference" or the "temptation to assert full control over the 'object' of study through ideologically suspect procedures," namely, "narcissism" and "scapegoating of the 'other'" (72). It is against this system of racial and ideological scapegoating that Logan rightfully challenges Western missionaries' characterizations of African marriage customs in terms of savagery and barbarism while failing to recognize the analogous relationship between this "other" cultural practice and their own upper-class matrimonial traditions. For Logan, it is important to recognize similar blind spots in the research findings on mass media influences and American youth. Whereas many of the studies attempted to frame the delinquency problem solely in terms of baleful mass media influences, Logan complicates this view by calling attention to other social explanations that might account for American youths' antisocial behaviors as well, such as the "yearning to earn a decent living and to escape sudden death or mutilation in another futile war" (Logan 1940, 427). Although Logan's study includes the print media and radio, we are most interested in his observations about "the influence of the movies on American Negro youth," which he confesses "has interested me for a number of years" (431).

Logan initiates his cinema discussion by acknowledging the importance of such studies, but he problematizes the focus on white attitudes: "I know of no survey that has completely analyzed the movie with respect to American Negro youth" (431). His purpose, then, is to fill this void. First, he considers black youth spectatorship by examining genre appeal as discernible through attendance patterns at specified black theaters. Focusing on Westerns, Logan observes that "'Westerns' have no great appeal to those who attend the Booker T., Republic, Lincoln, or Howard in Washington, [D.C.], the Royal and Asby in Atlanta" (431). He discovers a break in this pattern at other, more upscale theaters. Western epics, he concludes, were more popular at these theaters than were the "Buck Jones and Gene Autry canned goods." Logan then constructs the following generic topology and character archetypes of Hollywood films that black youth consumed:

> We have had the era of the pie throwing and the musical comedy, the gangster hero, the G-man hero and the gangster villain, the Dead End Kids and the Rejuvenated Brats, the Glorification of the Demi-Mondaine and the Retribution of Damaged Goods, the Child Wonder and the Adolescent in the Throes, the Good Old American Family, the Glamor of War and the Sale of Sex. (432)

Citing the Payne Fund Studies (a multiyear, multi-institutional survey that attempted to measure the behavioral influence of films on children), he indicates which film genres were dominant in a given year. Although Logan implies that such an accounting of films' thematic content and rates of diffusion for certain genres is useful, he is not convinced that these factors alone are adequate determinants of youths' overall social and cultural attitudes. As he puts it, "how can we judge the effects of these pictures upon impressionable youth? We could speculate interminably." He adds, "We must not make the mistake of jumping to the conclusion that the demonstrations of youth while in the cinema are earmarks of their conduct outside. . . . Nor should we conclude that every act of rowdyism committed by young people stems from something that they have seen in a movie" (432–33). After reflecting upon a specific instance of his and friends' own juvenile misconduct, he states, "No movie suggested that act of rowdyism to us" (433). For him, then, youthful outbursts in the theater are no more indications of delinquency than are the exuberant yells of fans at sporting events of their general demeanors. Considering the similarities in the two cases, Logan rejects researchers' "scapegoating" of the former while apparently ignoring the latter. He subscribes to the belief that the "frenzied cries, screams and yells" of youths in movies are basically harmless, especially when contained within socially regulated environments. In addition, Logan sees the process as likely cathartic, as "a kind of safety valve," but ultimately he concludes that "we should be rather chary in interpreting what those things mean" (425–33).

When he moves on to a consideration of the educational value of films, however, at first glance Logan's remarks seem to contradict his earlier position:

> I should hazard the guess that the movies that have the more permanent effect are those of an educational or propagandistic nature. Films that are really educational stand out in this group. It has been rather gratifying to observe the interest of students, most of whom are not history majors, in historical films. Their value is clearly demonstrable. "The Tower of London," "Robin Hood," "The Private Lives of Elizabeth and Essex" have meant more to my students, I modestly admit, than have my "brilliant" lectures on the appropriate subjects. Discussions in class have been more lively than those that followed a reading assignment on the same subject. (433)

What is striking about Logan's suggestion that educational and propagandistic films have more lingering effects is that he does not sufficiently unpack for his readers the social and cultural influences that support this contention, although his comments about historical films' pedagogical uses certainly allude to them. Although he has argued successfully against the tendency to make causal assumptions about film spectatorship and behavior, his contention that students can learn history from films poses the obvious concern—cannot students also learn antisocial behaviors from films as well? This question is answered by later research findings. Although the early research seemed to support the idea that films had a powerfully direct influence on audiences, later studies showed that nonmedia influences or "interpersonal networks," such as families and schools, vitiated these effects substantially (Lowery and DeFleur 1988, 165–67). With this in mind, Logan's example of his own experiences supports these later conclusions. Because the messages contained in historical films tend to be reinforced in school lessons, the theory holds that youths are more likely to retain this information, which explains Logan's point that such films are apt to create "permanent effects." According to this view, Logan's observations of the values and influences of historic films, for instance, can be seen as more nuanced than contradictory. (Of course, the issue of Hollywood films' historical accuracy is outside the scope of this discussion. And one presumes that Logan and other teachers availing themselves of films as a pedagogical tool would set the historical record straight for their students as the need arose.)

In his brief look at "propaganda" in films, Logan again touches on the anxieties generated by the prospect of World War II and the implications for race relations in the so-called social-consciousness films. Regarding America's prewar anxiety, he concludes that "'Ninotchka' is probably a much more effective vehicle against Communism than the strident labors of the Dies Committee" (Logan 1940, 433). Despite the fact that Hollywood evacuates the racial problem from such antilynching films as *Fury* (MGM, 1936) and *They Must Not Forget* (Warner Brothers, 1937), blunting the films' social impact, Logan still finds them "extremely effective arguments against lynching. . . . 'Black Fury' . . . told a more vivid story of the class struggle than a dozen tomes." He adds, "Many young Negroes who have not read The Grapes of Wrath will see the film. Suppose a faithful version of Native Son were to be produced!" These comments reveal Logan's optimistic view of the cinema, which he would like to see adopted by other professional educators. "The schools," he laments, "are definitely failing to take advantage of this marvelous aid" (433).

Logan's call for critical sobriety amid the social hysteria surrounding studies that attributed delinquency to the effects of mass media enacts an important intervention in the early history of mass media studies. Moreover, his call for a cautious and balanced approach to debates about mass culture, while it does not proffer concepts of resistant or transgressive readings of problematic film texts as such, clearly prefigures reconsiderations of popular culture by present-day cultural theorists. Logan does not deny the cinema's powerful influence, quite the contrary. Rather than give in to nostalgic desires for some imaginary ideal past or unattainable premedia society, or worse yet, repressive censorship measures, Logan insists that films be situated within their proper sociocultural context. This way their sway can be balanced against other social, cultural, and political institutions that similarly exert powerful influences on the attitudes of the nation's youth. Thus Logan points out that the cinema can be employed for constructive as well as destructive purposes. "For example," he writes:

Let us think of a course in Negro history that would include films portraying the life of Frederick Douglass, of Harriet Tubman, Booker T. Washington, and W. E. B. Du Bois, of Toussaint L'Overture. . . . If all of our
Negro universities and colleges would appropriate a certain sum for the
production of these pictures, I feel that would be making one of the most
significant steps in the whole history of education. The interest of Negro
youth in almost any type of picture in which Negroes play a role is according to my observation incontrovertible. (433)

In this passage, Logan touches on important themes that recur throughout the black film literature of this period and of the past, namely, the
need for films exploring historical topics that Hollywood willfully ne-
glected or consciously misrepresented, the underutilized educational potential of the cinema, and the desire of black spectators to experience
cinematic identification or *jouissance* with heroic black screen personae.
Clearly, Logan does not want to wait for, or count on, Hollywood to
become interested in these uplifting black historical themes. He wants
black educators and institutions to take the lead in crafting suitable black
screen heroes and heroines for black youths.

Finally, Logan also makes it clear that he does not accept the massifica-
tion or atomization theory of mass media effects through his discussion
of the different reception and exhibition contexts that distinguish the
various media. For him, the fact that some mass media messages are
encountered in the domestic sphere and others in the public makes broad
assumptions about their effects less generalizable. Another complicating
factor for such generalizations is that mass media messages targeted at
the domestic market, "rather than incorporating the bawdy 'masculine'
amusements of the urban streets [were] supposed to encourage genteel,
'feminine' forms of play" (Spigel 1992, 15), so that theoretically radio and
print messages would transmit a wide array of socially acceptable messages to counter "bawdy" amusements that pervade the public domain.[3]
Whereas Logan finds the public exhibition of films conducive to certain
quantifiable research methods, because attendance statistics indicate exactly what themes and narratives audiences are exposed to, he rightly
observes that media consumed in the domestic sphere are more difficult
to assess.

We do not know, especially in the case of the press and the radio, what
youth read and hear. And if we knew, we should have difficulty in deter-

mining the influence of each or of the three together. About all that we can conclude is this: No one of these three agencies utilizes to the best advantage its potential opportunities for good. (Logan 1940, 434)

By the mid-forties, the popular and scholarly presses also take up some of these issues. As with the Logan article, issues of spectatorship and cinematic portrayals of blackness predominate. The critical essays we will next consider raise issues of film history, the representation of history, content analysis, industry praxis, star discourse, and spectatorship.

Black Film Historiography

An important contribution to the forties film discourse is Lawrence Reddick's 1944 essay "Of Motion Pictures." Reddick's article pushes forward the incipient film historiography begun in 1919 by black filmmaker and critic William Foster, who wrote under the pseudonym Juli Jones.[4] Reddick takes a historical look at films over the decades, emphasizing such issues as cinematic form and content, star performance, and American films' racial ideologies. His essay is equally valuable for his cataloging of specific, unflattering traits that typify black screen characters in Hollywood, and his prescriptives for ways to bring about change in the motion picture industry. Reddick's essay originally appeared in the *Journal of Negro Education*.

Following Rayford Logan, Reddick (1944) frames his historical concerns in light of the milestone research conducted under the auspices of the Payne Fund, studies that emphasized "the immediate effects of motion pictures on their audiences" (3). For his project of interrogating the racial and political economy of black-themed film narratives, Reddick, however, conducts both synchronic and diachronic analyses of the cinema's racial discourse and "the social function of the movie in the realm of race relations" (20).

> The studies of the Payne Fund document what we have all guessed from our own impression; namely, that ideas of love, clothes, manners, and heroism among adolescents (and others, of course) are directly traceable to movies. . . . It is, therefore, important to inquire into what such a powerful instrument for influencing the attitudes and behavior of so many persons has had to say about the Negro. (3–4)

Compiling a "checklist" of 175 films, Reddick set out to determine which of these films could be classified as "pro-Negro," "anti-Negro," or "neutral" based on their figurations of African Americans. Of the 175, he found 75 to be "anti-Negro"; 13 were deemed "neutral," and only 11 were classified as "definitely pro-Negro" (4). In conducting a content analysis of this scope, Reddick wanted to draw analogies between the fact of films' known influences on matters of public tastes in fashions, or concepts about manners (which studies demonstrated are traceable to film), and public attitudes about racial difference. His twenty-two-page essay (one of the longest film articles of the period) is categorized as follows: (1) "The Early Years," (2) "Birth of a Nation," (3) "The Talkie," (4) "The Era of 'Gone with the Wind,'" (5) "Since 'Gone with the Wind,'" and (6) "Pattern of Change." In each of these subsections, Reddick groups, according to historical epochs, several "important films shown in the United States that have included Negro themes or Negro characters of more than passing significance" (4).[5]

Although space limits a full consideration of these six categories, an excerpt from his first section, "The Early Years," exemplifies Reddick's critical and methodological approaches. The following passage demonstrates Reddick's concerns beyond the pivotal concern with image considerations. The films' formal elements, thematic content, and sociocultural contexts are equally important to his analysis:

> Before 1915, despite constant improvements in technique and a rapidly expanding public interest in this cheap and thrilling amusement, the very best films of those days would be considered quite crude by modern standards. Uneven lighting and quick, jerky movements and melodramatic gestures of the actors appear amusing now. Yet to contemporary audiences these films were marvelous. Even in the beginning years, when the movies were principally "peep shows," the Negro was presented in an unfavorable light. . . . The very titles of popular favorites like *How Rastus Got His Turkey* and *Rastas Dreams of Zululand* suggest the type of low comedy of these split-reelers. *Coon-Town Suffragettes* was quite similar. (5)

Reddick's reminder that from the beginning the cinema inscribed African Americans in terms of a radical alterity to white norms is crucial to the development of his theses. It also suggests to his readers that derisive contemporary depictions of blacks are but continuations of previous misrepresentations of the black cinema subject, or object, in this case. As we can see, Reddick's approach is to explore the full spectrum of the cinema phenomenon so as to better assess the interlocking and interweaving of social, political, and cultural practices that contribute to cinema's powerful influence on the nation's collective racial unconscious over a four-decade span. Reddick situates his exegesis in the context of overt government campaigns to use the movies and their influence in national defense efforts after the attack on Pearl Harbor, which led directly to America's entry into World War II.[6] As an example of this strategic use of the cinema to influence public opinion in a specific direction, he offers the case of a wartime melodrama and its implied use value for the war effort. "Though there is no way of testing it, the movie play *Mrs. Miniver* probably did more to develop good will toward Britain among the masses of the American people than did all the speeches of all the diplomats combined" (4).[7]

In his discussion of *The Birth of a Nation*, Reddick reiterates points made in earlier critiques of the film. As with past criticism, his essay foregrounds the film's vexing duality. On the one side is the film's undeniable artistic contribution to world cinema history, which Reddick readily acknowledges. On the other is the venal racism that greatly compromises the film's narrative aspect, a venality that Reddick refuses to sublate in deference to the film's artistic innovations. "From the strictly artistic and technical point of view," he writes, "it was a masterpiece of conception and structure. Even today, it is important from this angle." Nevertheless, Reddick points out, "*Birth of a Nation* has remained, without question, the most vicious anti-Negro film that has ever appeared on the American screen" (6). He considers everything about the film, from the suppression campaign directed against it, to statistics about the film's reported box office receipts, to the film's contribution to the revitalization of the Ku Klux Klan (8).

His critique of the *Our Gang* comedies during the "talkie" period raises some interesting points. For Reddick, these films represent the first welcome break from the usual black stereotypical constructs. In his view, the films' fully integrated diegetic universe, where black and white children were not racially segregated, marked a significant advance over previous portrayals. At the same time, Reddick does disparage these films' "tendency to place the Negro child in a somewhat more ridiculous or subservient position" (9). Secondly, he finds the black child actors Sunshine Sammy, Farina, and Stymie to be "brilliant and winsome" and not likely to cause much dissonance for black spectators. The Buckwheat character, however, does not fare as well in Reddick's estimation. Nonetheless, he perceives the *Our Gang* films as important landmarks in the "attempt of Hollywood to do better by the Negro" since the advent of sound technology (9). Also in his "talkie" section, Reddick delves into the area of reception studies in his consideration of the press and audience responses to the black-cast films *Hallelujah, Hearts in Dixie, Emperor Jones*, and *Imitation of Life.*

His discussion of *Imitation of Life* brings to light the fundamental disparities existing between white producers of these narratives and the black audiences who consumed them. Reddick asserts that Fannie Hurst, who wrote the novel on which the film was based, "thought that Negroes should be a little more grateful for the 'break' which she had given them in her novel which carried over into the screen story." But Reddick reports that "editorials in the Negro press . . . Expressed annoyance and disgust at many scenes" (11). Reddick's observation vividly illustrates Stuart Hall's (1988) point that representation "is an extremely slippery customer" (27), and that reception is generally preconditioned by social and cultural factors such as racialized viewpoints. So that in terms of race, say, there can be an endless sliding of signifiers along the favorable/unfavorable representational spectrum depending on which racial group apprehends them. Reddick's short list of films "favorable to the Negro" (12) in this section includes only *Arrowsmith, Flying Down to Rio, The Spirit of Youth, Huckleberry Finn*, and *Dark Rapture.* For Reddick, these films are favorable because they treat African Americans as "dignified" three-dimensional characters with narrative agency and centrality. Unfortunately, however, these films are the exceptions to the rule.

In contrast, the films he considered unfavorable formed a long list indeed. Such British films as *Sanders of the River* and *Dark Sands* are singled out because although they constructed heroic black figures, Reddick asserts that these black heroes were crafted as alibis, "justifications and apologies for colonial imperialism" (13). It is important to note that Reddick makes this critique more than a decade before Roland Barthes's oft-quoted similar observation about an African soldier performing the same function for French imperialism. Reddick also identifies American films fitting this specious mode: the *March of Time* newsreels, *Judge Priest, Carolina, The Little Colonel, The Little Rebel, Steamboat 'round the Bend, So Red the Rose, Pennies from Heaven, King Kong, Baboona, When*

Africa Speaks, Trader Horn, The Green Pastures, Show Boat, and *Hypnotized.* What Reddick finds most disturbing about these film texts is their constant redeployment of the "stereotyped blackface minstrel tradition" (13), augmented now with denotations of black savagery and cannibalism, clearly crafted for the privileged gaze of the white spectatorial subject.[8]

In wrapping up his overview of the contemporary films on his list, Reddick focuses on *Gone with the Wind* and several films that follow it, such as *The Texan, Santa Fe Trail, Prisoner of Shark Island, Mr. Washington Goes to Town, Tennessee Johnson, Keep Punching, This Is the Army,* and *Tales of Manhattan.* Reddick has noticed that the racial discourse in these films has become especially efficacious because of their relative subtlety. Though he finds these films reeking with "anti Negro propaganda" (15), he also believes that their covert racism is potentially more damaging because they tend to smuggle in their racist ideologies through narrative indirection: "The social consciousness of the nation has developed to such a point that the inflammatory appeals of 1915 were not permissible in 1939. Perhaps there was little need for the former obviousness. The art of suggestion had matured" (15). Reddick sums up the danger of these newer approaches in the following statement that appears in his last subsection, "Pattern of Change":

> Directly and indirectly [the cinema] establishes associations and drives deeper into the public mind the stereotyped conception of the Negro. By building up this unfavorable conception, the movies operate to thwart the advancement of the Negro, to humiliate him, to weaken his drive for equality, and to spread indifference, contempt, and hatred for him and his cause. This great agency for the communication of ideas and information, therefore, functions as a powerful instrument for maintaining the racial subordination of the Negro people. (21)

The strength of Reddick's observation here is that it draws attention to some real effects of cinematic constructs "outside the sphere of the discursive" (Hall 1988, 27), and that these real effects too often naturalize black political and social repression. As impressive as Reddick's overall critical historiography is, his ability to chart out a sort of topology that isolates derogatory characteristics assigned to Hollywood's black characters and their social functions remains relevant even today.

Consider his twelve-point profile of the characteristics typically assigned to black character roles: (1) ignorance, (2) superstition, (3) fear, (4) servility, (5) laziness, (6) clumsiness, (7) petty thievery, (8) untruthfulness, (9) credulity, (10) immorality, (11) irresponsibility, and (12) a predilection for eating fried chicken and sliced watermelon (Reddick 1944, 5). Obviously, no one character is apt to display all of these negative traits at once. Nonetheless, the point about the general encryption of cinematic blackness along these lines holds. For example, Reddick's observation about the comedic function of the black film character is particularly insightful: "The Negro is exploited for comic relief. He is the clown, but seldom a magnificent clown; a buffoon, the butt of jokes, not the projector of them, except against himself" (4). As he cogently reveals, "the ceiling above which the Negro on the screen is seldom, if ever, permitted to rise is [significantly] lower than the ceiling for the Negro in American life itself" (5).

In summarizing his historical analysis of the black characters' disposition in the Hollywood cinema across four decades, Reddick identifies the following set of representational predicates that function to calcify the black stereotype:

1. That the Negro is usually presented as a savage or criminal or servant or entertainer.
2. That the usual roles given to Negro actors call for types like Louise Beavers, Hattie McDaniel, "Rochester," Bill Robinson, Clarence Muse, and various Jazz musicians.
3. That other groups such as Orientals, Mexicans, and South Europeans are sometimes presented unfavorably, but no religious or racial minority is so consistently "slandered" as the Negro.
4. That films have improved somewhat during the present war.
5. That when an attempt is made to improve the treatment of the Negro on the screen, the improvement usually takes place within the limitations of an all-Negro film.
6. That these limitations on the Negro are also important as limitations on the development of the movie as an art form and as an organ of democratic culture. (21)

Finally, we turn to a brief consideration of his prescriptions for effecting change in dominant industry practices and in the minds of film spectators. Reddick's strategy for intervening in traditional Hollywood practices of black representation marks another link with the past. Although he reiterates Loren Miller's call for a noncommercial cinema movement that could redress the imbalance of Hollywood's unrelenting racist discourse, Reddick also insists that "the main effort must be concentrated on the commercial film—Hollywood" (22). He is aware of the limitations of an alternative film movement if it is not supported by the mass of African Americans, who unwittingly authorize Hollywood's skewed vision of American life and culture through their continued, uncritical patronage. Reddick, like Miller before him, calls on citizen groups to embrace and support small-scale film productions that could be screened in churches, schools, libraries, YMCAs, and other civic and fraternal organizations. He is quick to point out that such alternative film programming strategies should be adopted in conjunction with the application of increased public pressure for improved representations of African Americans in the dominant film industry: "The strategy of those working for better treatment of the Negro accordingly must be worked out in terms of the profit motive of the industry. Hollywood will respond to the proper pressures just like everybody does" (23). Reddick believes that it is up to film audiences to encourage governmental agencies to make Hollywood accountable for its slanderous misrepresentations of African Americans, just as the military had prodded Hollywood to desist from its derogatory portrayals of Latin Americans, Chinese, and other groups considered then as wartime allies (24). "As a beginning," he proposes that "the government might ban the use of such terms as 'nigger,' 'darky,' 'pickaninny,' 'smoke,' 'sambo,' 'coon,' and 'WaCoon'" (24). In the following year, William Thomas Smith (1945) reports that indeed one small gain had been achieved as a result of "the abandonment by the studios of the word 'nigger' when speaking of a black electrical screen." Thus, black performers were no longer "unnerved" by this industrywide insult (14).

Content Analysis, Spectatorship, and Subjectivity in Melvin B. Tolson's "Big House" Theory of Cinema

Black film criticism in the forties also comprises articles concerned with close textual reading of specific texts and the representation of history in those works. Here the work of writer-poet-scholar-professor–political activist Melvin B. Tolson is central. Tolson's close textual analysis ushers in new, more philosophical critical paradigms. In his comparative analysis of *Gone with the Wind* and *The Birth of a Nation,* Tolson provides a prestructuralist approach to the semiotics of cinematic iconography through his formulation of the "big house" theory. It also leads him to important conclusions and observations about black spectatorship and black cinematic subjectivity.

From 1937 to 1944, Tolson wrote "Caviar and Cabbage," a feature column for the weekly African American newspaper, the *Washington Tribune,* which was published and circulated in Washington, D.C. Sandwiched between his 1940 noninterventionist articles about the escalation of World War II and America's increasing involvement were Tolson's two critiques of *Gone with the Wind.* Taken together, these two articles construct a dialectic whereby Tolson's resistance to news media propaganda advocating American involvement in World War II becomes the flip side of his resistance to Hollywood's propagandistic plantation dramas promoting the South's revisionist history of the Civil War and Reconstruction. In Tolson's view, both situations signify the denial of true democracy for oppressed black people in America.

The 23 March 1940 article, "*Gone with the Wind* Is More Dangerous than *Birth of a Nation,*" was the first of the duo to appear. Six months later, on 21 September, Tolson wrote "The Philosophy of the Big House." Both are searing indictments of Hollywood's antebellum plantation genre and the white supremacist blacklash politics it romanticized and reified. Whereas the former article was written shortly after the release of *Gone with the Wind* and reflects Tolson's visceral and spontaneous reactions to the film and the troubling documentary effect its status as a document about history could create, the latter essay, published months later, conveys Tolson's more contemplative stance toward the film, wherein his meditations on the film's racial economy and iconographic significations yield his philosophy of "the big house."

What frustrated Tolson most about *Gone with the Wind* was the film's ability to trade on the nation's racial imaginary and thus to circulate and indeed to be accepted as a mimetic equivalent to its historical referent.[9] Tolson understood that to the benighted of his generation such celluloid simulacra too often functioned to displace and ultimately to replace the more difficult and painful historical reality altogether. In his analysis of *Gone with the Wind*'s narrative point of view, Tolson observed in the "*Gone with the Wind* Is More Dangerous than *Birth of a Nation*" essay that

The Birth of a Nation was such a barefaced lie that a moron could see through it. *Gone with the Wind* is such a subtle lie that it will be swallowed as the truth by millions of whites and blacks alike. Dr. Stephenson Smith calls the moving picture the greatest molder of public opinion. And the Chinese say a picture is worth a thousand words. I believe it after listening to the comments of some of my friends on this movie, *Gone with the Wind.* (Tolson 1982, 213–14)

In acknowledging the increasing cultural capital being amassed by the cinema, Tolson concurs with the producers that this film was indeed more than mere amusement. He thus affirms that "A HISTORICAL picture is more than entertainment. Let us get that straight." It was the widely disseminated movie fanzines and billboard advertisements that proclaimed *GWTW* and *the* story of the Old South that were particularly vexing for him. By situating the narrative problematic of the film squarely in its monistic representation not as one story among many but as *the* story of the Old South, Tolson is clearly refusing this racialized and essentialized historicist perspective in much the same terms as those adopted by W. E. B. Du Bois in his book *Black Reconstruction.* Accordingly, Tolson is quick to point out that *GWTW* (in book or film form) could have presented the plantation drama from several vantage points, the viewpoint of the poor whites, the Negro slaves, the Yankees, the white masters, or any combination thereof. Instead, the narrative trajectory is confined to the point of view of the white masters exclusively. Thus Tolson admonishes his readers to "be not deceived" (214) by *GWTW*'s rhetorical enticements. As a master rhetorician himself,[10] Tolson understood completely their compelling power and allure.

Even though Tolson, as aesthete, begins his "*GWTW* Is More Dangerous" article with a paean to the "excellent acting" of Hattie McDaniel and the cast, as well as the film's "marvelous photography" (213), he is nonetheless determined to deconstruct, for his readers, the film's thinly veiled racist affront. In an instance of critical brilliance that anticipates some contemporary discussions in reception studies, Tolson discloses the secret of *GWTW*'s insidious biracial appeal for film audiences of his generation. In his attempt to awaken his readers to the cultural poison such racially divisive films contained, Tolson wrote, "If you put poison in certain kinds of foods, you can't tell it. If you beat a man long enough with your fists, you can slap him and he'll appreciate the slap." The tragedy, Tolson thought, is that "the Negro went to see one thing; whites went to see another. . . . The poor Negro has been kicked so often that he considers a slap a bit of white courtesy. Since *Gone with the Wind* didn't have a big black brute raping a white virgin in a flowing white gown, most Negroes went into ecstasies. Poor Sambo!" (214). And because the film comports with the unreconstructed South's conviction that "the North was wrong in freeing the Negroes" (215), who had an undying love for their white masters, "and hated the poor whites because they didn't own Negroes" (215), Tolson understood how white spectatorial pleasure was thereby assured. Absent these narrative enticements, how else, Tolson seems to ask, could one account for the popularity of a film yarn among both races about the Civil War that puts the motive forces of the film's plot under complete erasure? This confounds him because

> Half of the picture deals with the Civil War. But the Civil War comes like a spontaneous combustion. . . . Every critic in America will tell you that a truthful work of art must have motivation—causation. *Gone with the Wind* shows not a single economic or social or political cause that led to the Civil War. How could a civilization be "gone with the wind" unless there was something to MAKE it go? . . . The institution was built on the rape of Negro women, the hellish exploitation of black men, the brutalities of the overseers, and the bloodhounds that tore human beings to pieces. . . . These are the reasons why the Old South is "gone with the wind": The picture does not show that. . . . The picture aims to create sympathy for the white South. . . . Atlanta burns. But the picture does not tell us that *the Confederates set it afire!* [italics mine] (215)

Tolson's incredulity, it seems safe to say, is fueled by the historical travesty this much-celebrated film makes of the horrors of slavery visited upon dominated and oppressed African Americans, at the same time that the nation was fomenting anti-Hitler and antifascist sentiments against antidemocratic enemies abroad. In view of what he saw as obvious parallels in the two oppressive regimes, Tolson makes his exasperation at having to confront America's duplicity on the matter of democracy quite explicit.

On 4 May 1940, in response to a midnight bombing attack on a black residence in the nation's capital, Tolson wrote, "Hitler Blitzkrieg Strikes Near White House! Home Sweet Home—Death Trap in a Democracy" (Tolson 1982, 122). In this article, Tolson quotes Hitler's widely reported assertion that the Nazis were following American principles of handling the Negro problem to deal with their own Jewish problems. In tones mocking America's incipient consumer culture, Tolson concluded, "It seems that Hitler has nothing on the anti-Negro fascists in the Land of the Spree and the Home of the Burma Shave." Further, by directing his readers to the *Tribune*'s story of the bombing of a black home, replete with photos and an ironic headline reading "Not a Scene in Norway, but the Results of a Bombing Raid in Washington, D.C.," Tolson was suggesting to his readers that German Nazism was simply American racism's doppelgänger, and as such it represented an irrelevant distraction with which black America could ill afford to concern itself. For Tolson, the fact that America and the rest of Europe had turned a deaf ear to Ethiopia's pleas against Mussolini's antidemocratic aggression five years earlier was proof that something other than the noble cause of preserving democracy was inciting American fervor against Nazism and fascism. Besides, in Tolson's view, the matter was simply this: "If the President can hear the explosion of a bomb in Helsinki and Oslo, he should hear better the bombing of a law-abiding citizen's house at 1324 Harvard Street, Northwest, in Washington D.C." (122).

To contextualize Tolson's anti-interventionist position fairly, it is important that we recall that up to that moment, every antilynching bill had failed to pass in the U.S. Congress. It is against this backdrop that Tolson reminds his readers that "if the President can denounce German fascists 5,000 miles away, he can denounce anti-Negro fascists in Congress and the United States. Democracy begins at home" (122). Bear in mind, also, that Tolson wrote this article just six weeks after his "*Gone with the Wind* Is More Dangerous" essay, where he equates Nazism and fascism with Ku Klux Klan terrorism. In fact, World War II themes and terminology are recurring subtexts in the *Gone with the Wind* article. Most notable in this vein is Tolson's analogy between the film's pro-southern thematics and Goebels's Nazi propagandizing. Unfortunately, Tolson's reliance on American media for information about events in Germany during the early days of the war prompted him to surmise that "Hitler's persecution of the Jews is nothing compared to the KKK's hellish treatment of our black forefathers!" (216).

Under the subheading "Propagandistic Tricks in the Picture," he castigates the film's glorification of the Ku Klux Klan. In this section, Tolson grapples with the fact that white Americans seem to see all too well the evils of Nazism and fascism abroad, but that their persistence of vision

fails when it comes to recognizing equivalent evils at home. Most out-
rageous for Tolson during that historical moment was the nation's hypocrisy, made manifest by the popularity of *Gone with the Wind* and its
pro–Ku Klux Klan discourse when it was becoming increasingly apparent that blacks would be conscripts in the current war, forced to kill and
be killed to thwart Klan-like terror abroad just as they had in World
War I, when they were still prohibited from even voting against the ever-
present danger of Klan lynchings at home. *Gone with the Wind* thus
represented, for Tolson, a complete travesty and betrayal of the democratic ideals white America was currently championing. How could these
same democracy-loving citizens endorse such a film when, as he put it,
"Even the Ku Klux Klan is idolized. We see white gentlemen of the KKK
returning home at night, while a burly Yankee officer questions the innocent white ladies. Nothing is said about the brutalities of the KKK that
stank to high heaven. . . . I must give that Southern novelist and the white
producer credit for one thing; they certainly fooled the Negro and at the
same time put over their anti-Negro, anti-Yankee, KKK propaganda"
(214). For Tolson, then, the fact of America's romantic fixation on, and
filmic preoccupation with, the white South's anti-Negro plantation mythologies was evidence of one excruciating reality that African Americans had understood since the turn of the century; and that reality revealed at the article's conclusion was that "The South Won the Civil
War!" This was the message Tolson believed America was articulating to
its citizens and exporting around the world via lavish, racist plantation
dramas such as *The Birth of a Nation* and *Gone with the Wind*. Interestingly, this very point is echoed by Lawrence Reddick (1944) in his
analysis of *Gone with the Wind* as well. "Ideologically," says Reddick, "the
South had won the Civil War" (15).

Turning to Tolson's second article on *Gone with the Wind*, entitled
"The Philosophy of the Big House," written on 21 September 1940, it becomes apparent that his Big House theory functions ultimately as a metacritique of American racism. The big house, in Tolson's figuration, clearly
becomes a metaphor for American capitalism in which "the big fish eat
the little fish and color of the fish don't count" (1982, 67). Now Tolson did
not reach this enlightened state on his initial viewing of *Gone with the
Wind*. By his own account, it took time and special insight. Aided by what
he describes as the superior vision of his mind rather than that of his body,
Tolson is now ready to explain the hegemony of the big house:

Only after the lapse of months did I really see the big thing in the picture. . . . Now everything in *Gone with the Wind* could've been left out of both the novel and the picture but one thing. The movie could've had other characters, other settings, other happenings. Indeed, its author might've used another plot. But there was one thing Margaret Mitchell had to use to create *Gone with the Wind.* This novelist had to put into the book the Big House. The director of the movie had to use the Big House. Southern aristocracy could not be pictured without the Big House. The Big House is the most significant thing in the history of Dixie. (220–21)

Lest we think Tolson protests too much, it is important to recall some other southern-sympathizing plantation film dramas produced at this historical juncture, such as *So Red the Rose* (1935), *The Littlest Rebel* (1935), *The Little Colonel* (1935), *Can This Be Dixie?* (1936), and *Jezebel* (1938), to name a few popular films of the ilk.

For a society still reeling from the financial catastrophe of the Great Depression and on the brink of war, Tolson recognized the political economy symbolized by the big house in these antebellum films. They traded on America's nostalgia for an imagined past of economic stability and white aristocratic splendor as they helped ensure that the racial chasm dividing the black and white masses would remain intact during this volatile period of national crisis. While racial polarization was the fiction being naturalized on the screen, the reality of industrial slavery was uniting black and white workers in the growing labor movement that traversed the Mason-Dixon line. Tolson knew that mythological estates on sprawling southern plantations such as *Gone with the Wind*'s Tara and *Jezebel*'s Halcyon housed the nation's escapist fantasies and authorized these films' antiblack and antidemocratic themes.

In contrast to the sarcastic jeremiads he issued to his readers to dampen their enthusiasm for *Gone with the Wind* in the earlier article, here Tolson attempts to sway them with the cool voice of reason, as denoted by his title, "The Philosophy of the Big House." Even the opening sentence marks the different rhetorical strategy Tolson deploys in this essay. Rather than chide his readers for permitting themselves to be duped by the film's formal and narrative opulence, Tolson accepts their desire to experience this cinematic marvel. After all, it was one of the first full-Technicolor productions to come out of Hollywood. For *Gone with the Wind,* like *The Birth of a Nation* before it, producers deemed that no technological or financial extravagance was too much to lavish on a film that glorified what Ed Guerrero (1993) calls the "plantocracy" (15). And Tolson was resigned to the fact that African American film lovers were just as likely to be snared by it as were their white counterparts, even if, as we have already discussed, for different reasons. As a consequence, Tolson opens his second article on the film in a more conversational tone characterized by a direct address. "You saw the picture *Gone with the Wind.* I wonder if you saw the most significant thing in that melodramatic movie?" (220). This remark is contrary to one made in the earlier article. There he remarks indignantly, "I am not bothered much with what Negroes think about *Gone with the Wind.* Most of them won't think" (217). Tolson's turnaround on this point in the "Philosophy of the Big House" article points to his more sober consideration of the film as a potent cultural force in general. At issue now for Tolson is the need to disabuse his errant readers of the notion that this sugary racism is somehow less malignant. To this end, he sets out to recontextualize *Gone with the Wind* and its southern big house ethos within the long-standing tradition of antiblack rhetorics that have characterized the history of American arts and letters.

In the article's three subsections, "The Men and Women Who Write about the South," "What the Big House Means," and "The Negro and the Big House," Tolson begins to dismantle or tear asunder the pillars of racist assumptions undergirding the South's revisionist history codified in the big house. First Tolson informs his readers that cultural symbols can be found in all civilizations, from the pyramids of Egypt and the Via Appia of ancient Rome, to the bombing plane of Nazi Germany and the dollar sign of the United States (221). It is in this regard that Tolson wants his readers to comprehend the significance of the big house as symbolic of southern culture. It is Tolson's position, in this subsection, that T. S. Stribling's Pulitzer Prize–winning trilogy *The Forge, The Store,* and *Unfinished Cathedral,* Erskine Caldwell's *Tobacco Road,* Basso's *Courthouse Square,* Faulkner's *Sanctuary,* Langston Hughes's *Mulatto* and the one-act play *The Breeders,* by Randolph Edmonds, "develop, in some way, the history and tragedy of the Big House" (221). The implication here is that Tolson wants his readers to approach the film *Gone with the Wind* with the same critical consciousness they bring to other treatments of the African American in southern lore.

"What the Big House Means" purports to peel back the "veneer of glamour [that encases] the Big House, with its sweeping green lawns, its magnolia blossoms, its high-ceilinged rooms, its magnificent staircases, its waltzing couples, its mellow aristocracy, and stables of fine horses" (222). Tolson insists that his readers look beyond the material majesty of the big house to see that its opulence is built on exploitation, Jim Crow-ism, disenfranchisement, chauvinistic superiority, and above all the spirit of the Ku Klux Klan. For Tolson, failing to consider the stench of the slave cabins that invariably wafts through any open window of any big house is tantamount to sanctioning the bloodletting from the white and black masses on which the southern plantation is dedicated.

In the third section, "The Negro and the Big House," Tolson considers the most tragic component of the "hellish philosophy," that it has so entrapped the minds of too many African Americans. Again, rather than simply dismiss black audiences' admiration of McDaniel's transcendent portrayal of Mammy, as Tolson was wont to do in his earlier essay, here he demystifies the archetypal construct: "The black mammy in *Gone with the Wind* loved the Big House, for she received the crumbs that fell from the Big House table" (222). He further extends his appraisal of the mammy syndrome to "Negro teachers and politicians" who love the big house for the same degraded reason, "A man's body may have to accept crumbs, but a man's soul can demand his share of the dinner." Tolson then rounds out this deliberation with a maxim from Oliver Goldsmith, with comments likewise on England's big house system of government: "Ill fares the land, to hastening ills a prey / Where wealth accumulates, and men decay." By way of clarification, Tolson interjects: "It is well to remember that England has her Big House—Buckingham Palace, sur-rounded by the slums of London. Wherever there is a Big House, wealth accumulates and men decay." Thus Tolson sees in *Gone with the Wind* an enticing mirage, a mythic plenitude that obviates the starvation it exacts in a land of plenty. We accept the subterfuge. For as Tolson aptly puts it, "We want a democracy with Big Houses." "That, alas," he warns, "is impossible. A democracy cannot have a Big House with its cabins of wage-slaves" (223).

Years later, in an effort to wed his film criticism to the praxis of film-making, and thereby address filmically some of the issues discussed ear-lier, Tolson submitted a screenplay of his adaptation of George Schuyler's science fiction novel *Black No More* that ironically treats the subject of racial transformations, specifically racial "passing." On 21 March 1947, a representative from Paramount Pictures had the following reply: "Dear Professor Tolson . . . I am hastening to get the script of *Black No More* back to you. I enjoyed reading it and do feel the satirical idea behind it is amusing but I am still pretty sure it is a subject that the studio would have qualms about handling on the screen."[11] Interestingly, the subject was "handled" just two years later by Hollywood when a white writer's passing story was brought to the screen. That film, adapted from the work of Cid Ricketts Sumner, was entitled *Pinky*.

Industry Praxis and the Myth of the Southern Box Office

By the time Robert Jones and William Thomas Smith began their revisionist assessments of the myth of the southern box office, this potent alibi that had functioned effectively for decades to absolve Hollywood of its culpability in the marginalization of black themes and performers and its perpetuation of damaging antiblack stereotypes had become fully accepted and firmly entrenched in the minds of most American film critics, including African American critics. Carlton Moss, who wrote "Your Future in Hollywood" for the May 1946 edition of *Our World* magazine, apparently accepts this apologia. In his article, which surveys Hollywood's film productions featuring black characters and themes during the war years, Moss attempts to explain Hollywood's representational practices. Owing to the well-known fact that "profit is the primary motive of the men who control the making of motion pictures" (Moss 1946), Moss concludes that the black image in Hollywood is by necessity held hostage to the powerful sway of the southern box office and not to white producers' racial malevolence.

> A large percentage of the net profit of the industry comes from the 6,350 theatres, 31 percent of the total theatres in the country, which are situated in the deep South and border states. Especially does the South influence the use of Negroes in the industry. . . . There is a growing number of progressive-minded people in Hollywood. . . . But the strength of the democratic people in Hollywood is not yet strong enough to break through the Southern pattern that dominates. (Moss 1946)

Whereas Moss accepts this rationalization, William Thomas Smith (1945) and Robert Jones (1947) propose alternative explanations. In his essay "Hollywood Report," published a year later in *Phylon,* Smith convincingly contests such a naive view. Rejecting the assumption that Hollywood moguls were hostages of the South's control over the box office holy grail, and that these impotent moguls would "do better by the Negro" (Reddick 1944, 9) if they had the power, Smith counters:

> *If* they had the power . . . It is their claim that if a picture offends the South, the profits shown by that picture slump deeply. So that the way to make profits is, among other things, not to offend the South. Also they must not offend the Catholics, nor the Jews, nor the Mexicans. To offend the Negro apparently isn't a matter to be considered. . . . Those whom they seek not to offend are the exhibitors, the censors, and a few scraggly politicians who suffer acutely from Negrophobia. . . . The censors and the exhibitors of the South do not hesitate to use their shears on any scene in any picture which they consider objectionable. (W. Smith 1945, 15)

As Smith correctly points out, the South hardly needed Hollywood protection, since it routinely and without hesitation used its regional censorship powers to excise any and all scenes it deemed ideologically undesirable. The point Smith makes, then, is that just as the South refused to be held captive to Hollywood's cinematic discourse, in the same way, Hollywood should not permit the rest of the nation, and indeed the world, to be imprisoned by the demands of some southerners or any other constituencies for racist depictions of African Americans. Moreover, he is unwilling to abide the displacement of ethical responsibility and accountability for antiblack films onto the South by the true arbiters of power in control of this highly influential mass medium. Smith also rejects the essentialist view of the South that authorizes the perpetuation of this myth. He adds, "To those who realize that a majority of Southern people are not Negrophobists, the case is not without hope" (16).

Robert Jones is less sanguine in his approach. In his essay "How Hollywood Feels about Negroes," which appears in the August 1947 *Negro Digest* magazine, Jones is more pointed in his denunciation of the southern box office myth. For him, the day of true reckoning has finally come. He wants the "important people in filmdom" to own up to their power rather than mask it behind the myth of a tyrannical South wielding absolute power over Hollywood from afar. Knowing the unlikelihood of such an honest revelation coming out of the land of illusions and make-believe, Jones takes it upon himself to disclose a different set of power dynamics that belie the constant refrain that but for the South, black characters would receive a new deal in Hollywood. Not so, says Jones:

> Yes, flagrant prejudice is rampant in Hollywood—especially in high places where it counts. . . . the "important people" in filmdom are mostly hate-infected, money-grasping bigots who have dictated for years that the Negro shall appear on the screen as an inferior or not at all. . . . whenever the subject of decent treatment for Negroes has been suggested [,] their plea has been that Hollywood is in the business really to make but one thing—money—and to portray Negroes as ordinary humans would cut returns from Dixie. But their hiding behind Dixie's skirts is a pure phony, recent box office figures prove conclusively. (R. Jones 1947, 4)

Like Moss, who cites actual box office numbers in his discussion, Jones also utilizes box office statistics to support his argument. Unlike Moss, however, Jones uses the numbers to indict, not to acquit Hollywood, of outright racism. According to Jones, the lie is doubly exposed given the fact that the southern box office returns were healthy for "decent movies about Negroes but also by the relatively small business that comes from the South" (4). Additionally, Jones underscores his position by comparing the size differentials between southern and northern regional film markets:

> The Southern box office today totals roughly 8 per cent of the average national gross of a motion picture. Against this New York State, which has a law against racial discrimination, pulls 14.6 per cent of the national box office. Even more impressive is the total take of American movies abroad. In 1945 world box office returns were $2,235,000,000. Of that $285,000,000 or 37 per cent came from foreign markets. . . . No, the Southern box office excuse is all washed up and the movie industry as a whole stands exposed as the real culprit in the prejudice against Negroes. (5)

What Smith realizes at this early juncture is that contestations of powerful or big lies require equally big evidence if they are to be effective. Logically, then, if we accept Smith's numbers, it would seem that Hollywood would be more interested in catering to the more densely populated northern market in its quest for profitable returns on its production investments. Not content merely to expose the fallacy of the southern box office hindrance to better treatment of blacks in the cinema, Smith also reveals the limits of Hollywood's specious rationalizations of its racist representational practices by invoking the global box office dimen-

Chicago Defender 1934 story: The *Chicago Defender* helps debunk the Southern box-office excuse for cinematic racism. Courtesy of the *Chicago Daily Defender.*

sion to further destabilize this long-held alibi. This approach enables Smith to raise another important issue related to racial representations, and that is the issue of decentering the white subject from its traditional position of cinematic primacy so that a realignment of racial representations more consistent with a changing global marketplace might ensue. In an utterance that anticipates postcolonial debates about the cinema and the subaltern subject, Jones makes the following observations:

> Fortunately some movie executives have begun to see the hand-writing on the wall. Checking with their bookkeepers, they have discovered that while in 1946 some 45 cents out of every dollar of movie income came from overseas, this year the slice has dropped down to 30 cents. They are beginning to learn that the majority of the peoples of the world are colored, that they resent seeing every film hero as a well-to-do, fair-haired, glamorous Caucasian—usually Protestant American—and all villains and dull-witted clowns as dark-complected Latins or coloreds. (8)

In opening up the discussion to global considerations, Smith leads us directly into our next area of contemplation, Hollywood's "blackout" of cinematic toms, coons, mulattoes, mammies, and bucks during World War II.

Hollywood in World War II and Black Audiences as POWs

Carlton Moss began "Your Future in Hollywood" by quoting telling remarks from Hollywood insider Charlie Butler, "who for 24 years has been supplying Hollywood with Negro performers." Butler's comment "You see, we get the porter and maid parts and you don't need maids and porters when you're making mostly war pictures" succinctly illustrates the precarious predicament of African American performers and spectators caught up in Hollywood's representational exigencies. Hollywood's turn "toward a heightened king of realism" (D. Cook 1990, 456) in forties-era films is generally regarded by critics as a response to the "mood of disillusionment and cynicism [that] came over America" (463) in the aftermath of the Great Depression and World War II. Critics have also pointed out that Hollywood's turn to social relevance precipitated "what has come to be known as the 'Negro cycle'" (465) that signaled a temporary retreat from traditional representations of black themes and black character depictions. Although this representational shift marked a significant and welcome break with past stereotypical constructions of black otherness, for black film critics writing during that historical milieu, the change symbolized yet another instance of black cultural estrangement.

Moss revealed one of the black community's most complex forfeitures in Hollywood's wartime politics of representation, which was the reduction in employment opportunities for African Americans across the board in the entertainment industry. Citing Ben Carter, an actor-agent, Moss writes: "At present there are 78 Negro men and 67 Negro women on the rolls, a total of 145, against the 300 that were carried before the war" (Moss 1946). Moss also reports that the inability of blacks to obtain jobs in the industry's technical trades further exacerbated this erosion of black employment in Hollywood. Additional factors contributing to the near disappearance of black actors during the war years were the organized pressure campaigns against black stereotypes in films undertaken by the NAACP and the *Los Angeles Sentinel*'s Hollywood Fair Play Committee, spearheaded by *Sentinel* managing editor Leon Washington ("Negro Actor" 1942). One of the biggest problems in the protest efforts was the inability of black cultural and political leaders to reach consensus on how best to achieve reform in Hollywood. This unfortunate split resulted in black performers' railing against any interventionist attempt that threatened their jobs,[12] and writers' public condemnations of black actors for accepting demeaning roles that perpetuated racist stereotypes,[13] and complicating the scenario even more was Hollywood's reaction to this black political infighting. Robert Jones has described Hollywood's response in this manner: "The solution to protests against stereotyping the Negro has been quite simple for Hollywood; cut them out altogether" (R. Jones 1947, 6). Although Jones overstates the case somewhat, as Moss's article demonstrates, there was a severe cutback in the number of roles assigned to black actors at that time. William Thomas Smith also took note of the decline. Though he recognizes the general diminution of film production in Hollywood owing to wartime conditions, he also finds the disproportionate burden borne by black performers indicative of other, less benign, imperatives.

> Because of the war, Hollywood does not glitter quite as brightly as of yore, yet the films continue to be made, and with emphasis on social overtones. ... Despite almost frantic efforts at democratic preachment, as exemplified in the film crop of the past years, Hollywood's attitude toward the Negro actor, the Negro worker, and the Negro race remains unchanged; the democracy it preaches is as usual "For White Only." (W. Smith 1945, 13)

Interestingly, though, the reduction in the quantity of black roles was paralleled by the relatively improved quality of limited black roles available to black actors during the war years. While it is true that Hollywood modified its construction of black characters during the early forties, it should not be presumed that white producers achieved some sort of epiphany or conversion experience that fundamentally changed their attitudes toward African Americans.[14] In fact, Hollywood's short-lived and limited reformulation of cinematic blackness was the result of a necessary capitulation to the demands of generating pro-war sentiments in the hearts of all Americans, including blacks. Ralph Ellison has articulated an even more pressing concern that forced Hollywood's about-face on the issue of black representation during the war years. Ellison asks, in his 1949 essay "The Shadow and the Act," "Why these new attempts to redefine the Negro's role? . . . For one thing there was the war; for another there is the fact that the United States' position as a leader in world affairs is shaken by its treatment of Negroes (1972, 277). As Ellison surmises, Hollywood understood the political importance of breaking with its time-honored tradition of maligning African Americans through its endless parade of reprehensible screen stereotypes. It is also important to stress Hollywood's self-serving approach to redefining the black image even during this time of national crisis. David Cook (1990) has observed that during this era of heightened cinematic realism, the portrayals of African Americans as fully assimilated into the American mainstream only served to construct a mythological image of the nation as "a pure, democratic society in which Jews, blacks, Italians, Irish, Poles, and WASP farm boys could all live and work together, just as they had done in the ethnically balanced patrol squads of so many wartime combat films. This America, or wartime integration of course never existed," Cook writes, "but a nation engaged in a global war of survival had an overwhelming need to believe that it did" (463). Another clue to the disingenuousness of Hollywood's social consciousness where films dealing with blacks are concerned is the case of the reformulated black servant. It is true that Stepin Fetchit's "coon" as well as Clarence Muse's and Bill Robinson's "Tom" characters, for example, were anachronistic roles and therefore unacceptable character types for mass consumption at that moment. However, Hollywood did not depose these servile black icons from its representational pantheon. Instead, these figures were combined and transformed into the urbane manservant character of "Rochester," who became a ubiquitous cinematic presence in numerous Jack Benny film vehicles. Nevertheless, writing in 1945, Smith asserts, "Eddie Rochester Anderson continues as a unique person in that his parts in the Jack Benny films are not only large and hilarious but do not show him in a racially unfavorable light" (13).

In "The Future in Films," published in the July–September edition of *Opportunity* magazine, George Norford traces this progression of new black images further.

During the War several Hollywood firms undertook the production of such films as "Bataan," "Lifeboat," and the "The Ox-Bow Incident," in which Negro actors were more than incidentally involved. . . . With the exception of one, the roles played by the Negroes in these films were not necessarily "Negro" roles. Canada Lee was a seaman in "Lifeboat," Kenneth Spencer was a soldier in "Bataan," as was Rex Ingram in "Sahara." The exception was Lee Whipper who stalked through "Ox-Bow Incident," a symbol indicating the sanguinary Southern pastime of lynching. (Norford 1948, 108)

Norford found other signs of progress in these films in addition to their casting against racial type for the leading characters. In particular, he finds a progressive representational economy at work in the films' mise-en-scènes, particularly the sprinkling of black characters throughout many of the background scenes. When this seemingly minor point is contextualized within the history of the black press's long-standing campaign to get Hollywood to position black extras in background shots in films other than the prison and Tarzan genres (Buchanan 1968, 29), its importance becomes readily apparent. What Norford found so progressive about the appearance of black extras in *Baatan, Lifeboat,* and *The Ox-Bow Incident* was that for the first time, "people saw Negroes as an integral part of the scene. They were not 'different'; they were not caricatures; they were simple, understandable human beings" (1948, 108). Ralph Ellison echoes this sentiment in his discussion of the "human qualities" that characterize a later Hollywood film, the 1949 film *Intruder in the Dust* (1972, 281).

But the end of the war signaled Hollywood's desire to return to its prewar success formula, escapist entertainment. Consequently, this also meant the end to Hollywood's experiment with heroic depictions of African Americans as central figures in mixed-cast films, that is, until the decade's end. During the war years, however, "There was much cause for optimism," Norford comments. "But with the end of the war [Hollywood] summarily went back to its 'formula' films and even more 'formula excuses': that people go to the movies to be entertained and not to be preached at, and it proceeded to produce films that reflected just that" (1948, 109). Norford was resigned to the fact that Hollywood's platitudes, limited reforms, and antilynching films were merely reflex actions induced by "the artificial stimulus of the war." Nonetheless, he remained optimistic that the arrival of films such as *Gentlemen's Agreement* and *Crossfire* signified Hollywood's rediscovery of socially relevant themes that would pave the way for more socially conscious portrayals of African Americans.

The social problem films produced by Hollywood in the late forties did revisit issues of race and difference, as Norford hoped. However, in the main, these films once again constructed African Americans on screen as the "problem people," instead of people confronting the problems of a racist society. Ralph Ellison locates Hollywood's antiblack bias even in films that ostensibly challenge the nation's attitudes about race. In discussing the four films that made up the so-called Negro cycle produced by Hollywood in 1949, namely, *Intruder in the Dust, Lost Boundaries, Home of the Brave,* and *Pinky,* Ellison sums up the situation best in his critique that appears in *Shadow and Act:*

> We find that each of the films mentioned above deals with some basic and unusually negative assumption about Negroes: Are Negroes cowardly soldiers? (*Home of the Brave*); are Negroes the real polluters of the South? (*Intruder in the Dust*); have mulatto Negroes the right to pass as white, at the risk of having black babies, or if they have white-skinned children, of having to kill off their "white" identities by revealing to them they are alas, Negroes? (*Lost Boundaries*); and finally, should Negro girls marry white men or—wonderful non sequitur—should they help their race? (*Pinky*). Obviously, these films are not about Negroes at all they are about what whites think and feel about Negroes. And if they are taken as accurate reflectors of that thinking, it becomes apparent that there is much confusion. (1972, 277).

The confusion that Ellison refers to is Hollywood's attempt to reclaim and to reimpose the racial boundaries of America's prewar social order even though it had been discredited significantly by the harsh realities of the depression and the war (D. Cook 1990, 463). During the postwar years, Hollywood once again returned to a cinematic discourse privileging whiteness over blackness. Having fulfilled its duty to the national government and the War Information Office that had ordered filmic images of a happy, multicultural nation unified in battle against the enemy abroad, Hollywood now went about business as usual. For Ellison, *Lost Boundaries* was especially emblematic of this revitalized discourse of "whiteness."

> In *Lost Boundaries* the question evaded is whether a mulatto Negro has the right to practice the old American pragmatic philosophy of capitalizing upon one's assets. For after all, whiteness has been given an economic and

social value in our culture; and for the doctor upon whose life the film is based "passing" was the quickest and most certain means to success. Yet Hollywood is uncertain about his right to do this. (1972, 278)

Indeed, in the Hollywood postwar imagination, the biggest racial problem was blacks' usurpation of whiteness through the practice of passing. Just as in the 1934 film *Imitation of Life,* Hollywood and the mass audience were at once attracted to and repelled by this black racial masquerade. Paradoxically, *Lost Boundaries* and *Pinky* suggest that the most sympathetic black characters were what Ellison terms "white Negroes," black individuals who were simultaneously blessed and cursed for their foolhardy appropriations of white-skin privilege. Ellison remarks, "It would seem that in the eyes of Hollywood, it is only 'white' Negroes who suffer—or is it merely the 'white' corpuscles of their blood?" (279). These narrative failures, however, do not prevent Ellison from recommending these films, for he writes: "Despite the absurdities with which these films are laden, they are all worth seeing, and if seen, capable of involving us emotionally. . . . It is as though there were some deep relief to be gained merely from seeing these subjects projected upon the screen" (280).

At this point, Ellison shifts to considerations of spectatorship and the racial imaginary. Although he acknowledges the cathartic effect of these films, he worries that Hollywood and its privileged white spectators are in danger of misrecognizing these narrative fictions as material realities that the nation as a whole is better off for having confronted. "It is here that a danger lies," Ellison states. "For the temptation toward self-congratulation which comes from seeing these films and sharing in their emotional release is apt to blind us to the true nature of what is unfolding—or failing to unfold—before our eyes" (280). To subvert this tendency of white spectators, who, as a result of the nation's segregation politics, know too little about the realities of black life and experience and therefore are susceptible to Hollywood's imitations of that life, Ellison recommends racially mixed screenings of such films.

As an antidote to the sentimentality of these films, I suggest that they be seen in predominately Negro audiences. For here, when the action goes phony, one will hear derisive laughter, not sobs. (Perhaps this is what Faulkner means about Negroes keeping the white man's conscience.) Seriously, *Intruder in the Dust* is the only film that could be shown in Harlem without arousing unintended laughter. For it is the only one of the four in which Negroes can make complete identification with their screen image. Interestingly, the factors that make this identification possible lie in its depiction not of racial but of human qualities. (280–81)

Here Ellison puts his finger on what was likely one of the most frequently used tactics of subversion and resistance available to black spectators over the years, laughter instead of tears, or vice versa, if either ensured their specular pleasure. Just as surely as black audiences attenuated their spectatorial dissonance by reading against the grain in these films, we can extrapolate that similar decoding or misreading strategies were used to misread explicit antiblack character types so as to recode and reinvest such images with transcendent meanings to suit their own visual imaginings. Indicative of this transcendent reading practice are the reams of celebratory writings about these black purveyors of antiblack stereotypes in the black press. Many critics have ridiculed the black press's practice of treating the black bit performer as the "star" of a film. Alfred Buchanan, for one, has written derisively, "headlines constantly announced that a Negro actor or actress would 'star' in a play or motion picture when close observation later revealed that it was a bit part, and when reasoned speculation would reveal that it was likely to be an objectionable stereotype. The same pattern dictated that any show with a mixed or all-Negro cast was predicted as a sure success" (1960, 25). What such commentary fails to consider is that to black film audiences, the bit actors *were* indeed the stars. Moreover, it seems fair to conclude that black actors did not view the stereotypes as accurate reflectors of their existence, so they were free to enjoy the performances as just that, performance. (At the same time, it is true that black audiences presumed that white spectators believed the stereotypes were mirrors of the black experience, since most whites, by choice, had little if any contact with flesh-and-blood African Americans.) In the same way that black film spectators willfully inverted Hollywood's star hierarchy to transform the bit player into the star, they also recoded and reversed film genres through inappropriate responses to the films' intended meanings. Thus, as with the black subcultural practices of improvisation on classical musical forms and normative linguistic structures, black audiences reworked mainstream film images to suit their

Chicago Defender 1935 film advertisement. In the black press, it was not unusual for black supporting actors to be billed as *the* stars of their films as Bill Robinson's top billing over Lionel Barrymore in *The Little Colonel* ad attests. Courtesy of the *Chicago Daily Defender.*

own ends, which Ellison well understood in his appreciation of the black audience response to *Lost Boundaries* and *Pinky.*

Postwar Years and the Impact of Television

If the war years were not particularly beneficial to black film audiences or performers, they were wonderful for Hollywood. David Cook (1990) has remarked that "Hollywood enjoyed the most profitable four-year period in its history during the war" (460). However, during the postwar years, several domestic and international developments combined to reverse Hollywood's financial standing. As a result of an eight-month studio union strike, escalating postwar inflation, European protective tariffs, higher prices for film stock, and the 1948 "Paramount decree," which forced the five major studios to divest themselves of their theater operations, Hollywood was forced to adopt an austerity plan to cut production costs (461–62). Hollywood responded by curtailing its lavish productions, substituting for them more cost-effective films based on "high-quality scripts" (462). Out of this financial reorganization came the lower-budget "social consciousness," film noir, and "Negro cycle" genres. For a short period during the postwar years, the tables were now turned in favor of the black film spectators and performers.

In 1949 the *New York Amsterdam News* identified another factor that helped to spur the production of the "Negro cycle" films, which were extremely popular with black film audiences. On 1 October 1949, S. W. Carlington, the paper's film and entertainment editor, wrote an article entitled "Movies 'Courting Negro' to Boost Sick Box Office." Here Carlington reveals the true reasons behind Hollywood's sudden interest in producing films that would attract the black film audience. Under the subheading "Hunt for New Customers," Carlington writes, "The rapid rise of television as a major means of entertainment, and topflight radio programs 'stole' most of the ex-movie fans. On top of this, the record industry is runner-up as threat to the movies" (Carlington 1949, 3). While critics often regard the social consciousness awakened in Hollywood personnel who had been deeply affected by their war experiences as the primary reasons behind the production of the "Negro cycle" films (D. Cook 1990, 464–67), Carlington provides a more pragmatic view:

> People throughout the country are going less and less to the movies. To be exact, the national movie attendance dropped from 85 to 35 million. One does not have to be a business expert or an economist to understand that the loss of 50,000,000 paying customers is not a healthy sign and something must be done to recapture the old customers or find new ones. (3)

We might add that one need not be a psychoanalyst or sociologist to account for mainstream filmmakers' sudden discovery of socially relevant film topics. Carlington eliminates the need to look for imprecise psychological explanations for the production of these films. Even if certain directors were more prone to consider formerly taboo themes as a result of their personal feelings, there is little evidence to support this premise. Besides, Hollywood's box office bottom-line credo tends to negate these personal considerations. Moreover, Carlington's point is underscored by the fact that the "Negro cycle" films lasted for only a year. This hardly suggests that Hollywood producers and directors were responding to war-induced life-altering experiences.

Carlington raises another intriguing issue in his discussion of Hollywood's "hunt for new customers." Much has been written about the impact of television and radio on the movies during this period, but not particularly in terms of black spectatorship. Carlington provides information that helps us to understand better the role of music as a counterbalance to Hollywood's less-than-satisfactory output. In his reflection on the music industry and the black spectator, Carlington interjects another overlooked component in the diminution of Hollywood's audience during the postwar era.

> Negroes are the greatest record collectors in the world. They have used records plus radio to entertain themselves and their friends. Bigwigs in the music industry know these facts, and are trying to win them away from so much self-entertainment. (3)

This idea that blacks needed to be swayed from so much self-entertainment is provocative indeed. However, space does not permit an engagement with its fuller implications. Suffice it to say that the record industry was not alone in seeking to sway this potentially significant market from their self-entertainments. Even though the "race records" and black radio entertainment segments were produced in the segregated environments of the respective white industries, black audiences consumed these records and shows in the privacy of their homes, where neighbors could congregate without encountering the public indignities and humiliations that awaited them in the public sphere. Because Hollywood now found it necessary to cast aside concerns with the southern box office, it shifted its attention instead to luring black audiences from their self-entertainments. As Carlington writes, "To win over the Jew and the Negro, Hollywood had to present them in a favorable light" (3). With the production of *Gentlemen's Agreement, Crossfire, Home of the Brave, Lost Boundaries,* and *Pinky,* Hollywood set out to do just that, and Carlington reports that "the public went for them in a big way" (3). As the 1950s began, Hollywood went for a few black performers in a big way, the "Negro cycle" had run its course, and the "social consciousness" films were replaced by the "social problem" films. The social problem was, of course, the push for complete racial integration as the Civil Rights movement assumed national prominence. Against this backdrop, Hollywood produced its first group of bona fide black film stars for a national audience. Sidney Poitier, Harry Belafonte, Dorothy Dandridge, Ruby Dee, and Ethel Waters were 1950s box office draws for black and white audiences.

Although Hollywood in the 1940s failed to address the basic element of what the "Negro" wanted in films, the "consent decrees," the advent of television, and other significant industry changes convinced Hollywood that giving the black audiences some of what they wanted was the best way to get what it wanted, a reinvigorated box office. What comes close to articulating what the Negro wanted from Hollywood is Lawrence Reddick's (1944) commonsensical statement that "the overwhelming desire of the Negro people, as expressed through their critics, is to have Negro actors on the screen treated 'like everybody else'" (4).

Epilogue

As we have seen, the black critical discourse of the forties broke new ground, from intellectual considerations of the cinema in the context of the mass culture debates, to film historiography, to close textual analysis and investigations of exhibition and spectatorship. As the articles lengthened, the arguments became more sophisticated and intricately associated with larger social, cultural, and political developments. This set the stage for the next critical phase that ensued during the 1950s. The criticism in the fifties continued to develop along these same intellectual lines. Additionally it intersected with the growing Civil Rights movement, the phenomenal popularity of television, the advent of postwar suburban sprawl, and Hollywood's eventual capitulation to the inevitability of forced racial integration in America. As Hollywood began to fashion its integration dramas or "problem films" around the changing status of African Americans in mainstream society, contradictory notions of black sexuality (i.e., the smoldering sexuality of Dorothy Dandridge and Harry Belafonte vehicles, and the desexed film roles portrayed by Ruby Dee and Sidney Poitier), and new conceptions of the black domestic, black film critics followed these trends closely. In almost a replay of the thirties divisions of the literature into radical and assimilationist discursive formations, the fifties film literature tended to break down into camps of the scholarly and the popular. The early film writings of James Baldwin are exemplary of the former tendency, while the celebratory and less-critical strain is typified by the film articles appearing in *Ebony, Jet,* and *Sepia* magazines, and the still viable black newspapers. Unlike the thirties, with its politically marginalized radicalism, the more widespread populism of the Civil Rights movement prevented the two literary modes from becoming diametrically opposed in tone and intent. Thus the film criticism of the late forties, with its tone of guarded optimism about the new representational possibilities, ultimately gave way to the fifties' insistent agitation for even more progress on all fronts in Hollywood's newest regime of representation.

Notes

Introduction

1 See Ernest Kaiser's introduction to the 1969 reprint of Penn's text *The Afro-American Press and Its Editors* for a short biography on this impressive pioneer of black cultural preservation.

2 Black press historian James R. Grossman (1989) writes in *Land of Hope: Chicago, Black Southerners, and the Great Migration:* "Many migrants viewed migration as an opportunity to share—as black people—the perquisites of American citizenship. These included not only participation in what seemed to be an open industrial economy from which they had previously been excluded, but also good schools" (9).

3 This period was marked by the suffragists' movement and temperance societies, and the industrial revolution with its insatiable demand for human labor to run the machinery was in full swing as Taylor's scientific management system of mass production opened up unparalleled job opportunities for blacks in the Jim Crow era. Grossman (1989) reports in *Land of Hope* that "the packing houses in Chicago for a while seemed to be everything . . . recalled one migrant from Mississippi, 'the mecca was Chicago.' From 1916 to 1919, between fifty and seventy thousand black southerners relocated in Chicago, and thousands more passed through the city before moving to other locations in the North" (4).

4 For further discussions of the schisms that fragmented the black community along social, class, political, cultural, and caste lines, see, for example, Carter G. Woodson's *The Mis-education of the Negro* (1933); Manning Marable's *How Capitalism Underdeveloped Black America* (1983); E. Franklin Frazier's *Black Bourgeoisie* (1957); and Harold Cruse's *The Crisis of the Negro Intellectual* (1967). Even writers for the black press during the height of the Great Migration wrote articles and columns decrying the influx of uneducated, rural migrants to the already crowded and segregated black belts of the North and Midwest.

5 Tricia Rose credits James A. Snead for this phrase that refers to the cultural

means used by black people to cope with social transformation. See her interview with Mark Dery in "Black to the Future" (Dery 1994, 179–222).

1. *The Souls of Black Folks* in the Age of Mechanical Reproduction

1   In *The Sermon and the African American Literary Imagination*, Hubbard (1994) describes the African American's preacherly voice in this way: "Through his magnificently wrought oral poetry, the unlettered and semi-literate black preacher . . . moves the people beyond the boundary of hierarchical social order to the creation of new forms of human consciousness" (5).

2   In major debates between ministers who were in favor of the nickelodeons and those who were not, the Reverend Adam Clayton Powell took the former position: "The Abyssinian Church is surrounded by theaters and nickelettes as is no other church in the city, but I do not believe that they have affected our attendance in the slightest degree" (quoted in Walton 1910).

3   In his book *Before the Nickelodeon: Edwin S. Porter and the Edison Manufacturing Company*, Charles Musser (1991) observed that black characters were typically cast in films such as *The Watermelon Patch* as an outcast group, whose happy-go-lucky thievery suggests that "eating watermelon is the only pleasure in the world" (312).

4   Significantly, Walton's critical thrust is consistent with Benjamin's point that film's technical structure, in effect, could be made to evacuate the physical and moral shock effect from otherwise disturbing photographic images (1909, 44). Illustrating the moral crisis such an evacuation precipitates is Georges Duhamel's confession from "Scenes of Life in the Future": "I can no longer think what I want to think. My thoughts have been replaced by moving images" (quoted in Benjamin 1986, 44). To his credit, Walton is intent on disclosing, if not foreclosing altogether, the potential for psychological control and coercion inherent in the cinema's powerful imagery, alluded to by Duhamel. For our purposes, connecting these later observations by Benjamin and Duhamel is crucial because they evolve out of lessons learned as a result of the horrific encounter between art and the regime of fascism. And yet Walton comes to a similar realization about the overwhelming influence exerted by the cinema decades earlier.

5   Hans Magnus Enzensberger popularized this idea in the 1970s.

6   Lizabeth Cohen's (1989) study of mass culture among early-twentieth-century workers in Chicago was useful here. In her article "Encountering Mass Culture at the Grassroots," Cohen "credits hegemonic mass culture with blurring class lines" (6) to the extent that mobilizing class consciousness

among working-class groups to challenge bourgeois structures of domination becomes nearly impossible.

7 The black press made it possible for its readers at once to read and to be read. Henry Louis Gates, among others, has written extensively on the intricacies of African American signifying practices, tropes, and functions. Following this tradition, I am troping, here, on the doubleness of the term "read" as it often circulates in black vernacular discourse. There is a phrase in the African American vernacular tradition of signifying that admonishes, "Don't make me have to 'read' you," or, if the admonition fails, then the concomitant boast "Child, I 'read' him/her like a book" is uttered; and it is to this kind of verbal jousting that black critics' point about the polysemy and indirection inherent in black signifying rituals refers. Thus it is according to this logic that we must understand and interpret the "reading" (or the "dressing-down") the letter's author levels against one of the "Musical and Dramatics" column's errant critics. Basically, this letter's author has "read" through or deciphered the rhetorical indirection of the newly evolving film crit-speak and has set pen to paper to write a notification that the errant film critics' "signifying" on the orchestra director providing music accompaniment to the film under discussion was not appreciated.

8 In his influential book *The Cult of Information* (1994), Theodore Roszak revisits the legend of the Luddites, those infamous machine destroyers of the early industrial revolution. Discussing the reality and the mythology of England's working-class response to the threat posed by machine technology to their livelihoods, Roszak believes that "the original Luddites may have taken a bad rap. . . . Though they were desperate men fighting to feed their families, their hostility was carefully targeted. They asked how the machines were being used, by whom, for whose benefit—and then normally tried negotiating a better deal with their employers. Only when that effort failed did they feel forced to resort to violence" (xviii).

9 In a *Defender* article entitled "Moving Pictures Offer the Greatest Opportunity to the American Negro in History of the Race from Every Point of View" (1915), Juli Jones discusses the financial and cultural incentives for African Americans to become more active in the production of films. In addition to the economic benefits, Jones points out the international dimensions of black-produced films. He asserts that international interest in the plight of African Americans is enormous and singles out Brazil and South America as being "crazy to know more of the American Negro, and wanting to see some of his redeeming points" (6).

10 Lester Walton (1909c) writes about the failure of blacks to take "advantage of the laws in force which guarantee . . . the same rights and privileges in theaters" to blacks as to any other group. See also Walton's *New York*

Age article entitled "New Yorkers Have Gone 'Dippy' over the Movies" (1914b).

2. *The Birth of a Nation* and Interventionist Criticism

1   Even with the benefit of retrospection, too many mainstream film scholars and critics fail to fairly assess or adequately foreground African American oppositional literature in their revisionist historiographies of the film. Or when the film's potent racism is acknowledged, it is often rationalized or blunted by apologia or relativism. This abnegation surfaces even in such important revisionist assessments of Griffith's film as Michael Rogin's and Thomas Cripps's, among others. Consider, for example, the following representative phrasings from Cripps's *Slow Fade to Black* (1993b): "After a winter of cutting and editing, the final product with its benign Southern agrarianism, sentimental piety, and easy racial paternalism seemed far less racist than Dixon's novel. . . . The film was often paternalistic where the novel had been racist" (46). In his investigation of one black press response to the film, Cripps writes: "The foregoing [a critical synopsis] is not a fair recapitulation of *The Birth of a Nation* because it focuses on what Negroes saw at the expense of what critics saw" (51). It is telling here that Cripps opposes "Negroes" to critics, as if the two are somehow mutually exclusive categories. More troubling, however, is Cripps's disturbing attitude toward black spectatorship regarding the film. In positing his view of "what blacks saw" in *The Birth of a Nation*, Cripps explains, "They would have none of the compelling beauty, rich narrative form, painterly composition, or complex visual imagery. For them it was a rough and cruel racist slander upon Afro-Americans during Reconstruction" (52). It is not the case that black critics of the film were impervious to its artistic innovations and beauty. Instead, what some of these black critics lamented was the power and allure of the film's artful synergy when the racism and artistry combined.

Rogin, to a lesser degree, dilutes Griffith's racist vitriol by emphasizing what he terms Griffith's "conviction of truth beyond history" in these terms: "Contingencies and conflicting interpretations constitute history. Griffith's aim was to abolish interpretation . . . Griffith founded a preverbal art" (Rogin 1991, 318). Is not any representation of history, cinematic or literary, ultimately an interpretation? This situation begs a question similar to that posed by Siegfried Kracauer in another cultural context. To paraphrase Kracauer (1947, 18–19), is it for the sake of art or for the desire to serve the established order that present-day scholars and film buffs alike continue to shield Griffith's and Dixon's race-baiting film so ardently from the relevant

critiques of those African American writers and European American dis-
senters of that epoch, not to mention present-day calls for the film's censure?
It is equally important to stress here that the foregoing observation is not
meant to diminish the major debt we owe to Cripps and Rogin for their
dedicated scholarship and signal contributions to our contemporary reap-
praisal of the racial discourse in film historiography. The point is that often
the revelations that our heroes have feet of clay fall to those adversely affected
by the damaging activities of the hero in question. Accordingly, early-
twentieth-century African American writers and critics of *The Birth of a
Nation* would be willing and determined to name and castigate Dixon's and
Griffith's racist imperatives.

2 The *Iowa Bystander* was founded in Des Moines in 1894. Pride and Wilson
write in *A History of the Black Press* (1997) that this African American newspaper "built a circulation of more than 3,000 copies in a state sparsely populated by Negroes" (103).

3 Dixon's *Clansman* is also important because it constitutes what I am terming
the "pre-*Birth*" discourse, which is crucial to consider if a fair contextualiza-
tion of the film's ultimate power and influence is to proceed.

4 It is also important to recall that lynchings were not unheard of outside the
southern regions during this period. C.f. a *Defender* article that reports that
"during the twenty-one years ending January 1st 1903," 1,872 African Americans were lynched. Significantly the *Defender* makes the point that "only half
of the lynchings occurred in the South," with the remainder occurring out
West and points in between ("Birth of a Nation Will Not Be Shown in
Chicago" 1915, 8); also see Du Bois 1913, 337–40.

5 For a thorough investigation of this issue, see Allen and Gomery's *Film
History: Theory and Practice* (13).

6 See Charles A. Simmons's in-depth discussion of the politics of militancy in
black press in his recent book *The African American Press* (25–27).

7 As early as 1933, Woodson is insistent in *The Miseducation of the Negro* that a
fair assessment of the present African American condition escapes possibility if the historical context fails to be addressed. "The conditions of
today have been determined by what has taken place in the past, and in a
careful study of this history we may see more clearly the great theatre of
events in which the Negro has played a part" (9). The historical orchestra-
tion and manipulation of educational programs designed for African Americans in the wake of emancipation is of particular interest in this text. Woodson argues convincingly that blacks have been miseducated to act against
their own best interests.

8 See Du Bois's 1835 "The Propaganda of History" in *Black Reconstruction,
1860–1880*. Here Du Bois is proffering a corrective to the "frontal attack on

Reconstruction, as interpreted by the leaders of national thought in 1870 and for some time thereafter," whom he identifies as hailing "from the universities and particularly from Columbia and Johns Hopkins" (718).

9 Russell's unique reading serves to destabilize what Stuart Hall (1980) terms the "privileged position in the communicative exchange" (129) of Dixon's white supremacist message. As Hall observes, "In the moment when a historical event [which Dixon's plays attempt to dramatize] passes under the sign of discourse, it is subject to all the complex formal 'rules by which language signifies'" (129).

10 Russell comments in "The Sins of the Father" (1911a) on the fact that his interpretation of Dixon's earlier play *The Clansman* was not favorably received by the press. Because the community's sentiments were in favor of protesting against the play, none could appreciate his unique interpretation, and thus his review "manuscript was not accepted for publication" (6).

11 In an etymology of the term "mulatto" in his book *The Devil Finds Work* (1976), Baldwin deconstructs the term to better examine its particular sociopolitical ramifications as applied to the illegitimate children of slave masters: "Almost all mulattoes, and especially at that time, were produced by white men, and rarely indeed by an act of love. . . . The root of the word, *mulatto,* is Spanish, according to Webster, from *mulo,* a mule. The word refers to: (1) a person, one of whose parents is Negro and the other Caucasian, or white; and (2) popularly, any person with mixed Negro and Caucasian ancestry. A mule is defined as (1) the offspring of a donkey and a horse, especially the offspring of a jackass and a mare—*mules are usually sterile.* And, a further definition: in biology, a hybrid, *especially a sterile hybrid* [italics mine]. The idea of producing a child, on condition, and under the guarantee, that the child cannot reproduce must, after all, be relatively rare; no matter how dim a view one may take on the human race. It argues an extraordinary spiritual condition, or an unspeakable spiritual poverty" (59–60).

12 Jane Addams voiced her criticisms of the film in the *Chicago Defender.* However, her liberal views and writings were also printed in other black press outlets, such as in the National Urban League's house organ, the *Opportunity Magazine.*

13 Several studies of the history of the black press call attention to the existence of a significant white readership among the presses' circulation numbers. See, for example, Armistead S. Pride and Clint C. Wilson II's *A History of the Black Press* (1997) and James R. Grossman's *Land of Hope: Chicago, Black Southerners, and Great Migration* (1989), among others.

14 bell hooks clearly and cogently explains the survivalist imperative that motivates and produces black rhetorics of insurgency and resistance in her impor-

tant text, *Talking Back* (1989). I am indebted to her for popularizing and legitimating this familiar trope of the black folk and cultural experiences in America.

15 Joanne Braxton, in *Black Women Writing Autobiography: A Tradition within a Tradition* (1989), has noted that one black newspaper, the *New York Age*, "was on an exchange list with many white periodicals" (121); it is likely that a similar arrangement existed between the *Defender* and other Chicago white papers as well. It is certainly the case that black newspapers often reprinted news from white papers, which presumes such an arrangement to avoid copyright infringements. This factor of exchange is important because it negates the presumption that black newspapers circulated in a cultural and racial vacuum, even though it is often expected that blacks read the white dailies in addition to their own weekly newspapers.

16 For James Weldon Johnson's full review of the film and a scathing denunciation of one white paper's evaluation of the film, see Johnson's 1915 *New York Age* essay, "Perverted History."

17 Robert Sklar delves into the early cinema's fight for public acceptance in great detail and precision in *Movie Made America* (1976).

18 I borrow this concept of ensuring a willing "subjection to the ruling ideology" from Louis Althusser in his discussion of ideological state apparatuses. See Althusser's *Lenin and Philosophy* (1971, 133).

19 For a further discussion of white hegemonic investment in the South's revisionist historiographies in narratives of Reconstruction, see Du Bois's *Black Reconstruction in America* (1977).

20 See Alain Locke's essay "The Theoretical and Scientific Conceptions of Race" (1992) for a complete discussion of the black intelligentsia's efforts to combat theories of scientific racism (1–19).

21 For a then-contemporaneous guide to newspaper headline "characteristics and requirements," see Grant Milner Hyde's "Essentials in Headlines" (1926, 150–65).

22 Again, for a more thorough investigation of this miscegenation double standard, along historical lines, see Joanne Braxton's discussion of the mulatto question in *Black Women Writing Autobiography* (1989, 126).

23 These *Crisis* essays comport with what Antonio Gramsci (1985) has described as "the duty of journalistic activity (in its various articulations) to follow and monitor all the intellectual centers and movements which exist or are formed in the country" (405).

24 This was the thematic content of *The Birth of a Race* (Noble 1918) film that I screened at the Library of Congress in 1995. The scenario writers were listed as John W. Noble, Rudolph De Cordova, and George Frederick Wheeler. The title page also credits Noble with personal direction and supervision.

3. Cinephilia in the Black Renaissance

1   For a detailed account of *Freedom's Journal,* see Pride and Wilson 1997, 13.

2   Grossman's *Land of Hope* (1989, 3–9) explores in depth the Great Migration history of southern blacks to the city of Chicago.

3   I draw from Teresa de Lauretis's (1987) explanation of English uses of "cathexis" here. She says that what makes an individual "take up a position in a certain discourse rather than another is an 'investment' (this term translates the German *Besetzung,* a word used by Freud and rendered in English as *cathexis*)" (16). This sense of equating "investment" with "cathexis" is how I am explaining black spectators' excitement over these new images of celluloid blackness.

4   For an elaboration on this topic, see Walton 1912c.

5   Howard A. Phelps chronicles the shifts and developments in Chicago with the arrival of southern migrants in his essay "Negro Life in Chicago," which appeared in the May 1919 edition of *Half-Century.*

6   See Cathy Peiss's *Cheap Amusements* (1986) for a thorough treatment of the early cinema's socializing function among immigrant women at this time; also, a detailed discussion can be found in "Movie-Made Children," a chapter in Robert Sklar's *Movie-Made America* (1976).

7   See Jane Gaines's "The Scar of Shame" (1987) for a fuller treatment of the skin color problematic in 1930s black-cast films.

8   In addition to its monthly reports on lynchings in general, *Half-Century* reported specifically on lynchings and the returning black soldiers in both its October 1919 and October 1920 issues.

9   For more information on the relationship between the black press and its readers see Abby R. and Ronald Maberry Johnson's *Propaganda and Aesthetics* (1979); Grossman's *Land of Hope* (1989); and Vilma R. Potter's *A Reference Guide to Afro-American Publications and Editors* (1993). Potter examines the black readers' responses to, and expectations of, their presses. She notes that "these papers [and magazines] are read, and passed from hand to hand, and re-read until they are worn out" (17).

10 In its May 1919 edition, the magazine carried an editorial entitled "The New Negro Is Reading," on page 3. Here, the comments center on the benefits of newspaper and magazine reading as laying the foundations for the black masses' progression to more advanced literary texts, books.

11 In his article "The Melting Pot" in *Half-Century* (May), Shelton Fowler (1920) discusses at length the rationale for the African American's "demonstration of love for his country." For Fowler, the issue is best summed up in this way: "It is not the ambition of the Negro ever to take this country from the white man, but it is his ambition be a part of it, and with all the rights,

liberties and protection of an American citizen to do his bit to make this the greatest nation under the sun" (10).

12 Compare with Charles Musser's description of *The Great Train Robbery* in his book *Before the Nickelodeon* (1991, 254).

13 The May 1919 edition of *Half-Century* puts the total number of African Americans residing in Chicago in 1919 at 150,000, with most cramped into the Second Ward. In its June 1919 issue, *Half-Century* reports: "The war caused the migration of 500,000 Negroes from the South to the North" (12). The July issue of that year reports a "sixfold" increase in Detroit's black population in eight years (15).

14 In its "General Race News" department, the March 1919 *Half-Century* reported that the U.S. Department of Labor had to "cease granting permits for the importation of labor from the Bahamas, Jamaica and Mexico," although lumber, harvest workers, and fishermen were not affected by the ban (10).

15 Mark Reid's *Redefining Black Film* (1993) and Thomas Cripps's *Slow Fade to Black* (1993b) provide thorough investigations of early black filmmaking companies, and they proffer several reasons for the eventual demise of the black independent film movement.

16 Writers for *Half-Century* continually pressed black businesses to support black filmmaking enterprises. C.f. Juli Jones's "Motion Pictures and Inside Facts" (1919a), in which Jones writes: "Where does the fault lie? [He is referencing the lack of black film companies and theaters] It can be traced to the 'hog-it-all' desire of some of our business and professional men who will not enter any kind of proposition in which they are not head and shoulders over everyone else. . . . If Colored people with interest of the race at heart, would pool their money, stop fighting each other, and get down to business, they would reap unlimited returns, but would also do the race great service" (16–19). Jones also calculates the average amount of revenues generated by the scores of black film lovers and spectators.

17 The productions for the theater by Langston Hughes, Melvin B. Tolson, Countee Cullen, Lorraine Hansberry, and others typified the type of African American theater that Daugherty had envisioned earlier.

18 C.f. E. Franklin Frazier's *Black Bourgeoisie* (1957) for an unparalleled analysis of this class of African Americans; also, James Weldon Johnson's *Black Manhattan* (1968).

19 The term "Harlem Renaissance" is considered problematic in contemporary times because the emphasis on Harlem obscures the enormous contributions made by writers and artists hailing from other locales. See David L. Lewis's (1994) introduction in *The Portable Harlem Renaissance Reader*.

20 I am indebted to James Naremore's *Acting in the Cinema* (1988) for his illuminating discussions of the complex dynamics involving audience and

star interaction, specific acting styles, and ideological questions that combine in the concept of star discourse (2).

21 See a discussion of the church's prejudices against stage and film performers in Jean Voltaire Smith's "Our Need for More Films" (1922, 8).

22 That the black press was instrumental in encouraging the mass migration movement is not news. However, what is not so well known is that the papers and magazines were also adamant about the necessity for black migrants to resist southern promises that African Americans could expect improved race relations and economic opportunities in the southland. C.f. James Weldon Johnson's regular editorials on the subject in the *New York Age* during most of the early 1920s.

23 See Buchanan (1968) for an uneven treatment of black film writing in the *Defender* and *Courier* papers.

24 The *Amsterdam News* used its entertainment pages to justify its slightly higher rates. "Three pages devoted to the doings of the people in the amusement world places the Amsterdam News in the forefront of newspapers published by colored people in Greater New York and while our rates appear high to some, we continue to carry more display amusement advertising than all others" ("About Things Theatrical" 1923).

4. Black Modernist Dialectics and the New Deal

1 See "Period of Modernism and Consolidation in American Literature, 1930–1960," in Holmon and Harman (1992), 350.

2 In his essay "Art Is a Weapon," Cyril Briggs, the editor of the *Harlem Liberator*, insists that African American "artists and intellectuals have a significant contribution to make in the liberation struggles of the oppressed black masses (2). In an adjacent column of that 9 Sept. 1933 edition, J. C. L. advocates the necessity for African Americans to produce "their own films," as well as write protest letters to studios condemning stereotypes and sponsor "well-organized boycotts" (2).

3 Alfred S. Buchanan's (1968) dissertation "A Study of the Attitudes of the Writers of the Negro Press" focuses extensively on the black press's right to work campaign for black performers.

4 See Cedric J. Robinson's *Black Marxism* (1983); Harold Cruse's *The Crisis of the Negro Intellectual* (1967); and Mark Naison's *Communists in Harlem during the Depression* (1983) for detailed analyses of these political movements.

5 As early as 1923, the black press carried stories about African Americans' involvement with socialist politics; see, for example, "Socialism and the Negro" 1923, 12; "Race Woman Runs for Alderman on Socialist Ticket" 1923, 10; also, Naison 1983.

6 This was particularly true of white leftist film critics in Britain. Kenneth McPherson, the editor of the film journal *Close-Up*, devoted the entire August 1929 issue to the cinema, Africa, and African diasporic representation. This journal edition is notable for its inclusion of criticism written by African Americans in addition to its own critical discussions on the issue. See also the British Film Institute's journal *Sight and Sound*, which included articles on the Negro and the cinema by George Noble and William Harrison in its spring 1939 edition; and in 1935, the Left-oriented journal *The New Theater* included an interview with Duke Ellington, the important African American jazz musician. Here Ellington discusses his critical opinion of the play *Porgy*, which was adapted to film in 1959 by Samuel Goldwyn and the Universal studios as *Porgy and Bess.*

7 For a different treatment of the issue, see Cripps 1993a, 1993b.

8 See David Levering Lewis's *Harlem Renaissance Reader* (1994, xviii) for an interesting account of the ideological differences among these intellectuals that often ruptured along generational lines.

9 See Barksdale and Kinnamon 1972 for biographical and bibliographical information on Hurston (611–18).

10 See, for example, *The Cinema Book*, edited by Pam Cook (1985, 6–7, 26–27); "The Coming of Sound, 1926–32" and "The Sound Film and the American Studio System," in David Cook's *A History of Narrative Film* (1990, 253–354); and Sklar's *Movie-Made America* (1976, 152–54).

11 Loren Miller, a prominent black lawyer, journalist, and Communist fellow traveler, indicts the black press for its failure to counter sufficiently the antiblack themes in Hollywood films (see Miller 1934b).

12 Black writers and journalists have historically complained of the white newspapers' "long established practice of giving crimes among the city's half-million Negroes excessive prominence" (D. Robinson 1945, 169).

13 As with other films to which I have not had access, here I rely wholly on external sources. In this case, I defer to Lautier's review (1937) and John Walker's editorial comments from *Halliwell's Film Guide* (1995) for its description.

14 See a discussion of Capra and populism in Jeffrey Richards's 1976 article "Frank Capra and the Cinema of Populism."

15 This phrase is borrowed from David Levering Lewis.

16 Popular nightclub performer Bobby Short reveals not only that Razaf was a highly sought-after lyricist in black musical circles based on successful collaborations with such important musicians as Thomas "Fats" Waller, Eubie Blake, Fletcher Henderson, and Ethel Waters, to name a few, but that "white artists like Rudy Vallee, Benny Goodman, and Mildred Bailey also regularly included Razaf's songs" in their routines and radio fare (quoted in Singer 1992, xii–xiii). For a full accounting of this underappreciated giant of

American music, see Barry Singer's 1992 biography of Razaf, *Black and Blue: The Life and Lyrics of Andy Razaf.*

17 See, for example, "Harlem Pastors Are Called Upon to Take Position on Harlem Hootch Situation," *New York Age,* 13 Oct. 1923, 1. The article's subheading reads: "Editor of the New York Age Has Addressed a Letter to Ministers Urging Direct Action against the Bootlegging Interests Which Menace Community's Welfare." This article is typical of many that the *Age* reported during this era.

18 On 18 December 1937, for instance, the *New-Age Dispatch* carried a photo of the staff of Million Dollar Productions. Interestingly, in this photo, *Dispatch* film critic Harry Levette appears among the assembled interracial group. But the makeup of the company and the titles accompanying the names clearly attest to the fact that this is a white-owned and -operated company. Its black star, Ralph Cooper, and one other African American lend the company its necessary legitimacy with the black filmgoing public.

19 See James Weldon Johnson 1968; Frazier 1957; Cruse 1967; and Naison 1983 for more on this subject.

20 For a fuller engagement with sociopolitical currents that informed and in-flected oppositional filmmaking and cultural criticism in America during the silent era that reverberated into the early thirties, see Steven J. Ross's essay "Cinema and Class Conflict" (1990). For a continuation of many of these issues, see also Jonathan Buschbaum's "Left Political Filmmaking in the West: The Interwar Years" (1992).

21 Bogle admits that maid roles were abundant in Hollywood for years, but he differentiates between these maid roles and the mammy–Aunt Jemima cate-gory popularized by Beavers: "Before her there had been no distinctive mammy figure" (Bogle 1989, 62).

22 In *Shadow and Act,* Ralph Ellison (1953) observes that black audiences resist intended readings of films by inappropriate responses, such as laughter when the narrative clearly seeks to elicit tears, for example (280). Also, Mary Carbine mentions the extent to which black musical idioms such as jazz and blues that accompanied silent films in black neighborhoods helped audi-ences read the films against the grain. See her article "The Finest outside the Loop" (1990, 30–31).

23 The image of the mulatto does appear in Griffith's *Birth of a Nation.* I see these characterizations separate and apart from those proffered by *Imitation of Life.* In the first place, Griffith's mulattoes are portrayed by whites in blackface, and they are not sympathetic characters.

24 In fact, Washington looked white. "Press releases described her as looking French or Italian" (Bogle 1989, 60).

25 Arthur Draper's 1936 essay "Uncle Tom Will Never Die" considers the adverse effects plantation drama films had on the attitudes of white workers

who were beginning to join with black workers in forming sharecroppers, miners, and steelworkers unions.

26 I am borrowing Bill Nichols's (1981) conception of the function of the documentary film that "attempts to explain or describe some aspect of another culture to members of the [explicator's] own culture" (238) to discuss Cook's interaction with the reception issue as it pertains to the French audiences.

27 One of America's most renowned expatriates residing in France during this period, Josephine Baker sums up the lure of life abroad for African Americans in a letter to the *Chicago Defender* editor. Writing from Istanbul, Turkey, on 1 February 1934, Baker reports, "This is an interesting country and we are treated splendidly—just as in dear old France, where color means nothing but where merit, ability and real worth always find recognition. . . . I do wish you were with us; it would do you a world of good, I'm sure" ("Josephine Baker, Idol" 1934, 6).

28 My use of the term *panopticism* is inspired by Michel Foucault's (1979) extrapolation of Jeremy Bentham's architectural or brick-and-mortar prison house to describe individual society members' own coercive psychical mechanisms that must be deployed to maintain civil order. See Foucault's *Discipline and Punish,* 202–3.

29 See C. Robinson 1983; Cruse 1967; and the *Crisis* article "Negro Editors on Communism: A Symposium of the American Negro Press" (1932b) for rough estimates of the number of black communists in America during the thirties.

30 See Cornel West's "Marxist Theory and the Specificity of Afro-American Oppression" (1988, 17).

31 My use of this term comes from Hans Magnus Enzensberger (1974).

32 See Buchsbaum 1992, 131.

33 Mark Naison (1983) considers this dynamic and its impact on the party's activities in Harlem, where party whites and blacks often found it difficult to suppress their racial animosities (12–13).

34 On 15 March 1930, the *Defender* disclosed that a white self-styled African explorer named Daniel Davenport was ultimately responsible for the public revelation that his film *Jacko* was a hoax because he failed to pay Firpo Jack, a black janitor from Harlem, an agreed-on payment of $700. For the money, Firpo reports that "Davenport had given him a trick haircut and taught him to growl 'uga-uga-googie, woogie' . . . and that he was to assume the role of an 'African savage' who could not speak a word of English."

35 I borrow here from Clyde Taylor's particular use of Plato's "Noble Lie" as discussed in Taylor's article "The Ironies of Palace-Subaltern Discourse" (1993, 179).

36 See, for example, Camera Eye's "Screenings" columns dated 6 Jan. 1934 and 1 Jan. 1934.

37 See Philip Rosen's article "Document and Documentary" (1993) for a fuller explication of this concept.

38 See Platt's review of *Hallelujah* in his column dated 6 January 1934.

39 Platt considers *China Seas, Indo China, Good Earth,* and *Shanghai Madness* in one review, published on 16 December 1933, 6.

40 In Paul Arthur's (1993) discussion of documentary film production in the thirties, "Jargons of Authenticity: Three American Moments" (108), he adopts this term from Theodor Adorno.

41 See Phyllis Klotman's "The Black Writer in Hollywood, circa 1930" (1993, 80–92) for a discussion of Wallace Thurman's brief career as the only black writer in Hollywood during the thirties.

5. The Recalcitrant Gaze

1 See Constance Webb's (1968) discussion of Wright's attempts to secure $16,000 from "Mrs. Clara Florsheim, widow of the shoe manufacturer . . . [and] Mr. Marshall Field," the department store magnate (221).

2 Logan refers to the 1930s Payne Fund Studies of the effects of film on children, as well as later sources related to media studies, namely, I. Taylor 1939, 738–39; Bromley and Britten 1938, 12; and Thrasher 1940.

3 Although this quote from Lynn Spigel's book *Make Room for TV* (1992) refers to domestic penetration of women's magazines and novels, the radio soap operas and other family-oriented programming are obvious corollaries. And it is in this sense that her comments are applicable.

4 In June of 1919, William Foster, aka Juli Jones, Jr., wrote an article entitled "The Moving Picture: Their Good to the General Public and to the Color Race in Particular," for *Half-Century Magazine*. This is an early historical overview of the cinema with an emphasis on the international historical development of the medium. Even as Jones is careful to make the point that America was a latecomer to the artistry of film, as compared with its European counterparts, he still is interested in the early cinema's spectatorial allure for blacks: "Now the Negro lad or lass can see the pictures in his neighborhood theatre [*sic*] run by a white man who 'caters' to them or better still by a Colored man with a vision" (9).

5 Reddick (1944) compiled this list from "materials in the Film Library of the Museum of Modern Art" (4).

6 David Cook (1990) provides a detailed look at the cinema's role in World War II. See his excellent account in the essay "America at War" in his book *A History of Narrative Film.*

7 In a 1995 Turner Classic Movies interview, Greer Garson, the actress who portrayed Mrs. Miniver, reminisced about the war years when the film was

produced. She recalls being told by a high military official not to worry about her part in the war effort. His comment to her was to the effect that, "as long as you act in films like *Mrs. Miniver,* you are doing more for the war than if you had dropped a thousand bombs."

8 Manthia Diawara (1993b) discusses the privileging of white spectators in mainstream films in his essay "Black Spectatorship," in *Black American Cinema.*

9 I have extrapolated from Michael Renov's (1993) observations about the cognitive difficulties that arise when simulacral representations are mistaken as "the equivalent of their historical counterparts." In his essay "Toward a Poetics of Documentary," Renov is following Roland Barthes in warning against the "referential illusion" that "the referent is speaking for itself," when authorial agency is suppressed, as in documentary and actuality films (Renov quoting Barthes, 26–27).

10 In the thirties, Tolson was the director of Wiley College's debate teams, which Tolson biographer Robert Farnsworth (1982) says "had compiled an awesome record of success." He also reports that Wiley "defeated the national champions from the University of Southern California" in 1935 (50). Farnsworth informs us that "Tolson's debate team broke the color line in several states in the South, Southwest, and Midwest" (51).

11 Letter to Melvin B. Tolson, 21 March 1947. The Melvin B. Tolson Papers. Library of Congress. Container 1, Folder P–Q. Correspondent unknown.

12 Actress Freddi Washington, who portrayed Peola in the film *Imitation of Life,* disagreed vehemently with *Sentinel* publisher Leon Washington (no relation) on the best strategy to improve black roles in Hollywood. The debate is covered in the 19 September 1942 *People's Voice* article entitled "Negro Actor Film Committee Hindering Better Role Effect" (28).

13 See Nell Dodson's comments about black actors' "constant 'Uncle Tomming,' to get roles" in the 1942 *People's Voice* article "Headlines—Footlights" (28). She also disagrees with the *Sentinel* publisher's public statements disparaging Walter White's highly publicized meeting with Hollywood executives (28). See also Langston Hughes's (1943) critique of black performers in an article entitled "Round Table: 'Is Hollywood Fair to Negroes?'" (19).

14 David Cook (1990) offers an interesting perspective on the reality versus the perception of Hollywood's changed attitudes about escapist and social problem films during the war years in his book *A History of Narrative Film.*

Works Cited

"About Things Theatrical." 1923. *New York Amsterdam News*, 25 Apr.

Adams, Minnie. 1912. "In Union Is Strength." *Chicago Defender*, 24 Feb.

"The Ahjah Is Here." 1915. *Chicago Defender*, 16 Jan.

"Al Jolson Heads Petition Seeking Racial and Other Restrictive Enactments before City Body." 1938. *New-Age Dispatch*, 1 Apr.

Alexander, Howe. 1919. "Colored Motion Picture Drama." *Half-Century*, May.

"All-Talking Film Heads Regent Bill." 1928. *Baltimore Afro-American*, 3 Nov.

Allen, Robert C., and Douglas Gomery. 1985. *Film History: Theory and Practice*. New York: McGraw-Hill.

Althusser, Louis. 1971. *Lenin and Philosophy*. Trans. Ben Brewster. New York and London: Monthly Review Press.

Arthur, Paul. 1993. "Jargons of Authenticity: Three American Moments." In *Theorizing Documentary*, ed. Michael Renov, 108–34. New York and London: Routledge.

"As to Lynchings." 1915. Editorial. *Chicago Defender*, 1 May.

Atwood, Rose. 1920. "'A Man's Duty': Novelized." *Competitor*, Jan., 58.

Baker, Houston A. 1987. *Modernism and the Harlem Renaissance*. Chicago: University of Chicago Press.

Bakhtin, Mikhail M. 1981. *The Dialogic Imagination*. Ed. Michael Holquist. Austin: University of Texas Press.

Baldwin, James. 1976. *The Devil Finds Work*. New York: Dell.

"'Bargain with Bullets' Finished." 1937. *New-Age Dispatch*, 6 Aug.

"'Bargain with Bullets' to Premiere at Lincoln Theatre." 1937. *New-Age Dispatch*, 11 Sept.

Barksdale, Richard, and Kenneth Kinnamon, eds. 1972. *Black Writers of America: A Comprehensive Anthology*. New York: Macmillan.

Barthes, Roland. 1972. *Mythologies*. Trans. Annette Lavers. New York: Noonday Press.

Bazin, Andre. 1967. "The Ontology of the Photographic Image." In *What Is Cinema*, vol. 1, trans. Hugh Gray, 9–16. Berkeley and Los Angeles: University of California Press.

"Begins Work on New All Colored Cast Picture." 1937. *New-Age Dispatch,* 23 July.

Bell, George M. 1920. "Social Value of the Contemporary Drama." *Competitor,* Apr.

Benjamin, Walter. 1986. "The Work of Art in the Age of Mechanical Reproduction." In *Video Culture: A Critical Investigation,* ed. John Hanhardt, 27–52. Rochester, N.Y.: Visual Studies Workshop.

"Big Pictures Now Built on Great Stories." 1937. *New-Age Dispatch,* 27 Nov.

Bills, K. J. "Facts about *Birth of a Nation* Play." 1915. *Chicago Defender,* 11 Sept.

"*Birth of a Nation* Arouses Ire of Miss Jane Addams." 1915. *Chicago Defender,* 20 Mar.

"*Birth of a Nation* Barred by Mayor in Cedar Rapids." 1915. *Chicago Defender,* 5 June.

"*Birth of a Nation* Promoters after Mayor Thompson." 1915. *Chicago Defender,* 29 May.

"*Birth of a Nation* Run Out of Philadelphia." 1915. *Chicago Defender,* 25 Sept.

"*Birth of a Nation* Will Not Be Shown in Chicago." 1915. *Chicago Defender,* 1 May.

"The Black Vanguard." 1918. *Half-Century Magazine,* May.

Bogle, Donald. 1989. *Toms, Coons, Mulattoes, Mammies, and Bucks.* 1973. Reprint, New York: Continuum.

Bragg, Columbus. 1914. "On and off the Stroll." *Chicago Defender,* 1 Aug.

Braxton, Joanne M. 1989. *Black Women Writing Autobiography: A Tradition within a Tradition.* Philadelphia: Temple University Press.

Briggs, Cyrill. 1933. "Art Is a Weapon." *Harlem Liberator,* 9 Sept.

Bromley, Dorothy D., and Florence H. Britten. 1938. *Youth and Sex.* New York and London: Harper and Brothers.

Brown, Sterling A. 1935. "*Imitation of Life:* Once a Pancake." *Opportunity.* March.

Buchanan, Alfred Singer. 1968. "A Study of the Attitudes of the Writers of the Negro Press toward the Depiction of the Negro in Plays and Films: 1930–1965." Ph.D. diss., University of Michigan.

Buchsbaum, Jonathan. 1992. "Left Political Filmmaking in the West: The Interwar Years." In *Resisting Images: Essays on Culture and History,* ed. Robert Sklar and Charles Musser, 126–48. Philadelphia: Temple University Press.

Byrd, Pauline Flora. 1935. " 'Imitation of Life.' " *Crisis,* March, 91–92.

Camera Eye. "Screenings." 1933. *Harlem Liberator,* 23 Dec.

———. "Screenings." 1934b. *Harlem Liberator,* 23 Jan.

———. "Screenings." 1934c. *Harlem Liberator,* 27 Jan.

Carbine, Mary. 1990. " 'The Finest outside the Loop': Motion Picture Exhibition in Chicago's Black Metropolis, 1905–1928." *Camera Obscura* 23: 9–42.

Carlington, S. W. 1949. "Movies 'Courting Negro' to Boost Sick Box Office." *Amsterdam News,* 1 Oct.

"The Clansman." 1907. *Iowa State Bystander,* 8 Mar.

"The Clansman and Its Effects upon the Negro." 1906. *Baltimore Afro-American Ledger,* 17 Mar.

Clark, W. E. 1931. "'The Exile' at Lafayette Theatre." *New York Age,* 23 May.

Cohen, Lizabeth. 1989. "Encountering Mass Culture at the Grassroots: The Experience of Chicago Workers in the 1920s." *American Quarterly* 41: 6–33.

"Color Bars Louise Beavers from Film Award." 1935. *Pittsburgh Courier,* 2 Mar.

"Colored Men Organize Big Theatrical Circuit." 1919. *New York Age,* 12 July.

"Colored Voters Want another Councilman." 1915. *New York Age,* 11 Mar.

"Complains Race Movie Stars Repeat Same Roles Endlessly." 1937. *New-Age Dispatch,* 23 Apr., 1.

Cook, David A. 1990. *A History of Narrative Film.* New York: W. W. Norton.

Cook, Mercer. 1935. "'Imitation of Life' in Paris." *The Crisis,* June, 182.

Cook, Pam, ed. 1992. *The Cinema Book.* 1985. Reprint, London: BFI.

Cripps, Thomas. 1993a. *Making Movies Black.* Oxford and New York: Oxford University Press.

——. 1993b. *Slow Fade to Black.* 1977. Reprint, Oxford and New York: Oxford University Press.

Cruse, Harold. 1967. *The Crisis of the Negro Intellectual.* New York: William Morrow.

Dancer, Maurice. 1929. "'Hallelujah' One of Year's Big Successes." *Pittsburgh Courier,* 7 Sept.

Daniels, Fred. 1934. "Fredye Washington May Talk Herself Out of the Movies." *Pittsburgh Courier,* 21 Apr.

"Dark Manhattan Premiere." 1937. *New-Age Dispatch,* 15 Jan.

Daugherty, Romeo L. 1920. "Progress of the Drama." *Competitor,* Jan., 53–54.

"Debs Flays Bad Motion Picture." 1916. *California Eagle,* 18 Mar.

de Certeau, Michel. 1984. *The Practice of Everyday Life.* Berkeley and Los Angeles: University of California Press.

de Lauretis, Teresa. 1987. *Technologies of Gender: Essays on Theory, Film and Fiction.* Bloomington: Indiana University Press.

Dery, Mark. 1994. "Black to the Future: Interviews with Samuel R. Delany, Greg Tate, and Tricia Rose." *Flame Wars: The Discourse of Cyberculture.* Ed. Mark Dery. Durham, N.C.: Duke University Press.

Diawara, Manthia, ed. 1993a. *Black American Cinema.* New York and London: Routledge.

——. 1993b. "Black Spectatorship: Problems of Identification and Resistance." In *Black American Cinema,* 211–20. New York and London: Routledge.

"Discusses Fight Pictures." 1910. *New York Age,* 21 July.

Dismond, Geraldyn. 1929. "The Negro Actor and the American Movies." *Close Up,* Aug., 90–97.

Dodson, Nell. 1942. "Headlines—Footlights." *People's Voice,* 19 Sept.

Douglas, Ann. 1995. *Terrible Honesty: Mongrel Manhattan in the 1920s.* New York: Farrar, Strauss and Giroux.

Draper, Arthur. 1936. "Uncle Tom Will Never Die." In *Black Films and Film-Makers: A Comprehensive Anthology from Stereotype to Superhero,* ed. Lindsay Patterson. 1975. Reprint, New York: Dodd, Mead.

Du Bois, W. E. B. 1903. *The Souls of Black Folk.* 1969. Reprint, New York: Signet Classic.

——. 1910. "The Color Line." *Horizon,* Jan.

——. 1913. "Socialism and the Negro Problem." In *W. E. B. Du Bois: A Reader,* ed. Meyer Weinberg, 337–40. New York: Harper and Row.

——. 1915a. "The Clansman." *The Crisis.* May.

——. 1915b. "Fighting Race Calumny." *The Crisis.* May and June.

——. 1926. "Criteria of Negro Art." *The Crisis,* Oct. 1995. Reprinted in *W. E. B. Du Bois: A Reader,* ed. David Levering Lewis, 509–15. New York: Henry Holt.

——. 1933. "Marxism and the Negro Problem." *The Crisis,* May, 103.

——. 1935. *Black Reconstruction in America, 1860–1880.* 1977. Reprint, New York: Atheneum.

Dunbar, Paul Laurence. 1913. "To a Captious Critic." In *The Complete Poems of Paul Laurence Dunbar.* 1980. Reprint, New York: Dodd, Mead.

Ellison, Ralph. 1972. *Shadow and Act.* 1953. Reprint, New York: Vintage.

Enzensberger, Hans Magnus. 1974. "Constituents of a Theory of the Media." In *Video Culture: A Critical Investigation,* ed. John Hanhardt, 96–123. 1986. Reprint, Rochester, N.Y.: Visual Studies Workshop Press.

"Eugene V. Debs Flays Big Movie." 1916. *California Eagle,* 29 Jan.

"Extra! Five Burnings in South in Five Months." 1915. *New York Age,* 12 July.

Fabre, Michel. 1973. *The Unfinished Quest of Richard Wright.* Trans. Isabel Barzun. New York: William Morrow.

Fanon, Frantz. 1963. *Wretched of the Earth.* New York: Grove Weidenfeld.

Farnsworth, Robert M., ed. 1982. *Caviar and Cabbage: Selected Columns by Melvin B. Tolson from the Washington Tribune, 1937–1944.* Columbia: University of Missouri Press.

"Federation of Labor Condemns Lynching." 1915. *New York Age,* 23 June.

"Fight Film." 1910. Advertisement. *Moving Picture World,* 21 May.

"Fighting Race Calumny." 1915. *The Crisis,* May.

"Fighting Race Calumny II." 1915. *The Crisis,* June.

Fish, Stanley. 1987. "What Makes an Interpretation Acceptable." In *Contexts for Criticism,* ed. Donald Keesey, 347–56. Palo Alto: Mayfield.

"Fisher Writes Play for Motion Picture Company." 1915. *Baltimore Afro-American*, 18 Sept.

"'Flaming Crisis' Most Powerful Drama Screened." 1924. *Pittsburgh Courier*, 4 Apr.

"Foster Photoplay Company Licensed in Florida." 1914. *Chicago Defender*, 11 Apr.

"Foster, the Moving Picture Man Returns." 1914. *Chicago Defender*, 20 June.

Foucault, Michel. 1979. *Discipline and Punish: The Birth of the Prison*. Trans. Alan Sheridan. New York: Vintage.

——. "What Is an Author?" In *The Foucault Reader*, ed. Paul Rabinow, 101–20. New York: Pantheon Books.

Fowler, Shelton. 1920. "The Melting Pot." *Half-Century*, May.

Franklin, John Hope. 1989. "The Profession of History." In *Race and History: Selected Essays, 1938–1988*. Baton Rouge: Louisiana State University Press.

Frazier, Franklin E. 1957. *Black Bourgeoisie*. 1970. Reprint, London: Collier.

Gabriel, Teshome. 1985. "Towards a Theory of Third World Cinema." In *Cinemas of the Black Diaspora*, ed. Michael T. Martin, 70–90. 1995. Reprint, Detroit: Wayne State University Press.

Gaines, Jane. 1987. "The Scar of Shame: Skin Color and Caste in Black Silent Melodrama." *Cinema Journal* 26, no. 4: 3–21.

"General Race News." 1919. *Half-Century*, Mar.

"Gone Are Hey-Days of Slapstick Comedy." 1923. *Pittsburgh Courier*, 13 Oct.

Goodwin, Ruby Berkeley. 1920. "When Stepin Fetchit Stepped into Fame." *Pittsburgh Courier*, 6 July, pt. 2, p. 1.

——. 1929. "From 'Blackbird' Chorine to 'Talkie' Star." *Pittsburgh Courier*, 8 June, 6.

Graham-Du Bois, Shirley. 1978. *Du Bois: A Pictorial Biography*. Chicago: Johnson.

Gramsci, Antonio. 1985. *Selections from Cultural Writings*. Ed. David Forgacs and Geoffrey Nowell-Smith. Cambridge: Harvard University Press.

"'Green Pastures' Not Liked by Negroes." 1931. *New York Age*, 31 Jan.

Grossman, James R. 1989. *Land of Hope: Chicago, Black Southerners, and the Great Migration*. Chicago: University of Chicago Press.

Guerrero, Ed. 1993. *Framing Blackness: The African American Image in Film*. Philadelphia: Temple University Press.

Hall, Stuart. 1980. "Encoding/Decoding." In *Culture, Media, Language: Working Papers in Cultural Studies*, 128–38. London: Hutchinson.

——. 1988. "New Ethnicities." In *ICA Documents*, ed. Kobena Mercer, 2–31. London: Institute of Contemporary Arts.

"Harlem Pastors Are Called Upon to Take Position on Harlem Hooch Situation." 1923. *New York Age*, 13 Oct., 1.

Herring, Robert. 1929. "Black Shadows." *Close Up,* Aug., 97–104.

"'Hit the Nigger' New Film Insult." 1914. *Chicago Defender,* 38 Feb.

"Hollywood Screen Stars Protest Scottsboro Convictions." 1937. *New-Age Dispatch,* 21 Aug.

Holman, Hugh C., and William Harmon. 1992. *A Handbook to Literature.* New York: Macmillan.

Holub, Renate. 1992. *Antonio Gramsci: Beyond Marxism and Postmodernism.* London: Routledge.

hooks, bell. 1984. *Feminist Theory: From Margin to Center.* Boston: South End.

——. 1989. *Talking Back.* Boston: South End.

Hubbard, Dolan. 1994. *The Sermon and the African American Literary Imagination.* Columbia: University of Missouri Press.

Hughes, Langston. 1934. "Going South in Russia." *The Crisis,* May, 162–34.

——. 1943. "Round Table: 'Is Hollywood Fair to Negroes?'" *Negro Digest,* April, 19–21.

Hughes, Langston, and Milton Meltzer. 1967. *Black Magic: A Pictorial History of the African American in the Performing Arts.* New York: Da Capo Press.

Hyde, Grant Milner. 1926. *Handbook for Newspaper Workers.* 1921. Reprint, New York and London: D. Appleton.

"'Imitation' Sets New Record at Chicago's Metropolitan." 1935. *Pittsburgh Courier,* 23 Feb.

"Intolerance: D. W. Griffith, Producer of *The Clansman,* Forgiven." 1916. *Eagle,* 18 Nov.

The Investigator [pseud.]. 1920. "Is the Church Losing Its Hold on the People?" *Half-Century,* June.

"Is the Negro a Man?" 1906. *Iowa State Bystander,* 15 June.

Jackson, Faye. 1934. "Fredi Washington Strikes New Note in Hollywood Film." *Pittsburgh Courier,* 15 Dec.

——. 1937. "'Green Pastures' Star Gets Role in 'Spirit of Youth.'" *Pittsburgh Courier,* 6 Nov.

James, C. L. R. 1973. *Modern Politics.* Detroit: be wick/ed.

Jameson, Fredric. 1990. *Signatures of the Visible.* New York: Routledge.

Janken, Kenneth Robert. 1993. *Rayford W. Logan and the Dilemma of the African American Intellectual.* Amherst: University of Massachusetts Press.

"Japanese Make Strong Protest against Moving Picture Film before Welfare Committee of the City Council." 1916. *California Eagle,* 29 Jan.

JCL [pseud.]. 1933. "The Role Assigned the Negro in American Films." *Harlem Liberator,* 9 Sept.

Johnson, Abby Arthur, and Ronald Maberry Johnson. 1979. *Propaganda and Aesthetics: The Literary Politics of African-American Magazines in the Twentieth Century.* 1991. Reprint, Amherst: University of Massachusetts Press.

Johnson, George. n.d. "White and Negro Film Corporation, 1910–1940."
George Johnson Collection, UCLA Special Collections.

Johnson, James Weldon. 1929. "Color in the Films." *New York Age*, 19 Oct.

——. 1930. "A Director's Dilemma." *New York Age*, 4 Jan.

——. 1968. *Black Manhattan*. New York: Atheneum.

——. 1995a. "Perverted History." In *The Selected Writings of James Weldon Johnson*, vol. 1, ed. Sondra Kathryn Wilson, 156–58. New York: Oxford University Press.

——. 1995b. "Uncle Tom's Cabin and the Clansman." In *The Selected Writings of James Weldon Johnson*, vol. 1, ed. Sondra Kathryn Wilson, 12–13. New York: Oxford University Press.

"Jolson Denial Divides Negro Press." 1938. *New-Age Dispatch*, 15 Apr.

Jones, Juli [pseud.]. 1915. "Moving Pictures Offer the Greatest Opportunity to the American Negro." *Chicago Defender*, 9 Oct.

——. 1919a. "Motion Pictures and Inside Facts." *Half-Century*, May, 16–19.

——. 1919b. "The Moving Picture: Their Good to the General Public and to the Colored Race in Particular." *Half-Century*, June.

Jones, Robert. 1947. "How Hollywood Feels about Negroes." *Negro Digest*, Aug., 4–8.

"Josephine Baker, Idol of France, Writes Mr. Abbott." 1934. *Chicago Defender*, 17 Feb.

"Jottings Theatrical and Otherwise." 1914. *Chicago Defender*, 28 Mar.

"Karl Marx and the Negro." 1933. *Crisis*, Mar., 55–56.

Kellner, Douglas. 1989. *Jean Baudrillard: From Marxism to Postmodernism and Beyond*. Stanford: Stanford University Press.

Klotman, Phyllis. 1993. "The Black Writer in Hollywood, circa 1930: The Case of Wallace Thurman." In *Black American Cinema*, ed. Manthia Diawara, 80–92. New York and London: Routledge.

Kracauer, Siegfried. 1947. *From Caligari to Hitler*. Princeton, N.J.: Princeton University Press.

LaCapra, Dominick. 1987. *History and Criticism*. Ithaca, N.Y.: Cornell University Press.

La Mar, Lawrence. 1937. "All Sepia-Cast Films Triumph in Human Emotions and Theme Adaptation." *New-Age Dispatch*, 4 Dec., 1.

Langston, Tony. 1920. "Moral" and Movies." *The Competitor*, Feb.

Lautier, Lewis. 1933. Telegram to Walter White, 12 Sept. NAACP Files, Group 1, Box C 303. Library of Congress, Washington, D.C.

——. 1937. "Courier Critic Pre-views Mixed Cast Film: Lautier Says 'One Mile from Heaven' Opens New Field." *New-Age Dispatch*, 28 Aug.

Lee, James Melvin. 1917. *History of American Journalism*. 1923. Reprint, Garden City, N.Y.: Garden City.

Lewis, David Levering, ed. 1994. *Harlem Renaissance Reader.* New York: Viking-Penguin.

Library of Congress. 1993. *African American Mosaic: A Library of Congress Resource Guide for the Study of Black Culture.* Washington, D.C.: Library of Congress.

"Lincoln Motion Picture Company Making Good." 1917. *St. Louis Argus,* 5 Jan.

Locke, Alain. 1992. "The Theoretical and Scientific Conceptions of Race." In *Race Contacts and Interracial Relations,* ed. Jeffrey C. Stewart, 1–19. 1915. Reprint, Washington, D.C.: Howard University Press.

Locke, Alain L., and Sterling Brown. 1930. "Folk Values in a New Medium." In *Black Films and Film-Makers: A Comprehensive Anthology from Stereotype to Superhero,* ed. Lindsay Patterson, 25–29. 1975. Reprint, New York: Dodd, Mead.

Logan, Rayford. 1940. "Negro Youth and the Influence of the Press, Radio, and Cinema." *Journal of Negro Education* 9: 424–34.

"Louise Beavers Says Company Makes Movie, Trend Writer Says No." 1937. *New-Age Dispatch,* 12 February.

Lowery, Shearon A., and Melvin L. DeFleur. 1988. *Milestones in Mass Communication Research.* 2d ed. New York and London: Longman.

"Lynch Two in Georgia: Mob Spirit Again Rampant." 1915. *Defender,* 10 July.

"Lynching." 1915. *Crisis,* June, 71–73.

MacCannell, Dean. 1976. *The Tourist: A New Theory of the Leisure Class.* New York: Schocken Books.

Marable, Manning. 1983. *How Capitalism Underdeveloped Black America.* Boston: South End.

Marvin, Carolyn. 1988. *When Old Technologies Were New: Thinking about Electric Communication in the Late Nineteenth Century.* New York: Oxford University Press.

"Mayor Thompson Bars 'Birth of a Nation' from Chicago." 1915. *Chicago Defender,* 22 May.

"Mayor's Wife O.K.'s *Birth of a Nation:* Obnoxious Movie." 1915. *Chicago Defender,* 3 Apr.

McPherson, Kenneth. 1929. "As Is." *Close Up,* Aug., 85–90.

Micheaux, Oscar. 1919. "The Negro and the Photo-Play." *Half-Century,* May, 9.

Michelson, Annette, ed. 1984. *Kino-Eye: The Writings of Dziga Vertov.* Trans. Kevin O'Brien. Berkeley and Los Angeles: University of California Press.

Miller, Loren. 1934a. "Hollywood's New Negro Films." *The Crisis,* June, 8–9.

———. 1938b. "Uncle Tom in Hollywood." Crisis, Nov., 329.

"Million Dollar Production, Inc., Has Great Film." 1937. *Pittsburgh Courier,* 27 Nov.

"Modern Abolitionists Denounce Race Hatred." 1915. *New York Age,* 11 Mar.

Morris, Earl J. 1935. "Fredi Washington, 'Imitation of Life' Repeat at the 'Met.'" *Pittsburgh Courier*, 23 Feb.

——. 1937. "Morris Interviews 'Bojangles': Learns He Is Real Race Man." *Pittsburgh Courier*, 31 July.

Moss, Carlton. 1946. "Your Future in Hollywood." *Our World*, May.

"'Movies to Replace Books in Schools' Inventor States." 1923. *Pittsburgh Courier*, 2 June.

"Moving Pictures Doing Good Business." 1909. *Baltimore Afro-American Ledger*, 6 Nov.

"Moving Pictures of Tuskegee." 1910. *New York Age*, 20 Jan.

Murphy, Dudley. 1933. Letter to Walter White, 6 Oct. NAACP Files, Group 1, Box C 303. Library of Congress, Washington, D.C.

Musser, Charles. 1991. *Before the Nickelodeon: Edwin S. Porter and the Edison Manufacturing Company*. Berkeley and Los Angeles: University of California Press.

Naison, Mark. 1983. *Communists in Harlem during the Depression*. New York: Grove.

Naremore, James. 1988. *Acting in the Cinema*. Berkeley and Los Angeles: University of California Press.

"Negro Actor Film Committee Hindering Better Role Effort." 1942. *People's Voice*, 19 Sept.

"Negro Editors on Communism: A Symposium of the American Negro Press." 1932a. *The Crisis*, Apr., 117.

"Negro Editors on Communism: A Symposium of the American Negro Press." 1932b. *The Crisis*, May, 154.

"Negro Hater Defeated in 'White City Primary.'" 1915. *New York Age*, 11 Mar.

"Negro Motion Pictures." 1913. *New York Age*, 6 Mar.

"Negroes Charged 20; White Patrons 10 Cts." 1912. *New York Age*, 29 Aug.

"A New Departure in Movies." 1934. *Pittsburgh Courier*, 27 Dec.

"New Theater for Wilmington: One of the Finest in the Country of Its Kind Entirely Owned and Operated by Colored People." 1916. *Baltimore Afro-American*, 18 Mar.

Nichols, Bill. 1981. *Ideology and the Image*. Bloomington: Indiana University Press.

Nietzsche, Friedrich. "On Truth and Lies in a Nonmoral Sense." In *Philosophy and Truth: Selections from Nietzsche's Notebooks of the Early 1870s*, ed. and trans. Daniel Breazeale, 79–97. 1979. Reprint, Atlantic Highlands, N.J.: Humanities Press.

"No More Kiss! Hero Loses Reward." 1937. *California New-Age Dispatch*, 9 Apr.

Norford, George E. 1948. "The Future in Films." *Opportunity*, July–Sept., 108–10.

Null, Gary. 1975. *Black Hollywood: The Black Performer in Motion Pictures.* New York: Citadel.

"Opening of the New Angelus a Notable Success." 1916. *California Eagle,* 8 July.

Patton, Bernice. 1934. "Critics Weep at the Preview of 'Imitation of Life.'" *Pittsburgh Courier,* 8 Dec.

———. 1935a. "Bojangles Teamed Up with Shirley." *Pittsburgh Courier,* 16 Feb.

———. 1935b. "Edward G. Robinson's 'Tops' in Columbia's Latest Film: 'The Whole Town's Talking.'" *Pittsburgh Courier,* 23 Feb.

Peiss, Kathy. 1986. *Cheap Amusements: Working Women and Leisure in Turn-of-the-Century New York.* Philadelphia: Temple University Press.

Penn, I. Garland. 1969. *The Afro-American Press and Its Editors.* New York: Arno Press.

"Peter P. Jones Heads Moving Picture Company." 1914. *Chicago Defender,* 6 June.

"Peter P. Jones Takes Moving Pictures of Shriners." 1914. *Chicago Defender,* 23 May.

Phelps, Howard A. 1919. "Negro Life in Chicago." *Half-Century,* May, 12–14.

"Pictures of the Jeffries-Johnson Fight." 1910. *Moving Picture World,* 18 June.

Platt, Dave. 1933a. "Drama–Movie: Movie Snapshots." *Harlem Liberator,* 11 Nov.

———. 1933b. *Harlem Liberator,* 18 Nov.

———. 1933c. *Harlem Liberator,* 16 Dec.

———. 1933d. *Harlem Liberator,* 23 Dec.

———. 1934a. *Harlem Liberator,* 13 Jan.

———. 1934b. *Harlem Liberator,* 20 Jan.

———. 1934c. *Harlem Liberator,* 10 Feb.

———. 1934d. *Harlem Liberator,* 17 Mar.

———. 1934e. *Harlem Liberator,* 24 Mar.

———. 1934f. *Harlem Liberator,* 31 Mar.

Potamkin, Harry A. 1929. "The Aframerican Cinema." *Close Up,* Aug., 107–17.

Potter, Vilma Raskin. 1993. *Afro-American Publications and Editors, 1827–1946.* Ames: Iowa State University Press.

Pride, Armistead S., and Clint C. Wilson II. 1997. *A History of the Black Press.* Washington, D.C.: Howard University Press.

"The Race Is Misrepresented." 1915. *Baltimore Afro-American,* 9 Oct.

"Race Leaders Fight *Birth of a Nation.*" 1915. *Chicago Defender,* 24 Apr.

"Race Press Ignored by Big Film Interests." 1934. *Pittsburgh Courier,* 15 Dec.

"Race Screen Star Becomes Popular New York Favorite." 1923. *New York Age,* 31 Mar.

"Race Taking Advantage of Evening School." 1915. *New York Age,* 11 Mar.

"Race Woman Runs for Alderman on Socialist Ticket." 1923. *Pittsburgh Courier,* 3 Nov.

Razaf, Andy. 1937. " 'Bargain with Bullets' Is Reviewed by Andy Razaf." *Pittsburgh Courier,* 27 Nov.

Reddick, Lawrence. 1944. "Of Motion Pictures." *Journal of Negro Education.* Reprinted in *Black Films and Filmmakers: A Comprehensive Anthology from Stereotype to Superhero,* ed. Lindsay Patterson, 3–24. 1975. New York: Dodd, Mead.

Reid, Mark. 1993. *Redefining Black Film.* Berkeley: University of California Press.

Renov, Michael. 1993. "Towards a Poetics of Documentary." In *Theorizing Documentary,* 12–36. New York: Routledge.

"Resents Criticism." 1914. *Chicago Defender,* 18 July.

"Rex Ingram, 'Green Pastures' Star Broke; Refuses Comedy Role in Pictures." 1937. *New-Age Dispatch,* 18 Sept.

Richards, Jeffrey. 1976. "Frank Capra and the Cinema of Populism." In *Movies and Methods,* vol. 1, 65–80. Berkeley: University of California Press.

Robinson, Cedric J. 1983. *Black Marxism: The Making of the Black Radical Tradition.* London: Zed Press.

Robinson, Duane. 1945. " 'Mugging' and the New York Press." *Phylon,* April, 169–79.

Rogin, Michael. 1991. " 'The Sword Became a Flashing Vision': D. W. Griffith's *The Birth of a Nation.* " In *The New American Studies: Essays from Representations,* ed. Philip Fisher, 346–91. Berkeley: University of California Press.

Rosen, Philip. 1993. "Document and Documentary: On the Persistence of Historical Concepts." In *Theorizing Documentary,* ed. Michael Renov, 58–89. New York: Routledge.

Ross, Steven J. 1990. "Cinema and Class Conflict: Labor, Capital, the State, and American Silent Film." In *Resisting Images: Essays on Cinema and History,* ed. Robert Sklar and Charles Musser, 68–107. Philadelphia: Temple University Press.

Roszak, Theodore. 1994. *The Cult of Information: A Neo-Luddite Treatise on High Tech, Artificial Intelligence, and the True Art of Thinking.* Berkeley: University of California Press.

Russell, Sylvester. 1910a. "A Quarterly Review." *Chicago Defender,* 12 Mar.

———. 1910b. "Negro, Yiddish Theaters and Other Notes." *Chicago Defender,* 9 Apr.

———. 1911a. "The Sins of the Father." *Chicago Defender,* 8 Apr.

———. 1911b. "The Phoenix Theatre Shows Good Pictures." *Chicago Defender,* 1 July.

———. 1911c. "The Phoenix Theater Has Good Houses." *Chicago Defender,* 22 July.

———. 1911d. "New Year's Offerings." *Chicago Defender,* 30 Dec.

Sarris, Andrew. 1976. "Towards a Theory of Film History." In *Movies and*

Methods, vol. 1, ed. Bill Nichols, 237–50. Berkeley and Los Angeles: University of California Press.

"The Sentinel's Letter 'Keeps the Record Straight.' " 1938. *New-Age Dispatch,* 22 Apr.

"Sidelights on New Picture, 'The Exile.' " 1931. *New York Age,* 7 Mar.

"Sign Noted L.A. Screen Artists for MGM Picture." 1938. *New-Age Dispatch,* 3 Dec.

Simmons, Charles A. 1998. *The African American Press: A History of News Coverage during National Crisis, with Special Reference to Four Black Newspapers, 1827–1965.* Jefferson, N.C.: McFarland.

Singer, Barry. 1992. *Black and Blue: The Life and Lyrics of Andy Razaf.* New York: Schirmer Books.

Sklar, Robert. 1976. *Movie Made America: A Cultural History of American Movies.* New York: Vintage.

Sloan, Kay. 1988. *The Loud Silents: Origins of the Social Problem Film.* Urbana and Chicago: University of Illinois Press.

Smiley, J. Hockley. 1911. "Our Musical and Dramatic Critic." *Chicago Defender,* 23 Dec.

Smith, Jean Voltaire. 1922. "Our Need for More Films." *Half-Century,* Apr.

Smith, William Thomas. 1945. "Hollywood Report." *Phylon* 6, no. 1: 14–16.

"Socialism and the Negro." 1923. *Amsterdam News,* 28 Feb.

"Southern Editor Flays Movie That Depicts Woman in Love with a Dark-Skinned Man." 1923. *Pittsburgh Courier,* 22 June.

"Sowed the Wind, Reaping the Whirlwind." 1916. *California Eagle,* 29 Jan.

Spigel, Lynn. 1992. *Make Room for TV: Television and the Family Ideal in Postwar America.* Chicago: University of Chicago Press.

"St. Louis Theatre Group Sues Paramount Pictures." 1935. *Pittsburgh Courier,* 2 Mar.

"Stardom after 17 Years." 1937. *Pittsburgh Courier,* 28 Aug.

"States Theater Displays Vile Pictures." 1914. *Chicago Defender,* 5 May.

"Still Showing Vicious Picture." 1915. *New York Age,* 11 Mar.

"Stop Daily Lynchings." 1915. *Defender,* 18 Jun.

Strinati, Dominic. 1995. *An Introduction to Theories of Popular Culture.* London: Routledge.

"Talk of the Town." 1916. *California Eagle,* 1 July.

Taylor, Clyde. 1993. "The Ironies of Palace-Subaltern Discourse." In *Black American Cinema,* ed. Manthia Diawara, 177–99. New York: Routledge.

Taylor, I. Keith. 1939. *Intolerance by Radio.* New York: Macmillan.

Thompson, Kristin. 1986. "The Concept of Cinematic Excess." In *Narrative, Apparatus, Ideology: A Film Theory Reader,* ed. Philip Rosen, 130–42. New York: Columbia University Press.

Thompson, Louise. 1933. "The Soviet Film." *The Crisis,* Feb., 37.

Thrasher, Frederick M. 1940. "Education versus Censorship." *Journal of Education and Sociology,* 13, no. 295 (Jan.).

"Three Suits for Discrimination Filed against Producers of King Vidor's Movietone, 'Hallelujah': Harlem Business Men Refused Tickets for the Embassy Theatre Performance." 1929. *Pittsburgh Courier,* 31 Aug.

"To Make All-Colored Film." 1937. *New-Age Dispatch,* 6 Nov.

Toll, Robert C. 1974. *Blacking Up: The Minstrel Show in Nineteenth Century America.* New York: Oxford University Press.

Tolson, Melvin B. 1953. *Libretto for the Republic of Liberia.* London: Collier Books.

——. 1982. *Caviar and Cabbage: Selected Columns by Melvin B. Tolson.* Ed. Robert M. Farnsworth. 1937. Reprint, Columbia: University of Missouri Press.

"Too Much Pampering of White Writers by Negro Leaders." 1930. *Baltimore Afro-American,* 27 Sept.

Ukadike, Frank N. 1990. "Western Film Images of Africa: Genealogy of an Ideological Formulation. *Black Scholar* 21, no. 2 (Mar.–Apr.–May): 30–48.

"The Value of the Talkies." 1915. *Pittsburgh Courier,* 6 July.

Vann, Robert L. 1932. "Negro Editors on Communism: A Symposium of the American Negro Press." *The Crisis,* May, 154.

Vardac, A. Nicholas. 1949. *Stage to Screen, Theatrical Origins of Early Film: David Garrick to D. W. Griffith.* New York: Da Capo.

Vertov, Dziga. *Kino-Eye: The Writings of Dziga Vertov.* 1984. Ed. Annette Michelson. Trans. Kevin O'Brien. Berkeley: University of California Press.

"Vicious Picture Film Condemned by Censors." 1915. *New York Age,* 4 Mar.

Waldman, Diane. 1984. "From Midnight Shows to Marriage Vows: Women Exploitation and Exhibition." *Wide Angle* 6, no. 6: 39–48.

Walker, George. 1906. "The Negro on the American Stage." *Colored American Magazine,* June, 242–46.

Walker, John, ed. 1995. *Halliwell's Film Guide.* New York: Harper Collins, 1995.

Walton, Lester A. 1906. "Conspiracy of the White Press." *New York Age,* 13 May.

——. 1909a. "The Degeneracy of the Moving Picture Theatre." *New York Age,* 5 Aug.

——. 1909b. "Moving Picture Paper Takes Up the Age Crusade." *New York Age,* 26 Aug.

——. 1909c. "Negroes in New York Theaters." *New York Age,* 18 Nov.

——. 1910. "The Moving Picture Theater." *New York Age,* 15 Dec.

——. 1911. "Change Wrought by Motion Picture Craze." *New York Age,* 23 Feb.

——. 1912a. "The Influence of Moving Picture Shows." *New York Age,* 21 Mar.

——. 1912b. "Ban on Titanic Moving Pictures." *New York Age*, 2 May.

——. 1912c. "Negro Vaudevillians on the Color Question." *New York Age*, 17 Oct.

——. 1913a. "Jingle of Dimes at the Lafayette Is Faint." *New York Age*, 9 Jan.

——. 1913b. "The Motion Picture Industry and the Negro." *New York Age*, 5 June.

——. 1913c. "Motion Picture Concern Makes Film Ridiculing Race." *New York Age*, 16 Oct.

——. 1914a. "Want Representation on Film Censor Board." *New York Age*, 19 Mar.

——. 1914b. "New Yorkers Have Gone 'Dippy' over the Movies." *New York Age*, 4 May.

——. 1915a. "Colored Citizens' Weakness Shown in Photo Play Incident." *New York Age*, 23 Mar.

——. 1915b. "*Chicago Tribune* Laments over Barring of Photo Play." *New York Age*, 3 June.

——. 1915c. "Colored Men at Atlantic City Put O.K. on Photo Play." *New York Age*, 29 July.

——. 1918. "The Colored Soldier on the Screen." *Cayton's Weekly*, 7 Sept.

——. 1919a. "Stop German Opera; Un-American Film Allowed." *New York Age*, 15 Mar.

——. 1919b. "World to be 'Americanized' by Such Films as 'Birth of a Nation.'" *New York Age*, 7 June.

——. 1920a. "To Sue Company for Altering Race Film." *New York Age*, 10 Apr.

——. 1920b. "Sam Langford's Wallop Makes 'The Brute' a Screen Success." *New York Age*, 16 Sep.

——. 1921. "Bar Photo Plays in India Which Lower Prestige of White Races." *New York Age*, 24 Sept.

"Want Negro's Support on Female Suffrage." 1915. *New York Age*, 11 Mar.

Washington, Booker T. 1915. "Time to Fight Bad Movies Is Before They Are Shown." *Chicago Defender*, 22 May.

Webb, Constance. 1968. *Richard Wright: A Biography*. New York: G. P. Putnam's Sons.

West, Cornel. 1988. "Marxist Theory and the Specificity of Afro-American Oppression." In *Marxism and the Interpretation of Culture*, ed. Cary Nelson and Lawrence Grossberg, 17–33. Urbana: University of Illinois Press.

"What Will the New Year Bring?" 1918. *Half-Century*, Jan.

"Which Way Out for the Negro." 1935. *The Crisis*, May, 134.

White, Hayden. 1978. *Tropics of Discourse: Essays in Cultural Criticism*. Baltimore: The Johns Hopkins University Press.

White, Lucien H. 1922a. "New Method of Making Pictures in Natural Colors." *New York Age*, 17 June.

———. 1922b. *"Emperor Jones* Is Not Racial But Symbolic Study of Fear." *New York Age,* 25 Nov.

White, Walter. 1933a. Telegram to Louis Lautier, 19 Sept. NAACP Files, Group 1, Box 303. Library of Congress, Washington, D.C.

———. 1933b. Memorandum to Roy Wilkins, 21 Sept. NAACP Files, Group 1, Box 303. Library of Congress, Washington, D.C.

———. 1948. *A Man Called White: The Autobiography of Walter White.* New York: Viking.

"Why We Should Patronize the Grand." 1915. *Chicago Defender,* 20 Mar.

"Wild Cannibal Turns Out to Be Ex-Janitor." 1930. *Chicago Defender,* 15 Mar.

Winston, Brian. 1993. "The Documentary Film as Scientific Inscription." In *Theorizing Documentary,* ed. Michael Renov, 37–57. New York and London: Routledge.

Wood, Frank T., Jr. 1935. "Imitation of Life Again." *Crisis,* Sept.

Woodson, Carter G. 1990. *The Miseducation of the Negro.* 1933. Reprint, Trenton, N.J.: Africa World.

Index

Hubbard, Dolan, 14, 318 n.1
Huckleberry Finn, 287
Hughes, Langston, 233, 241, 262–65, 275, 297
Hurst, Fannie, 186, 218, 229, 287
Hurston, Zora Neale, 184–86
Hypnotized, 288

I Am a Fugitive from a Chain Gang, 247–48
Image criticism, 70, 160, 161, 247–48, 265, 285
Imitation of Life, 10, 192, 196, 217; accommodationist criticism and, 218–32; audience, 193, 220–21, 231, 287, 308; *Crisis* criticism of, 225–27, 231; French audience, 225–27; Hurst's novel compared with, 228–29; Peola discourse, 221–22; popularity of, 220–22, 231; southern mentality in, 219, 229–31; subversiveness in, 223, 225
"*Imitation of Life:* Once a Pancake" (Brown), 227–31
Immigrants, 25, 30, 92, 111, 258–59
Imperialism, 8, 287–88
Independent filmmakers, 8–9, 140–41. *See also* Black film industry; Interracial independent filmmaking
India, 167–68
Industry practices, 166–78
Informant-spectators, 90–92, 255–56
Ingagi, 248–49
Ingram, Rex, 188, 218, 306
Intellectuals, 144, 184–85, 190–91, 270; radicalism and, 233–34. *See also* Bourgeoisie
Intentionality, 127, 133
International cinema, 25–26, 35, 104–5, 167, 247; black-produced films and, 319 n.9; southern box office myth and, 301–2
Interracial filmmaking, 187–88
Interracial independent filmmaking, 114–16, 192, 193–205; accommodationist critiques of, 188–89, 217–18; Million Dollar Productions, 188, 201, 203, 328 n.18; promotional discourse

and, 199–205; radical critiques of, 268–69. *See also* Black film industry
Intolerance, 99–100
Intruder in the Dust, 306, 307, 309
"In Union Is Strength" (Adams), 42
Investigator (writer), 157–59
Iowa State Bystander, 60–67, 321 n.2
"Is the Church Losing Its Hold on the People?" (Investigator), 158–59

Jacko, 329 n.34
Jackson, Faye M., 203, 221–23
James, C. L. R., 90, 270, 276, 277
Jameson, Fredric, 70–71
Japanese Americans, 96–97, 98
Jazz Age, 144
JCL, 24, 239–40
Jeffries, James, 50–51
Jet, 314
Jewish American filmmakers, 148, 149–50, 252–53
Jezebel, 296
Jim Crow discrimination, 12, 54, 97, 111; segregated movie theaters, 24–25, 33, 38, 39, 175–77, 207; socialism and, 234; soldiers and, 143
Johnson, Abby Arthur, 3
Johnson, Charles, 186
Johnson, George, 9, 117, 188
Johnson, Jack, 50–51
Johnson, James Weldon, 30, 69–70, 75, 78, 145, 160, 176; accommodationist writings, 185, 189
Johnson, Noble, 9, 117
Johnson, Ronald Maberry, 3
Johnson-Jeffries fight, 49–51
Jolson, Al, 214–16
Jones, Juli. *See* Foster, William
Jones, Peter P., 112, 113–15, 119; technological innovations and, 166–70
Jones, Robert, 299–303, 304
"Jottings Theatrical and Otherwise" (*Chicago Defender*), 47–48
Journalist-reader dynamic, 5–6, 47–49
Journalists, as participant-observers, 37–38, 55
Judge Priest, 287

Anna Everett is Assistant Professor
of Film Studies at the University of California,
Santa Barbara.

Library of Congress Cataloging-in-Publication Data

Everett, Anna, 1954.
Returning the gaze : a genealogy of Black film criticism,
1909–1949 / Anna Everett.
p. cm.
Includes bibliographical references and index.
ISBN 0-8223-2606-x (alk. paper) — ISBN 0-8223-2614-0
(pbk. : alk. paper)
1. Afro-Americans in motion pictures. 2. African American
film critics—Biography. 3. Afro-American press—History—
20th century. I. Title.
PN1995.9.N4 E94 2001
791.43'01'508996073—dc21   00-010758